Cultural Sustainability and Regional Development

Meeting the aims of sustainability is becoming increasingly difficult; at the same time, the call for culture is becoming more powerful. This book explores the relationships between culture, sustainability and regional change through the concept of 'territorialisation'. This concept describes the dynamics and processes in the context of regional development, driven by collective human agency that stretches beyond localities and marked-off administrative boundaries.

This book launches the concept of 'territorialisation' by exploring how the natural environment and culture are constitutive of each other. This concept allows us to study the characterisation of the natural assets of a place, the means by which the natural environment and culture interact, and how communities assign meaning to local assets, add functions and ascribe rules of how to use space. By highlighting the time-space dimension in the use and consumption of resources, territorialisation helps to frame the concept and grasp the meaning of sustainable regional development. Drawing on an international range of case studies, the book addresses both conceptual issues and practical applications of 'territorialisation' in a range of contexts, forms and scales.

The book will be of great interest to researchers and postgraduates in sustainable development, environmental studies, and regional development and planning.

Joost Dessein is Scientific Coordinator of the Social Sciences Unit of the Institute for Agricultural and Fisheries Research (ILVO), Belgium and Visiting Professor at the Department of Agricultural Economics, Ghent University, Belgium.

Elena Battaglini, Senior Researcher, manages the Research Area on Environment & Regional Development of Istituto di Ricerche Economiche e Sociali (IRES), Italy. She is a member of the Scientific Board of the Italian Sociology Association (AIS), Section Environment and Territory.

Lummina Horlings is Assistant Professor at the Rural Sociology Group, Wageningen University and Research centre, The Netherlands.

Cultural Sustainability and Regional Development

Theories and practices of territorialisation

Edited by Joost Dessein, Elena Battaglini and Lummina Horlings

LONDON AND NEW YORK

First published 2016
by Routledge

2 Park Square, Milton Park, Abingdon, Oxon OX14 4RN
711 Third Avenue, New York, NY 10017, USA

Routledge is an imprint of the Taylor & Francis Group, an informa business

First issued in paperback 2017

British Library Cataloguing-in-Publication Data
A catalogue record for this book is available from the British Library

Library of Congress Cataloging-in-Publication Data
Cultural sustainability and regional development : theories and practices of territorialism / edited by Joost Dessein, Elena Battaglini and Lummina Horlings.
pages cm
Includes bibliographical references and index.
ISBN 978-1-138-83008-0 (hardback) -- ISBN 978-1-315-73743-0 (ebook) 1. Regional planning--Social aspects--Case studies. 2. Cultural policy--Case studies. 3. Sustainable development--Case studies. 4. Human ecology--Case studies. I. Dessein, Joost, 1971- II. Battaglini, Elena. III. Horlings, Lummina.
HT391.C85 2016
307.1'2--dc23
2015006436

ISBN: 978-1-138-83008-0 (hbk)
ISBN: 978-1-138-74353-3 (pbk)

Typeset in Times
by GreenGate Publishing Services, Tonbridge, Kent

Contents

Illustrations

Figures

Tables

Contributors

Jenny Atmanagara was Senior Researcher at the Institute of Urban Planning and Urban Design, University of Stuttgart from March 2012 until March 2014. Since then she has been leading the section on urban development at Baden-Württemberg International and is one of the core team members of the cluster agency Baden-Württemberg.

Marija Babović (PhD in Economic Sociology) is Associate Professor at the Department of Sociology, Faculty of Philosophy, University of Belgrade, Serbia, where she has been working since 1996. She is President of SeConS – Development Initiative Group, an NGO specialised in applied research and policy analyses. Her research focus is on sustainable development and gender equality.

Elena Battaglini (PhD in Spatial Sociology) is Senior Researcher, managing the Research Area on Environmental and Regional Development of ABT-ISF-IRES, Italy. Her main research focus is on regional endogenous development and its innovation processes. She teaches methods and techniques of spatial analysis in the Department of Architecture, Roma Tre University, Rome.

Lilian Blanck de Oliveira is Professor in the Postgraduate Program in Regional Development at the Regional University of Blumenau (PPGDR/FURB), Brazil. She is leader of the Ethos, Otherness and Development Research Group (GPEAD). Her experience is in the fields of Culture, Religion and Education.

Monica Caggiano (PhD in Environmental and Agricultural Economics) focuses her major research interests on social ecology and community development. She worked for several years in Italy and France on agricultural knowledge and innovation systems.

Leonardo Chiesi teaches Sociology in the School of Architecture, University of Florence, Italy. His interest is in social research methods for architecture and planning, and he studies how sociology and design can be mutually engaged. He has been involved in several architectural design and city planning projects and has an interest in the subjects of local identity, community processes and participation methods.

Annalisa Cicerchia is member of the Board of Directors of Associazione per l'Economia della Cultura and Professor of Economics and Management of Cultural Resources, Roma University Tor Vergata, Italy. She is Senior Researcher at the Italian National Statistical Institute.

Paolo Costa teaches Urban Sociology and Sociology of Design in the School of Architecture, University of Florence, Italy. He is interested in the relationship between social sciences and planning, architecture and design, with a focus on methodology and evaluation. He has been involved in several participatory strategies and in cultural mapping and co-design projects.

Joost Dessein (agronomist with a PhD in Social and Cultural Anthropology) is scientific coordinator of the Social Sciences Unit of ILVO (Institute for Agricultural and Fisheries Research) and Professor at the Department of Agricultural Economics of Ghent University, Belgium. He is the vice-chair of the COST-action IS1007 'Investigating cultural sustainability' and Series Editor of the Routledge Studies in Culture and Sustainable Development.

Reinaldo Matias Fleuri has a PhD in Education. He is Senior Visiting Professor at Instituto Federal Catarinense (CAPES and CNPQ fellow) researching on 'Intercultural and Ecological Challenges for Education on Science and Technology'. He is also Honorary Professor at Universidade Federal Catarinense (Brazil) and at the University of Queensland (Australia).

Luciano Felix Florit is Professor in the Postgraduate Program in Regional Development at the Regional University of Blumenau, Brazil (PPGDR/FURB). He is Leader of the Interdisciplinary Research Group on Development and Environment (GIPADMA). His research fields are the Sociology of Development, Environmental Sociology and Environmental Ethics, currently focusing on Environmental Ethics and Environmental Justice in Regional Development.

Ian Harris is Bangor University's Research Farm Manager. He lectures in GIS and has been the nominated researcher responsible for the spatial analysis components of a number of national and international projects funded by the EU, DEFRA, Environment Agency, NERC/ESRC, Natural Resources Wales and local government.

Paul Hebinck is a rural development sociologist at Wageningen UR, the Netherlands and University of Fort Hare, South Africa. He specialised in agrarian transformation processes in Africa with an emphasis on land reform and rights, peasant farming and rural livelihoods. He has substantial fieldwork experiences in Kenya, South Africa, Zimbabwe and Namibia.

Lummina Horlings is Assistant Professor at the Rural Sociology Group of Wageningen UR, the Netherlands. Her research deals with the question of how people contribute to sustainable place-shaping, including aspects such as leadership, self-governance, coalitions, values and sense of place. She is a member of the Cost Action 'Investigating Cultural Sustainability', the Research Committee of the Regional Studies Association (RSA), the RSA research network on 'The Place of Leadership in Urban and Regional Development' and member of the Policy and Advisory Panel of the Interreg IVB project 'Rural Alliances'.

Arwel Jones is Honorary Lecturer in Tourism, Sustainable Development, Heritage and Environmental Management, Bangor University, Wales. He is a founder member of the Welsh Responsible Tourism Group. As a regional development consultant he has undertaken over 150 assignments concerned with the optimisation of natural, built and cultural resources.

Hellen Kimanthi is a PhD student at the Department of Sociology of Development and Change, Wageningen University, the Netherlands. She holds a Master's Degree in International Development Studies from Wageningen University, specialised in the Sociology of Development. She has worked for more than four years as a Research Assistant on several development projects with different organisations in Kenya .

Mari Kivitalo is a PhD student in the Department of Social Sciences and Philosophy, University of Jyväskylä, Finland. She has previously worked as a junior lecturer for several years in the Unit of Social and Public Policy, University of Jyväskylä.

Kaisu Kumpulainen is a university teacher in the Master's Program in Cultural Policy in the Department of Social Sciences and Philosophy, University of Jyväskylä, Finland. She is the Chair of The Finnish Society for Rural Research and Development.

Nelson Mango is a Rural Development Sociologist and works for the International Centre for Tropical Agriculture (CIAT), Harare, Zimbabwe. His research work has focused on livestock, livelihoods, poverty and soil fertility (re)production in sub-Saharan African countries and Southern Asia. Currently he is involved in a new research project on Integrated Agricultural Research for Development through Multi-Stakeholder Innovation Platforms with conservation farming as an entry point in the Southern Africa region.

David Manuel-Navarrete is Assistant Professor in the School of Sustainability at Arizona State University, USA. He has worked in Chile for UNECLAC. His current research focus is climate change adaptation in Mexico.

Frans Padt trained as an environmental hydrologist and received a PhD in Political Sciences of the Environment. He has extensive experience in community and regional environmental planning as a researcher, educator, policymaker and consultant. Currently he teaches in the Department of Agricultural Economics, Sociology, and Education and the Department of Landscape Architecture at The Pennsylvania State University. His particular interests include the political, institutional and leadership aspects of community and regional environmental planning.

Siân Pierce is a lecturer in Human Geography, Bangor University, Wales. Previously Director of Studies for the Tourism and Heritage degrees in Bangor, her research interests are diverse, ranging from issues of rural governance to heritage, tourism and land management. Recent research projects have evaluated local festivals, events and community heritage projects with particular emphasis on local foods.

Michael Redclift is Emeritus Professor of International Environmental Policy in the Department of Geography, King's College, London. He is the author of 34 books, many of them concerned with the environment and sustainable development.

Katriina Soini is a cultural geographer working as Principal Research Scientist at the Natural Resources Institute Finland (Luke) and post-doc researcher at the University of Jyväskylä, Finland. She also holds an Adjunct Professorship at the University of Eastern Finland in Environmental Policy and Rural Studies. She is the chair of the COST-action IS1007 'Investigating cultural sustainability' and series editor of the Routledge Studies in Culture and Sustainable Development.

Eifiona Thomas Lane is a lecturer in Environmental Planning and Rural Geography, Bangor University, Wales. She works closely with public and voluntary initiatives including knowledge exchange at locality scale focusing on sustainable, healthy and prosperous communities. Recently she has been exploring the value of local place-based food networks within protected landscapes and also responsible interpretation of heritage for community benefit.

Rodrigo Wartha has a Bachelor Degree in History with studies in Education, Diversity and Indigenous Culture. He is member of the Ethos, Otherness and Development Research Group (GPEAD) of the Regional University of Blumenau, Brazil. His research focus is on indigenous culture in the Vale do Itajai, Santa Catarina.

Michael Woods is Professor of Human Geography at Aberystwyth University and Co-Director of the ESRC WISERD/Civil Society Research Centre, Wales. He is principal investigator on the European Research Council Advanced Grant GLOBAL-RURAL.

Series introduction

Katriina Soini and Joost Dessein

Achieving a more sustainable level of development is the biggest global challenge of the twenty-first century, and new approaches are urgently needed to ensure that development is much better aligned with the environmental, societal and economic challenges we are facing. Scholars and policy makers increasingly recognise the contribution of culture in sustainable development. The issue of culture is also being increasingly discussed in debates in various international, national and local arenas, and there are ample initiatives driven by local actors. Yet despite this increased attention there have been very few attempts to consider culture in a more analytical and explicit way within the frames of sustainability. The challenge of incorporating culture in sustainable development discourses, both scientifically and politically, arises from the complex, normative and multidisciplinary character of both culture and sustainable development. However, this difficulty should not be an excuse for ignoring the cultural dimension within sustainable development.

The Routledge Studies in Culture and Sustainable Development series aims to analyse the diverse and multiple roles that culture plays in sustainable development. It takes as one of its starting points the idea that culture in sustainability serves as a 'meta-narrative' that will bring together ideas and standpoints from an extensive body of academic research currently scattered among different disciplines and thematic fields. Moreover, the series responds to the strengthening call for inter- and transdisciplinary approaches that is being heard in many quarters, but in few fields more strongly than that of sustainability and sustainable development, with its complex and systemic problems. By combining and comparing the various approaches, in both the sciences and the humanities, and in dealing with social, cultural, environmental, political and aesthetic disciplines the series offers a comprehensive contribution to present-day sustainability sciences as well as related policies.

The books in the series will use a broad understanding of culture, giving space to all the possible understandings of culture from narrow, art-based definitions to broad, way-of-life based approaches, and beyond. Furthermore, culture is not seen only as an additional aspect of sustainable development – as a 'fourth pillar'– but rather as a mediator, a cross-cutting transversal framework or even as a new set of guiding principles for sustainable development research, policies and practices.

The essence of culture in, for and as sustainable development will be explored through the series in various thematic contexts, representing a wide range of practices and processes (e.g. everyday life, livelihoods and lifestyles, landscape, artistic practices, aesthetic experiences, heritage, tourism, agriculture, planning). These contexts might concern urban, peri-urban or rural contexts, and regions with different trajectories of socio-economic development. The perspectives of the books will stretch from local to global and cover different temporal scales from past to present and future. These issues are valorised by theoretical or empirical analysis; their relationship to the ecological, social and economic dimensions of sustainability will be explored, when appropriate.

The idea for the series is derived from the European COST Action IS1007 'Investigating Cultural Sustainability', running between 2011 and 2015. This network is comprised of a group of around 100 researchers from 26 European countries, representing many different disciplines. They have brought together their expertise, knowledge and experience, and based on that they have built up new inter- and transdisciplinary understanding and approaches that can enhance and enrich research into culture in sustainable development, and support the work of the policy makers and practitioners in this field.

Cultural Sustainability and Regional Development: Theories and Practices of Territorialisation explores the relationships between culture, sustainability and territorialisation. Here, the notion of territorialisation points to dynamics and processes stretching beyond localities and administrative boundaries. In this process the authors emphasise the role of nature in its interplay with culture, and the culturally varied ways in which people shape their territories.

The book contributes to our understanding of sustainable regional development by highlighting the time-space dimension of development and the varied ways in which people use resources. The cases represent different scales, a variety of locations and several continents (Europe, North and South America, Africa, Australia). The authors analyse these cases as the outcome of interaction between human intentionality, place-based characteristics and cultural history. Culture is not expressed only in practices and institutions, but also in the form of subjective perceptions, sense-making, and the construction of narratives and regional identities. The book provides empirical and theoretical insights into how these cultural expressions can contribute to sustainable regional development.

This publication is supported by COST

COST – European Cooperation in Science and Technology is an intergovernmental framework aimed at facilitating the collaboration and networking of scientists and researchers at European level. It was established in 1971 by 19 member countries and currently includes 35 member countries across Europe, and Israel as a cooperating state.

COST funds pan-European, bottom-up networks of scientists and researchers across all science and technology fields. These networks, called 'COST Actions', promote international coordination of nationally-funded research. By fostering the networking of researchers at an international level, COST enables breakthrough scientific developments leading to new concepts and products, thereby contributing to strengthening Europe's research and innovation capacities.

COST's mission focuses in particular on:

- Building capacity by connecting high quality scientific communities throughout Europe and worldwide;
- Providing networking opportunities for early career investigators;
- Increasing the impact of research on policy makers, regulatory bodies and national decision makers as well as the private sector.

Through its inclusiveness policy, COST supports the integration of research communities in less research-intensive countries across Europe, leverages national research investments and addresses societal issues.

Over 45,000 European scientists benefit from their involvement in COST Actions on a yearly basis. This allows the pooling of national research funding and helps countries' research communities achieve common goals.

As a precursor of advanced multidisciplinary research, COST anticipates and complements the activities of EU Framework Programmes, constituting a 'bridge' towards the scientific communities of emerging countries.

Traditionally, COST draws its budget for networking activities from successive EU RTD Framework Programmes.

COST is supported by the EU Framework Programme Horizon 2020.

1 Introduction

The role of culture in territorialisation

Lummina Horlings, Elena Battaglini and Joost Dessein

Notions on region, territory, place and space

Concepts such as place, region and territory are all terms that underpin crucial concepts in the processes of regional development. These concepts have taken on specific connotations concerning the different scientific, general and disciplinary paradigms that have succeeded one another over the course of time. The complex use of similar words in different cultures and languages, with slightly or strongly different meanings, illustrates the challenges we face when speaking of regional development. A variety of words are used to refer to the regional scale, such as *regione, région*, region, *territorio, territoire, territory, luogo, lieu*, place. There are analogies in the semantic thematisation among Southern European languages (Italy, France and Spain) which are less relevant in the English-speaking world. To illustrate this, in Italian the term *territorio* refers, on the one hand, to the sense of belonging to a place and, on the other, to its organisational principles: cultivation techniques, habitat, social rules that shape its land, nature and landscape. In the English definition the term territory indicates an area under administrative or state jurisdiction, understood as control and primary expression of social power exercised by the state.

Territory in scientific literature generally refers to territorial settlements and administrative or organisationally bounded areas. The size and nature of territories have changed from neighbourhoods and parishes to city-regions and beyond (Allen and Cochrane, 2010). Not all scholars automatically imply the existence of fixed and stable boundaries. Two conflicting traditions can be identified. Sack (1986: 1–2) treats 'territoriality' as a bounded space and as a spatial strategy approach:

> Territoriality in humans is best understood as a spatial strategy to affect, influence or control resources and people, by controlling area; and as a strategy, territoriality can be turned on and off. In geographical terms it is a form of spatial behaviour.

Raffestin and Butler (2012: 121) stress its 'relational' dimension and claim for compatibility and sustainability of the system:

> Territoriality can be defined as the ensemble of relations that a society maintains with exteriority and alterity for the satisfaction of its needs, towards the end of attaining the greatest possible autonomy compatible with the resources of the system.

Region is a keyword that has dominated geographical discourses since the field became institutionalised (Paasi, 2010). Scholars have reflected on the success factors of regional development (Pike *et al.*, 2006), on regional scales, questions such as how regions are performed, how regional governance is exercised, the issue of open versus bounded regions (Paasi, 2009a), fuzzy boundaries in regional planning (Haughton and Allmendinger, 2010), the relevance of regions for politics/policies of space (Allen and Cochrane, 2007), the significance of regions for food systems (Kneafsey, 2010) and for political ecology (Neumann, 2010). Paasi (2011) has sketched an overview of the historical evolution of the word 'region' and has distinguished the following three strata in the geographical thinking on space and region, characterised by partly overlapping meanings associated with these keywords: 1) Regional geographies, considering regions as unique, bounded units, on the basis of natural, cultural or other regional characteristics; 2) Spatial analysis and systematic approaches, categorising regions as formal or functional regions, stressing the need for mathematical and statistical methods for the purposes of generalisation and explanation. Researchers referring to the paradigm of rational mechanics and determinism in geography considered the physical environment as an influential factor in the use of the land; and 3) Space, region and social practice emphasising the relations between the social and the spatial. The new or reconstructed regional geography studies how places can be constructed by and are constitutive of social life, relations and identity (Paasi, 2011).

Place and space have a range of meanings as well, according to the context. Carter *et al.* (1993: xii) in their collection *Space and Place* state that 'place is space to which meaning has been ascribed'. The variety of definitions of place ranges from place as sites, places as subjective experiences to places as the product of social relations. To elaborate on this last approach and building on the rich literature on relational place and space (see, for example, Massey 1991, 1993, 2004, 2005; Cresswell, 2004; Amin, 2004; Jones, 2009; Woods, 2011) places in a relational sense are considered as geographically unbounded, as meeting places which are part of wider networks and relations and connected to other places through social, economic and political relations (Pierce *et al.*, 2011). Places are thus the outcome of networks, points of intersection, that integrate the global and the local (Massey, 2005).

Authors on region, territory and place all agree that complex spatialities or socio-spatialities matter in different ways.

> They matter materially. They matter in terms of discourses and representations that are mobilized around various spatial concepts. They matter through the ways in which space is performed. And, critically, they matter in terms of the everyday constructions of space that happen in the real world, as social

movements, neighbourhood organizations and other groups make the spaces that we academics try to think. (Merriman *et al.*, 2012: 8).

Conceptualising regional development

In the large body of literature on region, three types of interpretation of region can be distinguished: pre-scientific, discipline-centered and critical interpretations (Paasi, 2011). While in the past regions were often considered as pre-given and stable spatial units (Hudson, 2007) this essentialist view has been criticised (Jonas, 2012; Paasi, 2009b). According to the proponents of the 'new geography', the demarcation and the identity of a region cannot be taken for granted as pre-given facts (Messely, 2014; Messely *et al.*, 2014). Regions are fluid (Haughton and Allmendinger, 2010) and are historically contingent constructions, expressed in practices. In the words of Allen *et al.* (1998: 2): 'Regions are not "out there" waiting to be discovered; they are our (and others') constructions.'

Another debate, often intertwined with the essentialist-constructivist debate, centres on the territorial (understood as geographically bounded) versus relational conceptualisations of regions (Varro and Lagendijk, 2013; Messely, 2014). While some scholars focus on the importance of regions as administrative or governmentally bounded areas, relationally oriented scholars (see above) point to the importance of actors, relations and processes: 'What gives a place its specificity is not some long internalised history but the fact that it is constructed out of a particular constellation of relations, articulated together at a particular locus' (Massey, 1993: 66). These notions emphasise the importance of networks and connectivities (MacLeod and Jones, 2007) and have led to conceptualisations of regions as processes that are performed, limited, symbolised and institutionalised through practices, discourses and power relations that are not inevitably bound to a specific scale, but which may be networked in both time and space (Paasi, 2009b, 2009c). Such relations are expressed between the land and the economy, nature and society, rural and urban, as well as at the unique intersection of social, economic, cultural and political relations that are mapped over multiple localities, which results in the distinctiveness of places (Woods, 2011).

We argue here that it is productive to transcend the scientific division between regions as outcomes of social relations or as geographically bounded, administrative areas (see also Allen and Cochrane, 2007; Jessop *et al.*, 2008). Although a region is a relational and networked space, we can also understand regions from a spatial, bounded approach in a concrete context, such as in political debates where power is exercised, or in discussions on the constructing of regional identities (see also Messely *et al.*, 2014). Evidence can be found for the significance of regions and their boundaries as catalysts for regionalist movements, ethno-territorial groups and planning strategies (Agnew, 2001). Similarly, the identity-narratives created by regional activists and advocates and governmental bodies force us to study such 'politics of distinction' rather than denying their existence (Paasi, 2010: 171).

As Harvey (1973: 13) suggested, space is 'neither absolute, relative or relational in itself, but it can become one or all simultaneously depending on circumstances'. In regions the absolute, relative and relational aspects of space become fused in material practices (such as boundary-making), representations (such as mapping) and lived meanings (such as affective loyalities to territorial units) (Harvey, 2009: 174). Some scholars have attempted to bring together the terms territory, space, place and network in a 'TSPN framework' (Jessop *et al.*, 2008) or refer to assemblages of actors, representing different administrative scales, but which are still 'lodged' within a region and directed to regional aims (Allen and Cochrane, 2007).

In this book, both territorial bounded notions of region and region as relational/networked place are combined and considered relevant: 'In some cases place or region matters, sometimes boundaries are significant, sometimes not, at times networks and relations matter, while at other times scales and the processes of rescaling are of crucial importance' (Paasi, 2010: 406).

This book contextualises regions and regional development by analysing how practices and dynamics take place in selected regions. The key agency involved is human intentionality in interaction with the environment (see also Paasi, 2010: 2297; Relph, 1976). In the region identities are constructed as a result of the interplay between environment and culture. Nature, in its morphological, physical and climatic connotation, influences the practices of use and consumption of the resources in regions (Battaglini and Babović, 2015). A concrete example is the influence of '*terroir*' on the process of winemaking and the quality of the wine.

Territorialisation as co-production of society and environment

We introduce here the notion of 'territorialisation' (see also Brighenti, 2010) to describe the dynamics and processes in the context of regional development, driven by collective human intentionality and stretching beyond localities and geographical or administrative boundaries. Territorialisation thus is the outcome of the multi-scale interaction of structuring processes and agency/social relations, which are expressed in practices. This includes processes of boundary-making in the context of politics of place.

Building on the definition constructed by Turco (1988), when using the term 'territorialisation', we refer in this book to a process in which communities (although involved in unbounded networks) perceive the specific nature and characteristics of their place, attribute symbols to resources and to local peculiarities, and reify, structure and organise space. We are referring to a process of co-construction and co-evolution that is started along with a dialogic relationship, in which social configurations and the local environment, in its physical characterisations, both have agency.

Territorialisation can be studied from different methodological perspectives and theoretical starting points, such as practice theory (Schatzki, 2002), micro-sociology, actor-network theory (Callon, 1986; Law and Hassard, 1999; Latour, 2005), a TSPN framework theorising socio-spatial relations (see above; Jessop *et al.*, 2008), governance (Rhodes, 1997) or transition theory (Loorbach and Rotmans, 2006).

The interaction between humans and environment can be considered as *co-production* rooted in human intentionality and expressed in practices. This co-production is acknowledged in the theory on 'coupled' social-ecological systems which consider human society as dependent on natural systems (Gunderson *et al.*, 1995; Folke, 2006). Governance can enhance resilience and adaptive capacity in such coupled social-ecological systems (Janssen and Ostrom, 2006), influenced by learning capacity, social and ecological diversity, diverse knowledge and the self-organisation of these social-ecological systems (Folke *et al.*, 2005).

The concept of co-production used here, inspired by actor-oriented debates in rural sociology (Van der Ploeg and Marsden, 2008; Long, 2001), refers to the mutual constitution of the social and the natural, between society and environment and between man and living nature. Not only people but also the physical nature of territories have 'agency' (Ingold, 1992; Latour, 1993) with regard to the perceptions, meanings and values attributed by communities to resources. Environment and society, in dynamic interaction, are the protagonists of a process that is configured in time, conditioning the relationship between community and land, with a specific location, resources and climate. Both act and orient the quality and the direction of regional development, which we understand in this book as a process of territorialisation.

We argue here that territorialisation as a dynamic process has the following characteristics. First, territorialisation creates *differentiated outcomes* as a result of the intertwinement of globalisation and localisation. A key notion is that influences of globalisation and modernisation are not merely adopted but transformed into spatial varied outcomes, leading to 'territories of difference' (Escobar, 2001, 2008). Furthermore, the global does not only construct the local, but the global is co-constructed by the local (Massey, 1994), which is referred to in terms like glocalisation (Bauman, 1978) and hybridity (Woods, 2007).

Second, territorialisation is the result of *balancing endogenous and exogenous factors* (Ray, 2006). This refers to the debate on (neo-)endogenous development. The importance of endogenous actors has been acknowledged in regional development, for example in economic growth theory (Stimson *et al.*, 2011). In rural sociology, (neo-)endogenous development has been defined as the utilisation and celebration of local and regional characteristics as the basis of its economic activity and livelihood (Oostindie *et al.*, 2008). The emphasis here is on understanding the characteristics (natural, human and cultural) of a place that makes it special and/or distinctive (different from other regions), and how these may become the focus of sustainable economic activity (Vanclay, 2011: 59). This does not mean that regional development is considered merely from a perspective 'from within' because the significance and influence of unbounded factors are also acknowledged. Such unbounded factors can, however, be transformed into a self-constructed development model, creating autonomous capacity.

Third, territorialisation includes the *urban and rural* and all blurred mixtures in between. The rural-urban dichotomy has eroded in the context of metropolitan landscapes (Wiskerke, 2007), where urban and rural activities are becoming increasingly intermingled. These areas have become network societies, where local and international production and consumption are connected in a complex system, whereas governance implementation is still organised along sectoral lines. The blurring of rural-urban boundaries is especially relevant in the context of territorialisation in West European countries.

Fourth, territorialisation (based on a constructivist notion of region) encompasses not only cognitive actions but also *subjective perceptions, sense-making, the construction of narratives and place identities*. Regions are made meaningful and endowed with identities, subjectivities and difference (Escobar, 2001). Cultural practices, people's narratives, sense of place and the role of individual catalysts play a role in creating identities. Messely *et al.* (2014) stress the importance of individual catalysts in regional formation processes, people who stimulate synergies between the different aspects of the process, resulting in the (re)production of the region and its identities.

Territorialisation in the context of regional development can thus be understood as a 'fusion' between neo-endogenous regional development and the co-production of society and environment, transcending rural-urban boundaries and local-global divisions (see also Dessein, 2015).

Dimensions of territorialisation

To present territorialisation, we have developed an analytical framework that distinguishes three dimensions in territorialisation: the symbolic, reification and institutional dimensions. Although distinguished for analytical reasons, these dimensions are closely linked with each other and are mutually reinforcing.

The *symbolic* dimension: space becomes place. People reconstruct, represent, perceive or cartographically denominate a space with the aim of 'situating' and then 'placing' themselves. Here agency mediates sense and senses. People attach subjective cultural meanings to places in their appreciation of places. People make 'sense of their place' and add symbolic value to place in varied cultural contexts.

The *reification* dimension: from a place to a 'place to live in'. Place is structured through the occupation, use and transformation of the land. People use, re-use and add value to natural resources. Here agency mediates practices. Culture refers here to cultural practices. Cultural sustainability has been associated with the role of creativity and cultural activities for community vitality and community planning of urban and rural areas. Cultural practices are materialised in cultural heritage and cultural landscapes.

The *institutional* dimension: structuring place. In the process of defining functions and rules, it is the culture of a given community that shapes the frameworks that preside over the policies. Agency here mediates norms and rules. Culture refers here to cultural characteristics of institutions. Culture frames and shapes 'the rules of the game', routines, organisations and ways of cooperation and self-governance.

Territorialisation and sustainable development

The concept of sustainable development, born from the need to preserve the quality of the natural resources for the present and future generations, has been embodied in the international policy agendas starting from the 1972 Stockholm Conference. The best known definitions of this concept (and there are many; Latouche (1995) counted at least 154 definitions as early as 1995) are contained in the so-called Brundtland Report (WCED, 1987). The principles of the Brundtland Report have stimulated socio-economic research substantially, from the sociology and the economics of the environment to the more radical ecological economics, both in the theoretical and the applicative field. However, often a narrow approach of sustainable development is promoted, limited to efficient resource use, essentially referring to 'development' being understood as 'growth', and underestimating the connections to notions of space and place. The increasing centrality of a globalised economy has undermined the importance of specific locations, landscapes or places as critical components of sustainability (Escobar, 2001). In the way sustainability has been defined by the WCED (1987), notions of place, but also persons and permanence (time) have largely been neglected (Seghezzo, 2009: 546). Regions face all sorts of sustainability challenges on food, poverty, land-use, climate, energy and migration. These challenges are interrelated, but are often addressed separately in regional policy and science. We argue that notions on place, persons and time are to be connected with the difficulties of grasping and analysing the complex interactions that exist between social, cultural, economic and environmental dimensions of regional development.

The analysis of territorialisation provides more insight into the sustainability or non-sustainability of a region. The described dimensions allow us to study the characterisation of the natural assets of a place, the means by which nature and culture interact and how communities assign meaning to local assets, add functions and describe rules about how to use space. We believe therefore that the concept of territorialisation lends itself well to improving the framing of sustainable regional development, because it highlights the time-space dimension and the role of people in the use and consumption of resources. What counts in such studies are the relations that people and communities construct and normalise, in the time and in the places of their choice, with reference to resources and constructed local/regional specificities. Territorialisation includes expressions of a sense of belonging or the absence of these, and the identification of people with their inhabited space, according to tangible signs of recognition or difference, harmony or distance, both in its morphological and its organisational confirmation. Territorialisation thus has the potential to direct its goals also toward intra-generational and inter-generational equity with regard to the use of resources (Battaglini, 2014).

The role of culture in territorialisation

The call for culture is becoming more powerful to meet the aims of sustainability along with the increasing ecological, economic and social challenges. In the UN's

Sustainability Development Goals, which replaced the Millennium Development Goals in 2015, culture pops up in 4 of the 17 goals in the zero draft of this strategy (UN, 2014). Soini and Birkeland (2014), in their overview on culture and sustainability, have described seven different storylines on cultural sustainability. These storylines vary from conservative views focusing on preserving cultural heritage to more progressive, radical visions on eco-cultural resilience and cultural evolution. In the context of territorialisation it is relevant that the concept of cultural sustainability has been viewed as a dimension of sense of place (Vileniske 2008) and has been linked to local or place-based self-sustainable development (Magnaghi 2005). Doubleday *et al.* (2004: 389, cited by Duxbury and Gillette, 2007) note that discussions of sustainability incorporate 'both dynamic understandings of culture and the recognition that place matters because the practice that is in need of sustaining, as well as those that pose threats, happen in particular communities and in specific geographic contexts.' They note that serious discussions of sustainability require considerations of the dynamics of complex cultural arrangements in particular places, rather than assumptions of either people's or their ecological contexts.

We describe here three examples to illustrate the role of culture and cultural sustainability in territorialisation. First, the link between territorialisation and culture is evident in the theoretical notion of cultural landscape. Sauer (1925), for example, stressed the agency of culture as a force in shaping the visible features of the Earth's surface in delimited areas. Within his definition, the physical environment retains a central significance as the medium with and through which human cultures act. He defines 'cultural landscape' as fashioned from a natural landscape by a cultural group. Culture is considered the agent and the natural area is the medium, resulting in the cultural landscape.

Duxbury and Gilette (2007: 11) have linked both culture and sustainability to community development and people's engagement:

> Cultural development is a form of sustainable development that promotes a self-reliant economy and locally based cultural policy. Arts and culture are development tools that contribute to building networks and trust in the community, and help create a sense of place and occasions for sociability that draw people together who might not otherwise be engaged in constructive social activities.

Culture and sustainability have also been linked to values, referring to principles and motivations which guide people's actions, worldviews and sense making (Horlings, 2015). The Sustainable Development Research Institute mentions for example: 'the ability to retain cultural identity, and to allow change to be guided in ways that are consistent with the cultural values of people' (SDRI, 1998: 1; Duxbury and Gillette, 2007). The link between culture and sustainability is also visible in more radical pleas for a fundamental cultural or paradigm shift to enhance sustainability: 'Only in a rethinking of cultural value systems and ethical paradigms, by questioning foundations, attitudes and assumptions, there is some hope for moving toward sustainability' (Stefanovic, 2000: 6).

Objective and overview of the book

The overall purpose of this book is to elaborate on and provide more insight into the role of culture in territorialisation. This requires an interdisciplinary approach. We consider culture in this book as the fertile ground in which the dimensions of territorialisation can flourish, inspired by Francophone as well as Anglo-Saxon traditions. To summarise the above, we combine geographically bounded and relational space, the natural and the cultural, the material and the immaterial, and bring – again – the territory to the fore. By structuring the concept of 'territorialisation' in the described three-dimensional framework, we aim to show how the natural environment and culture are constitutive of each other. Territorialisation, then, is a process and a new lens to understand how culture mediates practices, symbolisation and institutionalisation in multi-scale spatial development.

The role of culture in this book not only refers to cognitive actions and practices, but also includes subjective perceptions, sense-making, the construction of narratives and place identities. The concept of territorialisation allows us furthermore to study the characterisation of the natural assets of a place; the means by which nature and culture interact; and how communities assign meaning to local assets, add functions and ascribe rules of how to use space. We believe, as argued above, that the concept of territorialisation lends itself well to grasp the role and meaning of culture in sustainable regional development because it highlights the dimensions of place, time and people in the use and consumption of resources. The chapters in this book contribute to the operationalisation of territorialisation by analysing how the dimensions of territorialisation play out in empirical cases, providing insight into how culture and agency mediate senses, practices, and norms and rules in different contexts.

The book is organised in 15 chapters to discuss these methodological, institutional, empirical as well as theoretical aspects of the role of culture. The chapters address concepts as well as practical applications in a range of places, contexts and forms: 1) on different scales (micro, meso, macro scales); 2) in different geographical locations; 3) on different dimensions of territorialisation; and 4) with a different balance of theoretical and empirical explorations.

The book shows how the cultural values attached by people, which are enmeshed in the institutional context, history, sustainability discourses and the intentions of people in interaction with their environment, shape sustainable practices and places. The cases provide geographical and institutional diversity. They are drawn from different continents, covering cases from Europe, Africa, Brazil, Australia and New Zealand, the Middle East, Canada and the USA.

Although the book is a collection of separately-authored papers, it arises from a closely-integrated series of debates over a three-year period. Some of the authors, writing from many disciplinary backgrounds, participated in the European COST Action 'Investigating Cultural Sustainability' and/or a working group on place-based approaches during a conference of the European Society for Rural Sociology in 2013. Here we provide a short overview of the chapters in this book.

Place can be considered as a vector of culture, a vehicle for the transference and ownership of human institutions as Redclift and Manuel-Navarette show in Chapter 2. Place is not simply a product of human agency. It is a cultural product, the filter through which agency finds expression, and subject to the structural binds of culture. With this perspective, the chapter examines what it is that makes places 'sustainable', both from a conceptual perspective and through the use of the ecotourism case material from the Mexican Caribbean. In Chapter 3 Woods explores the significance of processes of 'territorialisation' and 'de-territorialisation' in understanding the restructuring of rural places in the context of globalisation by drawing on assemblage theory (De Landa, 2006). He argues that assemblage theory offers an alternative perspective in which restructuring can be understood, not as the erosion of place-difference, but as the re-assembling of places, which is accompanied by processes of re-territorialisation and recoding. Applying this approach to examples from Australia, Canada and New Zealand, he illuminates the connections between culture and territorialisation in the form of cultural artefacts, symbols of identity, cultural expressions, organisation and the coding of places. In Chapter 4 Horlings adds a fourth 'worldview' dimension to the framework of territorialisation, to provide insight into the question why people would contribute to sustainable place-shaping. The dimensions of territorialisation are operationalised in this chapter as 1) way of life; 2) sense of place; 3) cultural practices; and 4) cultural characteristics of institutions. Horlings further describes how human values play a role in the first two dimensions, illustrating this via the case of an urban neighbourhood in the Netherlands. Battaglini and Babović attempt to understand how culture interacts with natural heritage. In Chapter 5 they build on the concepts of 'territorialisation' and 'affordances', as key concepts in their analysis of the rural Zlatibor region in Western Serbia, with wide touristic and agricultural potentialities. The main focus is on the affective, cognitive and selective dimensions of the values which people attribute to resources, and how processes of symbolisation and reification play a role in territorialistion. Chiesi explores the need for an integrated approach that brings together multiple scales of analysis. His analysis in Chapter 6 is supported by outlining a taxonomy of observable indicators of territorial behaviour, such as traces (non-intentional effects of behaviours), alterations (self-designed semi-permanent modifications to the environment), adaptations (actualisation of non-designed affordances) and signs (reference to content). Kivitalo, Kumpulainen and Soini attempt to understand culturally sustainable rural space in Finland. Chapter 7 analyses how culture manifests itself through lived, conceived and perceived rural space, following Lefebvre. Using the analytical framework of Horlings (2015) and Soini *et al.* (2012), the authors cross-read 'culture' and 'sustainability' based on data from Finnish villages. Dessein aims to understand and illustrate the process of territorialisation, with a focus on practices. In Chapter 8 he analyses coinciding rural development actions that take a natural resource (*in casu* saffron) as a catalyst for regional development. Drawing on empirical research on saffron cultivation in Morocco, he combines neo-endogenous development and co-production in a framework that distinguishes between 'weak' and 'strong' territorialisation. In Chapter 9 Cicerchia investigates the recent national and international policies to define and measure sustainable development and sustainable well-being, using indices and indicators. She investigates how these policies take spaces, places and territories into account as well as the different cultural milieux. Examples are UNESCO's Cultural Development Indicator Suite, Yale's Environmental Sustainability Index, OECD's Better Life Index and Italy's Fair and Sustainable Well-Being index. In Chapter 10 Chiesi and Costa frame the practices of 'co-design' and 'cultural mapping' within the discourse of place-based approaches to sustainable local development. Through the analysis of three Mediterranean case studies in Malta, Palestine and Syria, the chapter locates these practices within the general debate on methodology of social research, with some specific references to the action research paradigm. The authors then build a classification of cultural mapping projects, delving into the specific types of active community involvement. In Chapter 11 Padt explores how territories can purposefully be designed to attain greater sustainability at the territorial level and beyond. Territorialisation is a negotiation process that involves many actors which bring different scale frames to the table. The design process includes a review and critical evaluation of the actors' scale frames. He presents US case studies and a working method along the lines of the described dimensions of territorialisation to illustrate the design process. He argues that by 'scaling up, scaling in and scaling out' new, culturally mediated, territories can be created that help the case of sustainable development. Atmanagara aims to generate a better understanding of the role of culture in urban planning processes, which are considered to be the initiator and/or facilitator for developing solutions towards socio-ecological resilience. For this purpose, in Chapter 12 she explores and reflects on relevant strategies and measures of urban planning in Brussels and Ljubljana. She argues that culture can serve as a mediator in urban planning to develop adequate solutions to combat the impacts of global challenges and to foster urban resilience. Such an understanding of urban planning comes close to the storylines of eco-cultural resilience and eco-cultural civilisation within the concept of cultural sustainability (Soini and Birkeland, 2014). In Chapter 13 Thomas Lane, Pierce, Jones and Harris describe the governance-setting of Wales, which has a legal and well-documented commitment to sustainable development. Their chapter investigates implementation with regards to special places, often internationally asserted as meriting protection. Event-based regeneration, branding of sustainably managed goods and services are explored as means of re-producing place experience which can underpin these areas' successful resilience. The notion of European drivers and networks of influence is also discussed, combining a regional development framework with exemplars of community based projects relating to sustainable tourism, leisure and the broader green economy. Hebinck, Mango and Kimanthi explore the relationship between culturally embedded development situations and sustainability in Kenya. In Chapter 14 they describe how assemblages of seed practices, shaped by socio-technical networks, are well embedded and structured by cultural beliefs and associated kinship-based practices. This cultural repertoire provides hands and feet to a configuration that works in the daily practice of farming. It also explains why some farmers distance themselves from interventions aimed to change seed practices. They argue that sustainable development as a multitude of practices, which are continuously reassembled in time and space, needs to be cognisant of cultural notions of development. In Chapter 15 Caggiano reflects on territories in a metropolitan context to provide insight into how to analyse the interplay of culture, community and sustainable ways of life. Her analysis is based on field research on the *jardins partagés* in Paris. A *jardin partagé* designates a collective garden, set up and led by local associations on small public plots granted by the local authorities. The analysis suggests scenarios for sustainable futures beyond their confinements and beyond the rural-urban relationship, promoting place-based development. Florit, Blanck de Oliveira, Fleuri and Wartha associate the process of territorialisation of the State of Santa Catarina (Brazil) with European colonisation during the nineteenth century. In this context, they examine how the tourist regionalisation known as 'European Valley' is an update of coloniality in relation to indigenous people. This results in invisibility and maintenance of environmental inequities associated with strategies to cope with floods that currently sacrifice indigenous territories.

The editors and authors hope that this book will appeal to specialists in four major fields of research: regional development, geography, the social sciences (particularly those concerned with rural and urban development and governance) and sustainability. The questions raised in the book are of interest to researchers in the social sciences and humanities and those working in the environmental and physical sciences who may wish to work towards a more holistic perspective. The book is also directed towards those professionals and policy makers who implement or participate in local policies, regional development, planning and governance, social cohesion, place-based approaches and cultural diversity. This has become increasingly relevant in the context of emerging (regional, national, European) place-based policies, based on the potential of each place and ensuring equal opportunities for individuals irrespective of where they live. We hope to provide more insight in how to implement the much debated place-based dimension, including the role of culture in such place-based regional policies.

References

Agnew, J. (2001). Regions in revolt. *Progress in Human Geography,* 25: 103–110.

Allen, J. and A. Cochrane (2007). Beyond the territorial fix: Regional assemblages, politics and power. *Regional Studies*, 41: 1161–1175.

Allen, J. and A. Cochrane (2010). Assemblages of state power: Topological shifts in the organization of government and politics. *Antipode,* 42 (5): 1071–1089.

Allen, J., Massey, D. and A. Cochrane (1998). *Rethinking the region.* Routledge, London.

Amin, A. (2004). Regions unbound: towards a new politics of place. *Geografiska Annaler*, 86B (1): 33–44.

Battaglini, E. (2014). *Sviluppo Territoriale. Dal disegno di ricerca alla valutazione dei risultati*. Milano, Franco Angeli.

Battaglini, E. and M. Babović (2015). Nature and culture in territorialisation processes: Challenges and insights from a case study in Serbia. In: this book, Chapter 5.

Bauman, Z. (1978). *Hermeneutics and social science: Approaches to understanding*. Hutchinson, London.

Brighenti, A. M. (2010). On territorology. Towards a general science of territory. *Theory, Culture & Society*, 27 (1): 52–72.

Callon, M. (1986). Some elements of a sociology of translation: Domestication of the scallops and the fishermen of St Brieuc Bay, pp. 196–223 in: J. Law (ed.), *Power, action and belief: A new sociology of knowledge*. London, Routledge & Kegan Paul.

Carter, E., Donald, J. and J. Squires (1993). *Space and place: Theories of identity and location*. Lawrence & Wishart, London.

Creswell, T. (2004). *Place; a short introduction*. Blackwell Publishing, Malden (USA), Oxford (UK) and Carlton (Australia).

De Landa, M. (2006). *A new philosophy of society: Assemblage theory and social complexity*. Continuum, London and New York.

Dessein, J. (2015). Territorialisation in practice: The case of saffron cultivation in Morocco. In: this book, Chapter 8.

Doubleday, N., Mackenzie, F. and S. Dalby (2004). Reimagining sustainable cultures: Constitutions, land and art. *The Canadian Geographer,* 48 (40): 389–402.

Duxbury, N. and E. Gillette (2007). Culture as a key dimension of sustainability: Exploring concepts, themes, and models. Working paper no. 1. Centre of Expertise on Culture and Communities, Creative City Network of Canada/Simon Fraser University, Vancouver. Available at: http://tosca.vtlseurope.com:8098/arxius/pdf/E130054.pdf (accessed 10 November 2014).

Escobar, A. (2001). Culture sits in places: Reflection on globalism and subaltern strategies of localizaton. *Political Geography,* 20: 139–174.

Escobar, A. (2008). *Territories of difference: Place, movements, life, redes*. Duke University Press, Durham.

Folke, C. (2006). Resilience: the emergence of a perspective for social-ecological systems analysis. *Global Environmental Change,* 16 (3): 253–267.

Folke, C., Hahn, T., Olsson, P. and J. Norberg (2005). Adaptive governance of social-ecological systems. *Annual Review of Environment and Resources*, 30: 441–475.

Gunderson, L., Light, S.S. and C.S. Holling (1995). *Barriers and bridges to the renewal of regional ecosystems*. Columbia University Press, New York.

Harvey, D. (1973). *Social justice and the city*. Blackwell, Oxford.

Harvey, D. (2009). *Cosmopolitanism and the geographies of Freedom*. Columbia University Press, New York.

Haughton, G. and P. Allmendinger (2010). Spatial planning, devolution and new planning spaces. *Environment and Planning C, Government and Policy*, 28 (5): 803–818.

Haughton, G., Allmendinger, P., Counsell, D. and G. Vigar (2010). *The new spatial planning: Soft spaces, fuzzy boundaries and territorial management*. Routledge, London.

Horlings, L.G. (2015). The worldview and symbolic dimension in territorialisation: How human values play a role in a Dutch neighbourhood. In: this book, Chapter 4.

Hudson, R. (2007). Regions and regional uneven development forever? Some reflective comments upon theory and practice. *Regional Studies*, 41: 1149–1160.

Ingold, T. (1992). Culture and the perception of the environment, pp. 39–56 in: Croll, E. and D. Parkin (eds), *Bush base: Forest farm. Culture, environment and development.* Routledge, London.

Janssen, M. A. and E. Ostrom (2006). Resilience, vulnerability, and adaptation: A cross-cutting theme of the International Human Dimensions Programme on Global Environmental Change. *Global Environmental Change*, 16: 237–239.

Jessop B., Brenner, N. and M. Jones (2008). Theorizing sociospatial relations. *Environment and Planning D: Society and Space,* 26: 389–401.

Jonas, A. (2012). Region and place: Regionalism in question. *Progress in Human Geography* 36: 263–272.

Jones, M. (2009). Phase space: Geography, relational thinking, and beyond. *Progress in Human Geography*, 33: 487.

Kneafsey, M. (2010). The region in food – important or irrelevant? *Cambridge Journal of Regions, Economy and Society*, 3: 177–190.

Latouche S. (1995). *La Mégamachine. Raison technoscentifique, raison économique et mythe du progrès. Essais a la memoire de Jacques Ellul.* La Découverte-MAUSS, Paris.

Latour, B. (1993). *We have never been modern*. Harvester Wheatsheaf, Brighton.

Latour, B. (2005). *Reassembling the social: An introduction to actor-network-theory*. Oxford University Press, Oxford.

Law, J. and J. Hassard (eds) (1999). *Actor network theory and after.* Blackwell and the Sociological Review, Oxford and Keele.

Long, N. (2001). *Development sociology: Actor perspectives.* Routledge, London.

Loorbach, D. and J. Rotmans (2006). Managing transitions for sustainable development, pp. 187–206 in: Olshoorn, X. and A.J. Wieczorek (eds), *Understanding industrial transformation: Views from different disciplines.* Springer, Dordrecht.

MacLeod, G. and M. Jones (2007). Territorial, scalar, networked, connected: In what sense a 'regional world'? *Regional Studies*, 41 (9): 1177–1191.

Magnaghi, A. (2005). *The urban village: A charter for democracy and local self-sustainable development.* Zed Books, London and New York.

Massey, D. (1991). A global sense of place. *Marxism Today*: 24–29.

Massey, D. (1993). Power geometries and a progressive sense of place, pp. 59–69 in: Bird, J., Curtis, B., Putnam, T., Robertson, G. and L. Tickner (eds), *Mapping the futures: Local cultures, global changes*. Routledge, London.

Massey, D. (1994). A global sense of place, pp. 146–156 in: Massey, D. (ed.), *From space, place and gender.* University of Minnesota Press, Minneapolis.

Massey, D. (2004). Geographies of responsibility. *Geografiska Annaler*, 86 B (1): 5–18.

Massey, D. (2005). *For space*. SAGE Publications, London.

Merriman, P., Jones, M., Olsson, G., Sheppard, E., Thrift, N. and Y. Tuan (2012). Space and spatiality in theory. *Dialogues in Human Geography,* 2 (1): 3, published online.

Messely, L. (2014). On regions and their actors. An analysis of the role of actors and policy in region-specific rural development processes in Flanders. PhD thesis, Ghent University, Ghent.

Messely, L., Schuermans, N., Dessein, J. and E. Rogge (2014) No region without individual catalysts? Exploring region formation processes in Flanders (Belgium). *European Urban and Regional Studies*, 21 (3): 318–330.

Neumann, R.P. (2010) Political ecology II: Theorizing region. *Progress in Human Geography*, 34: 368–374.

Oostindie, H., van Broekhuizen, R., Brunori, G. and J.D. Van der Ploeg (2008). The endogeneity of rural economies, pp. 53–67 in: Van der Ploeg, J.D. and T. Marsden (eds), *Unfolding webs: The dynamics of regional rural development*. Van Koninklijke Van Gorcum, Assen.

Paasi A. (2009a). Bounded spaces in a 'borderless world'? Border studies, power, and the anatomy of the territory. *Journal of Power*, 2: 213–234.

Paasi, A. (2009b). The resurgence of the 'region' and 'regional identity': theoretical perspectives and empirical observations on the regional dynamics in Europe. *Review of International Studies,* 35 (S1): 121–146.

Paasi, A. (2009c). Regional geography I, pp. 2017–2227 in: Kitchin, R. and N. Thrift (eds), *International encyclopaedia of human geography*. Vol. 8. Elsevier, London.

Paasi, A. (2010). Commentary; regions are social constructs, but who or what 'constructs' them? Agency in question. *Environment and Planning A*. 2296–2301.

Paasi, A. (2011). From region to space, part II, pp. 161–175 in: Agnew, J.A. and J.S. Duncan (eds), *The Wiley-Blackwell companion to human geography*. Blackwell, Oxford.

Pierce, J., Martin, D. and J. Murphy (2011). Relational place-making: The networked politics of place. *Trans Inst Br Geog*, 36: 54–70.

Pike, A., Rodríguez-Pose, A. and J. Tomaney (2006). *Local and regional development*. Routledge, London.

Raffestin, C. and S.A. Butler (2012). Space, territory, and territoriality. *Environment and Planning D: Society and Space*, 30 (1): 121–141.

Ray, C. (2006). Neo-endogenous development in the EU, pp. 278–291 in: Cloke, P., Marsden, T.K. and P.H. Mooney (eds), *Handbook of rural studies*. SAGE Publications, London.

Relph, E. (1976). *Place and placelessness*. Pion, London.

Rhodes, R.A.W. (1997). *Understanding governance: Policy networks, governance, reflexivity, and accountability*. Open University Press, Buckingham Philadelphia.

Sack, R.D. (1986). *Human territoriality: Its theory and history*. Cambridge University Press, Cambridge.

Sauer, C. (1925). The morphology of landscape. *University of California Publications in Geography*, 22: 19–53.

Schatzki, T. R. (2002). *The site of the social. A philosophical account of the constitution of social life and change*. Pennsylvania State University Press, Pennsylvania.

SDRI, Sustainable Development Research Institute (1998). *Social capital formation and institutions for sustainability*. Workshop proceedings prepared by Asoka Mendis. November 16–17, 1998. Vancouver, Sustainable Development Research Institute. Available at: www.williambowles.info/mimo/refs/soc_cap.html (accessed 1 August 2014).

Seghezzo, L. (2009). The five dimensions of sustainability. *Environmental Politics*, 18 (4): 539–556.

Soini, K. and I. Birkeland (2014). Exploring the scientific discourse on cultural sustainability. *Geoforum*, 51: 213–223.

Soini, K., Kivitalo, M. and A. Kangas (2012). *Exploring culture in sustainable rural development*. The 7th International Conference on Cultural Policy Research, 9–12 July, International Conference on Cultural Policy Research.

Stefanovic, I.L. (2000). *Safeguarding our common future: Rethinking sustainable development*. State University of New York Press, Albany, New York.

Stimson R.J., Stough, R.R. and P.J. Nijkamp (eds) (2011). *Endogenous regional development: Perspectives, measurement and empirical investigation*. Edward Elgar, Cheltenham (UK) and Northampton (USA).

Turco A. (1988). *Verso una teoria geografica della complessità*. UNICOPLI, Milan.

UN (2014). Open Working Group Proposal for Sustainable Development Goals, Zero Draft. Available at: http://sustainabledevelopment.un.org/focussdgs.html (accessed 2 July 2014).

Van der Ploeg, J.D. and T. Marsden (eds) (2008). *Unfolding 'webs': Enlarging theoretical understanding of rural development*. Van Gorcum, Assen.

Vanclay, F. (2011) Endogenous rural development from a sociological perspective, pp. 59–69 in: Stimson R.J., Stough, R. and P. Nijkamp (eds), *Endogenous regional development: Perspectives, measurement and empirical investigation*. Edward Elgar Publishing, Cheltenham (UK) and Northampton (USA).

Varro, K. and A. Langendijk (2013). Conceptualizing the region – in what sense relational? *Regional Studies,* 47: 18–28.

Vileniske, I.G. (2008). Influence of built heritage on sustainable development of landscape. *Landscape Res*., 33: 425–437.

WCED (1987). *Our common future*. World Commission on Environment and Development. Oxford University Press, Oxford.

Wiskerke, J.S.C. (2007). *Robuuste regio's: dynamiek, samenhang en diversiteit in het metropolitane landschap. Inaugurale rede, 15 November*. Wageningen University and Research centre, Wageningen.

Woods, M. (2007). Engaging the global countryside: Globalization, hybridity and the reconstitution of rural place. *Progress in Human Geography*, 31: 485–507.

Woods, M. (2011). *Regions engaging globalization: A typology of regional responses in rural Europe*. Paper presented to the Anglo-American-Canadian Rural Geographers Quadrennial Conference, Manitoba, Canada, July.

2 'Sustainable places'

Place as a vector of culture. Two cases from Mexico

Michael Redclift and David Manuel-Navarrete

Introduction: the meaning of 'place'

In this chapter we examine what makes places 'sustainable', both conceptually and concretely, using case material from northern Mexico and the so-called 'Costa Maya'. Within most of the geographical canon 'space' has been given much closer attention than 'place'. McDowell (1997: 4) suggests this is because place is best seen as contextual: 'the significance of place depends on the issue under consideration and the sets of social relations that are relevant to the issues'. We argue that place is frequently used in a way that takes on meaning from the context in which it is employed, rather than conveying meaning itself. Modern science tends to disregard place by equating it with lack of generality (Casey, 1997). In physics, geography and social sciences, the use of coordinates, maps, statistics, and other simplifying and objectifying pictures have dominated the representation of places in spatial terms. The dimensions of space and actions within it have similar meanings for everyone. Consequently, space allows scientists to adopt a role of outside observers of places, while the modern concept of 'region' is often taken as a natural unit of spatial and social organisation (Curry, 2002). In social theories, space was assumed to be featureless and undifferentiated. It was often used for predicting patterns of land-use and economic activities without describing place in any real sense except as a product of historical accident (Johnson, 2002).

However, spatial representations of place were problematised during the second half of the twentieth century. Lefebvre (1974) and Foucault (1986) questioned the definition of absolute space in terms of Euclidean geometry, and claimed that regions are socially constructed. The human dimension of spatiality was emphasised and the notion of place acquired a renewed relevance, not only among the disciplines which traditionally deal with place (e.g. geography, planning, chorography and philosophy), but also among less related disciplines (e.g. anthropology, cultural studies, ecology, psychology and phenomenology). Researchers in these disciplines have made significant efforts to define the concept and formulate an adequate theory of place. Although it is not clear whether the adoption of a unique definition would be either possible or desirable, these multiple perspectives of place agree that places are more than geographic settings with physical or spatial characteristics; they are fluid, changeable, dynamic contexts of social interaction and memory (Harrison and Dourish, 1996; Stokowski, 2002).

In a path-breaking work Tuan (1977) argued that experiences of places involve perception, cognition and affection. Similarly, Relph (1976) identified three components of place: physical setting, activities and meanings. According to these authors, a place cannot simply be described as the location of one object relative to others. The concept of place has to integrate both its location and its meaning in the context of human action. As Tuan (1977) puts it: 'place is space infused with human meaning'. Along similar lines, Agnew (1987) studied the relationship between place and human behaviour and proposed a compositional view of places as constituted by economic, institutional and socio-cultural processes. Agnew identified three basic elements of place: location, locale and sense of place. Location is the role a place plays in the world-economy, locale the institutional setting of a place, and sense of place the identities that are forged and given meaning within places.

Recent thinking about place is greatly influenced by the work of Doreen Massey and Noel Castree. Massey (1994) suggested a more dynamic view of places as 'networks of social relations'. According to her, places are continually changing as a result of economic, institutional and cultural transformation. Places are not essences but processes, and places do not necessarily mean the same thing to everyone (Massey, 1994). Massey adds that the nature of a place is a product of its linkages with other places and not just a matter of its internal features. Places appear as points of intersection that integrate the global and the local. She writes that: 'displacement, most particularly through migration, depends … on a prior notion of cultures embedded in place' (Massey and Jess, 1995: 1). Determining place, 'drawing boundaries in space … is always a social act'. She adds that the dominant notion of place that we are all familiar with 'is one that arises as a result of the changes going on in the world around us' (Massey and Jess, 1995: 63). For Massey place is not a free-standing concept, but one that should be used transitively, attaching itself to another 'object' that might help to illuminate it. She ends by providing almost a 'place' advocacy, which she terms a 'progressive sense of place', through which geographers and others might take the part of communities and social classes.

Castree provides a rather different contribution to the conceptualisation of place. He argues that Marxist geographers were 'preoccupied with the inter-place connections more than specific place differences', in effect ignoring the saliency of place itself (Castree, 2003: 170). While broadly sympathetic to the humanistic geographers' perspective on place, which sought to 'recover people's sense of place … that is, how different individuals and groups … develop meaningful attachments to those specific areas where they live out their lives …' (Castree, 2003: 170), he invokes neurological circuit metaphors, 'switching points' and 'nodes' to suggest the degrees to which places are plugged into different sets of global relations. He argues that globalisation has resulted 'in an exciting and innovative redefinition of what place means', seeing 'place differences as both cause and effect of place connections' (Castree, 2003: 166).

The significance of place is that it has both cognitive and normative meanings. It involves the 'humanisation' of space, of territory. In this sense the experience of spatial relations is always a social construction; it is an inevitable consequence of human consciousness. It is impossible to distinguish a 'place' to which some group of people do not belong. (The obvious exception to this claim is the Antarctic – but even this has been colonised by research scientists.)

A sense of 'belonging', then, is a key element of the way space is socialised. What we 'belong to', of course, is itself a diachronic process, a liminal process in which the human actors themselves define place through the way their institutions evolve, as well as the territory they occupy. This sense of belonging is also suggested by the way they dress. One example of this is the border between the United States and Mexico on the Rio Grande River. When Mexico gained independence in 1823, most of the western and southern parts of the (now) United States were part of Mexico. Photographs of the Rio Grande from just after the Mexican Revolution of 1810 show very different styles of dress on each side of the divide. On the American side, ladies in long white 'Edwardian' dresses stand with men in smart, fashionable hats, while on the Mexican side the men resemble followers of Emiliano Zapata, with big broad brimmed hats and *campesino* attire. A 1912 image of Los Angeles (California) features a *zocalo* (main square) like any found in a large Mexican town, with the population dressed in typical Mexican clothing.

These images illustrate one of the key points in our argument: namely, that agency and culture mediate intention. Place is not simply a product of human agency; it is a cultural product. Agency gets filtered through place to find an expression that is subject to the bounds of culture (the opportunities and limits inherent in the local environment within which human agency works). The editors of this book refer to this in their treatment of 'territory' and territoriality: place is a vector of culture, a vehicle for the transference and ownership of human institutions, the sum of place and agency through which nature itself derives the power of agency. This sense of belonging and ownership is often involuntary, such as in the case of ghettos and prisons. Human institutions often imply 'ownership' and 'belonging', as we have seen, but people are often *dis*placed, rather than located in a place, and the places they inhabit are transgressive places, where they seek to retrieve the 'memory' of place and own it, just as Palestinians or Kurds today own a place-location that is no longer their own.

What factors make place sustainable? The first factor is the retention of culture and place through what the editors refer to as 'territorial belonging': the group awareness as nourished historically through daily social interactions over time. In diachronic terms we are referring to a 'given' historical process; in synchronic terms, to the active agency that is expressed in 'belonging' to a place. This contributes to a 'sense of place', and a way of life that is chosen, although the 'choice' is often made by our culture and through transgression rather than individual agency. Second, the way that we come to value the environment, an anthropogenic process, is not a 'given' in physical or spatial terms. To answer this question, we have considered one area in which place has been both constructed and deconstructed, largely around the labels that we attach to place in the litany (and taxonomy) of tourism. After considering a case from the Mexican Caribbean, we will return to the question of what makes a place (un)sustainable.

Eco-tourism in Mexico: the construction of place?

> Cancun, until very recently, was an unknown area. Formerly it was a fishing town but over a period of thirty years it evolved into a place that has become famous worldwide. It is located in the south-east of Mexico, with no more 'body' to it than the living spirit of the Mayas, a race that mysteriously disappeared and who were one of the great pre-Columbian cultures in Mexico. The only thing that remained was the land transformed into a paradise on earth …
>
> (Everest, 2002: 36)

The development of Cancun in the 1970s transformed the Yucatan peninsula from a unique ethnographic site of particular interest to archaeologists and anthropologists into a 'global space' for tourists. The coast south of Cancun, the so-called 'Mayan Riviera', is now one of the fastest-growing urban areas of Latin America, and plans are well advanced to take this process much further. Together with mass tourism, typified by the 'all-inclusive' hotels of Cancun itself, other more diversified forms of tourism have become established, which attempt to recombine several elements: the Mayan identity (real or imagined), closeness to nature, closeness to history (real or imagined) and the involvement of local communities. Under the sobriquet of 'communal tourism', 'sustainable tourism' and 'eco-tourism', distinct social groups have entered the tourist market, most of it geared to international tastes. Travelling in the remote interior of the Yucatan, in areas where the local population speaks little Spanish and practises 'slash and burn' agriculture, one hears the same refrain: 'How can we get started with *ecoturismo*?' Through these observations of the Yucatan, we examine some of the moral dimensions of these choices and the pursuit of more sustainable development.

We have considered three varieties of eco-tourism in the Mexican Caribbean – global 'eco-parks', official conservation areas or Biosphere Reserves, and local-level community or *ejido* initiatives. We examine each case from the standpoint of their moral claims and discursive constructions. Per case, we consider who the principal beneficiaries are and the wider implications of the observed practices towards more sustainable development.

'Eco-parks' on the coast of the Mexican Caribbean

After the development of Cancun in the 1970s, the Caribbean coast south of Cancun was opened up to developers, and with it one of the most alluring eco-systems in the Caribbean. Anyone travelling along this coast in the early 1970s, as the first author did, could leave the car on the narrow coastal road and explore a complex system of freshwater 'sinks' and cave systems cut into the limestone called *cenotes,* which are typical of Karst limestone areas. These freshwater lakes, many of them underground, are linked to tropical lagoons on the coast itself, and the rare passing tourist of the 1970s had unlimited and free access to them. Within a couple of decades most of these attractive, natural sites had been converted into 'eco-parks', tourist parks that combine the natural wonder of the original site with Disneyworld-like attractions. The lagoons and *cenotes* remain, but they have been embellished with new 'Mayan villages', restaurants, bars and other tourist attractions. Dolphins have been imported so visitors can 'swim with dolphins', and 'Mayan' dancers entertain the visitors with 'traditional' dances and music. The visitors mainly come for day trips from Cancun and Playa, paying up to 50 USD for an entrance ticket.

The accounts of eco-tourist development from brochures and tourist magazines suggest that words such as 'nature', 'natural' and 'sustainable' can be used to good effect in a number of ways. By cordoning off part of the coast and enclosing a salt-water lagoon, the developers of resorts like Xell-Ha, one of the most extensive 'Eco-Parks' south of Playa, were able to brand 'nature' with a company name and thus privatise it. Each of these 'parks' provides a variety of tourist facilities, including restaurants and shops, which sell a product that is both a 'natural' and a social construction. They promise a safe recreational experience, complete with limestone sinkholes or *cenotes,* which are developed for kayaking, swimming and snorkelling.

Eco-parks blur the line between the 'natural' and the 'human-made' in other ways. Many of the local staff working in the eco-parks are ethnically Mayan, but the restaurants and cafes that sell 'Mayan' cuisine and the bands that play 'Mayan' music are a counterfeit of the Mayan culture. This appears to work on some level: people sign the visitors' book, thanking the resort for offering them the chance 'to live among the Mayan people'. The reality and the illusion are often indistinguishable to them, particularly since the resorts claim to be 'ethical' both in their stance on ecology and in relation to the integrity of the Mayan culture represented there. The *ethnic* label 'Mayan' is the exact complement of the *eco* labels, such as 'nature', 'natural' and 'sustainable', which describe almost every activity presented to the visitors.

Biosphere Reserves

In contrast to the global eco-parks, the coast also boasts a major UNESCO designated Biosphere Reserve called Xian Ka'an, located to the south of the major resort areas. The Mexican government created this 1.3-million acre reserve in 1986. The following year it was designated as a World Heritage Site and ten years later, another 200,000 acres were added. Today the reserve accounts for 10 per cent of the land area of the state of Quintana Roo, with over 100 kilometres of coastline within the park boundaries. Several thousand Mayan people live there, and it houses 27 archaeological ruins.

Before declaring this reserve a more 'authentic' example of environmental protection than the global eco-parks, we might reflect on the meaning of 'nature' in this hybridised context. The Biosphere Reserve of Xian Ka'an is as much an artificial creation as the resorts of Xcaret or Xell-Ha, although its claims to conserve nature might sound more credible. It is supposed to be free from development, and provides only limited access to visitors with a serious interest in conservation ecology. These claims must be placed in context, however: most tourists who come to the Mexican Caribbean do not visit Xian-Ka'an, nor could it withstand mass tourism. Xian-Ka'an is able to fulfil this nature-conservation role because the nearby commercial resorts meet the needs of mass tourism. To fully appreciate the contribution of reserves like Xian-Ka'an, one also needs to consider the eco-parks with mass appeal, like Xcaret, Xell-Ha and Xpu-Ha, which have transformed the natural environment into something that can be more readily 'consumed'.

These observations suggest a pre-emptive 'environmentalism' that is designed to disarm the environmental critique and demonstrate that coastal developers have learned their lesson from bad publicity about Cancun. They have adopted the new language of sustainability, and reinvented these places within the changing context of sustainability rhetoric. It can be argued, however, that these parks do absorb increasing numbers of global tourists, many of whom would visit the Yucatan peninsula, with or without the eco-parks. They may act as 'honey pots', by attracting tourists away from areas of true ecological interest that would otherwise be threatened by a large number of visitors.

Other conflicts of interest over the environment are hidden behind the tourist-friendly rhetoric of eco-tourism. One example is the opposition being mounted by local peasant families (*ejidatarios*) to the Mexican electricity utility (CFE), which they claim has deforested their land. For the last several years, rallies to condemn these activities have been held nearly every day. Similarly, there has been much public criticism of the dangers and risks inherent in speculative development, notably in the construction of sub-standard hotels. Some of these hotels endanger tourist safety by practices such as running electric cables through hotel swimming pools; the local press denounces numerous avoidable hazards in these hotels. Ecological disasters, like the destruction of reefs, mangroves and turtle breeding grounds, now form part of the daily currency of political discussions on the coast. They serve to increase the efforts of some developers and to convince sceptical publics that their products are free from the taint of ecological risk or damage. The presence of tourism in these locations has moved the environmental debate towards greater consideration of their risk and security, as elements of a larger environmental vulnerability. These new 'consumer' concerns parallel the ecological vulnerabilities that drew some of the visitors to the area in the first place.

A full understanding of the 'Mayan Riviera' can be found in the 'rebranding' of the area's towns. Until 1999 the principal administrative unit (*municipio*) to the south of Cancun was called *Solidaridad* ('solidarity'), a name suggestive of the Mexican Revolution. Enthusiasts for the 'Mayan World' then suggested that it should be renamed 'Xiamen H'a', its original name in Maya, which is rarely used locally because most of the ethnically Mayan population has only a superficial knowledge of the language. A third, and dominant, view, supported by developers, was that the name Playa Del Carmen ('the Beach of Carmen') should continue to be employed, since it is well known in tourist brochures and had been successfully used to attract tourists.

The same place was thus being accorded three separate identities: an administrative identity, linked to the Mexican state; another conferring an ethnic identity; and the third exploiting the familiarity of the tourist connection. One view of the resurgence of interest in Mayan culture, especially among intellectuals and middle-class well-wishers, places these historical oppositions firmly within the camp of contemporary protest over environmental and ethnic abuses in the region. Others caution that both ethnic and environmental struggles in contemporary Latin America have failed to deliver a viable political platform and it may be dangerous to associate 'Mayan' identity with 'nature' and the oppositional politics.

Community and **ejido** *tourism*

Most of these examples of 'eco-tourism' rest on a guarantee of strong consumer demand from international tourist markets, combined with high levels of capital investment from a combination of private and governmental sources. The benefits of these 'hybrid natures' are communicated widely, notably on the internet, and command attention from prospective tourists in markets geographically remote from the sites themselves. The 'moralities' conveyed are complex – both for the consumer of the amenity, as well as for the provider in many cases.

New 'eco-tourist' initiatives are also developing on the Mexican Caribbean coast at a very different spatial level: that of the local community or '*ejido*'. An *ejido* is a peasant community in which community members share the usufruct to land, a result of the Mexican Revolution. In most cases today the agricultural land is worked privately, but many activities, and some resources, are still held in common. In the case of the Yucatan peninsula, one of the most important of these resources is the *cenote,* a natural well or sink-hole in the limestone carapace that covers the region that provides most of the groundwater, since there are no rivers. These *cenotes* are often very beautiful, and the clear, fresh water is a magnet for swimmers, divers and caving specialists. Since much of the water system is underground, it is often inaccessible without a guide and can be visited only if the *cenote* has been mapped and fully explored. Many *cenotes* are completely inaccessible, but others exist close to main arterial roads and resorts. In some cases, local communities provide snorkelling and diving gear to visitors, as well as tour facilities. The mouth of the *cenote* is used as an open-air market for selling artisan goods, hammocks, embroidered goods and pottery. For small communities, the attractions of the natural *cenote* provide access to tourists who would otherwise be lured by mainstream commercial agencies. The main visitors are thus young travellers, backpackers and domestic tourists. We can refer to the *cenote* as exhibiting agency, in that their existence confers value on local communities and their territory/culture. Without the material existence of the *cenote,* fewer opportunities would exist for the inhabitants to convey their sustainability goals in tangible ways. (This does not mean that the *cenote* is always exploited sustainably, however.)

An interesting case is that of Santa Catalina, a large *ejido* which was once a plantation dedicated to *henequén* (agave or henequen in English), the sisal-like 'cactus' that once provided the Yucatan with its principal source of foreign exchange. Henequen fibres were used until the early twentieth century for making ropes and carpets, before being replaced by synthetic fibres.

In the case of Santa Catalina, declining demand for henequen persuaded the original plantation owners to abandon their estate, which they agreed to sell to the former estate workers. There were few business opportunities in henequen production, thus the agricultural workers had to find other means of support besides their own *milpa* (maize) plots. They decided to take what we would describe today as the 'heritage' route, converting the old single-rail track and the wooden wagons which transported the henequen leaves into facilities for visiting tourists. The horse-drawn wagons pick up the tourists in the middle of the *ejido*, where there is a small restaurant and shop, and take them across the estate, visiting a number of *cenotes* en route, where the tourists descend into the holes, swim and snorkel, and eventually rejoin their party for the trip back to the village. The income from conducting these tours is small compared with that from global 'eco-parks' or specialist eco-tourist enterprises, but for the 120 families living on the *ejido*, it represents a significant source of income.

The community members are proud that they took the initiative and that it is still largely in their hands, although they are dependent on tour agencies to direct many of the tourists to their village. In their view what they offer has educational value, too, which most tourists would not gain elsewhere – they are introduced to the economy of a primary industry, combined with the attraction of a major recreational amenity. There is no doubt at all that their enterprise conveys 'sustainability' in a tangible form – the historic tracks and wagons are used, the landscape and ecology of the area is not destroyed, and they ensure that the beauty and splendour of the *cenotes* are not despoiled. To community members, their activities in encouraging 'eco-tourism' are morally defensible. Indeed, they represent an example of how local resources can be redeployed, especially in an area of high underemployment. This reinforces, rather than undermines, the idea of sustainability as a moral precept.

Many communities have established 'eco' or 'ethno'-tourist enterprises that use local resources and initiative. Often they need outside start-up capital, but in other cases, the existence of a community 'gatekeeper' is enough to stimulate activity. One branch of community eco-tourism consists of inviting foreign tourists to share their houses, or *palapas*, for brief periods, when the tourists are taught the Yucatan Maya language and introduced to the ecology of the area. These are obviously niche markets, but again they can be important to local communities with very limited cash incomes.

A more controversial example is provided by the 'Pueblo Chiclero' of Chachoben, inland from the so-called 'Costa Maya', located to the south of the Biosphere Reserve Xian Ka'an. This village was originally a settlement of *chicleros,* the men who tapped the resin known as *chicle* from the tropical *chicozapote* tree. This important historical industry employed over 100,000 workers at its height in the first half of the twentieth century (Redclift, 2004). The *chicle* resin was converted into chewing gum, and bought by large international companies, most notably the *William Wrigley Jr* Company. Because the history of chewing gum is largely unknown outside the region, it seemed to offer an opportunity for tourism, together with the development of the southern coast of the 'Costa Maya'. The state government of Quintana Roo and local private developers have already constructed a port for international cruise ships that visit the coastal town of Majahual. The tourists from the cruise ships are transported 50 kilometers inland along six-lane highways through the forest and mangrove swamps, to the community of Chachoben and the 'Pueblo Chiclero'. Here local guides take them into the forest to see how *chicle* was harvested, visit a *chiclero* encampment or *harto*, and learn something of the tropical forest ecology. This initiative was taken jointly by the local village and the state government, and appears to have strong local backing. Many of the people involved as 'guides' (who also have the opportunity to sell their artisan goods) take great pride in their families' history as *chicleros* and in their knowledge of the trees and animals of the tropical forest. From the perspective of the local community, this represents a 'sustainable' tourist option because it generates income locally, enabling the local people to reinvest profits from tourism.

The impacts of the new motorways and port can be questioned, however. Most infrastructure developments of this type bring enormous financial gains to a small number of rich developers, and locals are often forced to sell their land. On the other hand, some local people benefit, especially those living inland who seek better communication with the rest of the peninsula and want to benefit from some of the income generated from tourism. From the perspective of local, indigenous communities, eco-tourist developments like Chachoben and Santa Catalina chart a route into quite different moral territory, by suggesting ways in which *identity* and *self-determination* might be gained from what might otherwise be an exclusionary money-making enterprise.

Conclusion

The meanings of 'Mayan' and 'nature' are no longer (if they ever were) of local or parochial significance alone: they are now part of a global lexicon. They also carry messages across time, from the nineteenth century Caste War of the Yucatan and across space, to North America and Europe, the main sources of tourism to Mexico. The search for 'discovery' in the era of global tourism is not confined to wilderness areas nor wildlife expeditions; it also takes the form of new kinds of consumption, including tourist recreation, in which the process of transforming nature also transforms peoples' lives. In measuring the moral compass of these different forms of eco-tourism, one should be at least as much concerned with their indirect consequences, such as changes in development policy and the political demands generated by Mexican citizens exposed to mass tourism, as with the immediate effects, such as changes in land use and coastal defences. People, many of them from outside the area, have attachment to the places represented by the different forms of eco-tourism we have discussed, but do they 'belong' to them? In what sense have they 'chosen' the way of life associated with place, and does the existence or otherwise of choices make these places more or less sustainable?

Throughout the coastal zone dedicated to tourism, we find evidence of how the tourist economy has structurally transformed the environment. This is apparent from the pivotal economic role that nature affords in both tourism development and the local subsistence economy. The relatively buoyant labour market in areas like Playa Del Carmen has attracted people to work in the tourist sector, and served to reduce local peoples' cyclical dependence on subsistence agriculture and the village *milpa* (maize) zone. Tourism has created what is, in effect, a parallel and dominant economy based on the tourist dollar and the vicissitudes of the North American and European vacation seasons. In terms of the natural environment, the extraordinarily invasive capacity of tourism has privatised the shoreline. This robs the local people of access to the beaches, which are public property under Mexican federal law. Together with the effective privatisation of the shoreline, access to the marine environment has also been partially 'privatised' via dive centres, cruise ships and offshore facilities. The ocean was once an 'open access' resource, accessible to fishing communities and local people, but today it has become much more socially differentiated according to peoples' 'ability to pay'. Regardless of these places' contribution to the matrices of economic growth, they can hardly be called 'sustainable'.

The emergence of global resorts and eco-parks, all claiming to be concerned with environmental protection, forces us to examine some of the fundamental distinctions that are made between 'nature' as pristine wilderness and the managed nature of environmental protection. What are the ethical implications of branding nature in the form of 'green-washing' (i.e. the use of positive ethical associations surrounding conservation and sustainable development discourses) to raise the 'quality' of the marketable product (in this case, different forms of 'managed nature')?

First, it is unclear whether a clear distinction can be made between human, *produced* nature in places such as eco-parks, versus protected natural areas. The large Global Biosphere Reserve, Xian Ka'an, can only be visited via a guided tour that is organised by a travel company based in one of the resorts, or via a poor quality dirt road (that very few people take). The guided tours are restricted in size, but they provide many of the same activities as those of the eco-parks: snorkelling, floating in the *cenotes* and nocturnal observation of marine turtles. Considerable illegal development happens within the reserve and there are few effective planning controls. Although the environmental space occupied by the Biosphere Reserve has not been as thoroughly transformed as that of Xell-Ha and the other parks, it can be argued that Xell-Ha's existence protects the Reserve from further development. The eco-parks can be said to have become natural heritage sites in themselves, capable of withstanding saturation tourism, but without repelling the more adventurous prospective visitors from visiting areas like Xian Ka'an. Their overall contribution to global sustainability might indeed be significant.

Second, the use of terms like 'sustainability' depends entirely on the context in which these terms are employed; their power is essentially discursive. Much of the impetus for environmental protection on the coast of the Mexican Caribbean comes from the perceived need to internalise environmental costs, and to minimise the negative environmental effects of development. The interest of a minority of tourist entrepreneurs in cleaner, 'greener' tourist facilities is distinguishable from the wider questions of nature protection in the region. We do not know whether the tourists who visit the coast and express an interest in the environment are more concerned with the environmental standards in their hotels and swimming pools or if they actually care more about the welfare of the colonies of dolphins and marine turtles. It is likely that 'eco-tourists' come in various guises, and that the policy discourses surrounding sustainability and 'nature' appeal to different types of tourists. In addition, the way in which Mayan culture is invoked in many of the new tourist discourses is beginning to lead to a 'third' discourse about nature. This discourse seeks to identify traditional forms of sustainable livelihood practised by the Maya, and associates them with 'Mayan' views of nature.

The different temporal dimensions in which these policy discourses are employed have parallel spatial dimensions. The domain of human choice and consumption is heavily contested, and 'eco-tourism', however rhetorical, is a convenient label on which to hang contrary messages. 'Nature' and 'natural' places can be used by economists to suggest something that the market might help preserve, as well as something which is destroyed. This is the logic of tourist eco-parks. Other approaches to environmental management seek to regulate and 'manage' the environment in ways that control access to 'natural' places. This is the logic of the Biosphere Reserve. In practice, of course, the two currents often converge. The only person patrolling the principal beach at Xcacel (where marine turtles lay their eggs) is an employee of the tourist company developing Xpu-Ha, a hotel complex just a few hundred metres down the coast. When commercial developers have to provide the policing required by conservationists, the distinction between their respective interests becomes hard to find.

In the face of global eco-tourist development, it is not simple to draw a line between 'produced' nature versus the truly 'natural' and then decide which is more or less 'ethical'. Indeed, this kind of 'produced' nature development is designed to blur the very distinction between what is ethically conceived for human subjects and for non-human species. Discourses of the 'natural' increasingly combine human concerns with public access and recreation as well as with conservation goals, and need to be understood in terms of the structural processes which affect individual choices and lifestyles. Such discourses inevitably communicate a strong normative and 'moral' force. From the 'demand' side they include the ambiguously defined 'eco-tourism', and have served to underline the importance of different spatial and temporal perspectives on the meaning of 'place', 'sustainability' and 'nature'. The places tourists visit on the Mexican Caribbean are rarely the locations which evoke the past for the indigenous populations, i.e. the places where the native Maya fought off the white populations of Spain and Mexico in the centuries since the Conquest. Moreover, the sustainability of 'place' is even more elusive in the digital age. We are entering an age where not just the poor and ethnic minorities are displaced; in the new digital age, we are, in fact, all displaced people. Redefining what makes a place 'sustainable' is largely a question of discovering where digital and real, material space combine or conflict.

References

Agnew, J.A. (1987). *Place and politics: The geographical mediation of state and society.* Allen & Unwin, London.

Casey, E. (1997). *The fate of place: A philosophical history.* The University of California Press, Berkeley, CA.

Castree, N. (2003). Place: Connections and boundaries in an interdependent world, pp. 153–172 in: Holloway, S.L., Rice, S.P. and G. Valentine (eds), *Key concepts in geography.* SAGE, London.

Curry, M.R. (2002). Discursive displacement and the seminal ambiguity of space and place, pp. 502–517 in: L. Lievrouw and S. Livingstone (eds), *The handbook of new media.* SAGE Publications, London.

Everest (2002). *Everest tourist guide to Cancun and the Riviera Maya.* Everest, Leon, Spain.

Foucault, M. (1986). Of other spaces, heterotopias. *Diacritics*, 16: 22–27.

Harrison, S. and P. Dourish (1996). Re-place-ing space: The roles of place and space in collaborative systems, pp. 67–76 in: CSCW'96 (ed.), *Proceedings of the 1996 ACM Conference on Computer Supported Cooperative Work.* ACM Press. Boston, Massachusetts.

Johnson, T.G. (2002). *Where is the place in space?* Paper presented at the 2002 Southern Regional Science Association Meeting. April 12. Arlington, VA.

Lefebvre, H. (1974). *La Production de l'Espace.* Anthropos, Paris.

Massey, D. (1994). *Space, place, and gender.* University of Minnesota Press, Minneapolis.

Massey, D. and P. Jess (1995). *A place in the world.* The Open University, Milton Keynes.

McDowell, L. (1997). *Undoing place.* Edward Arnold, London.

Redclift, M. (2004). *Chewing gum: The fortunes of taste.* Taylor & Francis, New York.

Relph, E. (1976). *Place and placelessness.* Pion, London.

Stokowski, P.A. (2002). Language of place and discourses of power: Constructing new senses of place. *Journal of Leisure Research*, 34: 368–382.

Tuan, Y. (1977). *Space and place: The perspective of experience.* University of Minnesota Press, Minneapolis.

3 Territorialisation and the assemblage of rural place

Examples from Canada and New Zealand

Michael Woods

Introduction

The territorialisation of rural places has long been a focus of inquiry by geographers. On the one hand, rural places are culturally perceived as deeply embedded in their territories, if understood etymologically as a connection to the land or *terroir*. The traditional industries of rural areas have been based on exploiting the land and its natural resources, and the physical geography of rural places has historically determined their accessibility, shaped their settlement pattern, influenced their social and economic forms and left a mark on their sense of identity and cultural practices (Woods *et al.*, 2011). Yet, at the same time, defining and delimiting the territories of rural places, in the sense of a bounded space, has proved problematic. From the 1970s onwards, numerous attempts have been made in several countries to map and classify the division of rural and urban space, sometimes as governmental exercises (see for example Cloke, 1977; Isserman, 2005). However, these efforts have been rightly critiqued as methodologically flawed and analytically impotent (Cloke, 2006; Woods, 2009).

Moreover, the rise of the political economic perspective in the 1980s, with its attack on spatial fetishism, demonstrated that rural places, like all localities, are incorporated into wider social, economic and political structures, and that social relations in place are determined more by the global processes of capitalist accumulation and class struggle than by territorial factors. Territories might have relevance if they are understood as the spatial competence of local authorities that have sought to mediate broader processes, but which have no inherent agency. As the political economic approach threatened to undermine the usefulness of 'rurality' as an academic concept (Hoggart, 1990), the cultural turn responded by conceiving the rural as a social construct. This emphasised the cultural dimensions of rural being, but further detached rurality from territory. It held that different constructs of rural identity (and, indeed, place identity) could overlap across the same space, recognised that urban lifestyles might be performed in rural space, and conversely, that rural lifestyles could be performed in urban space (see Woods, 2011a). More recent relational approaches have reintroduced the material dimension of rural places (Heley and Jones, 2012; Murdoch, 2003; Woods, 2011a), but in stressing the connectivity of place have imagined rural places as spatial formations other than bounded territories. Rudy (2005), for example, dismisses the framing of Imperial Valley in California as a 'region' to reconceptualise it as a 'cyborg'.

In this chapter, I seek to recover the territorialisation of rural place by turning to assemblage theory, particularly as developed by Manuel De Landa. Proposed as a new ontology of society, assemblage theory offers an attractive way of conceptualising place, not only because of the emphasis it places on territorialisation and deterritorialisation as intrinsic features of assemblages, but also because it allows consideration of cultural expressions and affects as expressive components of assemblages. Assemblage theory further presents opportunities for analysing how places are reconfigured through processes of restructuring, such as globalisation, as illustrated through two brief case studies from Canada and New Zealand at the end of the chapter.

Assemblage theory and place

Assemblage theory, which has become fashionable in human geography in recent years, refers broadly to a relatively loose and diverse set of ideas and approaches that derive inspiration from the philosophy of Gilles Deleuze and Felix Guattari (Anderson *et al.*, 2012). Although Deleuze and Guattari never posited a clear definition of the concept, they repeatedly deployed assemblage in two senses: first, to refer to the composition of things as unstable collections of 'heterogeneous elements that may be human and non-human, organic and inorganic, technical and natural' (Anderson and McFarlane, 2011: 124); and second, to refer to the process of coming together (or *agencement* in the original French). The terminological inexactitude of Deleuze and Guattari has allowed subsequent writers to use and develop the concept with different inflections and emphasis, but Anderson and McFarlane summarise that the term assemblage 'is often used to emphasise emergence, multiplicity and indeterminacy, and connects to a wider redefinition of the socio-spatial in terms of the composition of diverse elements into some form of provisional socio-spatial formation' (Anderson and McFarlane, 2011: 124).

In this chapter, I particularly draw on the post-Deleuzian embellishment of assemblage theory by the Mexican-American philosopher Manuel De Landa, most notably in his 2006 book, *A New Philosophy of Society* (De Landa, 2006). In this, De Landa presents assemblage theory as a new ontology for understanding society through analysis of the components that comprise social entities, and helpfully outlines the principles of assemblage composition that provide a framework for analysis.

First, assemblages are composed of material components and expressive components. Material components are the physical elements that comprise an assemblage – both natural and manufactured, but also technologies and people. Expressive components are the affective characteristics and capacities that influence our perception of an assemblage. In De Landa's example (2006) of an ecosystem as an assemblage, he identifies the soil, sunlight, trees and animals as material components, and their forms, colours and habitats as expressive components. Moreover, individual components can perform both a material and an expressive role, such that the two are different ends of an axis, not discrete categories.

Second, and most importantly for this discussion, assemblages are subject to forces of territorialisation and deterritorialisation, the former giving an assemblage shape and the latter destabilising its form and unity. Territorialisation here need not necessarily be understood in its literal sense, but may refer to any form of diagram or matrix that holds the various components of an assemblage together; however, as De Landa (2006) makes clear, territorialisation can be literal in the claiming of ground, the occupation of space. As Anderson and McFarlane put it, 'assemblages always "claim" a territory as heterogeneous parts are gathered together and hold together' (2011: 126). Thus, in the example of the ecosystem, territorialisation is enacted through food chains (which do not have a geographical form), but also through the colonisation of particular sites by plants and animals and their adaptation to specific local environmental conditions. Deterritorialisation, meanwhile, is driven by factors including climate change, the invasion of exotic species and evolutionary mutation, which alter relationships between the components of the ecosystem and disrupt its geographical map.

Third, an assemblage is described and given an identity through the application of 'expressive media', such as language, in processes of coding and decoding. Thus, the use of the term 'ecosystem', and the body of scientific knowledge and theory that it implies, is an act of coding that describes and represents the assemblage to which it is applied. As theories are critiqued, language evolves and representations are challenged, the coding of assemblages may change, with old meanings stripped away through acts of decoding, and new representations constructed.

Fourth, assemblages are characterised by 'relations of exteriority'; in other words, they are defined not by their internal components, but by their relations to other assemblages and their external interactions. The capacities of assemblages, thus, 'do depend on a component's properties but cannot be reduced to them since they involve reference to the properties of other interacting entities' (De Landa, 2006: 11). Moreover, a component of an assemblage is not defined by its place in the assemblage, but rather by its capacity to interact with multiple relations, producing an independent interchangeability such that 'a component part of an assemblage may be detached from it and plugged into a different assemblage in which its interactions are different' (ibid: 10). Furthermore, this potential for the components of an assemblage to defect to other assemblages and, equally, for new components to be incorporated into an assemblage, means that assemblages are never settled, but are dynamic and constantly changing. As Anderson and McFarlane note, assemblage 'can only ever be a provisional process: relations may change, new elements may enter, alliances may be broken, new conjunctions may be fostered' (2011: 126).

The appeal of assemblage theory in contemporary human geography reflects its resonance with recent interests with relational geographies, non-representational theory and the politics of affect (Anderson *et al.*, 2012), but also perhaps the centrality that it affords to territorialisation. This may explain why many of the geographical applications of assemblage theory to date have focused on trans-local assemblages that operate across space, such as diasporic networks, the itineraries of peripatetic activists and disaster relief mobilisations. Certainly, applications in rural geography and rural sociology have been primarily concerned with such trans-local assemblages, including work on the global land-grabbing assemblage (Murray Li, 2014), global biofuel assemblage (Hollander, 2010), forest management (Murray Li, 2007) and rural microfinance (Rankin, 2008).

In contrast, there has been surprisingly little examination in geography of places as assemblages. The few exceptions include McFarlane's (2011) work on Mumbai and São Paulo, Venn's (2006) engagement with global cities and Rosin *et al.*'s work (2013) on Central Otago, the only study to focus on a rural area. Notably, Saskia Sassen has also written about cities as assemblages, but she makes clear that she uses the term only in its dictionary sense, and does not borrow conceptually from either Deleuze or De Landa (Sassen, 2006).

This neglect is especially curious given that De Landa himself sets a precedent by devoting a chapter in *A New Philosophy of Society* to considering cities and nations as assemblages. In it he works through the analysis of the city as an assemblage, identifying buildings as material components and an iconic skyline among the expressive components. Territorialisation, he proposes, occurs through processes including residential practices, such as that captured by Burgess's famous concentric model, whilst deterritorialisation follows from the disruption of these patterns, for example by gentrification. Meanwhile, the relations of exteriority of a city include the interactions between town and countryside, with De Landa suggesting that the classic market town and its relations to surrounding rural communities forms an exemplar of an economic assemblage (De Landa, 2006).

Starting from this model, it is not too difficult to image how rural places might be similarly deconstructed as assemblages. The material components might include the landscape, buildings, crops, livestock, wildlife, people, economic commodities that are produced or traded, and cultural artefacts, among others; while expressive components could include the aesthetic qualities attributed to the landscape, the emotional attachments of people to particular sites and localities and their sense of identity, and even the nebulous idea of the rural idyll as it is invested in an experience of calm, tranquillity and nostalgia.

The territorialisation of rural place might be expressed through its community structure and practices, its social stratification and the relations between established local families, but also through aspects that literally tie the place to territory: the settlement form and field system; the practice of working the land through farming or forestry and the intimate, embodied knowledge of territory which that imbues; the passing down of property through family inheritance; the identification of landmarks as symbols of place identity or boundary markers. However, these territorial forms are always contingent and subject to deterritorialisation and reterritorialisation through factors such as in- and out-migration, new building developments, the closure or rationalisation of local services, the amalgamation of municipalities, and so on.

From this perspective, the very description of a place as 'rural' is an act of coding that positions the place within collective geographical imaginations, and which implies certain associations and expectations that will vary from individual to individual and thus will always be contested. Furthermore, other practices of coding might also be observed, through acts of naming, mapping and measuring, and through formal representations such as eligibility for rural development funds.

Together, the multiple identities and mobilities of material and expressive components (as they might be part of several different assemblages simultaneously), the processes of territorialisation and deterritorialisation, and the acts of coding and decoding, connect a rural place to other places and other assemblages. The relations of exteriority of a rural place thus include its interactions with local towns and with the wider region, migration flows and commuting patterns, economic transactions and power relations to centres of political authority. As these are inherently unstable, rural places are always dynamic, always open to change. By adopting this assemblage theory approach to understanding rural place, we can posit a number of further observations about territorialisation and its relation to culture. First, territories do not make places – rather, territories are the outcomes of the territorialisation of places. This is an important counter to the environmental determinism of some earlier variants of regional geography, which suggested that the form and character of local cultures and economies were moulded by their territorial setting. As elements of the local environment are enrolled into a place-assemblage these will inevitably have a bearing on its form, character and culture. But as noted above, an assemblage cannot be reduced to the properties of its components and accordingly a place cannot be reduced to, or constrained by, its territory or environment.

Second, territorialisation does not necessarily result in bounded, discrete territories. The emphasis in assemblage theory on the exteriority of relations highlights the positioning of places within complex webs of social relations. The territorial form of a place-assemblage is consequently not as a discrete unit of smooth space, but as a knot, an entanglement of constellation of relations within these webs. As such, the territories of places have indistinct or fuzzy boundaries, with relations that spill over into and conjoin with other places (Jones and Woods, 2013). Moroever, they are dynamic, forever shifting their centre of gravity, claiming and deserting space, and sprouting relations that extend in new and unexpected directions. The decline in agricultural employment, for example, has shifted the locus of everyday life in rural communities away from the fields, whilst the closure of shops and schools means that significant elements of a community's social interactions may now take place in neighbouring towns and villages. Meanwhile, the maintenance of social relations between emigrants from rural communities in distant cities, their formation of hometown associations, celebration of local festivals, exchange of local gossip, and continuing involvement in community life through the mediating technologies of e-mail and Skype, might be seen as a new dimension of territorialisation for rural places.

Third, as processes of territorialisation and deterritorialisation involve the arrangement of material and expressive components, so they are closely implicated in the expression of culture through these components. Components of rural places include cultural artefacts such as folk dress, vernacular architecture and furniture, regional dishes and food products, folk songs and music, and so on. In some cases, such components can act as anchors to physical territory: recipes that use locally-grown produce, furniture made with local wood or stone, songs and poems that reference local landmarks. Yet the mobility of cultural artefacts can also make them agents of deterritorialisation, as they are exported to other places, enrolled into other assemblages and hybridised through contact with other cultures. Both these aspects are important for endogenous rural development strategies that commoditise cultural artefacts, valorising not only their material role as components of place, but also their expressive role: embodiments of nostalgia, authenticity, tranquillity, naturalness, wholesomeness, heritage and pleasure that can be taken away and plugged into the assemblage of the buyer's home.

Fourth, the coding of rural place is also a cultural act replete with references to territory. Codings that are applied to rural places from the outside are commonly informed by mainstream cultural discourses of the rural, and their associated stereotypes. These range from idealised notions of the rural idyll derived from media portrayals, through to negative stereotypes of the rural as backward, deprived and depraved. Such external coding frequently incorporates an imagined territorialisation of rural places as far-away, remote, isolated and difficult to get to, and thus as separated from mainstream urban society. At the same time, codings articulated from within rural places also assert territorialisation as differentiation, and are used to distinguish their communities from neighbouring places and people. Such coding of territorial differentiation is incorporated into, and expressed through, folk culture in the form of song, poetry, storytelling, humour, sporting rivalries and the use of dialect, which in many cases also reference and reinforce connections to the land and to the local environment, even after the material basis for such connections has been eroded.

Places as assemblages and rural restructuring

Rural places have been subjected to significant social and economic restructuring over recent decades, as economies have been diversified away from farming and other primary industries, populations have been reconfigured through flows of out-migration and in-migration, old class and power structures have been challenged, local services have been rationalised and reorganised, landscapes and habitats have been overlain with new environmental regulations and diverse elements from landscape features to cultural traditions have been commodified as tourist attractions. In popular discourse, these processes of restructuring are often presented as having diluted rural identity, diminished place-distinctiveness and depleted the cultural and economic sustainability of rural localities. It is perceived that places are all becoming the same, and certainly that they are all beholden to the same social and economic trends. Territorial differentiation seems less relevant.

Assemblage theory, as outlined in this chapter, offers an alternative perspective in which restructuring can be understood not as the erosion of place-difference, but as the reassembling of places as the substitution of material and expressive components is accompanied by processes of reterritorialisation and recoding. Take, for example, the impact of post-war agricultural modernisation. From an assemblage perspective we see that agricultural modernisation involved the introduction of new material components, including machinery and agri-chemicals, together with new farming practices that produced new territorialisations with larger farm units and larger fields, and led to new relations of exteriority as farmers increasingly produced commodities to contract for supermarkets and food processing corporations. The reduction in demand for farm labourers – a redundant material component – meanwhile prompted deterritorialisation in the form of changed social, labour and power relations in the village, the shift of everyday working life away from the fields, an increase in commuting to neighbouring towns for work and intensified out-migration. Depopulation led to abandoned properties which, in time, became enrolled in new assemblages of counterurbanisation as cheap property for migrants seeking to escape the city. Depressed agricultural villages were recoded as desirable places to live, attracting new in-migrants who brought with them not only new material components, but new expectations about the expressive roles of the village's components, reflecting their mental model of the rural idyll. Furthermore, as new in-migrants established their own social networks and activities, commuted to work and shopped at the nearest supermarket, they contributed to the further reterritorialisation of the village and the reconfiguring of its relations of exteriority. Thus, through these incremental changes, the assemblage of the village has been transformed, but it remains a place, an assemblage, a territory. Whether or not it is perceived as any less rural as a result is a question of coding.

The deployment of assemblage theory as an analytical tool in this way also resonates with the relational approach to researching globalisation in a rural context as discussed in Woods (2007), which positioned globalisation not as a force impacting on rural places from the outside, but as a phenomenon that is reproduced through rural places in acts of negotiation, contestation and hybridisation. In particular, deconstructing rural places as assemblages corresponds with the call in Woods (2007: 503) for research to examine 'the micro-processes and micro-politics through which place is reconstituted, treating human and non-human actants agnostically, and [being] sensitive to the historical legacies of past engagements with global processes and forces'.

The analytical potential of assemblage theory for examining the restructuring of rural places in the context of globalisation is explored through two brief illustrative case studies, from Canada and New Zealand, both in the final part of a restructuring process.

The outports of Newfoundland

The first case study concerns the small, remote fishing villages, called 'outports', of Newfoundland in eastern Canada. The outports were established by European settlers in the eighteenth and nineteenth centuries as part of the territorialisation of their emigrant communities, the locations reflecting the centrality of fishing as the economic driver of the colony, but also the harshness of the terrain and the climate. As place-assemblages, the outports are composed of material components including the rocky landscape, wooden buildings, boats, residents and the sea; combined with expressive components including the sense of isolation and qualities of resilience and community. Most important, though, were the fish, especially cod, that traditionally performed both material and expressive roles – as a commodity that provided the community with its income, and as a symbol of the community's identity and its reason for being.

The territorialisation of the outports reflected these components and their context. On land, the territorial reach was limited and defined by the inaccessibility of the location and the distance to larger settlements. However, the territorialisation of the outports also extended out to sea, encompassing regular fishing grounds and maritime features that were known intimately by the fishermen who worked the ocean.

The precarious existence of the outports highlighted the contingency of the relations that comprised them, and like all assemblages they were subject to constant change. The introduction of some new material components improved life – motors for boats, skidoos, communication technologies such as telephones and satellite dishes that reshaped their external relations. Other changes presented more serious challenges, the two most notable of which followed external acts of recoding.

The first challenge stemmed from the collapse of Newfoundland's major banks in the 1920s and the ensuing political and economic crisis that led to a narrow vote for the colony to join the Canadian confederation in 1948. The Canadian government, charged with rescuing the Newfoundland economy, imposed a new coding on the outports that represented many as unsustainable and unaffordable and demanded their evacuation. Between 1956 and 1965, 115 communities were resettled, in some cases involving a literal reterritorialisation as houses were transported across ice or floated across water (O'Flaherty, 2011). Often, the abandoned land remained part of the imagined territory of the community, but primarily as an expressive component – a site of nostalgia and remembrance, visited only in an annual pilgrimage.

The second challenge concerned the central component of the outports, the fish. The ocean had always been where the outport communities intersected with other fishing communities from both sides of the Atlantic, but during the twentieth century it became increasingly a point of intersection with a growing global fisheries assemblage, powered by industrial trawlers and large corporations. The intensified capacity of the global fisheries assemblage accelerated the depletion of the once-plentiful cod stock, to the point that the fish were recoded as an endangered species. In 1992, the Canadian Minister of Fisheries declared a moratorium on fishing for northern cod that was intended to last two years, but which was still in force at the time of this writing, 24 years later.

The moratorium removed cod overnight as a core material component of the outports. The loss of the central economic component in turn undermined the function of other material components, including fish storage and processing facilities, and many of the boats and workers, and fundamentally altered the relations of exteriority of the outports. The major response, however, was a dramatic act of deterritorialisation, as thousands of people left the outports for the provincial capital, St John's, and further afield. In hope that the moratorium might be lifted, many of these migrants retained ties to the outports, in some cases keeping property, such that in practice the migration served to extend the territorialisation of the outports, with geographically dispersed appendages. Moreover, some residents entered 'fly in, fly out' employment, working shifts in the offshore Newfoundland oil industry or the oil sand fields of Alberta.

At the same time, efforts to diversify the economy of rural Newfoundland focused on developing tourism, which in turn required the recoding of the outports and their components. Landscapes that were once perceived as hostile and threatening are now coded as unspoilt and exciting, and icebergs that were once risks to shipping are now natural wonders. The tourists attracted are themselves new material components in the outports, their arrival facilitated by transport assemblages involving aircraft and cruise ships, and creating new relations of exteriority with places in mainland Canada and the United States.

'The adventure capital of the world': Queenstown, New Zealand

The second case study concerns the rural resort town of Queenstown, in South Island, New Zealand, which has been transformed over the last two decades by its positioning as part of global tourism and amenity migration networks (see also Woods, 2011b). Originally established in the 1860s, Queenstown grew and crashed in a short-lived gold-mining boom before settling into existence as a farming community made possible by the introduction of merino sheep as a core material component. In the 1920s the introduction of another material component – a ski lift – prompted the coding of the town as a year-round resort, and the launch of a tourism industry that expanded to become the mainstay of the local economy, but which for fifty years was primarily fed by domestic visitors.

The reconfiguration of Queenstown as a global resort depended on two innovations that introduced two further new material components into the locality. The first was the fitting by entrepreneur William Hamilton of a water jet to a flat-bottomed boat, inventing a jet boat that could be manoeuvred swiftly in the fast but shallow rivers of New Zealand, and which within ten years was being used for commercial tourist trips on the Shotover river near Queenstown. The second innovation was the attaching of an elastic rope to Kawarau Gorge Suspension Bridge to create the world's first commercial bungee-jumping operation. Significantly, both these components also perform expressive roles in the Queenstown assemblage, as signifiers of thrill and adventure. This association, which connected with the growing global culture of adventure tourism, was further reinforced by the later coding of Queenstown as 'the adventure capital of the world' in the slogan of the local tourism agency.

The expansion of international tourism was facilitated by the upgrading of its airport, intersecting with budget transport assemblages. This enabled the arrival not only of adventure tourists, but also of more conventional tours, especially from east Asia. These latter tourists were attracted less by the search for adventure than by the mountain landscape, opportunities to consume New Zealand rural culture (albeit with the familiarity of Asian food and Japanese- and Korean-language gift shops, which had also been introduced as new material components) and by filming locations for movies including the Lords of the Ring trilogy, which recoded parts of the local landscape as 'Isengard', 'Lothlórien' and 'Dimrill Dale'.

International tourism reconfigured the territorialisation of Queenstown, reshaping its economic and labour market structures – by 2004, tourism contributed NZ$620 million to the local economy, and 50 per cent of employment was in accommodation, catering, retail or cultural and recreational services (Woods, 2011b) – and spatially opening up new areas to tourism, shifting the zoning of areas for conservation and recreation, and physically developing land for infrastructure. Reterritorialisation was further driven by the demand for new housing under pressure from a rapidly expanding population, including from international amenity migration. In the early 2000s it was estimated that up to a quarter of all property sales were to foreign buyers. These purchases injected foreign capital (and especially Asian capital) as the latest material component introduced to Queenstown, fuelling new housing and resort developments, whilst overseas investors and homeowners reshaped its relations of exteriority.

However, the subdivision of agricultural land for development sparked controversy, which focused on the coding of Queenstown as a place. On the one side, the neoliberal local government administration (whose territory had been expanded through municipal amalgamation) actively encouraged development with minimal land use planning controls, representing Queenstown as a business- and growth-friendly town. On the other side, conservation groups and amenity in-migrants campaigned for more controls, coding Queenstown as a fragile environment under threat from over-development. Queenstown's global relations of exteriority meant that the conflict overspilled the locality, soliciting interventions by external agents such as the actor Sam Neill, and being covered in the international media (see Woods, 2011b). Notably, though, it was the pro-development lobby that appealed to Queentown's local culture and its expressive components in its defence, presenting growth as consistent with the town's dynamics of change and its adrenaline culture:

> Progressive growth brings jobs and investment but areas of high scenic values throughout the district will be cherished and protected. Occasionally, used sparingly, if benefits can be proved. But there will be change, as there has been change since the establishment of Queenstown in the early 1860s.
>
> (Queenstown Mayor in *The Otago Daily Times*, quoted by Woods, 2011b: 377)

> Queenstown likes healthy entrepreneurs. This is an adrenalin-pumping beautiful place which can never be spoilt. It is a magnet.
>
> (Queenstown Mayor in *The Evening Post*, quoted by Woods, 2011b: 377)

In contrast, the antidevelopment campaigners were positioned as the representatives of an elitist, globalised culture that was external to Queenstown. Thus, through these arguments, the wealthy amenity migrants who objected to development were being rhetorically deterritorialised from Queenstown as an assemblage – despite their material presence – and the claim of local business elites to control the coding of place and its territorialisation was reaffirmed.

Conclusion

This chapter has commenced an exploration of the potential for assemblage theory to be employed to understand the reconstitution of rural places under globalisation and other processes of restructuring. In so doing, it aims to recover a concern with the territorialisation of rural place, which arguably has been marginalised by conceptual turns in rural geography since the 1980s. However, an assemblage theory perspective leads to a radically different understanding of territory, not as a discrete bounded space, but as the shape taken by place as an assemblage of heterogeneous components and relations. In this way, the territorialisation of a place has both spatial and non-spatial dimensions, and is shaped by the social relations that connect a place to other places and assemblages and which mean that the character of a place and its territorialisation are always dynamic and changing.

Moreover, the assemblage approach has the capacity to illuminate the connections between culture and territorialisation. Culture is intrinsic to the assemblage of place in a number of ways. Cultural artefacts are among the material components of place, and the expressive components of place include symbols of identity and affects such as emotion that are enrolled into cultural expression. The organisation, and substitution, of material and expressive components influence the territorialisation of a place, in some cases anchoring the assemblage in specific geographical sites, in others acting as mobile elements that can reshape the external relations of place. Equally, the coding of places draws on both local and global cultures to construct meanings that may include comments on the territorialisation of place. As such, culture is tightly implicated in territorialisation.

Indeed, the added value that an assemblage approach provides in exploring questions of territorialisation, cultural sustainability and regional development arguably comes from its agnostic treatment of both materiality and culture, recognising that components of place have both material and cultural/expressive roles, and that both are engaged in territorialisation. In a rural context, particularly, this includes the role that nature plays in the territorialisation of place. Natural components such as rock, soil, water and vegetation enrolled into place-assemblages serve to anchor place to a particular site. Yet, as they are enrolled into the place-assemblage, natural components are also extracted from their setting, modified, combined with other components and recoded as food, fuel, building material, fibre, etc., and acquire a mobility that contributes to the relations of exteriority of the place-assemblage and the stretching of its territorialisation. At the same time, the *in situ* reassembling of natural components into new material forms – stones into buildings, for example – or cultural forms – as parts of a 'landscape', for instance – can contribute to giving a place shape and identity, and thus is itself part of the process of territorialisation. In each of these settings the inclusion of natural components reflects their materiality, but their role is also defined by cultural expression. This can be observed in the two examples discussed in this chapter. In Newfoundland, the materiality of the cod and their incorporation into assemblages of fishing and trade explains the territorialisation of the outport communities but also underpins local cultural identity. When the cultural meaning of the cod is recoded by external environmentalists and politicians and the material role of the fish is suddenly transformed by the fishing moratorium there is a concurrent reterritorialisation of the outport communities, even if the expressive role of the cod lingers in local culture. In New Zealand, the mountain environment as a material component is central to the territorialisation of Queenstown, literally giving it shape, but the mountains also perform an expressive role reflecting cultural norms about rurality, adventure and environmental fragility that on the one hand attracts tourists and amenity migrants, but on the other hand stokes political debate about the impact of development.

An assemblage perspective therefore shows rural places to be anchored in particular sites through the enrolment of static material components, but also to be entwined in manifold external relations that are spatially diffuse. As such, it faces the same problem as other relational approaches to place: how does one identify where one place or locality ends and another starts? This lack of precision about the boundaries of place presents methodological challenges for locality research (see also Jones and Woods, 2013); however, careful application of De Landa's (2006) model provides a partial answer by revealing the act of drawing boundaries to be part of the process of territorialisation itself. In other words, whilst an assemblage approach rejects bounded territories as a starting point for locality research, it recognises that bounded territories are delineated to give a place-assemblage shape and to attempt to make it stable and governable. Territorial boundaries are thus part of the assemblage of place, and thus have meaning and influence, even if they are repeatedly breached by exterior relations and the mobility of components, or if tensions exist between multiple and non-congruent mappings of territory (see for example Rosin *et al.*, 2013).

This observation has implications for thinking about territory and sustainable development, pointing to the paradox that whilst rural sustainability initiatives often emphasise the endogenous development of local resources, sustainability can only be fully understood in terms of how the diverse components of rural localities interact with broader, complex ecological, economic and cultural systems through relations of exteriority, and that although bounded territories can provide a structure for policy intervention they are at best temporary and contingent fixes on a dynamic and networked world. Thus, in our examples, issues of environmental, economic and cultural sustainability were tied together for the Newfoundland outports in the management of cod stocks, yet the mobility of the fish across any notions of bounded territory and their alternative enrolment in the assemblages of industrial fishing (leading to a depletion of stocks) and of marine conservation (leading to the moratorium) means that the sustainability of the outports is dependent on exterior relations that extend beyond their formal territories. Similarly, attempts to introduce more sustainable modes of development in Queenstown have faltered on the limitations of local actors to control those parts of the Queenstown assemblage that extend beyond the formal territory of the district council, and which are defined by their external relations with the global economy, tourism and migration flows (see also Woods, 2011b for further discussion).

The brief examples discussed in this chapter hence point towards the insights that the application of an assemblage approach provide in understanding how places are constituted and reconstituted within broader currents of social and economic change, and how these are reflected in the territorialisation of place. Further research within this framework might probe questions about the nature of the material and expressive components that comprise places, how these are arranged and rearranged in processes of territorialisation and deterritorialisation, how they come to be mutated and substituted over time, how the relations of exteriority of place connect it into wider networks and how these may come to stretch or curtail its territorial expression, and, not least, about the role of culture in cohering and representing the territorialisation of place but also in opening up new opportunities and lines of flight that might lead to new territorial forms.

Acknowledgements

This chapter was written as part of European Research Council Advanced Grant 339567, 'The Global Countryside: Rural Change and Development in Globalization (GLOBAL-RURAL)'. The case study of Queenstown is based on earlier research, supported by the University of Wales Aberystwyth Research Fund.

References

Anderson, B. and C. McFarlane (2011). Assemblage and geography. *Area*, 43: 124–127.

Anderson, B., Kearnes, M., McFarlane, C. and D. Swanton (2012). On assemblages and geography. *Dialogues in Human Geography*, 2: 171–189.

Cloke, P. (1977). An index of rurality for England and Wales. *Regional Studies*, 11: 31–46.

Cloke, P. (2006). Conceptualizing rurality, pp. 18–28 in: Cloke, P., Marsden, T. and P. Mooney (eds), *Handbook of rural studies*. SAGE, London.

De Landa, M. (2006). *A new philosophy of society*. Continuum, London and New York.

Heley, J. and L. Jones (2012). Relational rurals: Some thoughts on relating things and theory in rural studies. *Journal of Rural Studies*, 28: 208–217.

Hoggart, K. (1990). Let's do away with rural. *Journal of Rural Studies*, 6: 245–257.

Isserman, A.M. (2005). In the national interest: Defining rural and urban correctly in research and public policy. *International Regional Science Review*, 28: 465–499.

Jones, M. and M. Woods (2013). New localities. *Regional Studies*, 47: 29–42.

Hollander, G. (2010). Power is sweet: Sugarcane in the global ethanol assemblage. *Journal of Peasant Studies*, 37: 699–721.

McFarlane, C. (2011). The city as assemblage: Dwelling and urban space. *Environment and Planning D: Society and Space*, 29: 649–671.

Murdoch, J. (2003). Co-constructing the countryside: Hybrid networks and the extensive self, pp. 263–282 in: Cloke, P. (ed.), *Country visions*. Pearson, Harlow.

Murray Li, T. (2007). Practices of assemblage and community forest management. *Economy and Society*, 36: 263–293.

Murray Li, T. (2014). What is land? Making-up a resource. *Transactions of the Institute of British Geographers*, 39: 589–602.

O'Flaherty, P. (2011). *Leaving the past behind: Newfoundland history from 1934*. Long Beach Press, St. John's, NL.

Rankin, K. (2008). Manufacturing rural finance in Asia. *Geoforum*, 39: 1965–1977.

Rosin, C., Dwiartama, A., Grant, D. and D. Hopkins (2013). Using provenance to create stability: State-led territorialisation of Central Otago as assemblage. *New Zealand Geographer*, 69: 235–248.

Rudy, A.P. (2005). Imperial contradictions: Is the Valley a watershed, region or cyborg? *Journal of Rural Studies*, 21: 19–39.

Sassen, S. (2006). *Territory, authority, rights: From medieval to global assemblages.* Princeton University Press, Princeton.

Venn, C. (2006). The city as assemblage: Diasporic cultures, postmodern spaces, and biopolitics, pp. 41–52 in: Berking, H., Frank, S., Frers, L., Low, L.M., Steets, S. and S. Stoetzer (eds), *Negotiating urban conflicts: Interaction, space and control.* Transcript, Bielefeld.

Woods, M. (2007). Engaging the global countryside: Globalization, hybridity and the reconstitution of rural place. *Progress in Human Geography*, 31: 485–508.

Woods, M. (2009). Rural geography: Blurring boundaries and making connections. *Progress in Human Geography*, 33: 849–858.

Woods, M. (2011a). *Rural*. Routledge, London.

Woods, M. (2011b). The local politics of the global countryside: Boosterism, aspirational ruralism and the contested reconstitution of Queenstown, New Zealand. *Geojournal*, 76: 365–381.

Woods, M., Richards, C., Watkin, S. and J. Heley (2011). Rural people and the land, pp. 57–66 in: I. Convery, T. Dutson, P. Davis and G. Corsane (eds), *Making sense of place: Multidisciplinary perspectives*, Boydell and Brewer, London.

4 The worldview and symbolic dimension in territorialisation

How human values play a role in a Dutch neighbourhood

Lummina Horlings

Introduction

Culture is crucial to sustainable development. Culture is seen as either connected to social sustainability or as a separate fourth pillar, captured in the notion of cultural sustainability. Storylines on cultural sustainability range from conservative views focusing on preserving cultural heritage to more progressive, radical visions on eco-cultural resilience and cultural evolution (Soini and Birkeland, 2014). Often these notions express a link between cultural sustainability and human values. Values are for example an aspect of the discourses on cultural diversity and cultural evolution (ibid., 2014). The Sustainable Development Research Institute refers also to values, describing cultural sustainability as: 'the ability to retain cultural identity, and to allow change to be guided in ways that are consistent with the cultural values of people' (SDRI, 1998: 1). The relevance of values has been emphasised: 'sustainability transitions may require radical, systemic shifts in deeply held values and beliefs, patterns of social behaviour, and multi-level governance and management regimes' (Westley *et al.*, 2011: 762). Radical visions consider current cultural value systems as a fundamental cause of sustainability problems and thus plead for changes in people's awareness, consciousness or attitudes (Stefanovic, 2000: 6). We argue that in the context of territorialisation, certain notions of cultural sustainability are especially relevant where culture plays a mediating role between people and the environment (see also Horlings, 2014; Horlings *et al.*, 2015). These notions, presented below, are rooted in what people consider as important values that guide their actions, perceptions and motivations.

The introduction to this book describes three dimensions of territorialisation. Territorialisation refers to a process of co-construction and co-evolution that starts with a dialogic relationship in which both the social configurations and the physical characteristics of the local environment have agency. A fourth dimension of territorialisation can also be described: the worldview dimension. The worldview dimension is relevant in the context of human intentionality, but does not refer to the role of nature on the co-production of territories, as nature itself has no intentions.

The reason to introduce the worldview dimension is that it plays an important role in the shaping of sustainable places. Not only the practical system and larger systems and structures (i.e., the political) are drivers of transformation to sustainability, but also individual and shared beliefs, values, worldviews and paradigms influence attitudes and actions (Hedlund-de Witt, 2011; O'Brien, 2013). The recognition of the important role of worldviews in societal transformation is growing. The act of changing worldviews, linked to notions of moral responsibility and awareness, is considered to be important to address the challenge of sustainability (Hedlund-de Witt, 2011, 2013; Hedlund-de Witt and Hedlund-de Witt, 2013; Hedlund-de Witt *et al.*, 2014; O'Brien, 2009). This is also referred to as change from the inside out (O'Brien, 2012; O'Brien and Sygna, 2013) or the inner dimension of sustainability (Horlings and Padt, 2013; Riedy, 2013). We have operationalised the four dimensions of territorialisation in this chapter as follows. In some instances they can overlap; for example, intentions of people can be underpinned by particular symbolic understandings of values and places.

Way of life: this is linked to the question of why people would accommodate sustainable change. Space becomes an action habitat, where agency mediates intention. Culture refers here to intentions, ethical and moral choices, rooted in values that drive our individual and collective actions. This refers to the worldview dimension of territorialisation.

Sense of place: this is linked to the question of how people shape, value, appreciate and are attached to places. People have a sense of place, attach meanings to place and add cultural value to place. Culture mediates senses. This raises questions on how cultural practices, people's narratives, identities, values and sense of place influence processes of territorialisation. This refers to the symbolic dimension of territorialisation.

Cultural practices: these have been associated with the role of art, creativity and cultural activities and practices for community vitality and community planning of urban and rural areas. This refers to the reification dimension of territorialisation.

Cultural characteristics of institutions: culture shapes 'the rules of the game', routines, organisations and ways of cooperation and self-organisation. One example is the variation in planning cultures (see also Atmanagara, 2015). This refers to the institutional dimension of territorialisation.

The key question in this chapter is how territorialisation can be understood as the variations and different expressions in time and space of (individual and collective) cultural values in processes of place-shaping. In the next section we first draw attention to the question 'what are values?' The remainder of this chapter is an analysis of the first dimensions of territorialisation. The worldview dimension of territorialisation is rooted in individual principles and motivations as well as in collective cultural values. The symbolic dimension of territorialisation includes subjective aspects of how people perceive and are attached to place, and how they appreciate place and construct place identities (Figure 4.1).

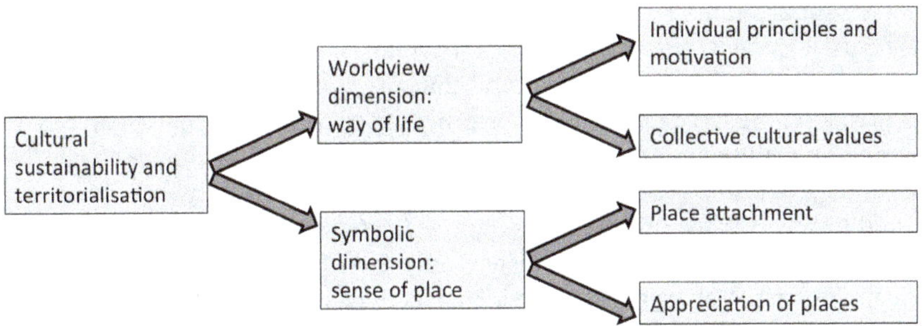

Figure 4.1 The worldview and symbolic dimension of territorialisation

Source: © Ina Horlings.

What are values?

Values are relevant for sustainable development in various ways: in the context of engagement, implementation and conflict, in relation to religious and ethnic aspects, in the context of educational strategies and development of sustainable competencies and in planning, with the challenges of implementing sustainable initiatives and aligning multiple stakeholders (Appleton, 2014). The development and engagement of the participant's values can, for instance, build co-creative capacity in sustainable development projects (Appleton, 2014: 1).

The value concept is central in understanding human behaviour. Theorists (Kluckhohn, 1951; Rokeach, 1973) have viewed values as the criteria people use to evaluate actions, people and events. When we think of values, we think of what is important to us in our lives, e.g. security, wisdom, pleasure or freedom. A value must be recognised as valuable, thus it has to become explicit – consciously recognised as a value and given that term.

In the literature the word 'value' is contested and has been given several meanings (see for an overview: Horlings, 2015). On the one hand values appear as abstract goals, beliefs or motivational constructs; Appleton describes values 'as concepts and objects for which individuals have a range of positive feelings' (Appleton, 2013: 23). On the other hand values appear in a more instrumental sense, as criteria or standards for evaluation or as a system for ordering priorities, for example in notions such as economic value, environmental values and nutritional value (see also Schwartz, 2006).

Values are a broader construct than attitudes. Attitudes can be considered to be emergent from values, and are therefore an expression of values. The characteristics of our attitudes are also shaped by the context, our behaviour, our beliefs and our level of understanding. These characteristics can therefore change, while our deeper values, some of which we are not even aware of, remain less malleable (Appleton, 2014: 22–23).

Much of the literature on values in the context of sustainable development refers to environmental values (Gilipin, 2000). Environmental scholars mention people's motivation for action towards sustainability based on environmental concerns. Our aim, however, is to go beyond this environmental perspective by emphasising the social and cultural dimension of sustainable development. Furthermore, we argue that values are not independent concepts that can be mapped or analysed as atomised issues. They are intertwined with the issues that matter to people and are therefore context-determined, culturally varied and connected to how we see ourselves and how we perceive our environment. Values such as freedom, solidarity and justice only gain meaning in real people and actual practices. Values can be considered as dynamic in space, place and time. Especially the three following notions can inform value-centred debates in the context of place and territorialisation.

First, value often refers to economic value and valuation. The dominant economic approaches assume that to make rational choices we must adopt some common measure of value and that money provides that measure (O'Neill *et al.*, 2008: 75). But to put a price on something does not reflect its value or benefit, only its scarcity; it is a reflection of the relationship between supply and demand under market conditions (Sagoff, 2008: 243). The concept of value encompasses far more than issues of use, benefit or utility. Money is an expression of value, but in fact not all values, or even most values, can be expressed in monetary terms. Shiva has criticised the dominance of an economic system which reduces society to the economy, and reduces the economy to the market: 'Economic systems influence culture and social values. An economics of commodification creates a culture of commodification where everything has a price, and nothing has value' (Shiva, 2014: 8).

The concept of values has been applied in the notion of 'shared value', defined as 'benefits relative to costs'. Shared value is a term used in the context of business and cluster development which points to the following aim: 'to enhance the competitiveness of a company while simultaneously advancing the economic and social conditions in the communities in which it operates' (Porter and Kramer, 2011: 7). The approach goes beyond a corporate social responsibility approach, by re-conceiving products and markets, redefining productivity in the value chain and building supportive industry clusters at the company's locations. Economic valuation is used for example in cost–benefit analysis (CBA) which is based on rationality assumptions and utilitarian welfare economics. This has been subject to both methodological and more fundamental critique, especially in those cases where 'priceless' valuables such as nature and culture are at stake. Broader approaches have been developed such as ecosystem services, based on the notion 'nature has value', which captures economic and non-economic value. In this approach values have been determined step by step by evaluating the attributes of the landscape, the ecological functions, how these functions provide services and the amount of benefit provided by the landscape (Halsey, 2014).

Second, values have been conceptualised as principles, preferences or appreciations. Here values are described as moral and subjective, expressing what is valued by people, what they appreciate or consider worthwhile, and what guides (the selection of) people's actions. This includes people's deeper motivations, passions and intentions, all of which express how precious something is for someone. Such values are inextricably tied to emotions, not objective cold ideas. Values are not rational principles of the mind, but also refer to people's will and heart (Scharmer, 2005). Appreciation stems from the Latin word 'appretiare', which means pay attention to strong points, qualities or what someone does well. People value and appreciate places and express social values in natural resource management. Several authors refer to the values people ascribe to resources or the environment (Battaglini and Babović, 2015; McIntyre *et al.*, 2008).

The third notion of value is used in a more ideological way, mostly on the societal systems level, to refer to worldviews, beliefs, levels of consciousness and value systems. Worldviews can be understood as inescapable, overarching systems of meaning and meaning-making. Worldviews contribute substantially to how humans interpret, enact and co-create reality (Hedlund-De Witt, 2013). Examples are an egocentric, ethnocentric, sociocentric, worldcentric or planet-centric worldview (Riedy, 2013).

The worldview dimension: way of life

The worldview dimension refers to what guides people's way of life and awareness of the much-needed transition to sustainable development. Long-term commitment to sustainable development resides within people's choices; it is grounded in people's deepest motivations, convictions and human intentionality. This leads to the question *why* people would contribute to sustainable change. Our reality is created by our beliefs. These beliefs, usually subconscious, are often the result of lifelong programming and represent a powerful influence on human behaviour. Studies in neuroscience indicate that as much as 95 per cent of our consciousness is actually subconscious. The subconscious mind is the storehouse of our attitudes, values and beliefs. From these beliefs, we form perceptions about the world and ourselves, and from these perceptions we develop behaviours (Lipton, 2005).

Values – and how we work with them – are a vital determinant for whether sustainable development will remain a dream or solidify into reality. A distinction can be made between motivations and cultural values. Motivations can be directed towards conservation but can also be open to change, and can contribute to self-enhancement and self-transcendence. Schwartz describes ten basic, motivationally distinct values such as power, hedonism, conformity, self-direction, etc., which are all recognisable in a variety of cultures across the globe (Schwartz, 2006). The assumption is that increased awareness of the source of passion, values, feelings and sense-making will lead to a more inspired (sustainable) use of our environment (Horlings *et al.*, 2009).

Cultural values have been explored in the context of the necessary transition towards sustainable development, which is understood as a vision of a utopian future society. Culture refers here to a process of transformation and cultural change. For example, sustainability has been linked to core values and roots of culture, not as a fixed state of affairs, but as a continuing process of change that implies authentic, positive or healthy self-development for humans, societies and nature.

Wilber's (2000) four-quadrant model, organised around an individual–collective and objective–subjective axis, offers a way to analyse the psychological, cultural, behavioural and social aspects of human society. The Spiral Dynamics model describes value systems as deriving from the interaction of 'life conditions' and 'capacities of the mind'. The term *vMemes* is used here to refer to the system of core values or collective intelligences that emerge at each level of human development (the v stands for value system). It stands for a unit of cultural information that changes and adapts over time as it is passed from one generation to the next (e.g., ideas, songs, theories, dances, habits, values, practices). The authors argue that *vMemes* comprise worldviews, belief structures, ways of thinking and modes of living – a cultural DNA map. Eight memes are observed. They are distinguished by different colours and divided into three tiers of human consciousness. The 'green' value system in particular has been associated with sustainable development (Beck and Cowan, 1996).

To date, only a few attempts have been made to analyse motivations and cultural values in the context of territorialisation. An example is Hamilton's (2008) empirical work in Abbotsford in Canada. She drafted a map of the city, inspired by Wilber's four quadrants and value systems, based on interviews with different types of respondents with different cultural backgrounds; in this way, she illustrated their varied motivations and culture.

The symbolic dimension of territorialisation: attachment and appreciation

People are involved in places via location, ecological participation, their sense of belonging and via cultural conformity or commonality (Pollini, 2005). Community attachment can lead to a sense of affinity or we-feeling, via values such as loyalty and solidarity. The other way round is also true: we-feeling can lead to community attachment. As territories have become more complex, the territorial *Gemeinschaft* has fragmented and differentiated and the ecological interdependence has decreased (Pollini, 2005).

This, however, has raised attention among sociologists to more subjective definitions of belonging and explorations of attachment to units of a particular size (home and neighbourhood, local community, region, nation, continent, etc.) (Gubert, 2000). Such research shows that 'the extension of increased frequency of relations across larger distances (continental and global) has not led to the superseding of local or at least noncosmopolitan attachments. Attachment to local ambits still largely predominates' (Gubert, 2000: 3134). People attach subjective cultural meanings to place, rooted in values. Values are the result of people interpreting social phenomena through negotiation and communication and have a geographical dimension (Davies, 2001: 82).

The subjective concept 'sense of place' is central in this approach, an attribute which is closely connected to community, personal memory and self, and which includes different senses (Relph, 1976; Vanclay, 2008). Sense of place is a multi-theoretical, complex and contested concept (Convery *et al.*, 2012: 6) that has been approached from a phenomenological and behavioural perspective. It has many components such as place attachment, place identity, place commitment and dependency, place satisfaction, belongingness or rootedness or community connectedness and community cohesion (Vanclay, 2008; Jorgensen and Stedman, 2006; Shamai, 1991; Soini *et al.*, 2012). This sense of place encompasses attachment to a place as well as processes of appreciation and evaluation. It includes material aspects, a symbolic dimension and social relations. As people are networked to places through social relations which stretch beyond geographical boundaries, they have a global sense of place as well as one that is locally specific (Massey, 1993; Escobar, 2001).

Sense of place has been linked to sustainability, suggesting that in spite of processes of globalisation, in order to create sustainable communities more people need to reconnect with a place that they call home, valuing the ancestral heritage that comes with development and maintaining a rooted sense of place (Hay, 1998). Sense of place can also inspire people to collective action as a response to unwanted spatial and sometimes unsustainable developments (Horlings and Hinssen, 2014), which should not be interpreted as ignorant or selfish NIMBY responses, but as founded upon processes of place attachment and place identity (Devine-Wright, 2009; see also Rogge *et al.*, 2011).

Towards a value-centred methodology

The worldview and symbolic dimensions described above are expressed in people's cultural practices. The challenge of a value-oriented approach is to create a dialogue between actors that is not based on personal interests but rather on shared values, and which is directed to the common good. Such a dialogue should have an 'inclusive' attitude towards sustainability, paying attention to the long-term social, cultural and economic aspects and the consequences of actions in time and place. This can refer to values such as social inclusion, esthetical aspects, solidarity, quality of life, etc.

The question then arises, 'how should we analyse and map values in the context of territorialisation?' The way people live out their daily lives has been studied using geographical, phenomenological, anthropological or ethnographic approaches. Research and evaluation of a participant's values can be done in many ways: via in-depth interviews, ethnographic observation, surveys, thematic and perceptive test evaluation, content analysis and associated literature, analysis of a participant's self-reporting and recording, psychometric testing, word association analysis, group participatory techniques, and so on (Appleton, 2014: 5). When testing values, one must consider espoused values and observed behaviour; but they are often not congruent (Schein, 2010: 25). People are not always aware of their values. Also they do not always act in accordance with their own values. Discourse analysis can be used to understand how people use language to accomplish social and emotional goals along with communicating ideas and how different ideas in turn reflect different worldviews and different priorities. The assumption here is that human language does not simply reflect the values and preferences of speakers, it also shapes them (Patthey, 2014).

We would like to give an overview here of some promising methods – which can be positioned in the context of participatory approaches – and then take a step further, with the aim of reaching a deeper understanding of the sense of place and values of people with regard to places.

Spatial mapping of values

The growing emphasis on place-based value-centered meanings urges social scientists involved in natural resource management to think in spatial terms and facilitate the integration of personal place-based values data into resource-based decision models. One example took place in the context of forest management and planning. McIntyre *et al.* (2008) collected data in a forest management area in Canada in three phases. Initially they used an interpretive approach (focus groups) to elicit values attached to the forest and to identify places associated with these values. In phase 2 participants were asked to mark valued places on a map of that same forest. Finally, in phase 3, a general user survey was implemented to explore broader recreation and tourism activity in the forest.

Mapping of assets

Another way of mapping is the assets based community development (ABCD) method, which builds on the assets and strengths of a community. It was developed by the Asset-Based Community Development Institute in the context of poor urban communities in large cities of the US. Gibson (2010) has also used this method in communities in Asia. Assets are being perceived as such by the residents and refer to what inhabitants perceive and experience as being qualities. Gibson distinguishes three elements of a community asset map: 1) business and physical resources; 2) local non-government associations as well as formal and governmental institutions; and 3) people and practices.

Mapping sense of place

Social and environmental psychology has developed and used scales and questions to measure sense of place. Using ethnographic and anthropological methods, sense of place has also been mapped, for example in the context of the complex and contingent sphere of the multiple, coexisting space–time trajectories that make up landscape. Deep mapping, as applied in the UK in place-based research, refers to processes of engaging with and evoking place in temporal depth by bringing together a multiplicity of voices, information, impressions and perspectives in a multimedia representation of a particular environment. Baily and Biggs (2012) included a wide set of participatory tools to retrieve data, building on conversational exchange, fieldwork, performative actions, sound and image work and a range of scholarly research methods and approaches. The deep mapping process in North Cornwall was loosely grouped into the steps of conversing, thread spinning and interweaving.

Appreciative inquiry (AI)

AI offers a promising approach for discovering values based on the principles of appreciative dialogue and social-constructionism.

> This is a transformation method for the development of potential of social systems. The positive images that the parties share in the future can give direction to achieve the transformation. The approach always starts with discovering the very best in the shared experiences.
>
> (Barrett *et al.*, 2010: 11)

This approach can be used to map values but also as a way to facilitate cooperation and joint learning in a multi-stakeholder process via different steps: discovery, dream, design and destination. The approach is centered not around problems but around positive strengths and possibilities for change, rooted in underlying principles of what people consider as important. It is a generative approach; the future and the seed for change are encompassed in the conversations and stories approach (Cooperrider and Whitney, 1999).

A case study of a deprived urban neighourhood in the Hague (the Netherlands)

Some of the above methods have been applied in empirical research in an urban neighbourhood in the Netherlands. We will describe this case here as an illustration of the above methods and in order to investigate the possibilities for 'value-oriented' empirical research in territorialisation.

Description of an urban neighbourhood

The Schildersbuurt is a neighbourhood in the Hague – a city with over 33,000 inhabitants – built in the nineteenth century. The district is multi-ethnic, and also remarkably young. A third of the inhabitants (33 per cent) are under twenty years old, while in the rest of the Hague this is 23 per cent. The Schildersbuurt is considered in policy-terms as one of the 40 problem districts of the Netherlands in terms of the need for extra investments from the national government to counter social, physical and economic problems such as low household incomes, high unemployment, poor integration of newcomers, health problems, school-dropout, criminality and a degraded habitat. The mobility within the district is high compared to other districts in the Hague. The combination of a young and at the same time relatively poor district means that many children and youth in the district grow up in poverty. These same youngsters are often considered the cause of many of the above-stated problems. The neighbourhood appeared in the news in 2014 as an example of a place where young Muslims chose radicalism.

The qualitative empirical research did not start with these problems, however. Instead, the researchers took an *appreciative approach* in order to retrieve insight into what people perceive as the strengths of their neighbourhood. The research carried out by Van der Schaar (2013) was implemented in the east part of the Schildersbuurt. Appreciative Inquiry was used here as a methodological tool for diagnosis. The focus was on the first step, the discovery phase. In addition, a combination of methods was used for data collection, such as desk research, interviews with experts and 42 semi-structured interviews with inhabitants of the eastern part of Schildersbuurt. The perceived qualities of the neighbourhood were inventoried using Gibson's method for assets mapping described earlier. Additionally, inspired by the deep mapping approach (Baily and Biggs, 2012), the interviews were complemented by eight walks through the neighbourhood with respondents to get insight into their 'sense of place'. The research included an inventory of what inhabitants considered important values, such as safety and social relations. The central question was: 'What do residents perceive as the qualities of their neighbourhood, what are important values underlying these qualities and how is this related to a certain sense of place?'

Sense of place

Sense of place was operationalised as place attachment, place identity and place dependence. A distinction was made between physical and social attachment. The findings showed a generally low level of physical attachment, influenced by the deteriorated state of many apartments and the fact that most people rent instead of own their homes. People also mentioned dirt and garbage in the public spaces and a lack of clear boundaries between public and private spaces. However, one of the neighbourhood squares, the Jacob van Campenplein, is an exceptional public space which appeared to be an important place for people, mainly for its social function as 'meeting place'.

Residents perceived an overall high social attachment towards their neighbourhood, resulting from their social networks and values, and felt especially connected to people with the same set of values. An ethnic and/or cultural segregation was visible in both the use of public places and in the activities undertaken by people. Language barriers and the tendency of migrants to network with people of the same ethnic background enforced this segregation.

Three main characteristics of the neighbourhood were highlighted by inhabitants as constructing a unique place identity: the multicultural character of the neighbourhood, the tolerant attitude of people living in the neighbourhood towards various lifestyles and the lively outdoor life (including the late opening hours of shops).

Place dependence of respondents was low overall because of the lack of facilities and the proximity to the centre of the Hague. Most respondents expressed not being dependent on the neighbourhood for their daily needs, their income or for secondary and higher education, sports and recreation. An exception are the many foreign (food) shops of the neighbourhood, which provide people with specific products.

Many respondents expressed that they would leave the neighbourhood if they had the financial resources to be able to do so. The low level of place dependency and the limited freedom of choice towards living in this location strengthens the ambiguous character of people's place sense of place.

Place qualities

The place qualities were – inspired by Gibson's assets mapping – categorised in qualities concerning the physical location, the institutions and the people and practices of the neighbourhood. Respondents mentioned three physical qualities: the square, the many foreign grocery stores and the coffee- and teahouses. Institutionally, the police officers, the residents' organisations, the municipality and the housing corporations were perceived positively, especially by people who were active in community development themselves. Other respondents were more critical, referring to the deteriorated state of their apartments and a lack of communication between the corporations and the respondents. Furthermore, the tolerant and active attitude and active engagement of inhabitants were mentioned. The research showed the somewhat ambiguous difference between opportunities and problems. Perceived qualities are linked with what people consider as problems. For example, if people consider the state of their houses as degraded, they appreciate people who act on this problem.

Linking sense of place, place qualities and values

Seven main values were found to be important for the inhabitants, based on the interviews: liveability of the physical environment; economic value; social networks and communal sense; multiculturalism; tolerance; safety; and taking responsibility for the liveability of the neighbourhood. The main concepts, sense of place, place qualities and values, appeared to be strongly interrelated. An example is the link between the value of communal sense, high social attachment and the quality of amenities such as shops. Communal sense is linked to the high social attachment among people of the same ethnic and/or religious background. Inhabitants appreciate place qualities such as the foreign grocery shops and the coffee- and teahouses, primarily for their social function, and more specifically for their role in facilitating the constructing and maintaining of social relations with neighbours of the same ethnic and/or religious background. The high social attachment among these specific groups therefore leads to appreciation of the foreign grocery shops and teahouses. This also works the other way around because foreign grocery shops and teahouses facilitate the opportunity for establishing and maintaining social relations.

Another example of the interrelations that were discovered are the links between the value of multiculturalism, aspects of the perceived place identity and the tolerant attitude of residents as a perceived quality. Most respondents mentioned that the multicultural character of the neighbourhood gives the area a unique and distinctive identity. Most respondents highly appreciated this multiculturalist character and gave it as a reason why they liked living in the neighbourhood.

The conclusion was that certain values influence people's perception and sense of place. In this specific urban neighbourhood the sense of place appeared to be strongly influenced by two factors: the involuntary character of living in the neighbourhood and the strong presence of facilities in the wider area of the Hague.

Critical questions can be asked if values were 'measured' objectively, as the sense of place reinforces the perceived importance of some values. For example, being faced with problems in the neighbourhood – which caused low physical attachment – made people aware of the importance of these factors for them. Furthermore, values influence what people perceive as qualities in the neighbourhood. Qualities regarding the physical characteristics, institutions and people and practices of the neighbourhood are all directly influenced by values people hold. These qualities in turn also influence people's sense of place. In spite of the critical remarks, the research indicates that values influence people's perceptions of a place – reflected in their sense of place and the perceived qualities of that place.

Concluding remarks

In this chapter, we have tried to provide some insights into cultural sustainable territorialisation, more specifically the worldview and symbolic dimensions as rooted in human values. Furthermore, some promising methods for mapping values have been identified and applied in an urban context. Empirically, the case study of an urban deprived neighbourhood in the Netherlands indicates that people's values influence people's sense of place and their perceived qualities of that place.

Values express what people appreciate about their place, they influence and prioritise actions and influence how people subscribe symbolic meanings to places. Places hinder or foster the fulfilling of what people consider as worthwhile, and this influences people's satisfaction with a certain place. However, more empirical research is necessary to underpin the assumed relationship between values, qualities and sense of place. Values can be analysed more in-depth and on larger spatial scales (where there is an increasing variety as well as complexity of physical characteristics and cultural values).

We plead for a value-oriented approach to territorialisation, based on a dialogue between citizens, and a sustainability approach that includes multiple values. In policies, multiculturality is often seen as a problem, leading to exclusion, non-integration and socio-economic problems or even enhancing criminality. This case study revealed, however, that citizens also perceive positive aspects of multiculturality such as the variety of people, businesses and multicultural meeting points.

The worldview and symbolic dimension of territorialisation offer insights into how values drive people's place-specific motivations, cultural sense-making and sense of place. Returning to the starting point of this chapter – the role of cultural sustainability in territorialisation – we have shown how this permeates the ecological, economic and social dimensions of sustainability. In other words, culture has a 'transversal' role in sustainability. It refers to the way people subscribe meaning to place and territories. Such cultural meanings are rooted in values which guide people's motivations to be involved in their place and take (sustainable) actions. Values do indeed have a geography.

References

Appleton, J. (2014). *Values in sustainable development.* Routledge, London.

Atmanagara, J. (2015) Culture matters. Planning processes and approaches towards urban resilience in European cities and urban regions: Two examples from Brussels and Ljubljana. In: this book, Chapter 12.

Bailey, J. and I. Biggs (2012). Either side of Delphy Bridge: A deep mapping project evoking and engaging the lives of older adults in rural North Cornwall. *Journal of Rural Studies*, 28: 318–328.

Barrett, F., Fry, R. and H. Wittockx (2010). *Appreciative inquiry. Het basiswerk.* Lannoo Campus/Scriptum, Leuven.

Battaglini, E. and M. Babović (2015). Nature and culture in territorialisation processes: Challenges and insights from a case study in Serbia. In: this book, Chapter 5.

Beck, D.E. and C.C. Cowan (1996). *Spiral dynamics. Waarden, leiderschap en veranderingen in een dynamisch model.* Altamira-Becht, Haarlem.

Convery, I., Corsane, G. and P. Davis (2012). Introduction: Making sense of place, pp. 1–8 in: Convery, I., Corsane, G. and P. Davis (eds), *Making sense of place: Multidisciplinary perspectives*. Newcastle University, Newcastle.

Cooperrider, D.L. and D. Whitney (1999). *Collaborating for change: Appreciative Inquiry.* Berrett-Koehler Publishers, San Francisco.

Davies, A. (2001). What silence knows: Planning, public participation and environmental values. *Environmental Values*, 10 (1): 77–102.

Devine-Wright, P. (2009). Rethinking NIMBYism: The role of place attachment and place identity in explaining place-protective action. *Journal of Community & Applied Social Psychology*, 19 (6): 426–441.

Escobar, A. (2001). Culture sits in places: Reflection on globalism and subaltern strategies of Localization. *Political Geography*, 20 (2): 139–174.

Gibson, K. (2010). *Community assets map*. Available at: www.communitypartnering.info/an40.html (accessed 22 December 2014).

Gilipin, A. (2000). *Environmental economics: A critical overview.* John Wiley and Sons, Chichester and New York.

Gubert, R. (2000). Territorial belonging, pp. 3128–3137 in: Borgatta, E.F. and J.V. Montgomery (eds), *Encyclopedia of sociology*. 2nd edn. Macmillan Reference, New York.

Halsey, J. (2014). Avoiding wrong turns on the road to ecosystem services valuation, pp. 255–263 in: Appleton, J. (ed.), *Values in sustainability*. Routledge, London.

Hamilton, M. (2008). *Integral city: Evolutionary intelligences for the human hive.* New Society Publishers, Gabriola Island, Canada.

Hay, R. (1998). Sense of place in developmental context. *Journal of Environmental Psychology*, 18 (1): 5–29.

Hedlund-de Witt, A. (2011). The rising culture and worldview of contemporary spirituality: A sociological study of potentials and pitfalls for sustainable development. *Ecological Economics*, 70: 1057–1065.

Hedlund-de Witt, A. (2013). Worldviews and their significance for the global sustainable development debate. *Environmental Ethics*, 35 (2): 133–162.

Hedlund-de Witt, A. and N. Hedlund-de Witt (2013). The state of our world, the state of our worldviews: The integrative worldview framework as a tool for reflexive communicative action and transformation, pp. 187–201 in: *Proceedings of the international conference 'Transformation in a changing climate'*, 19–21 June, University of Oslo, Oslo.

Hedlund-de Witt, A., De Boer, J. and J.J. Boersema (2014). Exploring inner and outer worlds: A quantitative study of worldviews, environmental attitudes, and sustainable lifestyles. *Journal of Environmental Psychology*, 37: 40–54.

Horlings, L.G. (2014). Cultural mapping: A value-centered and place-based perspective. Paper for the conference on Cultural Mapping, Coimbra (Portugal), 28–30 May.

Horlings, L.G. (2015). Values in place: A value-oriented approach toward sustainable place-shaping. *Regional Studies, Regional Science*, 2 (1): 256–273.

Horlings, L.G., Battaglini, E. and J. Dessein (2015). Introduction: The role of culture in territorialisation. In: this book, Chapter 1.

Horlings, L.G. and J.P.P. Hinssen (2014). Sustainable innovation in intensive animal husbandry; Policy and public protests towards a mega-farm in the Netherlands (Innovation sustainable dans l'élevage animal intensif; Politique et manifestations publiques envers une méga-ferme aux Pays-Bas). ESSACHESS. *Journal for Communication Studies*, 7, 1 (13): 125–145.

Horlings, I. and F. Padt (2013). Leadership for sustainable regional development in rural areas: Bridging personal and institutional aspects. *Sustainable Development*, 21 (6): 413–424.

Horlings, I., Remmers, G. and T. Duffhues, (2009). *Bezieling: de X-factor in Gebiedsontwikkeling*. Salsedo, Breda.

Jorgensen, B.S. and R.C. Stedman (2006). A comparative analysis of predictors of sense of place dimensions: Attachment to, dependence on and identification with lakeshore properties. *Journal of Environmental Management*, 79 (3): 316–327.

Kluckhohn, C. (1951). Values and value-orientations in the theory of action. An exploration in definition and classification, pp. 388–433 in: Parsons, T. and E. Shils (eds), *Toward a general theory of action*. Harvard University Press, MA.

Lipton, B.H. (2005). *The biology of belief: Unleashing the power of consciousness, matter, and miracles*. Mountain of Love/Elite Books, Santa Rosa, California.

Massey, D. (1993). Power geometries and a progressive sense of place, pp. 59–69 in: Bird, J., Curtis, B., Putnam, T., Robertson, G. and L. Tickner (eds), *Mapping the futures: Local cultures, global changes*. Routledge, London.

McIntyre, N., Moore, J. and M. Yuan (2008). A place-based, values-centered approach to managing recreation on Canadian Crown Lands. *Society & Natural Resources*, 21 (8): 657–670.

O'Brien, K. (2009). Do values subjectively define the limits to climate change adaptation?, pp. 164–180 in: Adger, W.N., Lorenzoni, I. and K. O'Brien (eds), *Adapting to climate change: Thresholds, values, governance*. Cambridge University Press, Cambridge.

O'Brien, K. (2012). Global environmental change II: From adaptation to deliberate transformation. *Progress in Human Geography*, 36 (5): 667– 676.

O'Brien, K. (2013). The courage to change: Adaptation from the inside-out, pp. 306–319 in: Moser, S.C. and M.T. Boykoff (eds), *Successful adaptation to climate change: Linking science and policy in a rapidly changing world*. Routledge, London.

O'Brien, K. and L. Sygna (2013). Responding to climate change: The three spheres of transformation. *Proceedings of the International Conference 'Transformation in a Changing Climate'*, 19–21 June, University of Oslo, Oslo.

O'Neill, J., Holland, A. and A. Light (2008). *Environmental values.* Routledge Introductions to Environment Series. Routledge, London.

Patthey, G.G. (2014). Understanding values using critical discourse analysis, pp. 37–45 in: Appleton, J. (ed.), *Values in sustainable development.* Routledge, London.

Pollini, G. (2005). Socio-territorial belonging in a changing society. *International Review of Sociology: Revue Internationale de Sociologie*, 15 (3): 493–496.

Porter, M. and M. Kramer (2011). Creating shared value. *Harvard Business Review* (Jan/Feb) 89: 62–77.

Relph, E. (1976). *Place and placelessness.* Pion, London.

Riedy, C. (2013). Terraforming ourselves: A causal layered analysis of interior transformation. *Proceedings of the International Conference 'Transformation in a Changing Climate'*, 19–21 June, University of Oslo, Oslo.

Rogge, E., Dessein, J. and H. Gulinck (2011). Stakeholders' perception of attitudes towards major landscape changes held by the public: The case of greenhouse clusters in Flanders. *Land Use Policy*, 28 (1): 334–342.

Rokeach, M. (1973). *The nature of human values.* Free Press, New York.

Sagoff, M. (2008). On the economic value of ecosystem services. *Environmental Values*, 17 (2): 239–258.

Scharmer, O. (2005). *Theory U: Learning from the future as it emerges.* Berrett-Koehler Publishers, San Francisco.

Schein, E. (2010). *Organizational culture and leadership.* 4th edn. John Wiley and Sons, San Francisco.

Shamai, S. (1991). Sense of place: An empirical measurement. *Geoforum*, 22 (3): 347–358.

Schwartz, S.H. (2006). Basic human values: An overview. Theory, methods and applications. Available at: http://segr-did2.fmag.unict.it/Allegati/convegno%207-8-10-05/Schwartzpaper.pdf (accessed 1 August 2014).

SDRI, Sustainable Development Research Institute (1998) *Social capital formation and institutions for sustainability.* Workshop proceedings prepared by Asoka Mendis. Sustainable Development Research Institute, Vancouver. Available at: www.williambowles.info/mimo/refs/soc_cap.html (accessed 1 August 2014).

Shiva, V. (2014). Caring for what we care about, pp. 7–17 in: Appleton, J. (ed.), *Values in sustainable development.* Routledge, London.

Stefanovic, I.L. (2000). *Safeguarding our common future: Rethinking sustainable development.* State University of New York Press, New York.

Soini, K., Hanne, V, and E. Poutaa (2012). Residents' sense of place and landscape perceptions at the rural–urban interface. *Landscape and Urban Planning*, 104 (1): 124–134.

Soino, K. and I. Birkeland (2014). Exploring the scientific discourse on cultural sustainability. *Geoforum*, 51: 213–223.

Vanclay, F. (2008). Place matters, pp. 3–11 in: Vanclay, F., Higgins, M. and A. Blackshaw (eds), *Making sense of place.* National Museum of Australia Press, Canberra.

Van der Schaar, A.M.P. (2013). *Sense of place in the Schilderswijk; On the relation of sense of place, qualities and values in the Schildersbuurt-oost.* Available at: http://edepot.wur.nl/246635 (accessed 1 June 2015).

Westley F. Olsson, P., Folke, C., Homer-Dixon, T., Vredenburg, H., Loorbach, D., Thompson, J. Nilsson, M. , Lambin, E., Sendzimir, J., Banerjee, B., Galaz, V. and S. Van der Leeuw (2011). Tipping toward sustainability: Emerging pathways of transformation. *Ambio*, 40 (7): 762–780.

Wilber, K. (2000). *Integral psychology: Consciousness, spirit, psychology, therapy*. Shambhala Publications, Boston.

5 Nature and culture in territorialisation processes

Challenges and insights from a case study in Serbia

Elena Battaglini and Marija Babović

Introduction

Swyngedouw (2007) asked whether particular natures and cultures exist in which the specific goals of sustainability could be addressed. We ask what kind of relationship between nature and culture would allow sustainable development policies to be constructed around it. Or whether it would be better to overcome the nature–culture dualism and speak instead about their mutual coproduction within the specific limits of time and space.

Some policies promoted in the name of sustainable development (where 'development' essentially refers to 'growth') have shown only minimal efficacy. Parallel to these failed policies are inappropriate analytical operationalisations; inaccurate insofar as they suggest that each specific time or space relates to the specific goals of sustainability. The difficulties found in the operativity of this concept can be traced back to the difficulties of grasping and analysing the complex interactions residing among the social, cultural, economic and environmental dimensions of the development of an area on each of these different scales.

In this chapter, we challenge the normativity inherent in the conceptual nature of sustainable development and its globalising logic, which could be located in any time and any place. Instead we choose to root it in real spaces and real timeframes. We therefore enter the debate on the 'territoriality' and 'territorialisation' of regional development because of its conceptual strength in framing place-based trajectories while still remaining grounded in the enduring features of the human experience and life trajectory.

Building on geographical tradition (Raffestin, 1980, 2012; Turco, 1988, 2009, 2010), we use the term 'territorialisation' to refer to a process in which communities settling in a place perceive the specific nature of the place, attributing symbols to resources and to local peculiarities, while reifying, structuring and organising the space. Both nature and culture, through their dynamic interaction, drive a process that is configured in time. They both condition the relationship between the settling community and the settled land with specific positions, resources and climates. Both act to orient the quality and direction of territorial development. As argued elsewhere (Battaglini, 2014; Battaglini *et al.*, 2015), we understand this to be substantially a process of territorialisation through which a 'space' becomes a 'place' (symbolisation), a 'place to live in' (reification), and thus a 'territory' (institutionalisation), orienting the socio-territorial tides among local communities and 'natural hybrids' (Latour, 1993, 1994). This could be framed as a process of coevolution (Norgaard, 1994) that we understand as coproduction (see also Horlings *et al.*, 2015): a dialogic relationship in which both the social configurations and the local environment in its physical characterisation have agency.

In this chapter, our main aim is thus to understand how culture interacts with natural hybrids within the development trajectories of social actors in a rural community. Specifically we examine the village of Sirogojno (630 inhabitants), in a mountainous region in western Serbia (Zlatibor) with good agricultural and touristic potentialities. We claim that the territorial bonds established by the local communities and their physical environment – in other words, between culture and nature – orient the quality and direction of place-based development, which we understand to be substantially a process of socio-territorial belonging, namely territorialisation.

The nature–culture interaction will be analysed in the context of the symbolisation and reification processes in territorialisation (see also Horlings *et al.*, 2015). Our analysis focuses on perceptions, meanings and values attributed to local resources along with the stages of the territorialisation processes that occur there.

The level of analysis was individuals and households. Qualitative empirical evidence was collected through biographical interviews with 14 local inhabitants of different ages and gender, visual methods (respondents were instructed to take photos of the resources or practices on their farm that are most valuable for their existence) and participatory observations on milk chain and raspberry production.

Theoretical underpinnings

The present debate on regional sustainable development tends to underestimate the relational dynamics of local communities with the natural, morphological and climate characterisations of the territories; or, put another way, the interaction between nature and culture within their paths of development, which we understand to be a process of territorialisation.

The debate about the so-called nature–culture divide is essentially between authors who downplay the role of nature as an autonomous actor, analysing it as a social construct, and others – mainly physical geographers and environmental historians – who assign agency to nature, de-emphasising its aspect as a social construct (Demeritt, 1994; Gerber, 1997). The latter do not recognise the agency of nature in terms of some intentional dimension (as with human intentionality), but rather through the contextual and relational aspects that hold between actor and structure (Bevilacqua, 1996; Dematteis and Governa, 2005).

Even sociology has indirectly confronted this dualism, in its preference for the concept of space to that of place or territory. Sociologists are concerned about falling into some form of environmental determinism and thus attempt not to overshadow the explanatory power of nonspatial sociological variables (Chiesi, 2010).

For us, studying places and their endogenous development (Stimson *et al.*, 2011) implies addressing the concepts of territoriality and territorialisation, and therefore tackling the black box of the relationship between nature and culture, which we claim both have agency.

In relation to these concepts, we can contrast two traditions: in Anglophone literature, these are analysed as approaches to spatial strategy (Sack, 1986; see also Vandergeest and Peluso, 1995; Buch-Hansen, 2003; Kumar and Kerr, 2013). In our chapter, territorialisation is conceived from a different perspective, reflecting the concept of 'human territoriality', promoted by the Swiss geographer Claude Raffestin since the 1970s. Referring to the works of Soja, Deleuze, Guattari and, above all, Lefebvre, Raffestin defines territoriality as 'the ensemble of relations that humans maintain with exteriority and alterity' (Raffestin, 2012: 139). Raffestin refers to space and nature as if they were not synonymous with, or at least not complementary to, a 'given' or 'first material offered to human activity' (ibid.: 122), but are an 'invention' or construction that allow actors to act (ibid.: 123).

From this perspective, he claims that space and its inherent nature is an 'original prison' that becomes a 'derived prison' (Raffestin, 1980) through the effects of culture. The spatial and temporal scale of territoriality structures the type of relations between communities, the resources available to mobilise the material state of resources, human subjective knowledge and emotions, and objective knowledge – whereas human constructions, actions and productions are the unique 'point of convergence of these three worlds' (Raffestin, 2012: 130).

Here we would argue that the representation of the values of the resources that drive production is also achieved by their specific natures. We would therefore challenge and complement Raffestin's arguments on the role of nature and culture, where both have agency.

Nature and culture among symbolisation process

Before being socially constructed – that is, 'produced' – natural resources open themselves to the senses of observers who initially perceive the materiality and physicality of such resources insofar as they might affect the actors' representations and actions.

From this perspective, we will focus on the local-level agency of networks in which social actors and natural hybrids are mutually and relationally coproduced. Networks here diverge in terms of their dimensions, functions and power, but all obey the same symmetric principle, related to the codetermination of nature and society. For this reason, here agency is intended to be collective and relational (see also Goodman, 1999).

One concept on which we rely to grasp nature's agency is that of 'affordances'. As indicated by Gibson (1986), affordances are the inherent properties of a natural resource which, by interacting with perceptions and values, induce a community to select and use resources for their own development paths. They therefore refer to the opportunities for action that the environment provides to social actors through the particular characteristics of the specific resource:

> the affordances of the environment are what it offers to the animal, what it provides or furnishes, either for good or ill. … An important fact about the affordances of the environment is that they are in a sense objective, real and physical, unlike values and meanings, which are often supposed to be subjective, phenomenal and mental.
>
> (Gibson, 1986: 127–129)

The concept of 'affordance' cuts across the dichotomy of the subjective–objective and helps us to understand its inadequacy. An affordance is equally a fact of the environment and a fact of behaviour. It is both physical and psychical, yet neither. An affordance points to both the environmental and to the observer (Gibson, 1986). Affordances arise, therefore, as 'means of action': they are latent in the environment and objectively measurable (regardless of an individual's ability to recognise them), but they are always in relation to the actors. Space arises or not, depending on the actor's capacity to perceive and to attribute value to a natural configuration.

Even environmental resources – through their outlets, their connotations and their morphological, physical and climatic conditions – inform the perceptions of the self and attributions of meaning. They thus have the power of agency in the use and consumption of resources. Consider the nature of a wine soil, its natural yeasts, how its microclimatic conditions influence both the grapes and the process of wine production itself. Through its tangible and intangible assets, the same agricultural landscape in which wine-grapes grow acts to condition the methods for marketing and positioning the wine produced. In essence, the physical nature of places possesses agency in relation to the perceptions, meanings and values attributed to the resources by local communities. It is in this sense that nature, too, has agency that contributes to driving the relationship between what is produced and the communities that territorialise specific local environments.

This is consistent with the body of literature on environmental history that recognises nature's agency and in which 'agency' is not conceptualised using the intentional dimension (human intentionality), but rather through the contextual and relational aspects between actor and structure (Nash, 2005). In writing this chapter, we have been inspired by the work of Piero Bevilacqua (1996), who examined the role played by the River Po in the construction of northern Italian agricultural properties and how wetlands affected the creation of the great estates of southern Italy. We also build on the studies of tidewater rice cultivation in colonial Georgia as described by Stewart (1996).

In our analysis, culture is operationalised dominantly in terms of values. We refer to 'use' values but also to what Clyde Kluckhon stated: 'A value is a conception of the desirable, expressed or implied, distinction of an individual or characteristic of a group, which affects the action selection between modes, means and aims available' (Kluckhohn, 1951: 395). In this regard, Sciolla (2012: 55) points to three crucial aspects that we wish to reinterpret in the light of our study: 1) an 'affective' dimension that involves the relationship between individuals and objects (the local resources), and which refers not only to opportunities but also to an internalised feeling of belonging; 2) a 'cognitive' dimension that refers to the actor's awareness of the specific choice that he or she is accomplishing in relation to that object, and which also appears to be rational and arguable; and 3) a 'selective' dimension that refers to the possible choices posed by, we would argue, the 'affordances' of that object.

Coproduction of nature and culture within processes of symbolisation and reification

Here we analyse the nature–culture interaction in two stages of territorialisation: symbolisation and reification. Within the symbolisation stage, attention is focused on the role of values, primarily in their 'selective' aspects of the appreciation of land and natural hybrids and the sense of belonging. Within the reification stage, on the other hand, attention is paid to the 'affective' and 'cognitive' aspects of values. The territorialisation patterns that emerge as the outcomes of these interactions are then described.

The symbolisation stage

Our study focused on the question, 'Which coproduction practices, or which "natural hybrids" are the most appreciated by respondents, and why?' Two basic types of recognition were found among the respondents: they could either identify 'favourite natural hybrids' or they insisted that all the products they cultivated were equally important. These findings are supported by data collected through both methods (in-depth interviews and visual methods). When respondents emphasised a certain type of 'favourite' product, their choice was also reflected in their photographs. Therefore, they could focus more on some resources and practices or choose diversity, which indicates their preferences. The photographs of the respondents who claimed 'everything is equally important' showed a much wider diversity.

The favourite products identified were mostly dairy products, raspberries and greenhouse vegetables. The selection and cognitive aspects of the appreciation and coproduction of these products is discussed in the section on reification. Note, however, that the reasons for the enjoyment of these products vary widely. The traditional dairy products are less economically profitable than the newer crops, raspberries and greenhouse vegetables. Although the income these novel crops produce is one of the the main reasons for their appreciation, the background of the valuation is more complex. Dairy products are an example of a truly endogenous resource: they are strongly rooted in the farming practices and consumption patterns of the area.

> Almost every household in the village has at least one cow. A cow means life for a peasant. If you have a cow, you always have something to eat. There is milk, cream, cheese, just add some bread to it ... A cow brings life into the house. Peasants' lives are centred around cows and milk. But we who are

> employed, we also like to have clean, healthy milk. We like to produce it for ourselves, for our children.
>
> (female respondent, age 53)

Raspberries, in contrast, are not part of the region's traditional production. Raspberry cultivation began here during the 1990s, with the development of the market for berries and the appearance of large exporters of frozen berries. The main reason for the introduction of this new crop at that time was its high market value.

> I had a friend. He started raspberry production, and at that time [in the early 1990s – author's note], it was very profitable. I saw how well others were doing in the raspberry business and how much they were earning. I was listening, and finally I decided to start my own raspberry production. When I planted my first raspberry yard, my father, who was still head of the household, told me 'Are you crazy, these aren't raspberries, they're blueberries!' He didn't know what raspberries were; he was 'old school'.
>
> (male respondent, age 68)

In instances where the respondents could not identify a few types of favourite product, several rationales were given: everything is important because (1) of the interdependence of various types of productions and products; (2) producing all of them decreases the risks and increases the overall resilience of the farm; and (3), together, the various products 'afford' to satisfy the diverse consumption needs of the household. As one 68-year-old male respondent put it:'In order to have good raspberries, you need to have natural fertilisers. For that, you need cows. For cows, you need grass, hay, alfalfa … It's all related and interdependent. Everything requires everything else.'

This diversified production due to self-consumption is strongly rooted in traditional farming practices and remains even when producers are aware that it is not always cost-effective.

> Don't ask me what we produce … Everything that is needed – from crops, to cattle, to raspberries. You have to manage to produce everything, my friend, like in the past. Everything was processed and preserved. It was all for use in the household. *Rakija* [a type of brandy – author's note] was produced, cattle were bred, chickens too, a bit of grain, and that's it … I still do this today … Each year, we produced vegetables for our own use: onions, carrots, beet, beans – all near to the house so we can have them to eat.
>
> (male respondent, age 48)

To understand further how the nature–culture interaction occurs within the various production practices, we now focus more on two cases as examples of either more endogenously or more exogenously driven 'natural hybrids', i.e. dairy products and raspberries. We examine the selection processes and cognitive aspects behind the valuation of these resources within the reification processes of territorialisation.

The reification stage

Why are some goods produced and others not? What influences the selection processes? Based on the research findings, it is clear that the process of selection is determined by the simultaneous interplay of various elements: some more objective, such as 'affordable' factors (the characteristics of the land and climate) and economic factors (in the form of market, subsidies and support programmes), and some more subjective – again in economic form (such as the use value attributed to the products) or through other nonmaterial values ('cognitive' and 'affective' values) ascribed to products and coproduction practices related to them.

In the case of dairy products, the motivation to produce was more endogenous. Traditionally, dairy products have afforded strongly related needs of households, based on nutritional habits and perceptions of healthy food. The local natural environment is favourable for this kind of production; grasslands and pastures abound. The whole region has traditionally been famous for livestock production. During the socialist period, when subsistence farming was dominant, milk and dairy products were strongly embedded in the region. The ongoing transition to the market economy since the 1990s has brought important changes. The previous practices of selling surplus dairy products to local cooperatives were dismissed due to the collapse of social cooperatives, altered legislation and new standards affected the trade in dairy products, and respondents were forced to find new solutions. The coping mechanisms in dairy production in the region are described and analysed in detail in Battaglini *et al.* (2015). It is important to note that dairy practices have transformed in response to transitional changes in a way that has enabled producers to maintain their nutritional habits and to provide stable income from the same resource. When they became unable to sell dairy products (such as cream and cheese) due to the restrictions of the regulations and the structure of the demand chains, farmers began to sell milk and to produce dairy products for personal consumption.

However, the adjustments that occurred in dairy production due to external factors influenced the practices of production. The mechanisms of selection and production were adjusted to market requirements, though some traditional knowledge and practices are still preserved. The selection of cow breeds was determined mostly by the desire to increase milk production for the market. Previously, farms had traditional breeds of cattle that were adapted to the local environment, or else they bred dairy cows with beef cows in order to provide both dairy products and meat for consumption within the framework of subsistence farming. Furthermore, milking technology and the preservation of milk are designed in accordance with market standards and to suit the dairy company that buys the milk.

Although many aspects of breeding cows and producing milk are new, having been acquired along with the standards for market production and modern veterinarian principles, some traditional knowledge is still in use.

> The selection of breeds is mostly influenced by the vet. Some of the old breeds of cows that were common 30–40 years ago don't exist anymore. But these cows were really good. They were good for giving milk, but also very resilient. They were healthy. They gave birth to calves easily; they didn't get sick. They were really resilient. They were not fed so much with concentrate. These breeds that we have now were introduced here 15 years ago.
>
> (female respondent, age 69)

Unlike the endogenous dairy products, raspberries are an example of exogenous, market-driven production on local family farms. The structure of the demand chains on the local fruit market was the key factor that influenced these selection processes. Prior to the transitional period, traditional fruit production mainly involved plums (used in the production of brandy), apples and some pears as well as wild berries collected from the surrounding woods. When large raspberry exporters appeared in the region, strengthening the demand chains for fresh raspberries, the local farms reoriented their production to this fruit.

> We still have plums that we collect and process. We make *rakija* for household consumption. We don't sell it, it's just for us and our friends. We had apples during the 1980s, about 50 acres of them. Those were fertile years. Grandfather used to invite schoolchildren to collect apples and keep them, just to remove them from the ground. You didn't have a market for it. Now the local company is active again, but it's hard to do business with them. You have to wait … for payment … We had a cooperative in Sirogojno that was liquidated. It was privatised for a small amount of money. If there was a demand for apples, I would produce them.
>
> (male respondent, age 48)

Besides market factors, the natural environment plays an important role in the development of raspberry production. First, the morphology of the terrain affords planting of raspberry yards. Hillsides enable good drainage during rainy seasons, which proved beneficial particularly during the severe floods and heavy and prolonged rain of spring and summer 2014. Despite the additional effort in cultivating this kind of terrain, our respondents explained that they intentionally planted raspberry yards on such plots in order to mitigate the risks of excessive water. Second, climate change, which can be seen in the consecutive years of dry seasons followed by floods, by sudden snows in May and mild winters, represents a serious challenge for raspberry producers. Their mechanisms for coping with these challenges include the choice of raspberry varieties, the introduction of mechanisation and insurance. In order to reduce environmental risks, some producers plant different types of raspberry that are resistant to different weather conditions. Others plant the old variety that is most suited to the local environment. Third, the configuration of the holdings, the small plots, gives the best return in raspberry production. Because they can provide a high income from a small area, the raspberry crop is greatly appreciated.

Raspberry production is relatively new in the local farming practices, thus the way in which knowledge of it is adopted and transferred differs from the way knowledge of dairy products is adopted and transferred. On account of the lack of traditional knowledge, public support services (such as institutes for agriculture and advisory services) and informal knowledge transfer among producers have played a more important role. The novelty of raspberry production is a significant challenge for farmers, many of whom find this kind of exploration and experimentation with new products exciting. This brings about new content and new practices and refreshes the 'monotony' of traditionally reproduced production practices.

> When I'm not sure of something, I consult the Institute for Plant Protection in Uzice. They give me advice on how to choose the variety of raspberry, how to protect them, and so on. But I learn a lot on my own. I keep a notebook for raspberry production. I try things and I record the results. Last year, when I bought an irrigation system, I experimented with how to feed the raspberries. I was testing, measuring, observing, and recording. If you add too many minerals, it is also not good. I learned a lot from experience in that way.
>
> (male respondent, age 48)

Raspberry production is perceived as hard work, but highly profitable. To develop a new raspberry yard requires an investment of energy, effort and care.

> My grandfather gave me that small plot of land last year when I decided to try raspberry production. Here in the photos you can see what I had to do to build the raspberry yard [shows photos]. I had to plow, create furrows manually, make channels, and remove all the stones, because when stones get hot or cold, they can destroy the raspberries. When you plow, the stones come out, so you have to take them out. I spent hours and hours in the raspberry yard every day. (…) This area is enough to give me an income equivalent to a total annual salary of my wife and me, together.
>
> (male respondent, age 32)

The previous narrative also indicates another important outcome of raspberry production: it results in interesting changes in the perception of the importance of different economic activities due to the increase in raspberry production. Traditionally, in this village and in the majority of others around Serbia, small landholdings meant that peasants would combine off-farm employment with agriculture. In their perception, off-farm employment was the 'main' economic activity, providing a regular salary and social benefits, while agriculture was an 'additional' activity that amounted largely to subsistence production and selling the surplus. With the economic crisis since 2008, problems in many companies in the region, low employment prospects and poor employment conditions, raspberry production has started to bring about comparatively better incomes. Some of our respondents realised that focusing more on this kind of production would not only compensate for the reduction in income from off-farm employment but would bring even greater economic benefit. Although many still consider raspberry production to be an 'additional' economic activity in addition to off-farm employment, some have fully shifted to raspberry production.

Besides generating a good income, raspberry production, like dairy production, is motivated by use values. Because it is consumed in the household, farmers are careful to produce healthy products.

The following narrative, like many others, indicates some forms of appreciation for raspberry production that are not related to economic values (whether market or use value). Interviewed farmers attribute 'cognitive' and 'affective' values to the production of raspberries: it is perceived as 'relaxing' in comparison to some other on-farm or off-farm work.

> I prefer to work on my farm than with people. It relaxes me. When I was young, I managed 22 workers in my company. I was the only one in the unit who did not drink, so you can imagine what it was like for me. Trust me, it was very hard to work with them. They wouldn't start work without two litres of *rakija*, and they finished with four litres. What can I say ....
>
> (male respondent, age 32)

> I love doing everything on the farm. But when I enter the raspberry yard – this is resting for me. It is not hard work, it's beautiful, and the smell is nice. When you cook raspberry, it smells really wonderful.
>
> (female respondent, age 69)

In addition to this, raspberry yards afford respondents to attribute selective aesthetic values to them: the raspberry yard is a place of beauty, and they are proud when their yards are tidy.

> In the raspberry yard, you get a lust for life. Of all types of work, I like most to work in the raspberry yard. It's such a nice feeling when you see the way it gets more beautiful each year. It grows, it's all in lines and orderly, green and red ... beautiful. Last year, I planted 40 plum trees up here above the raspberry yard. So now, when you look from afar, it all looks beautiful.
>
> (male respondent, age 48)

The patterns described and the processes of interaction between actors and nature, mediated by diverse values, influence the outcomes of territorialisation.

Main findings

The problems in defining 'territory' in the social and human sciences stem from the difficulty in 'conceptualising the interplay between physical space and the organisation of relations and functions that come along with it, ... [which] is in the first place an epistemological difficulty' (Mubi Brighenti, 2010: 59). We would argue that this difficulty relates to the black box of the dualism of nature and culture that we challenge in this chapter.

Our study had two aims: first, to relate developmental trajectories to the relationship between the settling community and the settled land with specific positions, resources and climates. We have claimed (Battaglini, 2014; Battaglini *et al.*, 2015) that what drives actors to select specific practices and life trajectories in relation to market and other external pressures are the perceptions, meanings and values attributed to what the local resources afford.

Land is the main natural resource of existential importance to the respondents. As our analysis illustrates, access to land, its type, quality and morphology 'afford' and strongly define the everyday practices as well as the long-term processes of territorialisation. At the same time, the distribution of land, as well as its valuation by actors during these processes, is influenced by cultural factors, specifically by social norms and values.

From this perspective, our findings indicate that successful territorialisation is addressed by coproduction practices that are shaped by a combination of local resource affordances and diverse values. It seems that the combination of economic and non-economic, market and non-market, traditional and modern values and practices leads respondents to become attached to the place they live over time. Opportunities to provide a satisfactory income, to produce and consume healthy food, and to live in a healthy and beautiful environment, are the key factors in their territorial bonding to Sirogojno.

However, the improvement in living conditions and the better economic opportunities in the village – especially those introduced by raspberry production – coupled with poor opportunities in the urban areas during the years of economic crisis, with high unemployment among young people, has probably contributed to the fact that the youngest generation in the families of our respondents have mostly remained in the village. Some of them had off-farm employment in nearby towns, but they continued to live in the countryside and to participate in agricultural production on the farm. Their decision to remain in the village is also of key importance for sustainable raspberry production in the future, as this is a labour-intensive activity.

The second aim of our contribution is to understand the process of territorialisation as a coproduction of nature and culture in which both have agency. As we have claimed, the concept that underpins nature's agency is that of 'affordances'.

The coevolutionary patterns that occur along the developmental trajectories described by our respondents could be also framed and understood in the perspective of time and space. The traditional knowledge shown by our respondents is strongly linked with seasonality and nature's inherent time. In other words, as Gerber stated: 'it remains true nevertheless that various time limits are imposed on the social constructions of nature by physical processes. Such time–space requirements of physical/biological processes support the idea of "agency" in nature' (Gerber 1997: 13).

If 'agency' here referred to the intentions of a nature capable of actively negotiating with the aims and expectations of human practices, we would agree with Gerber that it would be harder to explain how species extinctions and the ruthless exploitation of all life by humans could occur. Nevertheless, we join Nash

(2005) in that we need to consider agency in different terms, such as Latour's (1993) notion of agency dispersed among humans and natural hybrids in what he terms an 'actor-network'. We also agree with Ingold's (1992) efforts to challenge constructionism in social science by analysing 'organisms-in-their-environment' rather than 'self-contained individuals' with their culture confronting nature as the external world.

In our view, it is exactly this need that legitimises the concept of territorialisation, and which could allow scholars and practitioners to study development along with the coproduction of nature and culture within specific configurations of time and space.

Time and space have always played crucial roles in inquiries into nature as a social construct, as advanced by Harvey (1990). Building on Durkheim's reflections on religious life, Harvey stated that the notions of space and time employed by different social groups are objective and sufficient for that group's peculiar needs. They also function to organise the society's material practices and practices of self-propagation.

The case we have described shows that the time needed for physical processes to grow crops and guarantee their fertility cannot be shortened by any fertilisers, antibiotics or genetic manipulation. The traditional knowledge possessed by our respondents is strongly linked with seasonality and with nature's inherent timing. In this perspective, this could also corroborate our hypothesis of nature's agency.

In conclusion, in an attempt to answer Swyngedouw (2007), our results show that there are indeed singular natures and cultures interacting in which the specific goals of sustainability could be addressed. The endogenous trajectories followed by the Sirogojno community, its territorial bonding and its sense of valuing and esteeming what they have achieved on the farm level all depend on the time–space specific relations between the affordances of the resources available at the local level and the affective, cognitive and selective values attributed to them during the process of the symbolisation and reification stages of territorialisation.

In the social analysis of sustainable development trajectories, what counts are the intentions and conscious desires to 'sustain a particular situation' (Peattie, 2011: 22). These intentions drive actors to select specific practices and life trajectories in relation to the market and other external pressures.

Rather than adopting a globalising logic of sustainable 'transitions' that could occur any time and anywhere, we prefer to root sustainability in real spaces and in real timeframes; this is after all where transitions occur. As we have claimed, territorialisation has the conceptual strength to frame place-based trajectories, as it is grounded in enduring features of human experience and life trajectory patterns.

Some questions that need to be further developed in our study of territorialisation are as follows: how do national and local stakeholders perceive and reify the resources of the Zlatibor region? How do policies (local, national and other) enable or hinder Zlatibor's regional social andeconomic development? What are the development trajectories of the region and their relations with the territorialisation process of its inhabitants? What are the implications for the policies that underpin development? We expect that a deeper analysis of the institutional stage of the territorialisation patterns after the year 2000, and of the local configurations of market, state and society could help to answer these questions.

Our research in the Zlatibor region is still ongoing. Nevertheless, our observations thus far indicate that the operationalisation of the concept of territorialisation can produce results that are sufficiently robust and consistent to analyse the factors enabling or hindering endogenous development on the regional level for its focus on the interplay between environment and society.

Acknowledgements

This chapter was written as part of a COST IS1007 Grant. The case study is based on the research supported by the Italy and Serbia Bilateral Scientific Cooperation Agreement and fostered by the effective encouragement of ABT-ISF-IRES.

References

Battaglini, E. (2014). *Sviluppo territoriale. Dal disegno di ricerca alla valutazione dei risultati*. Franco Angeli, Milan.

Battaglini, E., Babović, M. and N. Bogdanov (2015). Framing resilience by territorialisation, pp.119–131 in Palovita, A. and M. Jarvela (eds), *Climate adaptation, policy and food supply chain management in Europe*. Routledge, London.

Bevilacqua, P. (1996). *Tra natura e storia. Ambiente, economia, risorse in Italia*. Donzelli, Rome.

Buch-Hansen, M. (2003). The territorialisation of rural Thailand: Between localism, nationalism and globalism. *Tijdschrift voor Economische en Sociale Geografie*, 94 (3): 322–334.

Chiesi, L. (2010). *Il doppio spazio dell'architettura. Ricerca sociologica e progettazione*. Liguori Editore, Naples.

Dematteis, G. and F. Governa (eds) (2005). *Territorialità, Sviluppo Locale, Sostenibilità: Il Modello SloT*. Franco Angel, Milan.

Demeritt, D. (1994). The nature of metaphors in cultural geography and environmental history. *Progress in Human Geography*, 18: 163–185.

Gerber, J. (1997). Beyond dualism: The social construction of nature and the natural and social construction of human beings. *Progress in Human Geography*, 21 (1): 1–17.

Gibson, J. (1986). *The ecological approach to visual perception*. Psychology Press, Taylor & Francis Group, New York and Hove, UK.

Goodman, D. (1999). Agro-food studies in the 'Age of Ecology': Nature, corporeality, biopolitics. *Sociologia Ruralis*, 39 (1): 17–38.

Harvey, D. (1990). Between space and time: Reflections on the geographical imagination. *Annals of the Association of American Geographers*, 80: 418–434.

Horlings, I., Battaglini, E. and J. Dessein (2015). Introduction: The role of culture in territorialisation. In: this book, Chapter 1.

Ingold, T. (1992). Culture and the perception of the environment, pp. 39–56 in: Croll, E. and D. Parkin (eds), *Bush base: Forest farm. Culture, environment and development*. Routledge, London.

Kluckhohn, C. (1951). Values and value-orientations in the theory of action. An exploration in definition and classification, pp. 388–433 in: Parsons, T. and E. Shils (eds), *Toward a general theory of action*. Harvard University Press, Cambridge, MA.

Kumar, K. and J.M. Kerr (2013). Territorialisation and marginalisation in the forested landscapes of Orissa, India. *Land Use Policy*, 30 (1): 885–894.

Latour, B. (1993). *We have never been modern*. Harvester Wheatsheaf, Brighton.

Latour, B. (1994). On technical mediation – philosophy, sociology, genealogy. *Common Knowledge*, 3 (2): 29–64.

Mubi Brighenti, A. (2010). On territoriology: Towards a general science of territory in theory. *Culture & Society*, 27 (1): 52–72.

Nash, L. (2005). The agency of nature or the nature of agency? *Environmental History*, 10 (1): 67–69.

Norgaard, R.B. (1994). *Development betrayed: The end of progress and a coevolutionary revisioning of the future.* Routledge, London and New York.

Peattie, K. (2011). Developing and delivering social science research for sustainability, pp. 17–33 in: Franklin, A. and P. Blyton (eds), *Researching sustainability: A guide to social science methods, practice and engagement.* Earthscan, London and New York.

Raffestin, C. (1980). *Pour une Géographie du Pouvoir.* LITEC, Paris.

Raffestin, C. (2012). Space, territory and territoriality. *Environment and Planning D: Society and Space*, 30: 121–141.

Sack, R.D. (1986). *Human territoriality: Its theory and history.* Cambridge University Press, Cambridge.

Sciolla, L. (2012). *Sociologia dei processi culturali.* Il Mulino, Bologna.

Stewart, M.A. (1996). *What nature suffers to groe: Life, labor, and landscape on the Georgia Coast, 1680–1920.* University of Georgia Press, Athens, Georgia.

Stimson, R.J., Stough, R.R. and P.J. Njikamp (eds) (2011). *Endogenous regional development: Perspectives, measurement and empirical investigation.* Edward Elgar, Cheltenham.

Swyngedouw, E. (2007). Impossible/undesirable sustainability and the post-political condition, pp. 13–40 in: Krueger J.R. and D. Gibbs (eds), *The sustainable development paradox.* Guilford Press, New York.

Turco, A. (1988). *Verso una teoria geografica della complessità.* UNICOPLI, Milan.

Turco, A. (2009). Topogenèse: la généalogie du lieu et la constitution du territoire, pp. 37–44 in: M. Vanier (ed.), *Territoires, territorialité, territorialisation: Controverses et perspectives.* Presse Universitaires de Rennes, Rennes.

Turco, A. (2010). *Configurazioni della territorialità.* Franco Angeli, Milan.

Vandergeest, P. and N.L. Peluso (1995). Territorialization and state power in Thailand. *Theory and Society*, 24 (3): 385–426.

6 Territoriality as appropriation of space

How 'engaging with space' frames sociality

Leonardo Chiesi

Life takes space very seriously. Every organism depends on its capacity to engage with its environment and every form of life reaches out to deal with space in some way or another. Humans are no exceptions; indeed, our relationship to space is so compelling, so nuanced, and so fundamental, that it has always demanded close scientific investigation (Tuan, 1974). However, only recently have studies generated a comprehensive perspective capable of delving into the specificity of 'engaging with space' of our species. Increasing theoretical and empirical evidence even shows that the dynamics of appropriation of space, in a word 'territorialisation', represent a key to understanding social life. As we shall see, territorialisation rests at the core of many social dynamics.

Regrettably, the debate on territorialisation tends to split into two main segments that scarcely communicate with each other, if at all. One camp studies territorialisation at the micro-scale of individual behaviour. Building on ethological studies of animal behaviour, sociologists, anthropologists and psychologists study the manifold aspects of human behaviour as related to space. The other camp studies territorialisation at the macro-scale of regional space. Here, mostly geographers, sociologists and economists study the implications of interactions between large groups and the environment, the management of resources and infrastructures, the development of cities, the relationship of cities with their surroundings, and so forth.

I plead instead for a unifying approach, where the micro- and macro-scale are consolidated within one theoretical framework. An experience-based approach like the one I propose here will hopefully help us integrate these two divided branches of the current debate; by understanding processes grounded in experience on the small scale, we can then expand to larger scales.

Breaking free from ethology

Research on human territoriality consolidated during the 1960s when social science scholars began to look at ethology with more interest. They realised that the vast knowledge about animal behaviour as related to space could yield promising results when applied to humans. In this scientific milieu, a whole research programme emerged and firmly positioned itself in the fields of sociology and psychology. Its premises could be summed up by a definition of territoriality that revolved around demarcation (constructing and communicating territories through marking behaviours) and defence of space (maintaining and restoring territories). Territoriality was then conceived as 'the act of laying claim to and defending a territory' (Hall, 1959: 146). It involves 'the mutually exclusive use of areas and objects by persons and groups' (Altman, 1975: 106) by means of 'repulsion through overt defense or some form of communication' (Dyson-Hudson and Smith, 1978: 22). The scientific discourse on territoriality has further been explored in the work of Sack (1986) and Brown (1987) and via classic reviews (Lyman and Scott, 1967; Altman, 1970).

This way of investigating generated a large corpus of knowledge that has helped us understand our relationship with space; however, by emphasising the control of resources via the demarcation and defence of space, this approach 'has distorted the picture of human territorial functioning by suggesting that territories become important only when they are violated or threatened' (Brown, 1987: 173).

Human territoriality can be a vehicle for much more subtle processes than animal territoriality, and we must go beyond this approach, imbued as it is with an outdated notion of either rationality or instinctiveness as the main avenues to the understanding of human behaviour. By breaking free from this ethological heritage, we will be able to appreciate how territories offer a great variety of opportunity for social organisation and we will come to a much broader understanding of how we relate to space and what kind of opportunities space affords us.

What we do to space; what space does to us

The current discourse on human territoriality also revolves around the much debated issue of the hegemony of nature versus culture; sometimes this dispute reaches the impasse of the unsolvable dilemma of the subject or object supremacy. The relationship between society and the environment is characterised by intense dialectics where neither society nor the environment prevails: space is simultaneously *shaped* by society, but is also capable of *shaping* society. The environment is continuously modified, planned and designed by society but, at the same time, the environment defines the conditions for social action and it thus helps to define society itself. This dialectic is expressed by the conceptual pair of 'place-making', i.e. the direction of the relationship where it is society that defines space (Prior, 1988; Baldry, 1999) and 'emplacement', i.e. the direction of the relationship where it is space that defines the possibility for social behaviour (Lefebvre, 1974) (see Figure 6.1).

When space is inhabited, it ceases to be a purely abstract geometrical quantity: humans extract from continuous and abstract space a bounded and significant identity (Gieryn, 2000). Tuan (2001) and others have described place as infused with meaning. The process of appropriation turns something inert and neutral into a 'place'. The appropriation is both material and immaterial, where society invests space with meaning but also physically shapes it into specific forms to suit a wide diversity of needs. During the 1980s a progressive shift towards a

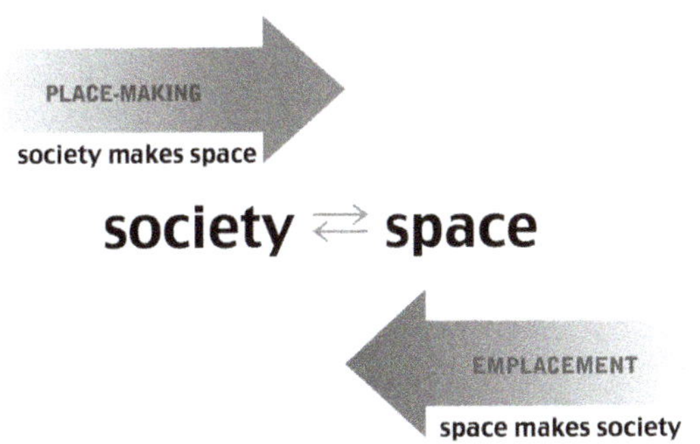

Figure 6.1 The dialectics between society and space

Source: © Leonardo Chiesi.

more diversified approach to territoriality began to consolidate, together with an emerging knowledge about the significance of space to humans (Brown, 1987). It then became apparent that space, and hence territory, could be considered as an elected key to understanding social action. These ideas echo the sometimes forgotten proposals by founding theorists such as Durkheim, advanced at the onset of social sciences as scientific discipline at the end of the ninenteenth century (Parker, 2004).

In this view, space is frame for action, in the sense that a fundamental component of sociality is situated in space. Social life is not indifferent to space: on the contrary, social life is deeply embedded in space. Space is not merely a container, but rather a producing element. Space is 'actively passive' because while it is socially made, it is also capable of making sociality (Thrift, 1983: 38): it is a product of practices and, at the same time, it produces practices. Territoriality must then be seen as a relational notion, where space ceases to be the mere result of social practice, but becomes an element of an ongoing dialectic relationship. Whenever we investigate this relationship, we must therefore always ask ourselves how we shape space while space is shaping us.

Territorialisation and sustainability

This mutual relationship between society and space is mediated by culture. It is through culture, broadly defined as shared sets of beliefs, values and behaviours, that this relationship becomes dynamic: culture can be thought of, in other words, as the human interface with space. If this interface deteriorates, the whole process of territorialisation is jeopardised and it could then be argued that the cycle of territorialisation/deterritorialisation (Raffestin, 1984) is a function of the deterioration of culture. Any reflection on a sustainable territory must take culture into account as a key factor, since territoriality is a process mediated by culture. When we adopt this perspective, it becomes clear that the recent trend where culture is considered a defining factor of sustainability (together with the long accepted ecological, economic and social dimensions) is just a late recognition of the possible role of culture as a vector of 'equity and fairness in the distribution of welfare, utilities and resources between generations' (Soini and Birkeland, 2014: 213).

Inter-scalarity

If we take our investigation further, and resolutely adopt a dialectic view of territoriality, we then must consider that our relationship with space is conveyed first by our experience of it (Griffero, 2010). With this phenomenological approach we are granted an important theoretical advantage: we can construct that we experience space at all possible scales through the body, be it the immediate proxemic space that surrounds the body, or the peripersonal space where we move freely, or the larger space reachable with all our sensory capacities. It does not matter whether I am trying a new office chair, I am inside a building appreciating its architectural space, promenading down Fifth Avenue, or walking down the hill in Chianti enjoying the Tuscan landscape. In all these cases, at such different scales, there is still a unifying principle: my body, with its measures, motor capacities and sensory abilities.

In this fashion, any space-related social practice, even the most abstract and apparently remote from direct experience (such as those related to territorial identity, as we shall see below), originates from a primary set of experiences. Obvious as it may seem, this conceptual choice will help us ground our analysis on a strong foothold, both theoretical and empirical, that will allow us to escape from the confinements of an exclusively small-scale approach. Many studies on territoriality investigate, for example, how we demarcate our temporary space in a library, or deal with intrusions during conversation, or defend our privacy in public space (see Baum *et al.*, 1974 and Brown, 1987 for a complete review). Conversely, we must also avoid the other extreme: an abstract conceptualisation where space is a node in a theoretical network at a very high level of generality (with concepts such as region, development, globalisation, and so forth) where it is difficult to define an object that permits empirical investigation (for examples, see Castells, 2010; Sassen, 2012; Grosby, 1995; also compare with Raffestin and Butler, 2012).

The only solid ground for our analysis of high-level scales can be found in low-level scales (namely those where we deal with primary experiential categories, rather than secondary abstract constructs) because the low-level processes are the constituents of high-level ones, and not vice versa (this idea, specifically applied to the spatial domain, is to be found in the work of Alexander (1977) and Hillier and Hanson (1984)). We might identify this epistemological movement 'from the ground up' as a constructivist approach to territorialisation, which focuses on outlining a unified theory of territorialisation that shows how there is consistency at different scales. This consistency emerges from the fact that any territorial experience, regardless of scale, happens with the engagement of the body-mind system with the surrounding environment.

Three modalities

When we conceive of territorialisation as appropriation of space through experience, we identify this process as it unfolds through the recognition of three sets of opportunities. Space allows for specific opportunities to humans, or, to put it differently, allows for the manifestation of three types of intelligence (see Figure 6.2). In regard to the surrounding environment we have developed three kinds of capacities of response, each with a high level of specificity, which in turn might correspond to specific neural architectures (see Gardner, 1983).

Space is first an opportunity for action. In other words, space is perceived as a set of affordances, as proposed by Gibson (1979). Second, space is also an opportunity to deal with signs. Space is, in other words, a support for encoding and decoding signs; i.e. inscribing signs as references to meaning, and decoding signs to extract meaning from signs previously encoded by others. Finally, space is an opportunity for aesthetic experience, i.e. for exercising taste as a structure of preferences that 'is dependent on perceptual interest and immersion' in space (Brady, 1998: 142).

Figure 6.2 Appropriation of territory as the result of three dominant modalities

Source: © Leonardo Chiesi.

Affordance

'Affordance' is an opportunity for action mediated by the environment, a concept proposed by Gibson in his groundbreaking work on perception (Gibson, 1979: 127–143). Gibson successfully demonstrated that we perceive such opportunities directly, independently of perceiving the qualities of properties of objects (such as colour, texture, and so on) and that this fundamental process characterises any form of living organism. The perception of what space affords entails a form of autonomous intelligence, which we use to work out how to do things in the three dimensions around the body. The psychology of perception, the research programme of embodied cognition (Mahon and Caramazza, 2008) and more recently neuroscience as applied to architectural space (Eberhard, 2008; Mallgrave, 2010) have shown us how to-be-in-the-world is inextricably linked to movement, and therefore to action (Petit, 1997). To put it more bluntly, as a neuroscientist has recently asserted, 'the reason for existence is action' (Krakauer in Firestein, 2012: 115). What space affords us is, in close vicinity, a myriad of proxemic affordances where we perpetually interpret the surrounding environment as a deposit of possibilities for action. Our body, thanks to its plasticity and sophisticated articulation, discovers opportunities for our fingers to dance on a computer keyboard, or for our back to adjust to the curves of a well-designed park bench for maximal comfort. On a different level, in space we find opportunities for movement, i.e. to translate our body through distance, and that is the quintessential process, at least for our species, to provide for food and shelter. Equally as vital as food and shelter are the opportunities that space presents for engaging in relationship: space favours or inhibits bodily contact, verbal and non-verbal exchange, and all of the possibilities for dialogue. This latter class of affordances, this set of spatial opportunities for sociality, strongly construe our experience of space, as it is through them that we let our natural disposition toward others unfold (Chiesi, 2014).

The catalogue of affordance is interminable because the very notion of affordance allows us to get rid of the problematic notion of 'function': the object itself is no longer seen as having one or more functions, but rather the subject is the one who discovers affordances in the object. This completely inverts the perspective: our capacity to individuate opportunities in space becomes key, rather than some objective qualities that predetermine its function(s).

Meaning

Space is also a support for signs. If we take the classic definition of sign as 'something which stands for something else' (Eco, 1974: 73), then it becomes obvious that much of what surrounds us is an opportunity to activate the process of signification, that is to make a connection between the sign (that which stands for) and its meaning (that which it is stood for). Whereas the sign is tangibly *out there* for us to perceive, the meaning is intangible (it is *in here*, in our minds). It is the result of a mental process and as such is unreachable in a direct manner. Space functions as a semantic device, where what we experience is not per se, but rather a reference to the separate worlds of meaning.

Whether it is a student at university filling her room with pictures from home, or a Bolivian family of *campesinos* spending more money on decorating their house gate, instead of repairing their roof, to declare their social status, or gang members spraying graffiti on street corners to mark where their turf begins, they are all making semantic statements. What dominates those statements is not what is immediately perceivable (the pictures, the decorations or the graffiti) but rather what is not visible yet so very present: a cluster of meanings (Rapoport, 1982; Gosling *et al.*, 2005). Space therefore provides a podium for the orchestration of signs with our need for projecting and introflexing meanings into the world and from it. It is only when we realise the pervasiveness of this process that we can understand how sometimes conflicts related to space and territory are only semantic battles with conflicting interpretations of signs by different strata of society: for instance, is a graffiti interpreted as an artistic expression or as vandalistic aggression (Mubi Brighenti, 2010)? Is an historic building a symbol of freedom or oppression (Lasswell and Fox, 1979; Goodsell, 2001)? Is the toponymy of an area and its traffic signs the focus of intense debate among the population as it reflects different visions of the future of the community (Chiesi and Costa, 2005; Castiglioni *et al.*, 2010)? These research questions are answered when meaning becomes the focus of investigation.

Taste

Whereas it is obvious to consider aesthetic experience as a universal and pervasive category of human experience, we have only recently acknowledged the specificity of the environment around us as an opportunity for aesthetic appreciation. Classically, this appreciation has been associated with works of art, especially painting and sculpture (Carlson, 2000). Indeed, the everyday sort of appreciation of the environment differs substantially from appreciating art, as it 'lacks the guidance of an artistic context' (Brady, 1998: 140; see also Brady, 2013). Our aesthetic experience of space is *continuous* as it unfolds within the flow of daily life (whereas works of art are discrete, and emerge from the ordinary into the extraordinary), *spontaneous* (that is, disengaged from critical discourse and reception, which provide the framework that sets the boundaries of our aesthetic experience of art, as described by Brady, 2003, 2013), and *interested*, in that it is inextricably connected to an affective investment that attracts or repels us. There is, after all, a clear evolutionary advantage in the development of such a response: it is reasonable to hypothesise that nature was the first source of what we have learned to call 'beauty' (Dutton, 2009). The natural environment grants us survival and the successful management of such dependence is also handled by this special set of internal processes, where what we experience through senses or what we 'taste' is construed as beautiful, pleasurable, noticeable … all of which responses imply a movement of appropriation or rejection in relation to the object, of *wanting more* or *wanting less* of it (Griffero, 2010).

What to look for: socio-environmental indicators

To put this theoretical approach into an empirical research framework means identifying indicators of these three dominant modalities of space appropriation. These indicators come in the form of observable phenomena that allow us to characterise the specific form of territoriality case by case. These indicators may be categorised into five groups (Chiesi, 2010): routines, traces, alterations, adaptations and signs (see Figure 6.3).

Routines are behavioural regularities that engage with the surrounding environment. They are complex sets of actions that become intelligible only if observed in their relation to space. All human behaviour obviously unfolds in space, and the process by which space frames action can always be analysed. Sometimes this framing is particularly salient for the researcher – this is when the notion of routine becomes theoretically useful (Figure 6.4).

Some routines produce tangible effects, that persist for some time and can thus be observed even after the routine has ended. Traces are a type of such an effect: they are space-related unintentional effects of behaviours, i.e. the non-deliberate products of our situated action in space. Although the space around us opposes any modification because of its own materiality, the constant and prolonged use of space *leaves traces*. In this sense, space is like a palimpsest on which users accumulate their involuntary contribution; the researcher then investigates this cumulative macro-text about the relationship between a given community and its environment. Much can be said, for example, by reading the *erosions* created by walking: people's perambulating is perhaps the most free and common practice of space appropriation that is vital to the life of the city the way we understand it today (Jacobs, 1961). More than one of the brightest theoreticians of the most recent decades have focused their attention on how we 'make a speech with our feet' (de Certeau, 1980: 150; see also Solnit, 2000 and Careri, 2002). Erosions are clues for the researcher to interpret the spatial needs of inhabitants. As examples, they could be needs in relation to going from one place to another, or to usability (Figure 6.5), or to very specific activities, such as those of children (Figure 6.6; see also Chiesi, 2010, Chapter 4).

Sometimes, specific activities also yield by-products, another type of trace, that can be used to investigate further the people–environment relationship on a case by

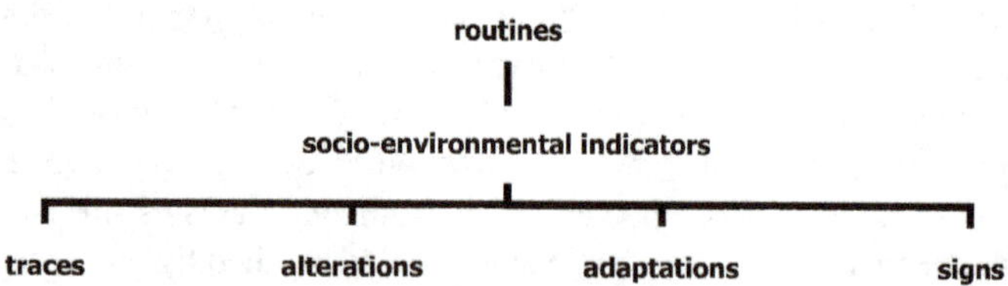

Figure 6.3 Socio-environmental indicators: forms of empirical evidence of appropriation of space

Source: © Leonardo Chiesi.

Figure 6.4 Routine as regular behaviour of appropriation of space. Children interpret a monument as a playground in a public park

Source: © Lorenzo Pagnini.

Figure 6.5 Traces as indicators of spatial needs and usability: shortcuts that reveal the walkers' actions where accessibility was designed only for cars (left); erosion, and lack thereof, that indicate usage or neglect in a public park (right)

Source: © Leonardo Chiesi.

Figure 6.6 Behavioural routines that produce trace. Erosion as a trace that shows an intense use of a specific area of a park (top). The trace is an indicator of a social routine of appropriation of space, e.g. children playing football (bottom)

Source: © Leonardo Chiesi.

case basis, in both public and private space. (This research approach has been taken to its fullest potential by Rathje, 1992; see also Rabow and Neuman, 1984.)

Alterations are self-designed and semi-permanent modifications to space: they are the results of the inhabitants' attempts to adjust the surrounding environment to their needs. They are, in other words, examples of spontaneous redesign, where people appropriate space with a variety of tactics, such as connecting or separating different segments of an area that were laid out differently in the original design (see Figure 6.7). It is not rare that people appropriate space by altering its relational affordances, by adjusting, for example, the arrangement of a seating scheme, sometimes in the direction of a sociopetal layout, i.e. with more relational content, or vice versa, towards a sociofugal layout, where people want more privacy and control over what happens around them (see Figure 6.7; Osmond, 1957). The variety of alterations is extremely wide and is only limited by people's inventiveness on the one hand and normative pressures on the other. In some highly regulated contexts, both formally and/or informally (such as, for example, medium-sized Middle-European towns) fewer alterations might be observed, in comparison to loosely regulated ones (such as, for instance, informal settlements in poor countries), where they abound.

Adaptations are actualisations of non-designed affordances and they are the results of a non-obvious interpretation of space through a creative insight. When people adapt space, they do not modify it as in the case of alterations, but rather they identify some opportunities that were not originally incorporated by those who designed it. Through adaptations people expand the catalogue of possibilities for action commonly associated with space, across different scales (see Figure 6.8). Adaptations reveal social creativity in that they show how we imaginatively construe the world around us, although we tend to lose this capacity with ageing (Defeyter and German, 2003). Adaptations have implications for the understanding of territorialisation, and their study is now having a profound impact on the world of object design (Maier *et al.*, 2009) and public space design (see Figure 6.9).

When we look around us, we see many references to the intangible world of meanings – we see signs. Unlike traces, alterations and adaptations, which help us to analyse the physical use of space, this type of socio-environmental indicator adds to the physical layers of the environment by dealing with our need for the attribution of meaning to the world, both in the sense of encoding meaning (actively placing meaning into the world), and decoding meaning (extracting meaning from the world; see the work of Rapoport, 1982 and 1990). Socio-environmental signs are key to analysing processes of territorialisation, as many are precisely the expression of the need for marking boundaries (see Figure 6.10), or otherwise affirm one's rights, factual or symbolical, over a portion of space (see Figure 6.11). Signs also allow for an investigation of the process of settling, which is triggered every time someone engages with a new territory. Using signs, we can study how people individualise space, personally or collectively. They distribute references that stop uniformity or serialisation in favour of some distinguishing feature that breaks anonymity and manifests the presence of subjectivity (see Figure 6.12). This possibility of exercising agency in the surrounding environment, which is tantamount to placing a portion of one's symbolic capital in space, has recently attracted considerable attention: preliminary findings show how this benefits general well-being (Knight and Haslam, 2010; Raanaas *et al.*, 2011); further, signs can be very good indicators of place attachment, especially when studying a community and its rootedness in a given territory (Milligan, 1998; Boğaç, 2009).

Figure 6.7 Example of alterations as indicators of a social need of redesigning relationship between regions of space (top): a barrier is transformed in an opening to make access easier in New York City. Social production of a socio-centripetal space by redesigning the layout of the benches (bottom): in the foreground, the benches repositioned by the inhabitants; in the background, the benches in a linear layout as they were arranged socio-centrifugally by the designers

Source: © Leonardo Chiesi.

Figure 6.8 Examples of adaptations as indicators of creative realisations of non-designed affordances: a telephone booth is turned into a public greenhouse (top left); an umbrella and a narrow street provide shelter in a public market in Trabzon, Turkey (top right); tyres as planters in Siena, Italy (bottom)

Source: © Leonardo Chiesi.

Figure 6.9 Adaptations and public space design: an adjustable bench that affords multiple arrangements with different relational implications

Source: © maO.

Figure 6.10 Example of sign as addition to form to evoke meaning. Children show a remarkable ability to use signs (line of stones on the ground as volleyball net) to create imagined worlds

Source: © Paolo Costa.

Figure 6.11 A different kind of line of stones on the ground: a Tuareg mosque in the Tassili n'Ajjer, Algeria. Signs allow for the creation of sacred space, which represents a prototypical form of its appropriation

Source: © Ugo Tonietti.

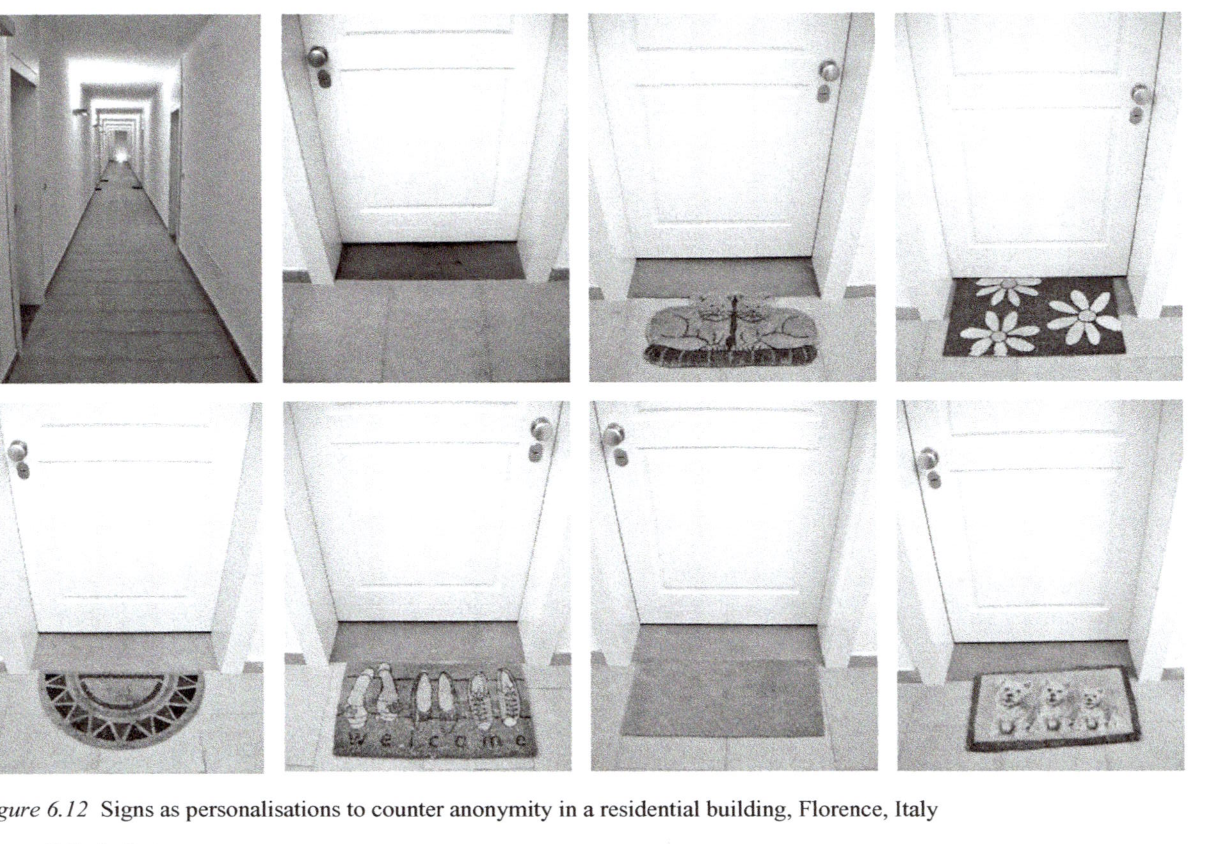

Figure 6.12 Signs as personalisations to counter anonymity in a residential building, Florence, Italy

Source: © Paolo Costa.

To sum up, socio-environmental indicators are manifestations of practices situated in space. Their empirical analysis allows the understanding of the dual process of appropriation of space on a case by case basis: how space becomes a *place* (that is, space invested by desire and practice in the sense of Deleuze and Guattari, 1972); and, contextually, how space emplaces sociality, as it frames practices in an active matrix that constrains, inhibits or favours specific social outcomes.

Open questions: micro versus macro and exclusion versus exchange

For the time being, conclusions can only be drafted as open questions and directions for future research. I am attempting to extrapolate these reflections to an analysis of macro-sociological categories. It is possible to construe regional processes, for example, in terms of affordance/meaning/taste dynamics. It is easy to see the analogy between low-level affordances as described earlier and the opportunities for actions afforded by regional mobility infrastructure. Or the analogy between the symbolic significance of borders in terms of national identity, and the need to demarcate space on a crowded summer beach. Or the comparison between the pleasure taken from making one's home beautiful and the pleasure derived from enjoying the landscape on a Sunday promenade. Further investigation may reveal what this possibility of moving across scales really entails: is it productive theoretically, or even more so empirically, to examine large-scale dynamics along the lines proposed here?

I find it interesting to investigate strategies at the individual or small-group level to illuminate the reasons why we seem less capable of managing the co-existence of different sets of opportunities on the larger scale, i.e. collectively. For example, in many regional (or even national) identity conflicts, the symbolic value of borders or independence (a meaning-oriented conflict) monopolises public discourse at the expense of any affordance-driven consideration, as can be seen in many regionalist independent movements in Europe since the 1990s. Some landscape conservation policies face similar challenges when trying to strike the balance between two kinds of affordance-based sets of opportunities (e.g. sustainability and energy production, as in the case of wind-produced energy) and the taste-based opportunities of a 'beautiful' landscape (Moraci and Fazia, 2013).

To end this discussion, I return to the beginning: the ethological heritage (or burden?) within the discourse on territoriality. Appropriation of space has been traditionally linked to defence, and as such, to exclusion. In other words, we are territorial in order to regulate the outsider's rights to space that we claim as our own. But as territoriality is certainly a modulator of engagement, and helps us regulate the degree and intensity of relationship we believe to be correct in any given case, we must not overlook how appropriation of space can also be a precursor of deeper and more open involvement with the other. Territoriality is better construed, therefore, as a neutral regulatory strategy for sociality, where engaging with space enables us to engage socially. In this regard, we can fruitfully borrow the notion of the two kinds of social capital, *bonding* and *bridging* social capital

(Putnam, 2000). Bonding capital is what makes for a stronger identity, and a more acute sense of 'we' as opposed to 'they'. It is a necessary component of any social dynamic, but if it is cultivated alone, it can become a principle of isolation. Bridging capital is, on the other hand, the kind of social ability that allows for dealing with the outside, the unexpected, the potentially dangerous but also inextricably interesting and enriching. In shorter terms, bonding social capital leads to exclusion, bridging social capital leads to exchange. They are both necessary, and territoriality generates a set of practices that can work both ways.

References

Alexander, C. (1977). *A pattern language: Towns, buildings, construction.* Oxford University Press, New York.

Altman, I. (1970). Territorial behaviour in humans: An analysis of the concept, pp. 1–24 in: Pastalan, L. and Carson D. (eds), *Spatial behaviour of older people.* Institute of Gerontology Press, Ann Arbour.

Altman, I. (1975). *Environment and social behaviour: Privacy, personal space, territory and crowding.* Brooks/Cote, Monterey.

Baldry, C. (1999). Space – the final frontier. *Sociology*, 33 (3): 535–553.

Baum, A., Reiss, M. and J. O'Hara (1974). Architectural variants of reaction to spatial invasion. *Environment and Behaviour*, 6: 91–100.

Boğaç, C. (2009). Place attachment in a foreign settlement. *Journal of Environmental Psychology*, 29 (2): 267–278.

Brady, E. (1998). Imagination and the aesthetic appreciation of nature. *The Journal of Aesthetics and Art Criticism*, 56 (2): 139–147.

Brady, E. (2003). *Aesthetics of the natural environment.* Edinburgh University Press, Edinburgh.

Brady, E. (2013). *The sublime in modern philosophy: Aesthetics, ethics, and nature.* Cambridge University Press, Cambridge.

Brown, B. (1987). Territoriality, pp. 505–531 in: Brown, B.B, Stokols, D. and I. Altman (eds), *Handbook of environmental psychology.* Wiley and Sons, New York.

Careri, F. (2002). *Walkscapes: Walking as an aesthetic practice.* Editorial Gustavo Gili, Barcelona.

Carlson, A. (2000). *Aesthetics and the environment: The appreciation of nature, art, and architecture.* Routledge, London and New York.

Castells, M. (2010). *The rise of the network society.* Wiley-Blackwell, Chichester.

Castiglioni, B., De Marchi, M., Ferrario, V., Bin, S., Carestiato, N. and A. De Nardi (2010). Il paesaggio 'democratico' come chiave interpretativa del rapporto tra popolazione e territorio: applicazioni al caso Veneto. *Rivista Geografica Italiana*, 117 (1): 93–126.

Chiesi, L. (2010). *Il doppio spazio dell'architettura. Ricerca sociologica e progettazione.* Liguori, Naples.

Chiesi, L. (2014). Situarsi nello spazio progettato, pp. 1–23 in: Chiesi, L. and S. Surrenti (eds), *L'ospedale difficile: Lo spazio sociale della cura e della salute.* Liguori, Naples.

Chiesi, L. and P. Costa (2005). Il Montalbano dal punto di vista dei suoi abitanti. Una ricerca su territorio, identità e senso del paesaggio nella campagna toscana, pp. 80–121 in: P. Baldeschi (ed.), *Il paesaggio agrario del Montalbano: Identità, sostenibilità e società locale.* Passigli, Florence.

De Certeau, M. (1980). *L'invention du quotidien: L'arts de faire.* UGE, Paris.

Defeyter, M.A. and T.P. German (2003). Acquiring an understanding of design: Evidence from children's insight problem solving. *Cognition*, 89 (2): 133–155.

Deleuze, G. and F. Guattari (1972). *L'Anti-Oedipe.* Les Éditions de Minuit, Paris.

Dutton, D. (2009). *The art instinct: Beauty, pleasure, and human evolution.* Oxford University Press, Oxford.

Dyson-Hudson, R. and E.A. Smith (1978). Human territoriality: An ecological reassessment. *American Anthropologist*, 80 (1): 21–41.

Eberhard, J. (2008). *Brain landscape: The coexistance of neuroscience and architecture.* Oxford University Press, Oxford.

Eco, U. (1974). *Trattato di semiotica generale.* Bompiani, Milan.

Firestein, S. (2012). *Ignorance: How it drives science.* Oxford University Press, New York.

Gardner, H. (1983). *Frames of mind: The theory of multiple intelligences.* Basic Books, New York.

Gibson, J. (1979). *The ecological approach to visual perception.* Houghton Mifflin, Boston.

Gieryn, T.F. (2000). A space for place in sociology. *Annual Review of Sociology*, 26 (1): 463–496.

Goodsell, C.T. (2001). *The American statehouse: Interpreting democracy's temples.* The University Press of Kansas, Lawrence.

Gosling, S.D., Craik, K., Martin, N. and M. Pryor (2005). The personal living space cue inventory. *Environment and Behaviour*, 37: 683–705.

Griffero, T. (2010). *Atmosferologia: estetica degli spazi emozionali.* Laterza, Roma, Bari.

Grosby, S. (1995). Territoriality: The transcendental, primordial feature of modern societies. *Nations and Nationalism*, 1 (2): 143–162.

Hall, E.T. (1959). *The silent language.* Fawcett Publications, Greenwich.

Hillier, B. and J. Hanson (1984). *The social logic of space.* Cambridge University Press, Cambridge.

Jacobs, J. (1961). *The death and life of great American cities.* Random House, New York.

Knight, C. and S. Haslam (2010). The relative merits of lean, enriched, and empowered offices: An experimental examination of the impact of workspace management strategies on well-being and productivity. *Journal of Experimental Psychology: Applied*, 16 (2): 158–172.

Lasswell, H.D. and M.B. Fox (1979). *The signature of power: Buildings, communication, and policy.* Transaction Books, New Brunswick.

Lefebvre, H. (1974). *Production de l'espace.* Anthropos, Paris.

Lyman, S.M. and M.B. Scott (1967). Territoriality: A neglected sociological dimension. *Social Problems*: 236–249.

Mahon, B. and A. Caramazza (2008). A critical look at the embodied cognition hypothesis and a new proposal for grounding conceptual content. *Journal of Physiology*, 102 (1): 59–70.

Maier, J., Georges, R.A., Fadel, M. and D.G. Battisto (2009). An affordance-based approach to architectural theory, design, and practice. *Design Studies*, 30 (4): 393–414.

Mallgrave, H. (2010). *The architect's brain: Neuroscience, creativity, and architecture.* Wiley-Blackwell, Chichester.

Milligan, M. (1998). Interactional past and potential: The social construction of place attachment. *Symbolic interaction*, 21 (1): 1–33.

Moraci, F. and C. Fazia (2013). Impatti delle energie rinnovabili sul paesaggio. Eolico, alternative offshore in ambiti marini. *Territorio della Ricerca su Insediamenti e Ambiente*, 11: 145–156.

Mubi Brighenti, A. (2010). At the wall: Graffiti writers, urban territoriality, and the public domain. *Space and Culture*, 13 (3): 315–332.

Osmond, H. (1957). Function as the basis of psychiatric ward design. *Mental Hospitals*, April: 23–29.

Parker, S. (2004). *Urban theory and urban experience: Encountering the city*. Routledge, London.

Petit, J.-L. 1997. *Les neurosciences et la philosophie de l'action*. Vrin, Paris.

Prior, L. (1988). The architecture of the hospital: A study of spatial organization and medical knowledge. *The British Journal of Sociology*, 1: 86–113.

Putnam, R. (2000). *Bowling alone: The collapse and revival of American community*. Simon & Schuster, New York.

Raanaas, R.K., Evensen, K.H., Rich, D., Sjøstrøm, G. and G. Patil (2011). Benefits of indoor plants on attention capacity in an office setting. *Journal of Environmental Psychology*, 31 (1): 99–105.

Rabow, J. and C.A. Neuman (1984). Garbaeology as a method of cross-validating interview data on sensitive topics. *Sociology & Social Research*, 68 (4): 480–497.

Raffestin, C. (1984). Territorializzazione, deterritorializzazione, riterritorializzazione e informazione, pp. 69–82 in: Turco, A. (ed.), *Regione e regionalizzazione*. Angeli, Milan.

Raffestin, C. and S.A. Butler (2012). Space, territory, and territoriality. *Environment and Planning D: Society and Space*, 30 (1): 121–141.

Rapoport, A. (1982). *The meaning of the built environment: A nonverbal communication approach*. SAGE Publications, Beverly Hills.

Rapoport, A. (1990). *History and precedent in environmental design*. Plenum Press, New York.

Rathje, W.L. (1992). *Rubbish! The archaeology of garbage*. HarperCollins, New York.

Sack, R. (1986). *Human territoriality: Its theory and history*. Cambridge University Press, Cambridge.

Sassen, S. (2012). *Cities in a world economy*. SAGE Publications, Thousand Oaks, CA.

Soini, K. and I. Birkeland (2014). Exploring the scientific discourse on cultural sustainability. *Geoforum*, 51: 213–23.

Solnit, R. 2000. *Wanderlust: A history of walking*. New York: Viking.

Thrift, N. (1983). On the determination of social action in space and time. *Environment and Planning D: Society and Space*, 1 (1): 23–57.

Tuan, Y. (1974). *Topophilia: A study of environmental perception, attitudes, and values*. Prentice-Hall, Englewood Cliffs, NJ.

Tuan, Y. (2001). *Space and place: The perspective of experience*. University of Minnesota Press, Minnesota.

Webb, E. and D. Campbell (1966). *Unobtrusive measures*. McNally, New York.

Zeisel, J. (1984). *Inquiry by design*. Cambridge University Press, Cambridge.

7 Exploring culture and sustainability in rural Finland

Mari Kivitalo, Kaisu Kumpulainen and Katriina Soini

Introduction

Rural areas across Europe and the world are undergoing rapid changes. Declining populations, the weakening of traditional livelihoods and the introduction of new livelihoods challenge the social and cultural structures and dynamics of rural areas. These areas can be seen as territories, characterised in particular by nature and nature-based livelihoods. The sustainability of rural development has been actively discussed in research since the introduction of sustainable development in 1987 by the WCED report 'Our Common Future' (WCED, 1987) and it has also become a key phrase in rural policy on various scales. Despite the popularity of the notion, the conditions of sustainability often remain undefined.

In this chapter we explore sustainability of rural culture in a territorial context. We observe how culture acts as a mediator in everyday life as well as in the structures and policies shaped by human (cultural) agency and nature. We apply an analytical framework based on the notions of culture and agency in territorialisation (Horlings, 2015), as well as an analytical framework for rural sustainability (Soini *et al.*, 2012). We understand 'rural' as a triad space which results from social processes within conceived, perceived and lived space (Lefebvre, 1991). In this chapter we focus on lived space. Thus, we discuss how culture manifests itself in the everyday life of rural people and communities and how these people construct and give meaning to rural places.

Our empirical analysis is based on two independent qualitative case studies conducted in central Finland. Finland is one of the most rural countries in Europe (OECD, 2008). About 91 per cent of the total land cover is considered as rural and one-third of the population (1.6 million) lives in rural areas, which are predominantly characterised by nature and natural resources. Similar to many other European countries, rural areas in Finland are currently under transition. Modernisation of agriculture and forestry, together with the globalised economy, have dramatically changed the conditions of livelihoods. New activities such as nature-based tourism, bioenergy production, local food production and the mining industry contribute to these new livelihoods. In addition to long-term trends affecting rural development, the seasons affect the rhythm of rural life. Finland has approximately 500,000 summer cottages, most of which are located in rural areas (Official Statistics of Finland, 2012). The summertime population of small rural communities doubles or even triples, which has many implications for local social and cultural dynamics.

Finland has 320 municipalities for local-level administration which act as fundamental, self-governing administrative units. Villages are rural communities within these municipalities; in one-third of Finnish villages, the village association is run by volunteers who maintain the village hall and organise local activities (Rural Policy Committee, 2014). According to Finnish rural policy, local communities should take more responsibility for providing local services and development in rural areas. The increasing role of local communities and non-governmental organisations in rural development is a part of the ongoing restructuring of the municipalities towards larger administrative and service units.

This chapter focuses on everyday life and the future prospects of local inhabitants and communities. Through two studies, we reveal various aspects of culture and agency in rural territory. The first study, the socioanalysis of rural residents in Keuruu municipality, is comprised of 35 semi-structural interviews of the inhabitants (Kivitalo, 2015). Keuruu is the municipal centre located at the crossroads of two provincial districts; Keuruu has 13 villages, with a total of 10,000 inhabitants. Like many other remote post-agrarian communities, Keuruu has experienced depopulation since the late 1980s. The vast majority of the population is Finnish speaking (over 98 per cent) and the population density is low, approximately 8 inhabitants per square kilometre. About 12 per cent of the surface is comprised of water. The multitude of small lakes are an essential element of this rural landscape, which helps to attract leisure residents who use the nearly 2,000 summer cottages in the area. The service sector is the biggest employer in Keuruu, at almost 70 per cent. The remainder of employees work in industry (24 per cent, and agriculture and forestry (6 per cent). In 2012 the unemployment rate in Keuruu was over 13 per cent, almost 3 per cent higher than the Finnish average (Official Statistics of Finland, 2012).

The second study analyses the role of village associations in rural development in three small villages in central Finland: Huikko (pop. 200), Kyynämöinen (pop. 400) and Ylä-Muuratjärvi (pop. 150). The settlements in the villages are scattered and remote. There are a few public or private services or jobs in the communities, but no basic commercial services such as grocery stores. In Kyynämöinen there is a village school, but the other two villages no longer have municipal services. All three villages have an active village association which organises local events, practises development work and takes care of the village hall. The study is based on 12 semi-structural interviews of chairmen of village associations and a discursive reading of village plans and strategies (Kumpulainen, 2012).

In the following sections, we define rural as lived space within territorialisation; we introduce the framework of our analysis for operationalising culture and sustainability and apply it to our empirical studies; and we discuss the multiple interconnections between culture and sustainability.

Figure 7.1 Case studies in Central Finland

Source: © Hanna Huitu.

Rural as lived space

'Rural' has been defined in a number of ways (e.g. Cloke, 2006). Most of the definitions consider rural either as an area or as a socio(political) construction that is distinct from 'urban' (Cloke, 2006; Urry, 1995). Going beyond dichotomies such as rural/urban and material/imaginative, we consider rural space as a triad space. Following the theory of social space of Henri Lefebvre (1991; see also Halfacree, 2006, 2007), rural space consists of three moments, which are interconnected and together form a dialectic triad. Perceived space (i.e. spatial practices) refers to local activities and structures. The conceived space (i.e. formal representations of space) is produced particularly through research, policies and legislation. The third aspect, lived space (i.e. representational space) refers to local culture; how rural space is experienced and lived in. It is subjective and constructed through everyday life, meanings, symbols and values related to places (Lefebvre, 1991; Shields, 1999) resulting in a local identity, sense of place and place attachment. Rural space as a social product signifies space as an unstable and constantly changing process (Dogshon, 2008).

We argue that culture is embedded within all three moments of which rural space consists. However, in this chapter we focus on the third moment of the triangle – rurality as lived space. Lived rural space takes place in homes, tourist attractions, natural places, community halls and villages that are lived and represented through the experiences of human beings as agents (Agnew, 2011; Tuan, 1977). The lived space emphasises the meanings and symbolism constructed through the everyday life of local people. Local actors have a significant role in producing lived space, but places also reflect broader spatial relations (Massey, 2005; Woods, 2010).

Territorialisation, understood as the interplay between human and nature and culture, emphasises the eventual, processual and relational characteristics of a territory (Horlings *et al.*, 2015; Brighenti, 2010). Each territory is a unique composition of agents, nature and structures; flows, rhythms and boundaries manifest tensions over its inner plurality, stability, order, consensus and hegemony. This interplay is both rooted in nature and grows along with the imaginative world of symbols and narratives in culture. Territorialisation is about constant change of actors and relations, processes of exits and extensions of a territory. Territorial configurations and reconfigurations thus exist and become manifest in various scales and degrees (Brighenti, 2010).

We focus on the processual and subjective characters of territorial place-making (Halfacree, 2006, 2007) in which cultural meanings, representations, values and interpretations of territorial practices are constructive characters of lived space (see Horlings, 2015) and sustainability. Culture and sustainability are thus understood as intertwined but ambiguous processes happening in lived space. Narratives represent rural cultures and different cultural trajectories in lived space. They are also acts of imagination that enable social relations, recognition and distinction of members within territorialisation (Anderson, 1983; Brighenti, 2010). We apply a constructivist scope for understanding culture and sustainability within territorialisation; while acknowledging the agency of nature in territorialisation, we focus only on human constructions of nature (see Horlings *et al.*, 2015).

Operationalising 'culture' and 'sustainability'

There are several ways to approach culture in the context of place. Culture has, for instance, been considered as local identity (Hernandez *et al.*, 2007), creative industry (Drake, 2003), cultural heritage (Giaccardi and Palen, 2008) or as an instrument in place promotion (Vanolo, 2008). We operationalise culture through four dimensions (see below) that Horlings (2015) considers as key elements for place-based development. These are manifestations of place-based culture, which has a mediating role in shaping rural space.

- The worldview dimension – culture as intentions, ethical and moral choices, rooted in values that drive individual and collective actions.
- The symbolic dimension – culture mediating senses as sense of place, place attachment and local identity.
- The reification dimension – culture as cultural practices, which shape places and images of places. Cultural practices are materialised especially in cultural heritage and cultural landscapes.
- The institutional dimension – cultural characteristics of institutions, routines and planning that structure places.

The second part of our framework concerns sustainability. In the multidisciplinary research project 'Cultural Sustainability of Rural Finland' the frames of sustainability within the rural context were examined in respect to the rural livelihoods, landscape, well-being and community life. The research identified four binaries through which the sustainability of rural space could be defined at the more general level: spatial, temporal, diversity and ethics (Soini *et al.*, 2012). As noted by Cloke and Johnston (2005), binaries simplify and also shape reality. However, they are needed in science, policy and everyday life to discuss and define the phenomena in question. These four binaries are briefly described below.

The spatial dimension of sustainability refers to the spatial imaginaries between different scales, from local to global. All spatial scales are relational concepts, although 'global' is thought of as a more simple and abstract spatial category than 'local', which can refer to a village, region or nation depending on the phenomena in question (Cox, 2005). The concept 'global' is often seen as a threat to sustainability, while local, place-based development and local governance are favoured and seen as supporting not only ecological but also social sustainability (Soini and Birkeland, 2014). Local and global are not always seen as opposite, however; they can also be seen as mutually constitutive and translocal (Brickell and Datta, 2011). For instance, local, place-based economies are part of the global economy (Woods, 2010) and, in nature conservation, local (traditional) ecological knowledge can be completed or activated using global scientific knowledge (Soini, 2007). Therefore, rather than arguing for locally- or globally-driven development, the question should be asked: what is the 'local' in question and how should the various scales be handled in a sustainable manner?

The temporal dimension of sustainability refers to the relationship between permanence and change. The concept of sustainable development is an oxymoron, as it refers both to change (development) and stability (sustainability) (Redclift, 2005). 'To sustain' implies continuation, but 'to develop' implies change. For this reason, the focus is often shifted to the resilience and adaptability of systems (Hollings, 2001) instead of stability. Resilience assumes permanence of some constituents of the systems, which are challenged by the constant changes in society, environment and culture. 'Breaks' or 'ruptures' within the system may be necessary for adapting new more sustainable cultural schemes in relation to changing context. If both permanence and change are needed for sustainability, then what should be sustained in culture? When is such change culturally sustainable?

Diversity has been discussed both in relation to environment and culture (Convention on Biological Diversity and Convention on Cultural Diversity) (Heyd, 2010; Blanc and Soini, 2015). The concept of cultural diversity refers usually to multiculturalism: the rights of ethnic and language minorities. The recognition of and participation of different cultural identities and groups is the foundation of liberal and multicultural society (Kymlicka, 1995; Parekh, 2006). Cultural diversity is seen as a source of creativity; innovations contribute to cultural reproduction (UNESCO, 2005). Biodiversity in turn refers to the diversity of living organism at genus, species and ecosystem level (CBD, 1992), which is seen as a necessary basis for sustainable ecological systems. Many scholars and policies have found analogies between the two: the more diverse the system (biological or cultural) is, the more adaptable ('sustainable') it is when confronted with change. Biodiversity and cultural diversity may also enhance each other (e.g. Heyd, 2010; Pilgrim and Pretty, 2010). However, while cultural diversity can create a source for cultural reproduction, concurrently diverse interests and practices also constitute threads for conflicts and dissolution (Bourdieu, 1979). The third binary thus concerns the balance between diversity and cultural homogeneity.

The ethical dimension of sustainability concerns (cultural) rights and responsibilities towards nature and other people. Rights are seen as important in reports related to culture and sustainability (UNESCO, 2005) and are perceived as the foundation of a liberal and multicultural society (Kymlicka, 1995; Parekh, 2006). While recognising the rights of individuals and communities and nature, the core idea of sustainability is the responsibility of nature and other people within and between generations (Mearns and Norton, 2010). The fourth binary thus concerns the balance between rights and responsibility regarding sustainability. Who has authority to make decisions on local development and who is responsible for the place?

Cross-reading culture and sustainability in rural Finland

In the following we cross-read 'culture' (Horlings, 2015) and 'sustainability' (Soini *et al.*, 2012) in order to localise the culture within the frames of sustainability in lived rural space, focusing on cultural manifestations in the narratives and interpretations of the interviewees (Figure 7.2).

Reflecting the four binaries of sustainability we identify cultural characteristics and tensions represented within lived rural space and illustrate them with representative quotations from the data.

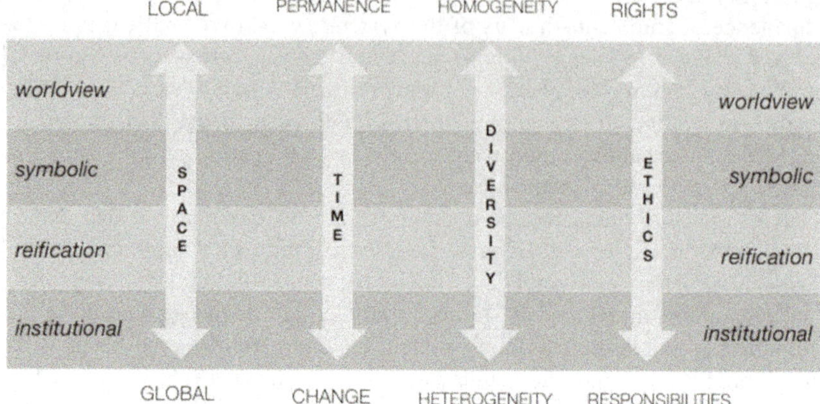

Figure 7.2 The framework for analysing the relation between culture and sustainability

Source: © Mari Kivitalo, Kaisu Kumpulainen and Katriina Soini.

Spatiality

'This morning when I was jogging I thought how wonderful it is to run along that sandy path, framed by bluebells, daisies and cow parsley' (Remigrant). Rural residents describe nature, its aesthetics and resources through everyday practices based on natural resources such as picking berries, fishing, hunting, hiking, etc. The connectedness to nature reflects the worldviews of local residents, as well as the values and resources the places afford.'I need open space and fresh air around me … I will never be urban' (Farmer). Life in rural areas is often seen as opposed to urban life, in particular because of the natural environment. Increased awareness of (global) environmental problems make people appreciate even more the unpolluted nature in the rural environment, with its lakes, forests and fresh air. Rural living represents a counterforce and escape from global society.

> We are here because of the rural fresh air. Nature and soundscape, there is not much pollution here. Not many roads cross nearby, but still, we are a decent distance from the centre of town. This was an ideal place [to move into] … There is a lot of space here. Many people can gather here.
>
> (New resident of an eco-community)

For many residents rural places are specific and irreplaceable; they create an overall sense of belonging, where they feel culturally and socially connected. Embedded cultural and social relations cannot be abstracted from their material basis: 'Everything is here' (single mother).

The sense of belonging is also built and maintained through reification and symbols. Village houses, local craftwork and myths are described in the local cultural traditions and histories. Local associations such as the village associations or hunting and fishing communities organise events, promote village planning and conduct development projects related to cultural heritage, livelihoods and landscape. The sense of belonging is a resource for rural development policy. Associations maintain and reconstruct local territory and connectedness among residents.

'Well, for us it has been defined in such a way, which I agree, that the village and surrounding area would remain populated' (Chairman of the village association). Local promoters represent villages as a permanent, 'eternal' place that local people are willing to work for. Letting the village die is not an option.

Temporality

'When I inherited this place, I remember saying that I would not leave this place otherwise than feet ahead [dead]' (Public officer, part-time farmer). The strong sense of belonging is typical for people whose families have been rooted in a rural area for generations. Especially among farmers, the sense of belonging is derived from multi-generational land ownership and inherited social positions. The relation is constructed and maintained through inherited narratives as pre-assigned positions and dispositions.

> Actually there was nobody except me, since I was the only male among siblings. The day I was born I was chosen to be the heir of this farm, so actually there was no other choice … Of course I have been rooted in this earth and I have liked it.
>
> (Farmer)

Seasons give rhythm to the local collective action. In summertime, the rural places become socially and culturally diverse. People from different locations interconnect and participate in summer festivals, theatre and other local activities. The summer season is also an important source of income for village associations and their image building. 'For Midsummer's Eve, people come from farther and farther away, coming here for the midsummer celebrations, not somewhere else. This shows that we have made the village known somewhere at least' (Chairman of the village association). Community projects, local festivals and a local identity are a part of constructing the future, partly derived from local traditions but also through strategic reasoning. Village associations are promoters who make plans for the village, thus constructing the future. Either starting up a new active phase or losing a local school or another essential service may act as a catalyst for more organised forms of co-operation and projects. 'It is partly a tradition, but I guess it is also partly ambition for the village you are working for, to try and keep the village alive and thriving' (Chairman of the village association).

From the temporal perspective, active and passive phases alternate. Project planning and implementation add new rhythms to the traditional multi-generational timespans and seasonal cycles. Maintenance of traditions and an orientation to the future are constantly in dialogue.

Diversity

'There are foreign people coming in here from Russia. Some of them live along this road. They are good workers' (Labourer). The overall local social and cultural map is diverse. It is comprised of individuals (both native and immigrants) with different values, socio-economic backgrounds and worldviews. Newcomers and leisure residents bring viability and diversity in rural communities. Encounters with permanent and leisure residents are seen as an important arena for representing the rural way of life. 'We have gone fishing and since they are urban, they wonder about agriculture and forestry. We have spent evenings together, gone to festivals, had a sauna, gone hiking in nature, and that sort of thing' (Public officer, part-time farmer).

Some people living in a village do not participate in community life; some active members in village associations do not live in the village. In other words, 'insiders' and 'outsiders' are defined more by participation in community life rather than by where they live or the amount of time they have been living there. Furthermore, people living in a rural territory do not necessarily form one unified community, but rather segregated and autonomous communities. For example, eco-communities represent alternative worldviews and a way of life that is separate from traditional rural cultures and communities: 'We do not socialise much with our neighbours, since there are already so many of us' (Newcomer, resident of an eco-community).

Different values and worldviews are present and become visible in local decision-making processes or when they affect local livelihoods. Social distances between socio-economic groups may consequently prevent interaction, and diversity may also lead to contradictions when it comes to sharing resources (in particular physical and economic resources). 'Why should we attract people [to move] here if someone does not naturally want to move here?' (Public officer, part-time farmer). Many village associations manage projects to write local histories and preserve cultural heritage. Selected memories are represented as shared heritage of the rural culture.

Ethics

> I have learned that it is important to work: This place is not for leisure … you always have to do something, less in the wintertime, but in summer we work long hours … It is the attitude towards working. You always have to do something in order to survive.
>
> (Public officer, part-time farmer)

Moral values are constructed through local practices. Peasant values have traditionally dominated and they still often guide the rural way of life. This rural ethic is about trust and a social responsibility which extends beyond private life to the community, creating a feeling of safety among the residents.

> It is about communality and taking care of neighbours ... If your child is out in a village you do not need to be worried since someone can always tell you where your child is. It is a safe environment for children, being in the countryside where nature and grandparents are close.
>
> (Remigrant)

A safe environment includes a strong sense of responsibility to nature throughout the generations. This is how rural people interpret and safeguard nature and the environment they live in. Traditions give rise to meanings of nature and respecting natural resources; the traditions remain alive in local discourses and ethics. For example, the protection of vulnerable species is part of hunting culture: 'For the past few years I have not been hunting birds since the number of fowl has diminished, but now the population is reviving slightly' (Landowner).

Moreover, peasant values such as the tradition of mutual help and cooperation are a kind of hidden cultural resource. These values are revived, for example,when village associations try to motivate people to participate in local development activities: 'Do we feel that our village and keeping it alive is important and that everyone wants to get involved' (Chairman of a village association).

Since the 1990s, Finnish rural policy has emphasised the responsibility of individuals and local communities in providing services and infrastructure to the villages (such as fire-fighting, roads and water management). An official objective is to increase the village association's responsibility for rural development. It is expected that giving them authority will encourage the local residents to take responsibility for their local welfare.

> Because of the increasing size of municipalities, there is a growing demand for local community action in the future to ensure the implementation of local democracy and to promote active citizenship. Village associations and NGOs producing local services can also employ local people and prevent social exclusion.
>
> (Rural Policy Committee, 2014: 30)

The increased responsibility given to local people over rural development concerns the lived space because the responsibility is emerging from personal and collective commitment and attachment to the place. Culture is the glue that binds societal (extra-local) demands with individual actors.

Reflections

The spatial imaginary in lived rural space is strongly connected to the local environment and nature, reflecting spatial connections between the local and global world (Massey, 2005). People give nominal value to the situated and local rural places, which are thick with meanings (Sack, 1997). Rural places are a basis for a sense of belonging and a strong place-identity. People also compare local rural places to urban spaces, illustrating that binaries such as rural–urban are a central part of geographical imagination (Cloke and Johnston, 2005). Local activities and development are not solely based on the local resources or needs, but their value and use are increasingly defined and organised by non-local institutions and multiple relations, and the tension between the local and the non-local world becomes materialised in rural space.

Permanence and change are both part of the development of rural space. Lived rural space is a temporal process (Lefebvre, 1991; Massey, 2005) mediated through culture between the past and the future. Although the meaning of agriculture as a livelihood has dramatically diminished and many farmers have had to shift from traditional food production to other livelihoods, the peasant values still have a dominant role in the worldviews and values of local people. The sense of belonging is often represented through naturalisation of relations, social order and inheritance. Traditional rural life and worldviews have been oriented towards seasonal work and tasks in the cycle of nature. New livelihoods and practices which are affected by institutional processes gradually introduce new temporalities. This results in a variety of time-spaces which do not necessarily converge with lived space. For example, recently implemented community development practices are project-based and more wave-like by nature (Kumpulainen, 2012). In the long run, new rhythms may lead to a deep integration of territorial transformations into rural cultures.

It is more difficult to define one's position in a territory in structured or categorised ways because the relations are so varied and complex (e.g. Brighenti, 2010). Boundaries between various rural communities have weakened, which has changed the interpretation of the 'insiders' or the 'outsiders' (Relph, 1976). Cultural diversity, values and identities are materialised through local life and participation in local community. Cultural diversity in rural territory compounds social diversity. It can be a resource for local development in rural space, but it can also cause conflicts and segregation. The important question is how to connect people with different aims and interests, and, in particular, how to find the means to involve them in local development with common aims. Therefore, sustainability is not about diversity itself but about recognition, dialogue and negotiation between diverse cultural meanings, values and identities.

Concerning the ethics of sustainability, the questions of rights and responsibilities towards the community and nature are essential. Our results have confirmed that many of the rights and responsibilities arise from traditions and emotional bonds toward the place, which are handed down through the generations. Traditions enhance cultural coherence and social relations while, at the same time, the rural community is not 'all-inclusive', nor do all the residents want to get involved. Yet, these conceptions of rights and responsibilities are gradually changing along with rural space owing to the increased social and cultural diversity and connectedness with the world beyond the local. Deconstruction of state relations, enhancing the role of individuals and communities in local development, has been a global trend since the 1980s (Boltanski and Chiapello, 2007). This shift stretches also to rural communities and emphasises the actors' sense of responsibility when managing rural lived space. In terms of sustainability, people should have a right to the place, but the responsibilities are given by higher-level policies. In times of transition, the responsibility for rural space results in a larger negotiation of power and authority between territorial assemblages, the public sector and civil society.

Conclusions

When exploring the narratives of culture, we identify the concurrency between the peasant culture and breaking of new cultural flows encountering each other in lived rural space. Our analysis indicates that sustainability of culture within a rural territory takes place between various spatio-temporal and socio-ethical scales. Tensions are found not only between local or global, permanence or change, diversity or homogeneity, rights or responsibility, but in various forms of culture (Horlings, 2015) between them (see Figure 7.2). The empirical analysis confirms that various trajectories of sustainability arise from differences in cultural dimensions.

Lived rural space stems from traditional peasant representations, affections and imaginary, which creates continuity from the past but does not resolve questions under the present circumstances. Competing imaginaries break traditional rural trajectories and create new spans. Spatial, temporal and ethical encounters with diverse actors and ways of life make sustainability and culture a plural and complicated system of relations, similar to territory, which is neither subject nor object but rather movement within space (Brighenti, 2010).

In this chapter, we have located rural cultures within lived rural space, between the everyday life and the diverse meanings constructed by local people. We have observed focal tensions that challenge the sustainability of rural culture and make it more complex. These tensions range from changing spatial and temporal relations to the diversity of actors and ethics. Rural cultural sustainability cannot be summarised as common normative abstractions or guidelines, as there is no single homogenous rural culture to be sustained but rather multiple cultures that sustain rural development. Considering culture as an important dimension of sustainable development in rural territories, culture represents and creates wider relations between human and nature, past, present and future, the materialised and the imagined world.

References

Agnew, J. (2011). Space and place, pp. 316–330 in: Agnew, J.A. and D.N. Livingstone (eds), *The SAGE handbook of geographical knowledge*. SAGE Publications, London.

Anderson, B. (1983). *Imagined communities*. Verso, London.

Blanc, N. and K. Soini (2015). Cultural and biological diversity: Interconnections in ordinary places, pp. 75–90 in: De Beukelaer, C., Pyykkonen, M. and J.P. Singh (eds), *Globalization, culture and development: The UNESCO convention on cultural diversity*. Palgrave Macmillan, Basingstoke.

Boltanski, L. and E. Chiapello (2007). *The new spirit of capitalism*. Trans. Gregory Elliott. Verso, London.

Bourdieu, P. (1979). *La distinction: Critique sociale du jugement.* Les Éditions de Minuit, Paris.

Brickell, K. and A. Datta (2011). Introduction, pp. 3–20 in: Brickell, K. and A. Datta (eds), *Translocal geographies: Spaces, places and connections*. Ashgate, Aldershot.

Brighenti, A.M. (2010). On territorology towards a general science of territory. *Theory, Culture & Society* (SAGE Publications, Los Angeles, London, New Delhi and Singapore), 27 (1): 52–72.

CBD (1992). *Convention on biological diversity*. Available at: www.cbd.int/convention/text (accessed 22 April 2014).

Cloke, P.J. (2006). *The handbook of rural studies*. SAGE Publications, London.

Cloke, P. and R. Johnston (2005). Deconstructing human geography's binaries, pp. 1–20 in: Cloke P. and R. Johnston (eds), *Spaces of geographic thought*. SAGE Publications, London.

Cox, K.R. (2005). Local : Global, pp. 175–198 in: Cloke, P. and R. Johnston (eds), *Spaces of geographical thought*. SAGE Publications, London.

Dogshon, R.A. (2008). Geography's place in time. *Geogrfiska Annaler*, 90B (1): 1–15.

Drake, G. (2003). 'This place gives me space': Place and creativity in the creative industry. *Geoforum*, 34 (4): 511–524.

Giaccardi, E. and L. Palen (2008). The social production of heritage through cross-media interaction: Making place for place-making. *International Journal of Heritage Studies*, 14 (3): 281–297.

Halfacree, K. (2006). Rural space: Constructing a three-fold architecture, pp. 44–62 in: P. Cloke, T. Marsden and P. Mooney (eds), *Handbook of rural studies*. SAGE Publications, London.

Halfacree, K. (2007). Trial by space for a 'radical rural': Introducing alternative localities, representations and lives. *Journal of Rural Studies*, 23 (2007): 125–141.

Hernandez, B., Hidalgo, C., Salazar-Laplace, E. and S. Hess (2007). Place attachment and place identity in natives and non-natives. *Journal of Environmental Psychology*, 27 (4): 310–319.

Heyd, D. (2010). Cultural diversity and biodiversity: A tempting analogy. *Critical Review of International Social and Political Philosophy*, 13: 159–179.

Holling, C.S. (2001). Understanding the complexity of economic, ecological, and social systems. *Ecosystems*, 4 (5): 390–405.

Horlings, L. (2015). The worldview and symbolic dimensions in territorialisation: How human values play a role in a Dutch neighbourhood. In: this book, Chapter 4.

Horlings, L., Battaglini, E. and J. Dessein (2015). Introduction: The role of culture in territorialisation. In: this book, Chapter 1.

Kivitalo, M. (2015). Maaseutukaupungin sosiaalinen tila. Sosioanalyysi asukkaiden positioista ja dispositioista. *Rural town as social space. A socioanalysis of rural residents' positions and dispositions*. Unpublished DSoc.Sciences thesis, Department of Philosophy and Social Sciences, University of Jyväskylä. Yhteiskuntatieteiden ja filosofian laitos, Jyväskylän yliopisto.

Kumpulainen, K. (2012). Kylätoiminta ja aktiivisen kylän tuottaminen. Jyväskylä: Jyväskylän yliopisto. Village action and the production of an active village. Department of Philosophy and Social Sciences, University of Jyväskylä, Jyväskylä.

Kymlicka, W. (1995). *Multicultural citizenship: A liberal theory of minority rights*. Clarendon Press, Oxford.

Lefebvre, H. (1991). *The production of space*. Blackwell, Oxford.

Massey, D. (2005). *For space*. SAGE Publications, London.

Mearns, R. and A. Norton (eds) (2010). *Social dimensions of climate change: Equity and vulnerability in a warming world.* World Bank, Washington DC.

OECD (2008). *Rural policy reviews: Finland.* OECD, Paris.

Official Statistics of Finland (2012). *Population structure* (e-publication). Helsinki: Statistics Finland. Available at: www.stat.fi/til/vaerak/2012/vaerak_2012_2013-03-22_tie_001_en.html (accessed 17 September 2014).

Parekh, B. (2006). *Rethinking multiculturalism: Cultural diversity and political theory.* Palgrave Macmillan, New York.

Pilgrim, S. and J. Pretty (eds) (2010). *Nature and culture: Rebuilding lost connections.* Earthscan, London and Washington DC.

Redclift, M. (2005). Sustainable development (1987–2005): An oxymoron comes of age. *Sustainable Development*, 13: 212–227.

Relph, E. (1976). *Place and placelessness.* Pion, London.

Rural Policy Committee (2014). *A countryside of opportunities: National Rural Policy Programme 2014–2020.* MEE Publications, Regional development 9/2014, Ministry of Employment, Helsinki.

Sack, R. (1997). *Homo geographicus: A framework for action, awareness, and moral concern.* Johns Hopkins, Baltimore.

Shields, R. (1999). *Lefebvre, love and struggle: Spatial dialectics.* Routledge, London.

Soini, K. (2007). Beyond the ecological hot spots: Understanding local residents' perceptions of biodiversity of agricultural landscapes. *Annales Universitatis Turkuensis*, AII, 206.

Soini, K., Kivitalo, M. and A. Kangas (2012). *Exploring culture in sustainable rural development.* The 7th International Conference on Cultural Policy Research, 9–12 July. International Conference on Cultural Policy Research.

Soini, K. and I. Birkeland (2014). Exploring the scientific discourse on cultural sustainability. *Geoforum*, 51: 213–223.

Tuan, Y. (1977). *Space and place: The perspective of experience.* Edward Arnold, London.

UNESCO (2005). *Convention on the protection and promotion of the diversity of cultural expressions.* UNESCO, Paris.

Urry, J. (1995). *Consuming places.* Routledge, London.

Vanolo, A. (2008). The image of the creative city: Some reflections of branding in Turin. *Cities*, 25, 370–382.

WCED (1987). *Our common future.* Report of the World Commission on Environment and Development. Available at: www.un-documents.net/our-common-future.pdf (accessed 6 April 2014).

Woods, M. (2010). The political economies of place in the emergent global countryside: Stories from rural Wales, pp. 166–178 in: Halseth, G., Markey, S. and B. David (eds), *The next rural place in global economies.* CABI, Wallingford.

8 Territorialisation in practice

The case of saffron cultivation in Morocco

Joost Dessein

Introduction

Rural areas all over the globe are subject to dynamic change processes. They challenge the existence of rural areas, creating an urgent need for creative developments. These processes result from a twofold pressure. First, globalisation processes expose large parts of the world to similar influences (Simon *et al.*, 2010), creating uniformisation (Taylor, 1999). Wiskerke (2009) has shown how places have become increasingly interchangeable due to processes of disconnecting, disembedding and disentwining. Simultaneously, and closely linked to globalisation, counter movements lead to divergence and localisation, returning the processes of globalisation to place-specific forms (Taylor, 1999). Swyngedouw (2004) combined these in his concept of glocalisation.

These diverse processes include political, economic, social, environmental and cultural aspects as well as the complex interrelation between them. Coined as 'rural restructuring' (Floysand and Jakobsen, 2007: 208), they entail new modes of governance (Pike *et al.*, 2006; Shucksmith, 2010) and an increasing mobility and connectivity of goods and services, people and knowledge among various regions, including rural as well as urban areas (Hedberg and do Carmo, 2012).

We use the notion of 'territorialisation' to describe the dynamics and processes in the context of regional development that are driven by collective human intentionality; these stretch beyond localities and fixed regional boundaries (Horlings et *al.*, 2015). Political, societal and scientific attention is growing for the role and position of places in rural development – as well as the opportunities and challenges of place-based characteristics and assets in processes of rural development (Messely, 2014). Transcending the (mostly scientific) dichotomies 'essentialist/constructivist' and 'territorial/relational' (for an overview, see Messely, 2014), we consider regions to be the interplay of geographical conditions and social practices, conditioned by political, cultural, economic and natural factors. More specifically, we want to explore territorialisation as the complex interplay of neo-endogenous rural development and co-production in the context of a development arena.

For the past 50 years or so, rural development has been approached from different angles and continues to be subject to shifting paradigms and policies. These shifts have led to a 'new rural paradigm' (OECD, 2006) that emphasises the competitiveness of rural areas, valorisation of local assets and the exploitation of unused or insufficiently used resources (Messely, 2014). It involves a multi-actor, multi-level and multi-sector process, including numerous key actors such as farmers and national and local governments, and a gradual shift from government to more governance-like approaches (High and Nemes, 2007). The renewed focus on place-based or endogenous development, based on using the endogenous resources of a region, promotes territorially-focused integrated rural development (Messely, 2014: 26) and aims to maximise the retention of benefits within the local territory by valorising and exploiting local resources.

However, given the abovementioned processes of globalisation and rural restructuring, it has become clear that no regional development can happen in isolation as there are numerous and diverse links with other levels: actors and institutions from other localities interfere in the processes of endogenous rural development (Shucksmith, 2010). The concept of neo-endogenous rural development refers to this interplay of endogeneity (bottom-up approaches, focusing on the local territorial level) and various manifestations of the extra-local:

> Neo-endogenous development retains a bottom-up core in that local territories and actors are understood as having the potential for (mediated) agency, yet understands that extra-local factors, inevitably and crucially, impact on – and are exploitable by – the local level.
>
> (Ray, 2006: 281)

The perspective of neo-endogenous rural development encompasses a developmental idea rooted in the assumption that two different types of resources should be utilised side by side. 'Endogenous' refers to internal resources (physical, social, political, cultural, and so on), unique to a particular community, local control over these resources and local redistribution of economic gains (Oostindie *et al.*, 2008). The prefix 'neo-' stands for external, extra-local resources that are offered by the state, non-governmental organisations and supranational institutions and organisations (Gorlach and Adamski, 2007). Central to the approach is that a local area has, or must acquire, the capacity to assume some responsibility for bringing about its own socio-economic development. In terms of (rural) development, the neo-endogenous approach has two other primary characteristics. First, economic and other development activities are reoriented to maximise the retention of benefits within the local territory by valorising and exploiting local resources, both physical and human. Second, development is contextualised by focusing on the needs, capacities and perspectives of local people; the development model emphasises the principles and processes of 'local participation' in the design and implementation of action and through the adoption of cultural, environmental and 'community' values within a development intervention (Ray, 2006). Messely (2014) argues that neo-endogenous rural development is best organised at the level of territories, which should be seen as the result of local, autonomous bottom-up initiatives combined with top-down, official interventions by the government.

A second component of the territorialisation concept is 'co-production': considering the rural (and rural region) as a place where the ongoing encounter, interaction and mutual transformation of people and living nature is located. Particularly important is the coinciding and often mutually reinforcing shaping and transforming of the social and the natural, which leads to specific natural conditions (e.g. landscapes, agricultural products and breeds, hydrological conditions) as well as particular social, cultural, economic and political relations and institutions (e.g. social networks, family relations, local traditions and identities, producer-consumer relations). As such, not only people but also physical nature have agency that can transform perceptions, meaning, values and actions of local actors. This co-production and the importance of such a transformative agency is also acknowledged in the theory on 'coupled' social-ecological systems which considers human society to be dependent upon natural systems (Horlings *et al.*, 2015; Westley *et al.*, 2013).

This human-nature encounter occurs through a wide range of different practices that are spatially and temporally bounded (van der Ploeg and Marsden, 2008). Hence, co-production is subjected to an ever-changing relationship between people and living nature. All over the globe, the obvious interrelation of people and nature, particularly in the context of agriculture, is being challenged either from within or from the outside. It leads to a wide range of agricultural practices, ranging from culturally embedded ways of production to a disconnected agriculture, (partly) independent from local natural conditions, and detached from or transforming the prevailing social conditions.

Territorialisation in the context of regional development can thus be understood as the combined processes of neo-endogenous development and co-production. Neo-endogenous development refers to the interplay of endogenous and exogenous forces while co-production refers to the interplay of the social and the natural environment (Figure 8.1). Strong territorialisation can be found with a balance between the endogenous and exogenous forces influencing development in a context of a strong human-nature interrelation (i.e. strong co-production). Weak territorialisation, by extension, occurs under conditions of an unbalanced relation between exogenous and endogenous forces combined with a disconnected human-nature nexus.

The role of culture in territorialisation is manifold, as shown by Horlings *et al.* (2015). It entails the symbolic, reification and institutional dimensions, where culture refers to sense of place, cultural practices and the cultural characteristics of institutions. This chapter presents a case study of 'territorialisation in practice' in Morocco. It centers around a 'territorialised complex good' (Landel *et al.*, 2014): a good with an ensemble of often non-codified 'territorial attributes' such as knowledge, emotions, images and experiences that are anchored in a territory. We describe the good in a case study of saffron as a culturally embedded product that catalyses practices of weak and strong territorialisation. We first describe the methodological approach followed by a description of the context. In the results section, we focus on a number of actors that engage in development activities. Finally we discuss the results, and return to this framework for territorialisation.

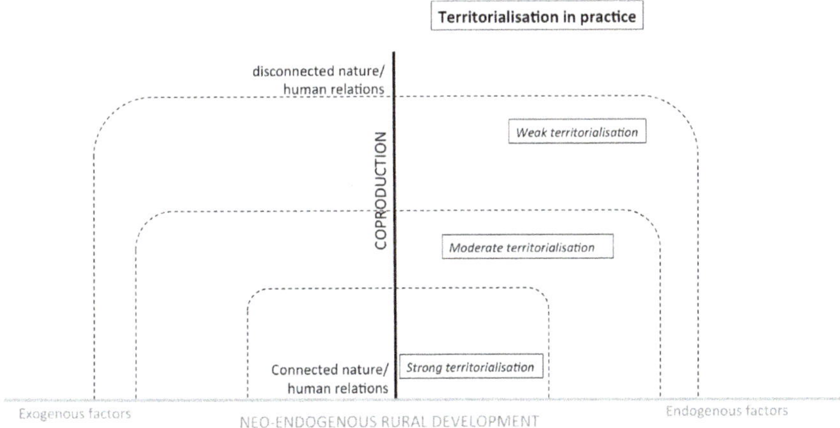

Figure 8.1 Territorialisation as the combined processes of neo-endogenous development and co-production

Source: © Joost Dessein

Methodology

The aim of this contribution is to understand and illustrate the process of territorialisation with a focus on practices. Being inspired by an actor-oriented interface approach, we look at 'sites of social discontinuity, ambiguity and cultural difference [...], by exploring how discrepancies of social interest, cultural interpretation, knowledge and power are mediated and perpetuated or transformed at critical points of confrontation and linkage' (Long, 2001: 89). Such an analysis must be grounded methodologically in the study of everyday life, in which actors seek to deal cognitively and organisationally with the problematic situations they face.

We look at coinciding rural development actions that take a natural resource (*in casu* saffron) as a catalyst for regional development. More specifically, we take the materialisation of two development dynamics (the House of Saffron and the Saffron Inn). Taking these as starting points, we look at several dynamics related to the cultivation and marketing of saffron. Multiple sources of evidence were used, including open and semi-structured interviews, informal conversation, reading grey literature and document analysis. The goal was to understand what kind of relationships the different actors within the arena have built with each other, and what roles these relations played in the logic of their interventions and actions. Interviews were held in the local Tamazight language (more commonly known as 'Berber') with the help of a French-speaking interpreter during March and September 2012. Ten households were interviewed, with explicit attention to maximising diversity in livelihood and economic status. These interviews were complemented with a number of informal talks with randomly chosen respondents (farmers and non-farmers, men and women). Six developers were also interviewed, including administrators, development agents and researchers. Interviews and documents were translated from French to English by the author.

Context

Taliouine, Souss-Massa-Drâa

The Taliouine community is situated in a mountain range in the crossing of the High- and Anti-Atlas, in the province of Taroudant, region of Souss-Massa-Drâa, southern Morocco. The name 'Taliouine' refers to the many natural springs and brooks in the area.

Between 1994 and 2011 the urban population of the Taroudant province increased by 3.3 per cent. However, the Taliouine municipality did not follow this provincial trend and showed an increase of only 1.6 per cent, presumably because the neighbouring localities are perceived as more dynamic and attractive. The current Taliouine population is set at an average of 115 inhabitants per km².

Taliouine is situated in the semi-arid climate zone, characterised by moderate temperatures (9°C–25.8°C) and a very irregular topography. Altitude varies between 980 m and 1,160 m. Rainwater provisioning is variable and dependent

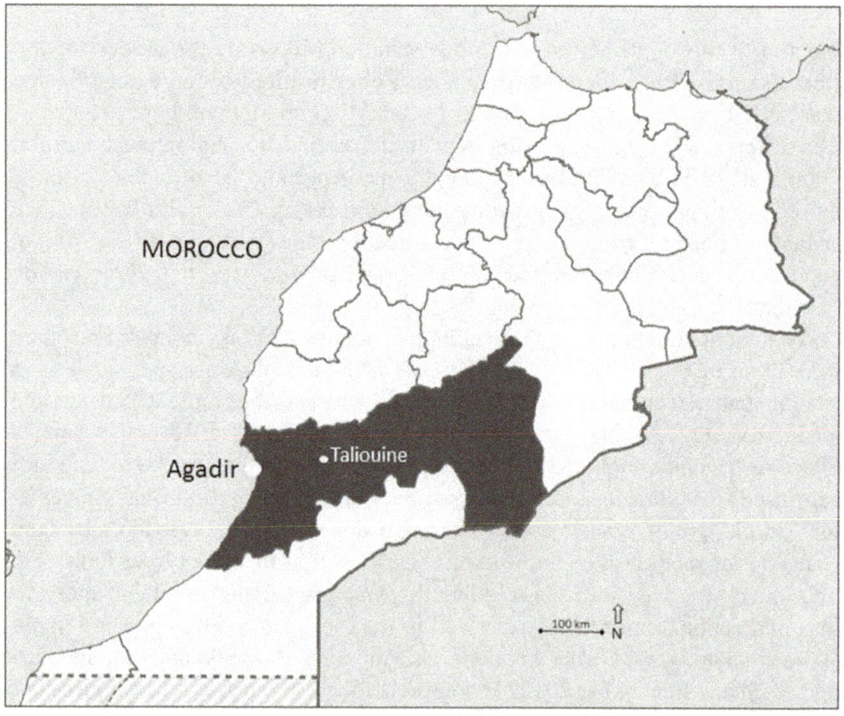

Figure 8.2 The region Souss-Massa-Drâa in Morocco, and the indication of Taliouine

Source: © Joost Dessein

on alternating wet and dry seasons. Within the Moroccan context, Taliouine is a rather deprived area. Only 64 per cent of the households in Taliouine are connected to the public water network (the national average is more than 86 per cent). The electricity connectivity is comparable with urban areas, however; 89.6 per cent of the households are connected to the public network, although power outages are common. The community is a rather isolated enclave. In the north, the High Atlas forms a natural barrier. Taliouine is only accessible via the road from Agadir. The nearest bus station is 120 km away, the nearest railway station 370 km. The closest hospital is in Taroudant, 110 km from Taliouine. The local medical services are limited to a modest health centre with very limited resources. Taliouine has a high percentage of illiteracy compared to the national percentage (35.5 per cent compared to 29.5 per cent), especially among women (more than 50 per cent). In addition to a few public schools (four primary, one comprehensive school and one secondary school), Taliouine has six private pre-schools with a capacity of 300 children and one religious Koranic school with a capacity of 80 pupils.

The active population of Taliouine is 31 per cent, comparable with the provincial percentage. However, there is a significant difference between men and women: women represent only 10 per cent of the active population (which is slightly higher than the provincial percentage). The major economic activity in the municipality is agriculture. Of a total of 43 km^2, 25 per cent of the land is occupied by agriculture, of which 18 per cent is irrigated. However, unfavourable topographic conditions in combination with traditional practices limit the productivity and the profitability of the agricultural sector. The most important cultivated crops are wheat and barley, followed by fruit trees such as almonds and olives; cattle are also bred for meat and dairy production. A limited handicraft sector (pottery and tapestry) and tourism sector are also present. The market is the commercial centre of the municipality, with an abattoir, a grain market, a food market and a market for phytosanitary products and household goods.

Saffron cultivation

In addition to their main agricultural activities, most farmers cultivate a small field of saffron, but never as a major crop. The cultivation of saffron (the stamen of the crocus flower, *Crocus sativus L.*) is said to have been introduced by the Arabs in the Maghreb around the ninth century. The initiatives of the government and external private investors have led to an increase of the cultivated saffron area from 500 ha (2008) to 1000 ha (in 2013). This huge increase is mainly due to the implementation of drip-irrigated cultivation systems, steered by external actors, with a focus on national and international markets.

The cultivation requires intensive irrigation (35–50 mm per hectare per week from September to November), mainly using water pumped from wells. The division of water is organised according to particular social structures (see below). Saffron cultivation in Morocco is carried out traditionally without chemical inputs. Its production requires a large amount of skilled labour during planting and harvesting. The average yield varies from 2–6 kg/ha during the 5–6 year production cycle, with a maximum reached during years 3–5. The Taliouine region produces five tonnes of saffron per year, making Morocco one of the world's five largest producers of saffron. Most of the saffron produced in Morocco is also sold in Morocco. Taliouine is the major national saffron provider, which has attracted a number of notable banks to the region. The international saffron trade is rather limited.

In Taliouine, culture and traditions are embedded in daily life, including agricultural production. Tamazight culture is interwoven with Arabic, Muslim and Jewish cultural influences. In saffron cultivation, these cultural traditions are passed on to the next generation, and include, among others, the organisation of a labour force during planting and harvesting, the patterns of trading cooperations on the market, the dynamics of land ownership, the sharing of water and the medicinal, culinary and artistic use of the crop. Typical is the role of saffron in the local social security system. As saffron can easily be stored, it is a much appreciated and highly valued way of saving capital to be used for irregular expenditures (such as weddings or funerals, hospitalisation or precious gifts). Saving capital through storing saffron is the act of responsible and caring family elders, as 'saffron is less volatile than money, which is so easily spent'. In 2010, 'Taliouine Saffron' was awarded Protected Designation of Origin status.

Results: two houses and development dynamics

In the results section below, we narrate two different development trajectories, both materialised in a building (the House of Saffron and the Saffron Inn) and shaped by a number of actors.

Development 'from beyond' and the House of Saffron

When entering the mountain town Taliouine along the long, winding road from Agadir, the centrally located Saffron House (*la Maison du Safran*) catches the eye. This impressive, brand-new building houses a permanent exhibition on the cultivation of saffron, serves as a selling point for well-marketed saffron products and is moreover the coordination centre for an institutionalised saffron market. The objective is to contribute to the development of a saffron distribution network and to centralise all the producers' organisations.

The House of Saffron was founded in 2010 by the Moroccan government as part of the Green Morocco Plan (*Le Plan Maroc Vert*), a new agricultural strategy intended to modernise agriculture and integrate it into the world market, improve human development, upgrade natural resource management and enhance sustainable growth. This governmental attention is not new. Since Moroccan independence in 1956, the government has always invested in agricultural development. The government has supported huge irrigation projects; a regulated market for agricultural commodities; and a number of strategic development plans aiming to increase agricultural production, employment and income, and

Figure 8.3 The House of Saffron (top) and serving saffron tea in the Saffron Inn (bottom)

Source: © Joost Dessein

to reduce environmental degradation and improve education, social services and infrastructure. The policy of the Green Morocco Plan aims to develop efficient, market-oriented agriculture with private investment for high-value commodity chains, and to increase the income of the most vulnerable smallholders especially in dry and mountainous zones through public and private intensification projects that will create a shift towards more profitable commodities. The plan includes reforms of land tenure, water policy and taxation and the reorganisation of the Ministry of Agriculture and Marine Fisheries. The second pillar of the plan, 'Improvement of agricultural income and fight against poverty', specifically mentions the importance of state-driven interventions for niche products such as saffron, among others.

Inspired by the Green Morocco Plan and its Axis 2, and referring to 'sustainable development of rural regions, using an integrated approach', a scientific research project was launched by two Moroccan research institutes. To fulfill the funding criteria, a European socio-economic agricultural research institute was invited to join the consortium. A European private company specialising in irrigation techniques was added as well. The sequence that the project group chose is striking: it characterises their particular approach to 'improving the efficiency of saffron cultivation, and optimisation of the use of water and energy resources, the marketing system and sustainable development'. The project proposal outlines the context of saffron cultivation as a challenged environment in terms of water provisioning, energy use and the creation of added value for 'local products' (*produits du terroir*), and describes the cultivation of saffron as '*still* the object of artisanal practices. [...] Concerning the cultivation of saffron [...], the ancestral competences that are continuously perpetuated because of the traditional practices, *call for* the adaptation and adoption of modern techniques for cultivation and valorisation' (emphasis added). In other words, the need for new methods of cultivation and valorisation (production, conservation, treatment and commercialisation) is motivated by the assessment of the present-day methods by the external researchers, rather than by an evaluation of these methods by local actors who actually engage in these production methods. Interestingly, after formulating the general research objectives (setting up a process of modernisation of saffron cultivation on an experimental plot with the focus on water and energy consumption, developing an appropriate marketing system, introducing the innovation to the cultivators and evaluating the research results) all but three of the nine themes for research and action are related to technical issues, with three dedicated to marketing, commercialisation and sustainable development. The three-year research plan started with two years of only technical research, leaving the third year (and only 11 per cent of the budget) for evaluation of the project, extension and dissemination of the results. The three non-technical topics were outsourced to the foreign scientific partner, whose role was actively curtailed by the national partners. During the course of the project, it became clear that only the huge high-tech drip irrigated experimental plot would receive the full attention of the research consortium. Talking to a farmer during a field visit, the project director clearly formulates: 'we are here to do actions that will improve your harvest'. Local actors (male and female cultivators, traders, users, leaders) and their cultural practices are not involved or included in the project set-up or execution in any way.

Instead of being an attractive demonstration site and platform for knowledge exchange for local farmers, the high-tech irrigated plot became an attractor for foreign investors who considered the presence of this research consortium, and its relationship with the Green Morocco Plan, as a moral support and a window of opportunity for their own private investment plans. One example is Mr X, a wealthy investor from Rabat, who returned to Morocco after spending a decade abroad in the telecom business. Neglecting existing local systems of labour division, access to land and water distribution, he hired five adjacent plots of (temporarily) fallow land to obtain a sufficiently large area and quickly installed a high-tech irrigation system, including a protective security system. Mr X's initiative was welcomed by the governmental and research actors, and he was invited to guide external visitors through his field as an example of 'a private investor in the development of local product with huge potential for the regions'. When questioned about the challenge of finding sufficient skilled manual labour to plant and harvest the bulbs of such a huge plot – taking into account that at the beginning of the planting season that year's available labour is already ascribed to particular farmers according to specific family structures – he stated that he would 'rely on cheap migrant workers from Spain or Italy'. He was not concerned about the eventual loss in quality resulting from using unskilled labourers for this very specific work, because even with lower quality, 'this is still saffron from Taliouine, so I can sell it as saffron from Taliouine'. However, this investor never reached the harvest stage. A few months after installing the equipment, a number of local landowners, who claimed their right to cultivate these plots because Mr X had denied ancient family rights, accused him of unlawful occupation of the land, and chased him away from the area. Despite this, the impetus of such investors has doubled the cultivated acreage in the past six years.

Development 'from within' and the Saffron Inn

A little further down the main street, not far from the House of Saffron, is the Saffron Inn (*Auberge du Safran*) which tells a different story. Established in the 1990s by a Taliouine man educated in Europe and recently married to a Frenchwoman, the Saffron Inn is a local initiative that started as a small restaurant ('In those days, I served four tables only'). In the wake of spontaneous growth, the Saffron Inn now includes a restaurant, a hotel and even a swimming pool. Moreover, the owner offers excursions to passing tourists interested in the cultivation, marketing and use of saffron and in Tamazight culture. The owner is proud of his own family ties with saffron cultivation (a number of generations have grown saffron) and he also works in the cultivation himself. ('I know what I'm talking about. I'm one of them! And my mother is growing saffron here [in the village].')

The Saffron Inn is part of a larger dynamic that is exemplified in the broader network of guesthouses, often the result of local investors who, returning home after a number of years earning money abroad, invest in their home village. The guesthouses often work together as exemplified in a circuit called 'the Land of Saffron' managed by Maroc Inédit, a Moroccan association that specialises in eco-tourism and travel in solidarity with the locals. These tourist activities include visiting the farms, cooking workshops, consuming saffron teas and food, and sale of saffron products. In addition, the NGO *Migration et Développement* (Migration and Development) enriches this dynamic with cultural activities, such as organising the annual saffron festival during the October harvest (including activities such as dance, concerts, craft exhibitions and cooking with saffron).

This shift is remarkable: based on guidelines from governmental tourism departments, and because of the lack of knowledge, skills and agency to challenge these guidelines, tourism was regarded as an external activity, without local consumption, and – more importantly – without any possible link with the local community. 'In those days', a guesthouse owner says, referring to the 1990s, 'the local people were even not allowed to talk to tourists!' Tourists were just seen as 'threatening strangers' passing through, who brought all their food from Agadir and got information from their Agadir-based guide or traveller's books. Visiting a saffron field did not include a meeting with the owners or workers, and could even be limited to a view from the bus. A big former hotel, located next to the historical Kasbah, is now a near-empty reminder of these earlier times.

Due to the agency of the local investors, and supported by organisations such as the NGO and the eco-tourism association, the current saffron tourism illustrates how new dynamics are being grafted onto the long existing and ever-changing territorial and socio-cultural embeddedness of saffron, which can be exemplified in two characteristics: co-production leading to territorial attributes, and the social structure based on *sociétés* (associations).

The co-production of people and nature in the saffron cultivation leads to 'territorial attributes' (Landel *et al.*, 2014) of the area. The micro-climate, the soil conditions and altitude, together with a history of isolation and trading, gave rise to the cultivation of this very particular crop. That in turn has led to specific landscapes, local architecture and irrigation systems, local breeds, etc. Saffron also plays a key role in the local cuisine, health care and arts. Referring to this interrelation of man and nature, a farmer says that 'It is the Souss cow [a specific local breed] that ploughs the Souss land'. An important aspect of this co-production is the role of tacit, often non-codifiable, knowledge about saffron cultivation, harvesting and storage.

A critical point in the cultivation of saffron is the harvest, which can only be done by women. This work is extremely labour intensive and requires a high level of skill and experience. Sufficient water must be available during specific stages of the growth of the flower. Therefore, to quote the head of a family, the 'real gold of Taliouine is even not the saffron, but the skilled labour (*main d'oeuvre*). And the water, of course.' Two key responsibilities of the *sociétés* (associations) are to organise the scarce labour (the number of square metres that can be harvested is calculated based on the availability of women during the harvest) and the distribution of the available water. These self-governing, age-old yet flexible clusters of families structure the society and are the result of geographical, religious and commercial historic processes. Based on the available saffron stock, the *sociétés* gather to negotiate the price of saffron on the local market (the *soukh*). They have only very limited, if any, relations with external, national or international saffron traders or other actors.

Territorialisation in practice and missed opportunities

The economic, social and cultural setting of saffron cultivation has created an arena in which diverse battles are recently being fought. These battles are fed by diverse visions of whether and how a territory should develop. As shown in Figure 8.4, this discussion section will situate the abovementioned activities as a result of dynamics along the two axes of co-production (the interplay of the social and the natural environment) and neo-endogenous development (the interplay of endogenous and exogenous forces). We then discuss the position of new forms of cooperatives (based on Table 8.1), and how these are emblematic of missed opportunities to create territorialisation.

The Saffron Inn and the House of Saffron occupy different positions in Figure 8.4. The Saffron Inn serves as a prototype of connected human-nature relations: human activities (social, cultural, economic) and natural processes co-evolve and mutually influence each other. Constituted by and constitutive of the natural environment, saffron cultivation also constitutes new human activities (excursions, accommodation, consumption). The Saffron Inn also balances endogenous resources (natural environment, local knowledge, local entrepreneurship, etc.) with extra-local resources, such as the organisation Maroc Inédit or the NGO *Migration et Développement*. This leads to a strong territorialisation. In contrast, the activities of the House of Saffron are closely linked with the Green Morocco

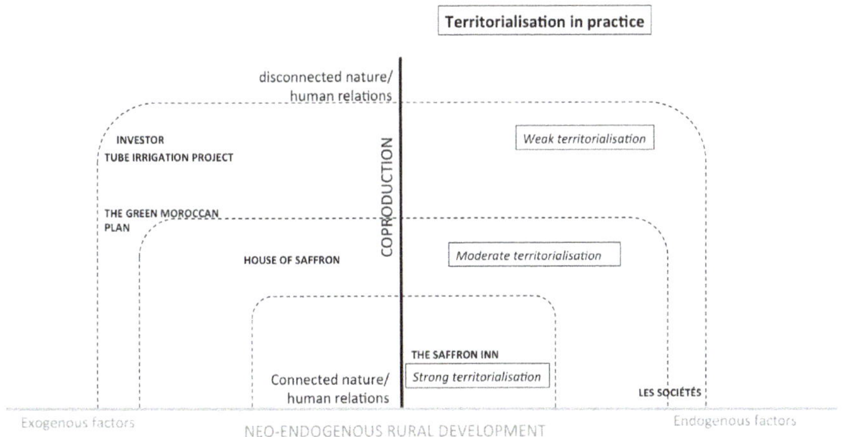

Figure 8.4 Position of the development activities in the territorialisation scheme

Source: © Joost Dessein

Table 8.1 Arguments for the position of actors and activities in Figure 8.4

	Co-production – (dis)connection of nature-human	*Neo-endogenous development – balance of external and endogenous factors in development*
The Green Morocco Plan	Connecting: recognises the importance of local products and local context Disconnecting: aim is land reform and new irrigation systems to increase production	Focus is merely on the crop (the product), while the process of production (including local knowledge and practices) is not taken into account. Technology, expertise and the organisation of the market are exclusively based on external factors
Foreign investors	Connecting: – Disconnecting: saffron cultivation is considered as independent from local circumstances. Labour is imported; distribution of water and land is disconnected from the natural, social and cultural conditions	Except for the locally-available soil and water, saffron cultivation by foreign investors relies entirely on external production factors (labour, irrigation technology, capital, bulbs, market)
Research project	Although recognising the present human-nature nexus, the project aims to disconnect them, formulated as 'the adaptation and adoption of modern techniques for cultivation and valorisation'	The research project relies almost entirely on external factors (technology, academic knowledge, relations with governmental powers)
House of Saffron	Connecting: making saffron a 'theme'; putting saffron on the agenda Disconnecting: the envisioned business model, exemplified in the organisational model of the commercial activities in cooperatives	Endogenous factors: confirming the status of saffron as an important natural resource External factors: the involvement of external managers; the intricate intertwinement with governmental bodies

	Co-production – (dis)connection of nature-human	*Neo-endogenous development – balance of external and endogenous factors in development*
The Saffron Inn	Connecting: the scale of the activities, the involvement of local people, the integration of saffron cultivation and tourism activities, respect for local culture of saffron cultivation Disconnecting: –	External factors: the expertise, experiences and capital of returnees; the alliance with NGOs and other associations Endogenous factors: involvement of local personnel, grafting of activities on local natural and human resources, re-investment of money in the area
Sociétés	Connecting: the interrelationship of natural conditions and the socio-cultural environment, resulting in the way saffron cultivation is reflected in the natural environment (plots, terraces, irrigation system, etc.) and the socio-cultural organisation (labour division, power distribution, etc.) Disconnecting: –	Endogenous factors: their approach of saffron cultivation relies entirely on endogenous factors (knowledge, social capital, natural resources, marketing chains, etc.) External factors: –

Plan and as such are based much more on disconnected human-nature relations, although still acknowledging the importance of local ways of cultivation and the local natural resources. While the House of Saffron still recognises the importance of endogenous development factors (such as the natural environment, but also the role of cooperatives), the Green Morocco Plan defends a development model that is almost exclusively based on external factors, such as high-tech irrigation, scaled-up farming and an ultra-productivist model of agriculture that might lead to the depletion of natural resources (see also Akesbi, 2012). In the tube irrigation research project and the activities by the foreign investor, the endogenous development factors and the connected human-nature relations are no longer relevant: they are situated in the upper left corner of the above scheme, characterised as weak territorialisation. In the lower right, the position of the *sociétés* illustrates the imbalance in their external and endogenous factors that also leads to weak territorialisation potential: despite their strong nature-human connection, their introverted relations prevent genuine development processes from taking place.

Local actors do acknowledge the need for new processes that can (re)vitalise the cultivation and commercialisation of saffron and that can tackle technical issues such as irrigation problems, the post-harvest storage of saffron or the uncontrolled import and export of crocus bulbs. They also recognise the role of external actors in assisting in these processes. But at the same time, they do value the embeddedness of saffron cultivation in their natural, social and cultural environment. This precarious situation is illustrated in the way the state, as probably the most powerful external actor, is dancing on a tightrope when trying to catalyse the dynamics of saffron cultivation. Already in the early 1980s, acknowledging the importance of uniting producers to strengthen their position in the value chain, the Moroccan Ministry of Agriculture installed cooperatives. However, instead of grafting these on the already long-established *sociétés*, hence linking external and endogenous factors and confirming the nature-human nexus, the new cooperatives were created artificially, based on criteria (composition, distribution of formal positions, mechanisms of control and enforcement) that were designed and implemented by external technocrats. After years of malfunctioning (including non-payments and fraud), the cooperatives led to distrust between the government and local actors and a lack of enthusiasm to join the cooperative. The launch of almost twenty new cooperatives in the context of the Green Morocco Plan repeated this external set-up (no cooperatives based on the structure of the *sociétés* are allowed), and the chairs of the cooperatives as well as the director of the House of Saffron are said to be appointed by high political officials who have no knowledge about the cultivation and marketing of saffron. Their focus is on large-scale saffron cultivation. Family elders complain that 'Even the visit of the King [in January 2011] didn't help to restore this trust' and question the objective of the government ('Does the government want to improve our saffron cultivation, or to make money?'). As a countermovement, NGOs such as *Migration et Développement* are installing their own cooperatives. Acting as catalytic go-betweens rather than leaders, these cooperatives are in the hands of local producers, and promote family based, small-scale saffron cultivation.

Conclusion

Between the Weberian ideal-types of non-territorialisation and complete territorialisation, the cases in this chapter on saffron cultivation in Taliouine have illustrated different hybrid trajectories of 'territorialisation in practice'. The House of Saffron and the Saffron Inn exemplify different approaches to regional development based on different levels of connectedness of human-nature relations and differences in the balance of exogenous and endogenous factors.

Strengthening the territorialisation of the region implies processes of reconnecting disconnected human-nature relations, and of rebalancing the relative importance of exogenous and endogenous factors. This coincides with findings of Wiskerke (2009) who stresses the importance of (re)connecting stakeholders, re-embedding goods and services, and intertwining the various economic and non-economic activities and roles in processes of sustainable regional development. Building on the experiences in saffron cultivation, we emphasise the importance of 'territorialised complex goods' in such processes of regional development. Culturally embedded products can support connected human–nature relations as well as the balancing of exogenous and endogenous factors, leading to strong territorialisation.

References

Akesbi, N. (2012). The 'Green Morocco Plan': Strengths and weaknesses of the Moroccan agricultural strategy (*Le 'Plan Maroc Vert': Forces et faiblesses de la stratégie agricole Marocaine*), pp. 777–797 in: *l'Annuaire Marocain de la stratégie et des relations internationales AMSRI*. Harmattan, Paris.

Floysand, A. and S. Jakobsen (2007). Commodification of rural places: A narrative of social fields, rural development, and football. *Journal of Rural Studies*, 23 (2): 206–221.

Gorlach, K. and T. Adamski (2007). Neo-endogenous development and the revalidation of local knowledge. *Polish Sociological Review*, 4 (160): 481–497.

Hedberg, C. and R.M. do Carmo (eds) (2012). *Translocal ruralism: Mobility and connectivity in European rural spaces*. Springer, Dordrecht.

High, C. and G. Nemes (2007). Social learning in LEADER: Exogenous, endogenous and hybrid evaluation in rural development. *Sociologia Ruralis*, 47: 103–119.

Horlings, L. Battaglini, E. and J. Dessein (2015). *Introduction: The role of culture in territorialisation*. In: this book, Chapter 1.

Landel, P.-A., Gagnol, L. and M. Oiry-Varacca (2014). Territorial resources and tourist destinations: Couples with a bright future? *Journal of Alpine Research/Revue de géographie alpine*. Online at: http://rga.revues.org/2334 (accessed 19 November 2014).

Long, N. (2001). *Development sociology: Actor perspectives*. Routledge, London and New York.

Messely, L. (2014). *On regions and their actors: An analysis of the role of actors and policy in region-specific rural development processes in Flanders*. PhD thesis, Ghent University, Ghent.

OECD (2006). *The new rural paradigm: Policies and governance*. OECD rural policy reviews. OECD Publications, Paris.

Oostindie, H., van Broekhuizen, R., Brunori, G. and J.D. van der Ploeg (2008). The endogeneity of rural economies, pp. 53–67 in: van der Ploeg, J.D. and T. Marsden (eds), *Unfolding webs: The dynamics of regional rural development*. Koninklijke Van Gorcum, Assen.

Pike, A., Rodriguez-Pose, A. and J. Tomaney (2006). *Local and regional development*. Routledge, Abingdon.

Ray, C. (2006). Neo-endogenous rural development in the EU, pp. 278–291 in: Cloke, P., Marsden, T. and P. Mooney (eds), *Handbook of rural studies*. SAGE Publications, London.

Shucksmith, M. (2010). Disintegrated rural development? Neo-endogenous rural development, planning and place-shaping in diffused power contexts. *Sociologia Ruralis*, 50: 1–14.

Swyngedouw, E. (2004). Globalisation or 'glocalisation'? Networks, territories and rescaling. *Cambridge Review of International Affairs*, 17: 25–48.

Simon, C., Huigen, P. and P. Groote (2010). Analysing regional identities in the Netherlands. *Tijdschrift voor Economische en Sociale Geografie*, 101: 409–421.

Taylor, C. (1999). Two theories of modernity. *Public Culture*, 11: 153–174.

van der Ploeg, J.D. and T. Marsden (2008). *Unfolding webs: The dynamics of regional rural development*. Van Gorcum, Assen.

Westley, F. R., Tjornbo, O., Schultz, L., Olsson, P., Folke, C., Crona, B. and Ö. Bodin (2013). A theory of transformative agency in linked social-ecological systems. *Ecology and Society*, 18 (3): 1–16.

Wiskerke, J.S. (2009). On places lost and places regained: Reflections on the alternative food geography and sustainable regional development. *International Planning Studies*, 14 (4): 369–387.

9 Is there a place for place?

How spaces and places are included in the measures of sustainable development and well-being

Annalisa Cicerchia

The need to go beyond GDP: three steps

In 1934, Simon Kuznets, one of the fathers of the System of National Accounts and of the GDP, explicitly warned that 'the welfare of a nation can scarcely be inferred from a measure of national income' (Kuznets, 1934: 7). On 18 March 1968, senator Robert Kennedy (1968) delivered his famous speech on the failure of the GDP (it 'measures everything except that which is worthwhile'). He was not alone in his opinion: contemporary distinguished academic communities in the US agreed with him, and the Social Indicators Movement, which advocates social indicators as tools for measuring societal progress and development, was already on its way.

Ciommi *et al.* (2013) distinguish three main stages in the evolution of measures of progress related to (or alternative to) the GDP. The first stage, peaking in the 1920s and 1940s, is the material stage, which focused almost solely on economic indices (GNP or GDP). This stage is characterised by a macro approach which left very little to micro (and, consequently, also to place-based) phenomena.

From the 1950s to the end of the 1980s, the second, social stage explored the social preconditions and dimensions of well-being. A number of new measures were developed, including Bauer's Social Indicators (1966), Buthan's Gross National Happiness (Royal Government of Bhutan, 2009) and Nordhaus and Tobin's Measure of Economic Welfare (Nordhaus and Tobin, 1972). The OECD List of Social Indicators (1982) and Index of Social Health (1986) by Miringoff and Miringoff (1999) also deserve mentioning. Regional and sub-regional differences and inequalities started to be noticed.

The end of the 1980s was marked by the publication of the Brundtland Report (World Commission on Environment and Development, 1987), which boosted the popularity of the notion of sustainable development. In 1992, the UN Summit in Rio de Janeiro introduced that concept into political debate. The third stage is thus global, both in geographical scope and in content, the stage where economic, social and environmental indicators merge in a variety of new approaches. International projects of this type are the UN Human Development Index (UNDP, 1994); Cobb's Genuine Progress Indicator (Talberth *et al.*, 2006) and the UNDP Gender Empowerment Index (1995); and, later, the Sarkozy

Commission (Stiglitz *et al.*, 2008), the European Commission GDP and Beyond projects (2009), the OECD Better Life Initiative of 2009 (OECD, 2011), the UN General Assembly's Resolution on Happiness (United Nations General Assembly, 2011) and the UN World Happiness Report 2012 (Helliwell *et al.*, 2013), among others.

How do space, place and territory fare in these new approaches? In theory, their weight should be significant. The very concept of sustainability is built on the quality of the relationship between human communities and their ecosystems. The notion of the ecological footprint is even more embedded in the human–ecosystem relationship. The idea of 'glocality' also pushed the idea of the global relevance of lifestyles and actions happening on the smallest local level and their role in sustainability. Cultural minorities, local traditions, national and ethnic identities have increasingly gained relevance, sometimes also generating severe conflicts, as seen in recent history in Europe and elsewhere. The need for super-national sustainable development policies goes hand in hand with the need for finer sub-national interventions: in 2009, for instance, the independent report submitted by Fabrizio Barca to the EC Commissioner for Regional Policy in preparation for the 2020 strategy advocated 'A place-based approach to meeting European Union challenges and expectations'. A place-based development policy is i) a long-term development strategy aiming at reducing under-utilisation of resources and social exclusion of specific places, through the production of integrated bundles of public goods and services, ii) determined by extracting and aggregating people's knowledge and preferences in these places and turning them into projects, and iii) exogenously promoted through a system of grants subject to conditionalities and multilevel governance. In a place-based development policy, 'a place is not identified by administrative boundaries, nor by any other ex-ante "functional" criteria ... rather a place is endogenous to the policy process, it is a contiguous area within whose boundaries a set of conditions conducive to development apply more than they do across boundaries' (Barca, 2009 in Böhme *et al.*, 2011: 17).

One could expect that the new measures devised for a different appraisal of development, progress or well-being would be key to the territorial dimension. The present exercise investigates three of these measures: one by UNESCO, one by OECD and one by the Italian National Statistical Institute (ISTAT) and the Italian National Economic Development and Labour Council (CNEL). We explore to what extent they take space, place and territory (SPT) into consideration. Our interest is confined to the acknowledgement of the topic and its conceptualisation; we do not consider the massive methodological and statistical discussion that the actual or attempted measurement of well-being entails.

Beyond GDP: three new proposals and the territorial issue

From the multitude of new measures of development, progress and well-being, we have chosen three candidates for an in-depth investigation of the recognition they grant to SPT. We preferred sets of indicators to synthetic indexes because the components are easier to track and they do not have a conceptual and/or statistical weighting system. The chosen three sets of indicators were developed between 2009 and 2011, with special emphasis on the role they do (or do not) attach to SPT:

- UNESCO's Culture for Development Indicator Suite (CDIS);
- OECD's Better Life Index;
- ISTAT–CNEL's Equitable and Sustainable Well-being (BES).

The different geographic scopes of the three systems represent valid examples of different ways to tackle the challenge of how to go beyond the GDP. UNESCO's approach focuses on culture and its possible contribution to development; the OECD uses a dynamic and multifaceted description of well-being; and ISTAT–CNEL introduce sustainability and equity into the theoretical frame. Despite all having different outcomes, they all tackle the role of culture in territorialisation.

Each of the three indicator sets can be considered unique, but nonetheless they are related and share relevant aspects. The first is 'Data come first, indicators follow'. In other words, none of the indicator sets is based on specifically designed and targeted data collections. None has given rise, so far, to surveys expressly meant to feed the set of proposed measures with data, but one – UNESCO's – keeps track of those indicators for which no data are presently provided. The systems are thus built on data from existing official statistics which are gathered for a variety of purposes, but in which the measurement of well-being was seldom, if ever, included. In the two international sets considered here, the data are quite obviously the result of statistical activities carried out independently in different countries. Apart from possible semantic mismatches – a risk common to all cross-cultural data sets – the main consequence is that the identification of a list of ideal measures has been necessarily followed by progressive adjustments to adapt them to the available data: the indicator creation process has been ultimately shaped by those data which were at hand and were comparable.

Second, with a few exceptions, they all favour objective indicators: they record quantities, behaviours, states or conditions; they refer to individuals as well as to groups, laws and norms. Only in rare cases do they focus on opinions, expressed values or feelings. This leads to a distinct difficulty in seeing the relevant phenomena from within and in appreciating the role played by sense-making in attaining well-being.

Third, while SPT are both the root and the meaningful setting of any human activity related to well-being and the proposed measures are focused on well-being, no explicit definition of SPT is made in any of them.

Finally, all the systems considered here are open projects. Study and discussion on themes, approaches, methodologies and indicators are still ongoing, and some aspects, like territorialisation, that at present might appear neglected or underestimated, could be reconsidered.

For each set of measures we have asked the following questions:

- Are SPT covered at all? At what level (basic dimension/indicator)? How intensively (frequency and/or strategic role)? Directly or indirectly?
- Are SPT introduced as a finer, more detailed view of the phenomena, aimed at identifying differences and/or inequalities in distributions?
- Are SPT seen as sources/beneficiaries of specific/unique contributions, positive or negative, to development/well-being?

UNESCO's and OECD's systems compare national performances, while the ISTAT–CNEL system compares the 20 Italian regions (NUTS II). This complicates the adoption of an SPT-aware perspective, as the fine indicators capable of grasping the essential characteristics of places and territorialisation are often not found at the national level and/or are not adequately harmonised for the international level. However, the notion of territorialisation we refer to does not equal a micro approach. It is rather a matter of concepts taken into consideration; thus territory-oriented indicators could be found even among national level measures.

UNESCO's Culture for Development Indicator Suite (CDIS)

UNESCO's research and advocacy initiative (CDIS) was created to use data to illustrate and measure the contribution of culture to development processes. CDIS is made up of 22 quantitative indicators, covering 'the economic, social participation, governance and institutionality, communication, heritage, education and gender equality dimensions of culture and development', as defined in the Report of the World Commission on Culture and Development (1996).

The 2001 Universal Declaration on Cultural Diversity adopted a definition of culture which describes the basis of its relationship to human development processes:

> Culture should be regarded as the set of distinctive spiritual, material, intellectual and emotional features of society or a social group, and that it encompasses, in addition to art and literature, lifestyles, ways of living together, value systems, traditions and beliefs.
>
> (UNESCO, 2001)

CDIS has three key axes:

- Culture as a sector of economic activity.
- Culture as a set of resources that add value to development interventions and increase their impact.
- Culture as a sustainable framework for social cohesion and peace, essential to human development.

Described and defined along these lines, culture appears likely to be further analysed in terms of SPT. As a sector of economic activity, culture is locally specialised, often in form of district, fuelled by site-specific cultural and professional *milieux*. As a complex of resources, the production, selection and historic stratification of these *milieux* is strictly tied to the local geography and eco-systems and to the ways they interact in time with resident and incoming human groups. Social cohesion is deeply rooted in a shared sense of belonging, and belonging to a place is the first and foremost of those human experiences that build identity and social ties.

The 22 indicators in UNESCO's CDIS are distributed among seven dimensions and sub-dimensions. Each sub-dimension in turn is represented by at least one indicator. At their present state of development, the measures proposed in CDIS are divided into three groups: fully developed indicators, indicators needing further development and indicators for which no data is provided.

In the fully developed indicators, SPT appear directly only in one case: 'Distribution of selected cultural infrastructure relative to the distribution of the country's population'. The indicator highlights territorial inequalities in the distribution of cultural infrastructures (museums, exhibition venues, libraries, etc.).

Two indicators relate to SPT only indirectly: they address cultural minorities, who, in some cases, are spatially concentrated or belong to special places: 'Index of promotion of the participation of representatives of cultural professionals and minorities in the formulation and implementation of cultural policies, measures and programmes that concern them' and 'Minority Languages: percentage of annual broadcasting time for indigenous and tribal peoples'.

In the subset of indicators for which data are not provided, SPT can be found in eight cases: 'Per cent of revenue/profit reinvested in community development or heritage management', 'Entrepreneurial opportunities for local communities', 'Retention of local customs and language', 'Incorporation and implementation of local ideas in heritage management', 'Presence of heritage authority or planner in local community', 'Level of support for conservation/development projects in local communities', 'Stakeholder collaboration' and 'Availability of resident advisory boards'.

The SPT content that we can infer from the proposed measures is only hinted at. Hardly evoking the symbolic, reification and structural dimensions, the first three indicators point only to differences or inequalities in the distribution of/access to goods and services. Among the eight indicators not covered by data, those pertaining to the section of social effects and socio-cultural fabric evoke something related to the symbolic dimension (retention of local customs and language), the reification dimension (incorporation of local ideas in heritage management) and the structural dimension (presence of authority, support for projects, stakeholder collaboration and resident advisory boards). In all cases, however, the reference is indirect; none account for SPT as a key element in the sustainability of culture.

Table 9.1 UNESCO's Culture for development indicator suite (adapted from UNESCO, 2014)

Dimensions	*Sub-dimensions*	*Indicators*
Economy	1. Added value of cultural activities to GDP 2. Employment in culture 3. Household expenditures on culture	FULLY DEVELOPED INDICATORS 1.1 Added value of cultural activities: contribution of characteristic cultural activities to GDP 1.2 Employment in culture 1.3 Revenues of employees in culture 1.4 Expenditures in culture: spending on final market goods and services INDICATORS NEEDING FURTHER DEVELOPMENT 1.5 Expenditures on culture: percentage of expenditures in advertising for the financing of cultural products in GDP 1.6 International trade of cultural activities INDICATORS FOR WHICH NO DATA IS PROVIDED 1.7 Government expenditures on culture
Education	1. Complete, fair and inclusive education for all 2. Valorisation of interculturality, cultural diversity and creativity in the first two years of secondary school 3. Training of professionals in the cultural sector	INDICATORS NEEDING FURTHER DEVELOPMENT 2.1 Knowledge of cultural diversity (students aged 14) 2.2 Self-reported participation in formal and informal courses on cultural diversity (students aged 14) 2.3 Courses on language instruction, moral education, and the social sciences and humanities in school or at tertiary level 2.4 Participation in arts courses in formal and informal education 2.5 Course modules on the arts 2.6 Rates of adults' participation in training activities in culture INDICATORS FOR WHICH NO DATA IS PROVIDED 2.7 Acquired knowledge on culture by adults 2.8 Offer of courses for adults/professionals in culture

Dimensions	*Sub-dimensions*	*Indicators*
Heritage	1. Promotion and valorisation of heritage	FULLY DEVELOPED INDICATORS 3.1 Register of cultural heritage assets 3.2 Employment in the cultural heritage sector 3.3 Public attitude towards heritage 3.4 Participation in heritage related activities INDICATORS NEEDING FURTHER DEVELOPMENT 3.5 Government resources dedicated to heritage 3.6 The existence and status of heritage legislation in the various countries 3.7 The status of the implementation of UNESCO conventions 3.8 Experiences in the participatory heritage management INDICATORS FOR WHICH NO DATA IS PROVIDED Sustainability components – Economic effects Income distribution – Percentage income seepage into communities – Employment and income multipliers on tourism expenditures – Changes in rate of purchase of local products, value and variety – Percentage of tourism contribution to local economy – Comparative ratio of wages in tourism sector to local average wages Capital formation in communities/investment – Percentage of local/foreign ownership of tourism establishments – Per cent of revenue/ profit reinvested in community development or heritage management – Entrepreneurial opportunities for local communities Demand for Heritage Products – Per cent of repeat visitors – Consumer spending by demographic variable

Continued

Table 9.1 UNESCO's Culture for development indicator suite, *continued*

Dimensions	*Sub-dimensions*	*Indicators*
Heritage	1. Promotion and valorisation of heritage	Sustainability components SOCIAL EFFECTS Socio-cultural fabric – Retention of local customs and language – Changes in the satisfaction with heritage integrity and security – Cultural education – Number and types of training opportunities available for heritage employees – Level of promotion of heritage tourism – Quantity and quality of heritage interpretative material Local oriented policy – Incorporation and implementation of local ideas in heritage management – Presence of heritage authority or planner in local community – Level of support for conservation/development projects in local communities – Stakeholder collaboration – Availability of resident advisory boards – Level of public–private partnership Sustainability components PHYSICAL EFFECTS Preservation/Loss of heritage resources – Level of erosion, vandalism, theft and destruction of heritage – Level of protection of sites and other heritage resources Rate of ecosystem conservation – Recycling rate – Formal control required for development of sites and use densities – Number of endangered species – Level of loss of vegetation Assessment of environmental impact of tourism – Natural environment accounting and life cycle analysis – Use of renewable resources – Recycling rate – Use of environmental impact assessment – Per capita discharge of solid waste – Per capita discharge of waste water

Dimensions	*Sub-dimensions*	*Indicators*
Communication	1. Freedom of expression	FULLY DEVELOPED INDICATORS
		Rights and Legal Framework:
		4.1. Number of censorship cases
		4.2 Freedom of Expression
		Infrastructure and Access:
		4.3 Minority Languages: percentage of annual broadcasting time for indigenous and tribal peoples
		4.4 Media Availability and Culture
		4.4 a. percentage ownership concentration of TV, radio, newspaper and internet access
		4.4 b. spectrum allocation; broadband availability
		4.4 c. number of broadcasting channels per capita
		Content and capacity:
		4.5 Percentage of annual television broadcasting time on ‘Arts and culture’
		4.6 Percentage of graduates in the arts
		4.7 Percentage of those new cultural products released (book titles on arts, recreation and literature, movies)
		4.8 Percentage of stories that clearly challenge or reinforce stereotypes on women

Continued

Table 9.1 UNESCO's Culture for development indicator suite, *continued*

Dimensions	*Sub-dimensions*	*Indicators*
	2. Access and internet use	INDICATORS NEEDING FUTHER DEVELOPMENT Rights and Legal Framework: 4.9 Number of cultural events per capita 4.10 Access to information data/legal country data Infrastructure and access: 4.11 Minority Languages: proportion of population taught in minority language 4.12 Government funding of cultural activities Content and capacity: 4.13 Funds dedicated to cultural grants by country
	3. Diversity of media content	INDICATORS FOR WHICH NO DATA IS PROVIDED Infrastructure and access: 4.14 Minority Languages: percentage internet usage amongst minority groups; percentage minority language/community/cultural newspapers; Number of translations in minority languages; rate of reading, viewing or listening to language-based cultural products translated into and from minority languages, compared to all cultural experience Content and capacity: 4.15 Number of Civil Society organisations dedicated to cultural pursuits 4.16 Percentage of all professions in the arts 4.17 Numbers of professionals and amateurs involved in cultural activities

Dimensions	*Sub-dimensions*	*Indicators*
Governance and institutionality	1. Standard-setting framework for culture 2. Policy and institutional framework for culture 3. Distribution of cultural infrastructure 4. Civil society participation in cultural governance	FULLY DEVELOPED INDICATORS 5.1 Index of development of the standard-setting framework for the protection and promotion of culture, cultural rights and cultural diversity 5.2 Distribution of selected cultural infrastructure relative to the distribution of the country's population in administrative divisions immediately below State level 5.3 Index of promotion of the participation of representatives of cultural professionals and minorities in the formulation and implementation of cultural policies, measures and programmes that concern them
Social participation	1. Participation in cultural activities 2. Trust 3. Freedom of self-determination	FULLY DEVELOPED INDICATORS 6.1 Participation in cultural activities 6.2 Distrust or dislike of other cultures 6.3 Interpersonal trust 6.4 Freedom of self-determination 6.5 Computer use INDICATORS NEEDING FURTHER DEVELOPMENT 6.1 Adjusted participation rates in cultural activities
Gender equality	1. Levels of gender equality 2. Perception of gender equality	FULLY DEVELOPED INDICATORS 7.1 Gaps between women and men in political, education and labour domains and in gender-equity legislation 7.2 Targeted gender legislation 7.3 Level of positive assessment of gender equality (subjective)

OECD's Better Life Index

When comparing the measures used by UNESCO and the OECD, one must keep in mind that UNESCO's measures apply in principle to all countries in the world, while the OECD focuses exclusively on OECD countries. Despite differences between low-income and higher-income OECD countries, they still have much in common.

The conceptual framework used by the OECD distinguishes between current and future well-being. Current well-being is measured for two broad domains: material living conditions (income and wealth, jobs and earnings, housing conditions), and quality of life (health status, work–life balance, education and skills, social connections, civic engagement and governance, environmental quality, personal security and life satisfaction). Future well-being (or sustainability of well-being) is assessed through indicators of different types of 'capital' that drive well-being over time (FOC, 2014).

Intensive work is being done to improve the proposed set of measures, and the project is far from finished. Many indicators in the OECD list point to SPT in multifaceted and significant ways.

Four indicators deal directly with SPT: 'Dwellings without basic facilities' (the percentage of the population living in a dwelling without an indoor flushing toilet for the sole use of their households), 'Rooms per person' (the number of rooms, excluding kitchenette, scullery/utility room, bathroom, toilet, garage, consulting rooms, office, or shop, in a dwelling, divided by the number of persons living in the dwelling), 'Satisfaction with housing' (this indicator is built on responses to the question: 'Are you satisfied or dissatisfied with your current housing, dwelling, or place you live?'), 'Satisfaction with the quality of the local environment' (the indicator is based on responses to two questions: 'In the city or area where you live, are you satisfied or dissatisfied with the quality of air?' and 'In the city or area where you live, are you satisfied or dissatisfied with the quality of water?').

Five indicators relate to SPT indirectly: 'Quality of support network' (this is a measure of perceived social network support. The indicator is based on the question: 'If you were in trouble, do you have relatives or friends you can count on to help you whenever you need them, or not?' and it considers the respondents who respond positively), 'Frequency of social contact' (the proportion of people who report socialising (i.e. face-to-face contact) with friends and relatives living outside the household at least once a week), 'Assault' (based on the question: 'Within the past 12 months: have you been assaulted or mugged?'), 'Feeling of security' (based on the data drawn from the Gallup World Poll in the question: 'Do you feel safe walking alone at night in the city or area where you live?'), 'Commuting time' (the number of minutes spent commuting on a typical day by all kind of workers).

The OECD's well-being measures range from appreciating the physical comfort attainable in the house and in the local area to satisfaction with life, the physical setting and the network of social relationships, the perceived invisible network of social support and the personal feeling of safety or the self-reported victimisation. The balance of subjective and objective indicators helps to render an image of the

Table 9.2 OECD's Better Life Index (adapted from OECD, 2011)

Dimensions	*Indicators*
Housing	Dwellings without basic facilities Housing expenditure Rooms per person Satisfaction with housing
Income	Household net adjusted disposable income Household net financial wealth
Jobs	Employment rate Job security Long-term unemployment rate Personal earnings
Community	Quality of support network Frequency of social contact
Education	Educational attainment Student skills Years in education
Environment	Air pollution Water quality Satisfaction with the quality of the local environment Consultation on rule-making
Civic engagement	Voter turnout
Health	Life expectancy Self-reported health
Life satisfaction	Life satisfaction
Personal security	Feeling of security Self-reported victimisation Domestic violence on children Homicide rate
Work–life balance	Employees working very long hours Commuting time Time devoted to leisure and personal care

many possible ways SPT impact on well-being. Although the OECD indicators, which mainly focus on institutionalisation and reification, are not able to cross the boundary of the symbolic dimension and to tell us something about it, they nonetheless establish a continuum leading very close to where subjective perceptions and sense-making, the construction of narratives and place identities take place and shape the operational world of individuals and communities.

Italy (ISTAT–CNEL): Equitable and Sustainable Well-being measures (BES, Benessere equo e sostenibile)

In 2010, Italy joined the most advanced assessments being developed all over the world when CNEL and ISTAT committed to producing a measuring tool capable of identifying the underlying elements of well-being in Italy. The process has been carried out by involving some of the leading experts in the various subjects relevant to the general definition of well-being (health, environment, employment, economic conditions, etc.) as well as thousands of citizens via polls and surveys, along with meetings held with institutions, social stakeholders and NGOs. As in the other two cases considered here, the set of indicators of Equitable and Sustainable Well-being is not definitive, and the project is still open.

BES is based on 129 indicators divided into 12 dimensions of well-being, including one devoted to landscape and cultural heritage.

SPT are directly and indirectly represented in six out of 12 dimensions, through 25 indicators: 'People suffering from poor housing conditions', 'Satisfaction with family relationships', 'Satisfaction with friendship relationships', 'Friends or neighbours to rely on', 'Fear of being a victim of a sexual crime', 'People who feel safe walking alone after dark', 'People who are afraid of being a victim of crime', 'Decay or degradation in the neighborhood', 'Density of historic/artistic buildings', 'Per capita current expenditure of municipalities for cultural heritage management', 'Illegal building rate', 'Urbanisation rate of areas subject to building restrictions', 'Urban-sprawl-induced erosion of rural areas', 'Depopulation-induced erosion of rural areas', 'Historic rural landscapes', 'Regional programmes for landscape protection and rural development', 'Historic parks/gardens and other urban parks of significant public interest', 'Conservation of the historic urban fabric', 'People who are dissatisfied with the quality of landscape of the place where they live', 'Concern for landscape deterioration', 'Contaminated sites', 'Protected land areas', 'Protected marine areas', 'Areas of special biodiversity interest', and 'Time spent commuting'.

The main distinctive character of BES lies in the qualitative importance it grants to SPT themes by devoting a whole dimension to landscape and cultural heritage among the key factors of well-being. A first set of proposed measures concerns the territorial (regional) distribution of cultural heritage assets. Other indicators quantify the direction and intensity of policies, rules and public investment devoted to preservation, protection and maintenance of cultural and natural assets. Finally, a few subjective indicators measure perceptions (safety, degradation, neglect, etc.) and values (satisfaction, aesthetic appreciation, etc.).

BES shows similarities to the OECD's measures, such as those concerning the physical quality of housing, the sense of perceived safety and the reliability of a social network. But the reference to the historic landscape and cultural heritage characterises the system: the indicators point to the objective (in the absence of data on the subjective), built and institutionalised side of the symbolic dimension and the sense-making process, albeit at the regional level, which is probably still sub-optimal. The indicator 'percentage of municipal public expenditure allocated

Table 9.3 ISTAT-CNEL's Equitable and Sustainable Well-being measures (adapted from ISTAT, 2013)

Dimensions	*Indicators*
Health	Life expectancy at birth
	Healthy life expectancy at birth
	Physical component summary
	Mental component summary
	Infant mortality rate
	Age-standardised transport accidents mortality rate
	Age-standardised cancer mortality rate
	Age-standardised mortality rate for dementia and illnesses of the nervous system
	Life expectancy without activity limitations at 65 years of age
	Overweight or obesity
	Smoking
	Alcohol consumption
	Sedentary behaviour
	Nutrition
Education and training	Participation in early childhood education
	Percentage of people having completed at least upper secondary education
	Percentage of people having completed tertiary education
	Percentage of early leavers from education and training
	Percentage of people not in education, employment or training (Neet)
	Percentage of people participating in formal or non-formal education
	Literacy level of students
	Numeracy level of students
	Percentage of people with high level of ICT competencies
	Cultural participation
Work and life balance	Employment rate of people 20–64 years old
	Non-participation rate
	Transition rate (12 months' time-distance) from non-standard to standard employment
	Share of employed persons with temporary jobs for at least 5 years
	Share of low wage earners
	Share of over-qualified employed persons
	Incidence rate of fatal occupational injuries or injuries leading to permanent disability
	Share of employed persons not in regular occupation
	Ratio of employment rate for women 25–49 years with children under compulsory school age to the employment rate of women without children
	Share of population aged 15–64 years working over 60 hours per week
	Asymmetry index of family work
	Share of employed persons who feel satisfied with their work

Continued

Table 9.3 ISTAT-CNEL's Equitable and Sustainable Well-being measures (adapted from ISTAT, 2013) *continued*

Dimensions	*Indicators*
Economic well-being	Real per capita adjusted disposable income
	Disposable income inequality
	People at risk of relative poverty
	Per capita nominal net wealth
	People living in financially vulnerable households
	People living in absolute poverty
	Severe material deprivation rate
	People suffering poor housing conditions
	Index of subjective evaluation of economic distress
	People living in jobless households
Social relationships	Satisfaction with family relationships
	Satisfaction with friendship relationships
	Friends or neighbours to rely upon
	Percentage of children aged 3 to 10 years who play with their parents
	Provided aids
	Social participation
	Volunteer work
	Association funding
	Non-profit organisations
	Social co-operatives
	Generalised trust
Politics and institutions	Voter turnout
	Civic and political participation
	Trust in the Italian parliament
	Trust in judicial system
	Trust in political parties
	Trust in local institutions
	Trust in other institutions (fire brigade, police)
	Women and political representation in Parliament
	Women and political representation at regional level
	Women in decision-making bodies
	Women in the boards of companies listed on the stock exchange
	Median age of members of Parliament
	Length of civil proceedings

Dimensions	*Indicators*
Security	Homicide rate
	Burglary rate
	Muggings rate
	Robbery rate
	Rate of physical violence on women
	Rate of sexual violence on women
	Rate of domestic violence on women
	Fear to undergo sexual crime
	People feeling safe walking alone after dark
	People who was afraid of being victim a crime
	Elements of decay in the neighbourhood
Subjective well-being	Overall life satisfaction
	Leisure time satisfaction
	Expectations about the future
Landscape and cultural heritage	Endowment of cultural heritage buildings
	Per capita current expenditure of Municipalities for cultural heritage management
	Illegal building rate
	Urbanisation rate of areas subject to building restrictions
	Erosion of rural areas from urban sprawl
	Erosion of rural areas from abandonment
	Presence of historic rural landscapes
	Quality assessment of Regional programmes for rural development with regard to landscape protection
	Presence of Historic Parks/Gardens and other Urban Parks recognised of significant public interest
	Conservation of historic urban fabric
	People that are not satisfied with the quality of landscape of the place where they live
	Concern about landscape deterioration
Environment	Drinkable water
	Quality of marine coastal waters
	Quality of urban air
	Urban parks and gardens
	Areas with hydrogeological risks
	Contaminated sites
	Terrestrial protected areas
	Marine protected areas
	Areas of special naturalistic interest
	Concern for biodiversity loss
	Material flows
	Energy from renewable sources
	Emissions of CO_2 and other greenhouse gasses

Continued

Table 9.3 ISTAT-CNEL's Equitable and Sustainable Well-being measures (adapted from ISTAT, 2013) *continued*

Dimensions	*Indicators*
Research and innovation	Research intensity
	Patent propensity
	Percentage of knowledge workers on total employment
	Innovation rate of the productive system
	Percentage of product innovators
	Productive specialisation in high-tech and knowledge intensive sectors
	Internet use
Quality of services	Beds in residential health care facilities
	Waiting lists
	Citizens who benefit from infancy services
	Elders who benefit from home assistance
	Irregularity in electric power distribution
	Percentage of population served by natural gas
	Irregularity in water supply
	Urban waste disposal
	Separate collection of municipal waste
	Prison overcrowding
	Time devoted to mobility
	Density of urban public transport networks
	Composite index of service accessibility

for heritage preservation and maintenance' is justified not so much in financial terms, but rather as a proxy measure of the public choice in favour of cultural heritage out of many possible competing alternative allocations.

Conceived as new tools for orienting and evaluating sustainable and effective development policies, the perspective assumed by the three systems is mainly a top-down one. True enough, ISTAT–CNEL did promote a vast survey for weighting the key factors of well-being, and OECD's Your Better Life Index website allows its visitors to allocate their own preferred weights to the various dimensions. In essence, however, the (presumably benevolent) decision-maker has perfect knowledge of what is good for the well-being of his fellow citizens – the measures follow that knowledge. The territorialisation process has relevant bottom-up dynamics, almost always pluralistic and often conflicting, which hardly fit into that vision. Moreover, grasping the symbolic dimension of place or the intangible culture via top-down, objective indicators like those proposed in the three systems we are discussing is a very difficult task. 'Feeling at ease' in different places (home, neighbourhood, school, workplace, city, etc.), the awareness of the *genius loci* or of the cultural meanings of places, landmarks, etc., the ability to access and to take full advantage of the resources locally available are basic requirements for sustainable endogenous development. Measuring them and transforming them into policies is the challenge that lies ahead.

Concluding remarks: well-being and cultural sustainability

Despite the long-standing debate, there is no shared, univocal definition of well-being. The Stigltz-Sen-Fitoussi Report lists eight basic dimensions of well-being:

1 Material living standards (income, consumption and wealth);
2 Health;
3 Education;
4 Personal activities including work;
5 Political voice and governance;
6 Social connections and relationships;
7 Environment (present and future conditions);
8 Insecurity of an economic as well as physical nature.

Culture is not among the dimensions, nor is it mentioned in that report. It is clear, however, that each of the eight dimensions is culture-laden, culture-defined and culture-bound. Different cultures will fill each dimension in their own way.

In January 2014, four relevant international organisations (IFACCA, Agenda 21 for Culture, IFCCD and CAE) advocated the inclusion of a goal focused on culture in the Post-2015 Development Agenda: *Ensure cultural sustainability for the well-being of all.*

The document states that culture plays both an instrumental and constitutive role in development; it is both a means and an end. It contains an instrumental and transversal value, supporting and strengthening interventions in development areas but it is also a development priority in its own right, the constitutive basis of our life and, thus, a desirable end in itself. And, listing ten key targets (to orient policies and hence indicator-building), the document devotes one target to culture and sustainability:

> Build on culture to promote environmental sustainability. Access to essential environmental goods and services for the livelihood of communities should be secured through the stronger protection and more sustainable use of biological and cultural diversity, as well as by the safeguarding of relevant traditional knowledge and skills. Indeed, there is a significant interrelationship between culture and environmental sustainability due to the intrinsic link between cultural diversity and biodiversity, its ability to influence more responsible consumption and its contribution to sustainable management practices as a result of local and traditional knowledge.
>
> (IFACCA *et al.*, 2014: 9)

May those words inspire our future actions.

References

Barca, F. (2009). *An agenda for a reformed cohesion policy: A place-based approach to meeting European Union challenges and expectations* (independent report prepared at the request of Danuta Hübner, commissioner of Regional Policy). Ministry of Economics and Finance, Rome.

Bauer, R. (ed.) (1966). *Social indicators*, MIT Press, Cambridge, MA.

BG-FOC Friends of the Chair group on broader measures of progress (2014). *Some national, regional and international efforts and practices in the measurement of sustainable development and human well-being*, UN Statistical Commission, Forty-fifth session 4–7 March, Item 3(c) of the provisional agenda. Programme review: broader measures of progress (Mimeo).

Böhme, K., Doucet, P., Komornicki, T., Zaucha, J. and D. Swiated (2011). *How to strengthen the territorial dimension of 'Europe 2020' and EU Cohesion Policy*. European Union, ERDF, Warsaw.

Ciommi, M., Gigliarano, C., Chelli, F.M. and M. Gallegati (2013). *Behind, beside and beyond the GDP: Alternatives to GDP and to macro-indicators. Deliverable D3.1.* Seventh Framework Programme, European Commission. Available at: http://eframeproject.eu/fileadmin/Deliverables/Deliverable3.1.pdf (accessed 10 November 2014).

European Commission GDP and Beyond Projects (2009). Available at: http://ec.europa.eu/environment/enveco/pdf/SWD_2013_303.pdf (accessed 30 April 2015).

FOC – Friends of the Chair group on broader measures of progress (February 2014). *Some national, regional and international efforts and practices in the measurement of sustainable development and human well-being*. Statistical Commission Forty-fifth session 4–7 March, Item 3(c) of the provisional agenda. Programme review: broader measures of progress. Available at: http://unstats.un.org/unsd/broaderprogress/pdf/BG-FOC-Broader%20measures-Practices%20on%20broader%20measures%20of%20progress.pdf (accessed 20 May 2015).

Helliwell, J., Layard, R. and J. Sachs (eds) (2013). *World happiness report.* The Earth Institute, Columbia University, New York. Available at: www.earth.columbia.edu/sitefiles/file/Sachs%20Writing/2012/World%20Happiness%20Report.pdf (accessed 20 May 2015).

IFACCA, Agenda 21 for Culture, IFCCD and CAE (2014). *Culture as a goal in the post-2015 development agenda.* Available at: http://media.ifacca.org/files/cultureasgoalweb.pdf (accessed 10 November 2014).

ISTAT (2013). *Trends in well-being.* ISTAT, Rome. Available at: www.misuredelbenessere.it/fileadmin/upload/docPdf/Report_on_Equitable_and_Sustainable_Well-being_-_11_Mar_2013_-_Trends_in_well-being.pdf (accessed 30 April 2014).

Kennedy, R.F. (1968). *Remarks at the University of Kansas. March 18, 1968.* Full text: http://tinyurl.com/q4ygjgq (accessed 30 April 2014).

Kuznets, S. (1934). *National income, 1929–1932.* 73rd US Congress, 2nd session, Senate document no. 124, 7.

Miringoff , M. and M.L. Miringoff (1999). *The social health of the nation: How America is really doing.* Oxford University Press, Oxford.

Nordhaus, W.D. and J. Tobin (1972) Is growth obsolete?, pp. 1–80 in: Nordhaus, W.D. and J. Tobin (eds), *Economic research: Retrospect and prospect.* Vol. 5: *Economic Growth.* National Bureau of Economic Research. Available at: www.nber.org/chapters/c7620 (accessed 15 November 2011).

OECD (2007) *BRIDGE's gender and indicators cutting edge pack.* Available at: www.bridge.ids.ac.uk/reports_gend_CEP.html Indicators (accessed 7 May 2015).

OECD (2011). *How's life? Measuring well-being.* OECD Publishing, Paris.

Report of the World Commission on Culture and Development (1996). Available at: http://unesdoc.unesco.org/images/0010/001055/105586e.pdf (accessed 30 April 2015).

Royal Government of Bhutan (2009). *Tenth five-year plan. 2008–2013.* Gross National Happiness Commission, Thimphu. Available at: www.grossnationalhappiness.com (accessed 7 May 2015).

Stiglitz, J., Sen, A. and J.-P. Fitoussi (2008). *Report by the commission on the measurement of economic performance and social progress.* Available at: www.stiglitz-sen-fitoussi.fr/documents/rapport_anglais.pdf (accessed 16 January 2015).

Talberth, J., Cobb, C. and N. Slattery (2006). *The genuine progress indicator 2006: A tool for sustainable development.* Available at Redefining Progress: http://rprogress.org/publications/2007/GPI%202006.pdf (accessed 16 November 2009).

UNDP (1994). *Human development report 1994.* UNDP, New York.

UNDP (1995). *Gender empowerment index.* Available at: http://hdr.undp.org/en/content/gender-development-index-gdi (accessed 30 April 2015).

UNESCO (2001). *Universal declaration on cultural diversity.* Available at: http://unesdoc.unesco.org/images/0012/001271/127162e.pdf (accessed 30 April 2014).

UNESCO (2011). *Analytical framework.* Available at: www.unesco.org/new/fileadmin/MULTIMEDIA/HQ/CLT/pdf/Conv2005_CDindicators_Analytical_en.pdf (accessed 30 April 2014).

UNESCO (2014) *Culture for development indicators.* Methodology Manual. Available at: http://en.unesco.org/creativity/system/files/digital-library/CDIS%20Methodology%20Manual.pdf (accessed 9 February 2015).

United Nations General Assembly (2011). *Happiness: Towards a holistic approach to development.* Resolution adopted by the General Assembly on 19 July. Available at: www.un.org/en/ga/search/view_doc.asp?symbol=A/RES/65/309 (accessed 13 November 2014).

World Commission on Culture and Development (1987). *Our creative diversity: Report of the World Commission on Culture and Development.* Available at: http://unesdoc.unesco.org/images/0010/001055/105586e.pdf (accessed 23 April 2015).

10 Making territory through cultural mapping and co-design

How community practices promote territorialisation

Leonardo Chiesi and Paolo Costa

Human territorialisation (Chiesi, 2015) is a spontaneous and fundamental social process that has been the subject of intense debate since the mid-twentieth century. This debate has started to take territorialisation out of the unreflexive realm and instead turn it into an increasingly deliberate collective practice. We have therefore studied the ways in which two community practices, cultural mapping and co-design, can impact the process of human territorialisation.

Design in a social perspective

When we say 'design', we mean the wide set of practices, and related knowledge, by which intentions are inscribed in space (Adorno, 1967). In this view, any design act is the result of the intersection between two sets of intentions: those of the designer and those of the users (Figure 10.1). Designers conceive a spatial device with a purpose and advance an hypothesis on how it will be used. On the other side, users receive the device and invest it with their own intentions. When the act of design is successful, these two sets of intentions tend to overlap, as the users accept the designers' intentions and make them their own. But this is only one of three possibilities – the users may also not accept the designer's proposal or the users may also read into the spatial device an opportunity not intended by the designer. This means that when thinking about design in a social perspective, we must always consider the degree of congruence between the conceptual world of the designer and that of the user (Rapoport, 2005; Chiesi, 2010), and focus our analysis on the overlap between the two. Cultural mapping and co-design are two community practices with a strong relationship with design; they help to avoid an inadequate degree of congruence, thus minimising the chance of unsuccessful projects.

Cultural mapping and co-design

Cultural mapping is a process of collecting, recording, analysing and synthesising information in order to describe the cultural resources, networks, links and patterns of usage of a given community or group (Stewart, 2007; Duxbury *et al.*, 2015). The expression of the culture of a place encompasses a wide variety of

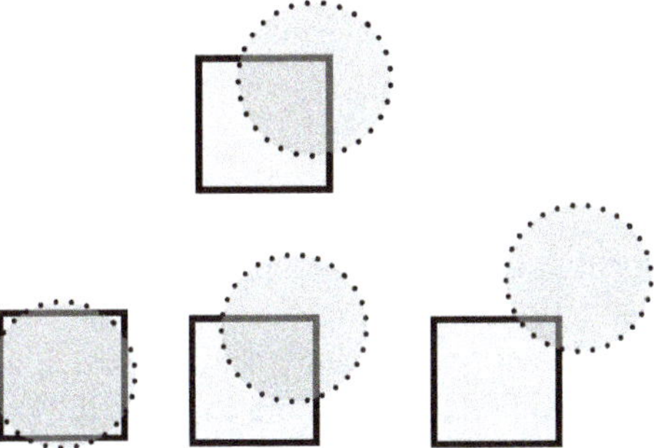

Figure 10.1 Design in a social perspective. Different degrees of congruence between two sets of intentions: those of the designer (square) and those of the users (circle)

Source: © Leonardo Chiesi.

tangible and intangible aspects of its past, present and even future life, each with a very specific nature. The description and analysis of each of them needs a specific set of tools that are chosen on a case-by-case basis. The choice of tools also depends on the goals of the cultural mapping process.

The relationship of cultural mapping with design can be multifaceted and acts mainly *ex ante*. As output, cultural mapping can produce a set of knowledge about a specific site or community that can be used as input for a design process that will take place there in the future. This knowledge contributes to subsequent design decisions that are more connected to the context and are better accepted and shared by the stakeholders who have been involved somehow in the cultural mapping process (e.g. citizens, end-users, partners, local authorities, and so forth). In some cases – and especially through tools that adopt a participatory approach, such as community mapping or participatory photography (Hague and Jenkins, 2004) – the involvement in a cultural mapping process of a community produces what we may call an 'identity effect' – a set of intangible outcomes that can indirectly foster a stronger sense of attachment of the community to its own place and its future. This place attachment is a crucial element of territorialisation.

Co-design – originally used in the industrial design field to create objects that are closer to the end-user's needs (Sanders and Stappers, 2008) – is a community practice that can adopt some typical cultural mapping tools (e.g. maps, photography or storytelling). It can operate at any levels of scale: from the design of small objects, such as street furniture, to service design, from architectural and urban design to urban and regional planning.

Other participatory design tools, in contrast, usually consult users before the design process starts, to study their peculiarities or needs, or long after it has started, to test ideas or prototypes (Simonsen and Robertson, 2013). Co-design, on the other hand, invites stakeholders to participate in the creative stage of design; their knowledge-built-on-experience can thus directly contribute to the design. This further reduces the distance between the design output and their needs and it can foster a stronger sense of attachment to design decisions. Because of their involvement, stakeholders do not see the design decisions as external impositions but rather as the result of their own action.

Relation with action-research

We believe that cultural mapping and co-design are particularly relevant to the research community because these methodologies are excellent instances of what is generally referred to as 'participatory action research' (Whyte, 1989) or, more recently, 'action-research' (Bradbury and Reason, 2001). Both cultural mapping and co-design offer a framework for transforming the object of study as well as simultaneously advancing knowledge about that same object. In other words, while trying to address social problems using the strongly reflexive and critical attitude typical of scientific practice, action-research has produced relevant theoretical outcomes (Friedman and Rogers, 2009; Gustavsen, 2008; Poonamallee, 2009). Cultural mapping and co-design both share the action-research assumption that academic research should be used to reduce the effects of oppression, symbolic domination (Bourdieu, 1998) or any form of inequality in general. To accomplish this goal, members of relatively powerless groups are involved in the construction of knowledge, in a critical examination of the world around them and in action to address social problems (see Stringer, 2007 and Hardina *et al.*, 2007 for an extensive critique). By giving researchers the chance to engage with the challenges of social situations that need change, action-research brings social science (and scientific research in general) closer to society.

Territorialisation

Community mapping and co-design practices promote territorialisation because they focus on the community's relationship with space. In contrast to most of the community techniques currently available, these practices specifically entail reflection on the surrounding environment. In the case of cultural mapping, space is the substratum of what is being mapped; in the case of co-design, space is almost invariably the active matrix for the design process (see Chiesi, 2015). The community is thus compelled to reflect on space and its implications, which pulls space out of the domain of the unreflexive. This process can foster many forms of territorialisation that are intended as bottom-up appropriation of space; it thus constitutes an antidote to the deterioration of space. One hypothesis is that de-territorialisation is also caused by a progressive decay of the spatially related elements diffused within a given culture and community mapping and co-design favour precisely the collective and deliberate elaboration of such essential components of culture.

Strategic choices: three key dimensions

Community projects can be classified by placing them on a three-dimensional space created by three coordinates (Chiesi and Costa, 2015). Projects usually operate in a budget-controlled and heavily purpose-oriented mode; the researcher-practitioner is therefore forced to choose a well-defined scope to pursue. The classification outlined below is meant to describe and evaluate the variety of the choices available, and to help those choices to be more deliberate. This is a fuzzy classification (Kosko, 1993) with heuristic value, rather than an epistemological typology that professes to capture the nature of reality: it is supposed to have practical value, rather than ontological. As such, this typology apprehends the majority of community practices as carried out today, but it does not exclude the possibility of cases that do not fit well with it.

Cultural mapping and co-design projects can be categorised by placing them along three axes – continua defined by a pair of extremes (Figure 10.2). The relationship between the opposites that define each axis is a trade-off: moving along the axis tends to decrease the salience of one in favour of the salience of the other. In this sense, the principle that defines the pole of the continuum tends to disappear but never disappears completely, even at the furthest point.

The first axis is defined by the identity/knowledge pair of opposites: on the one side are projects that intend to maximise the 'identity effect' while projects designed to produce data, or their 'knowledge effect', are found on the other side. The 'identity effect' is that largely intangible cluster of outcomes related to the community or group's self-awareness of resources and potential; in other words, it concerns the process of empowering the group towards a stronger sense of itself. The 'knowledge effect' concerns producing a maximal amount of data.

The second axis is defined by the pair past/future. Past-oriented projects are more interested in cataloguing heritage such as cultural assets stratified during the long duration of an historical past. Future-oriented projects strive to shape the community's tomorrow by mapping emerging resources, potential networks

Figure 10.2 A three-dimensional space to classify cultural mapping and co-design projects

Source: © Leonardo Chiesi and Paolo Costa.

and relationships, and by helping its members envision a desirable scenario for their development.

Finally, the third axis defines whether the cultural mapping project aims to promote an internal or external response. Is the main strategic objective to elicit a reaction from the insiders, some kind of reorganisation of resources or some self-managed initiative from the members of the group? Or is the intent of the project to help the community to engage in meaningful social, cultural or economic relations with the outside world? Is, for example, the purpose of the project to help the group become more visible from the outside as a first step towards rehabilitation or empowerment? Or is the purpose to attract economic resources from external operators that might see desirable opportunities in the community?

These questions must be answered early in the planning process. In the following case studies, we illustrate how this classification becomes useful and how these strategic choices might have a different impact on territorialisation.

Raising children's awareness about cultural heritage in Bethlehem

In 2007, one of the most visible contrasts in the urban landscape of Bethlehem, Palestine, was between the historical buildings that had been carefully restored by international organisations and other old buildings in private hands that were located just beside them. The latter often showed very visible alterations made by their inhabitants to satisfy their changing needs, usually with solutions and materials that highly compromised the buildings' historical value and which had little or no coherence with the surroundings. In short, such alterations were not culturally sustainable.

The sharp contrast between these two kinds of interventions was a sign of a deep cleavage between two completely different ways of seeing value in the very same stones, which led to clashing attitudes toward the buildings. This contrast also pointed to the lack of a coordinated approach to preservation that somehow involved citizens. So far they had been just passive actors of top-down interventions that often felt to them like yet another form of occupation of their territory.

This was the context at the beginning of the development of the Bethlehem Area Conservation and Management Plan (BACMP), the first case of adoption of a comprehensive and participatory approach to develop an urban plan in the Occupied Palestinian Territory. The plan aimed to preserve the cultural and environmental assets of the three Palestinian historic towns of Bethlehem, Beit Sahour and Beit Jala, and to contribute to creating sustainable conditions to revitalise them (Serrini, 2012). One of its goals was to develop a set of rules to define what kind of interventions, restorations and changes could be made to the buildings in each area of the towns according to their historical and cultural value. But no rule would have been accepted by the owners – and hence implemented by the municipalities – without a shared consciousness of the value of the historical heritage that those rules were trying to preserve. The main goal of the broad participatory strategy that we coordinated in the BACMP project was therefore to build this shared awareness. One of the actions adopted in the strategy was a community mapping process in the three towns.

Community mapping is a particularly powerful cultural mapping tool to involve local communities and reconnect them with their territory (Clifford and King, 1996). Despite its many different styles and variations (Corbet, 2009) one of its principles is that all the steps needed to produce a community map (analysing, selecting, prioritising and representing) push participants to develop a shared idea of the features that are particularly relevant in their place.

The main actors involved in this process were children aged between 11 and 14 years at nine schools located in the three municipalities. At that age, children were ready to actively and independently participate in the process but still young enough to form their views about their place without being overly strongly influenced by the views of their families.

For thirteen weeks the children were involved in a series of activities located both inside the schools and outdoors (Figure 10.3). The activities included a few lessons with experts and many visits to the streets of the children's towns, to see and touch what children slowly started to recognise as a tangible part of their own cultural and historical heritage. The children learned that their heritage also included human activities and features which were the intangible counterpart to its tangible elements. The main relevance for the BACMP project was that this long process helped the children to understand how the value and the preservation of their heritage were not only related to the most visited historical sites – such as the Nativity Church complex – but were also connected to the conditions of the rest of the cities' public and private spaces and to all decisions related to them. In short, they learned that heritage was far more connected to their own daily lives than they had known before.

The tangible outcomes of the project were maps, drawings and three-dimensional models made by the children using different techniques. But for the BACMP, the achieved intangible outcomes were much more relevant than the tangible maps created.

The children were the active participants but the project indirectly involved a wider audience: the teachers, other citizens participating in the activities, and the children's peers and their families who heard from the children what they were doing and learning in the project. A series of final events was another chance for them to show the products of their work to the rest of the community and to share how the whole process allowed them to discover a new sense of what their place and its heritage meant to them.

Reconnecting people to their place in San Pedro de Macorís

The city of San Pedro de Macorís lies on the southern coast of the Dominican Republic, at the estuary of the Higuamo river. In the first quarter of the twentieth century, thanks to the sugar cane industry, San Pedro was more attractive and cosmopolitan than the capital city. It was the only destination on the island of the Pan-American seaplane line connecting the United States to the Caribbean islands and South America.

Figure 10.3 Some of the activities of the Community Mapping process in the Bethlehem Area. Below, the making of one of the final maps

Source: © Bethlehem Area Conservation and Management Plan (BACMP).

A crisis ensued in San Pedro when the sugar cane market started to decline. In 1998, Hurricane Georges dealt San Pedro another heavy blow. Tourists no longer visit the city, preferring the beaches and the high rise hotels of Juan Dolio, a resort a few kilometres west of San Pedro. Despite some signs of resurgence, San Pedro is still a town with big social problems characterised by densely populated informal settlements and high crime rates. Only a few signs of its glamorous past remain in the historical centre. The Edificio Morey, the first three-storey cement building in the whole country (1915), was once the best hotel in town, but is now just a boarded-up monument to the crisis. Parco Duarte, the main square, has lost all its appeal; people now avoid its central tree-lined pathways. Towards the river, the boulevard that separates the cathedral square and the informal settlements of La Barca is – to use Lynch's categories (1960) – an impenetrable edge that separates two districts, with two populations that avoid all contact with each other.

These were the study areas of a workshop that we coordinated in 2012, with 30 advanced students of the School of Architecture at the local Universidad Central del Este. After a training in participatory techniques and co-design, the students were asked to involve citizens to fulfill the following goals: to develop new concept designs to renew Parco Duarte; to find new functions to regenerate the Edificio Morey; and to plan new strategies to reconnect La Barca and the city centre.

In Parco Duarte, the students attracted the citizens' curiosity and participation by locating their temporary headquarters in the square's central gazebo and by decorating it with the workshop banners. This helped students to gather citizen stories about the past, the present and the future of both the square and the city. This relationship inspired a set of design ideas that were then discussed again with citizens and modified according to their opinions and advice.

The same boards that boarded up the Edificio Morey were used – first to display photos, articles and documents that shed light on its glorious past; then to post the citizens' points of view about its possible new functions (Figure 10.4). These then formed the basis for a series of design proposals, which were again displayed on the boards to gather feedback from the citizens.

Because the interactions took place right *in* the study areas, both the citizens and the students were led to experiences that sometimes went far beyond the verbal exchange of information that the students were trying to produce. Some inhabitants of La Barca, for example, invited students inside their neighbourhood, which is usually off-limits to outsiders. Beside the emotional impact of discovering a place in their own city that they had never visited before, those students had the opportunity to see directly both how the people of La Barca lived inside the neighbourhood and how they related with the rest of the city. Further, the other citizens' surprise at seeing outsiders so interested in their place and their lives was another sign – if one were needed – for architects of the intensity of the social seclusion and the urgent need for reconnection with the city.

The results were different in the three areas (Parco Duarte, Edificio Morey and La Barca) due to the different forms and degree of the citizens' involvement. For Parco Duarte the proposals had a higher level of detail, correlated to easier interaction with the citizens. For the Edificio Morey and La Barca, the viability

Figure 10.4 Involving citizens in San Pedro de Macorís, working on the boards that boarded up the Edificio Morey, once a modernist landmark in the town

Source: © Leonardo Chiesi and Paolo Costa.

of the proposals was much lower. But even though some of the proposals were sometimes naïve, they were the result of an involvement that was a first step towards fostering the citizens' agency and their sense of connection and attachment to their own places. Although with different implications, this was true also for the students, because the process led to a change in their opinion about their city. From being a place that they had so far neglected, San Pedro and its community became interesting and potential fields for action for their future roles as architects and planners.

Involving citizens to co-design their own place

Marsaxlokk is a fishing village with a population of 3,000 located on the south-east coast of Malta. In 2010 it was involved in the project 'Mare Nostrum', together with other four port-cities of the Mediterranean: Carthage (Tunisia), Rhodes (Greece), Tartus (Syria, until 2011) and Tyre (Lebanon). All five cities share two cultural elements: Phoenician origin and a strong relationship with the sea. Through a wide range of research and participatory tools, the project aimed to make those cultural elements more meaningful, preserved and accessible by giving the citizens a greater role in the cities' regeneration strategies.

The historical cultural heritage of Marsaxlokk is relatively rich considering its small size. It includes a Phoenician archeological site, other historical and naturalistic elements in the surroundings and a range of symbolic and tangible aspects of the relationship with the sea, such as the characteristic decorations on the local fishing boats. The residents of Marsaxlokk were generally aware of the value of this heritage; but this was not very visible to the visitors, who usually only went to the village for the many fish restaurants on the waterfront and for the Sunday market, which was less and less related to fishing activities.

In 2012 we organised a six-day co-design workshop to change this relationship with cultural heritage in Marsaxlokk. The participants – about fifty local citizens and a dozen advanced architecture and design students from the Faculty for the Built Environment of the University of Malta – were invited to co-design an information strategy for the visitors of Marsaxlokk. The information strategy had to display the map of the city and the heritage trails that had been designed in previous stages of the project. But it also had to adopt creative ways to increase the visitors' awareness of Marsaxlokk's cultural heritage; and it had to be felt by citizens as 'theirs'.

Both the promotion before the workshop and the visibility of the hall that hosted the workshop generated a relatively strong and constant participation throughout all six days. This contributed to a much closer and structured interaction among participants than in the case of San Pedro. After an introduction to the workshop goals, the citizens started to work in groups with designers who had been previously trained in co-design. The sessions in the first two days were mainly occupied by citizens telling stories about themselves and their place and about how they related to it. This knowledge was annotated on maps of Marsaxlokk, of Malta and of the heritage trails, and on some other personal materials – such as old prints, family photos, newspapers articles that citizens brought with them (Figure 10.5). This stage helped designers to understand better from the citizens what Marsaxlokk had been in the past and what it was in the present, and what they expected it to be in the future. But it also inspired some design ideas on how to give projects a stronger relationship with the meaning of the tangible and intangible elements of the cultural heritage to the people of Marsaxlokk.

In the following days, these early ideas were transformed into design sketches. The citizens repeatedly discussed them with the designers and often called for design improvements, relevant both to them and tourists. Sometimes the citizens even proposed new ideas that were then developed by the designers. In this way, the citizens, with their knowledge about the local context, and designers, with their creativity and skills, both contributed to shape the final projects.

On the last day of the workshop, a Sunday, all the design proposals were displayed in an exhibition. Many people who had come from the rest of the island to attend the Sunday market (and who were in fact the main potential final users of the communication strategies) visited the exhibition, together with many other citizens who had not participated in the workshop. All the viewers were also invited to give their feedback on the projects with the aim of generating further improvements.

The design proposals were but one of the final outcomes of the process. The workshop was a chance for designers to appreciate that working with

Figure 10.5 Designers listening to stories about the village as told by community members in the early stages of the co-design workshop in Marsaxlokk

Source: © Davide Virdis.

non-professionals could be enriching and inspiring. For local participants it was a chance to bring about a reflexive attitude towards their heritage. As some of them explicitly mentioned, the experience disclosed how the heritage was connected to their everyday life and to their past, making them feel part of it. This made them understand that it was possible for them to actively contribute to designing the future of their community, even if many of them were too old to experience that future personally.

Discussion of the three cases in relation to the three dimensions

Each of the three abovementioned classifying dimensions (identity/knowledge, past/future, inside/outside) works as a trade-off. Any specific community practice cannot produce or relate to the maximum expression of the opposite poles of each dimension simultaneously. This can be achieved only by adopting more complementary practices that then act as tactics of a broader strategy. We now discuss the three cases to clarify this point.

The effects produced by community processes such as the one adopted in the Bethlehem area are obviously related to the first side of the identity versus knowledge dimension. By building maps in the Bethlehem area, children discovered its cultural and historical value and connected that value to their own life. Much more important than the maps themselves was the identity effect related to their reinforced sense of attachment to what they had mapped, and their deepened caring for its preservation and for the consequences of actions affecting it. The maps did not contain any data or knowledge useful for the planners. The process was only indirectly connected to the planning activity, as the new awareness produced was strategic to prepare the community for a better acceptance of the plan and of its effects, increasing the likelihood that the citizens would perceive the plan as a tool to manage their own historical heritage instead of it being an unwelcome top-down imposition.

At the other end of the identity/knowledge dimension, other kinds of community practices produce forms of knowledge that can complement more traditional social sciences data. These practices help to sketch a portrait of the community that is particularly deep, alive and connected to the processes that shape the locals' experience and everyday life. Co-design goes a step further, closing the gap between the production of this knowledge and the design phase. In San Pedro and in Marsaxlokk the designers needed a deeper understanding of the social and cultural context for which they were designing because such an understanding could make their projects more grounded and linked to that context. In these knowledge-focused processes, the identity effect produced was mostly a side effect. When the identity effect became stronger, as in the case of La Barca in San Pedro, the knowledge produced was more abstract and allowed only very general design decisions.

The three case studies are examples of tactics oriented towards both the poles of the past versus future dimension. Even though the effects of any process usually take place in the future, those effects can be created by looking back in time. In the case of Bethlehem, learning about its past led to acknowledgment of the value of an historical heritage.

When a community process is linked with a design stage the aim of which is to make something or to find a solution to a problem, those involved usually orient their gaze more to the future. This is particularly true for most co-design experiences, where design (future-oriented by definition) is a fundamental part of the process. Then the future of the community can be addressed in the short term, for example by designing something tangible on a small scale – like in Marsaxlokk – or in the longer term, such as by designing a complex strategy that will be enforced in years through a series of smaller steps. But other cultural mapping tactics that are not directly related to a design stage can also be oriented towards the future of the community. That would be the case, for example, for a process that focuses on specific cultural features that are related to youth and their activities (music, recreation, sport, etc.). It all depends on the focus of the map – what is mapped – and the strength of its connection with the future.

The last dimension, inside versus outside, is related to the internal or external origin of the reaction the practices are trying to stimulate. Different cultural mapping and co-design processes can point toward each of the opposite poles of this dimension, depending on how they have been designed. Both in Bethlehem and in San Pedro, for example, all of the actors directly and indirectly involved in the processes were from the same community; therefore, so were the reactions and the processes that the practices were trying to produce or activate. In other cases, such as in Marsaxlokk, the aim of such processes is to activate or capture a response that comes from outside, regardless of whether local citizens are involved in the practice.

How cultural mapping, co-design and the three dimensions play out in relation to cultural sustainability and territorialisation

The practices of cultural mapping, co-design and the three dimensions are connected to cultural sustainability as related to community development (Duxbury and Gillette, 2007). We focus here on some of the aspects and meanings that, according to Soini and Birkeland (2014), have been most commonly highlighted in the scientific discourse on cultural sustainability.

Cultural mapping is related to cultural sustainability if we stress the idea of culture as heritage – something handed down from previous generations and passed on to future ones. By definition, cultural mapping is a tool to list the tangible and the intangible instances of the cultural capital of a place. This is true whether cultural mapping aims to produce identity effects – as in the community mapping project in Bethlehem – or whether the aim is to build knowledge (in the form of a catalogue of those instances) that could then be used in a subsequent planning or design stage. For example, a community mapping process designed for the city of Tartus (Syria) aimed to list all tangible and intangible cultural instances of the city to then link them in touristic itineraries to attract visitors (Chiesi and Costa, 2015).

Cultural mapping processes can also successfully highlight another aspect of cultural sustainability: the human-nature relationship. Depending on the process design, cultural mapping can either lead to the study of the past to discover forms of the human-nature relationship that are more sustainable than in the current times or can focus on the future to seek new solutions that may guarantee so-called eco-cultural resilience. Much depends, of course, on how the participants are challenged with the constraints of any design stage. This is particularly relevant in co-design processes. In Marsaxlokk, for example, the locals placed the greatest emphasis on the cultural aspect of having a respectful relationship with the sea, and the architects' task was to propose ways to communicate that to visitors. Architects, designers and planners come from disciplines that increasingly address environmental issues in their research and practice. By working with those professionals, the non-expert participants have the chance to understand better how those issues are relevant in the decision-making process, be it related to a specific design problem or to the policy-making process.

Cultural mapping also helps to reveal the cultural diversity of a place and can represent the different perceptions and values related to its cultural capital. These differences can be highlighted during the steps of confronting and discussing what should go on the map. For instance in Bethlehem, the question of what had to be mapped revealed different opinions between the participating children and their teachers. When reading the maps after their workshop, administrators sometimes had yet another point of view. Cultural mapping can sometimes highlight strong inequalities in a community, while co-design can try to address this situation by developing new ideas for intervention. In San Pedro, for example, the architects realised – and then showed to the other citizens – the depth of the social and cultural cleavage in the spatial edge between the area of La Barca and the rest of the city. This new awareness reinforced their desire to search for a design that could somehow reduce the starkness of that socio-cultural-spatial border.

The cultural vitality of a community (Hawks, 2001) is strictly related to the above-defined 'identity effects' that cultural mapping processes can generate. In this respect, co-design can catalyse further cultural vitality, mixing those energies with creativity and transforming them into projects or even tangible products. In turn, these products can become a kind of stage to showcase the enhanced vitality in new ways. For instance, the Marsaxlokk citizens saw their self-designed information boards as not only a way to show their identity to visitors, but also as an ongoing way to continue to act on behalf of their community, for example by taking care of the boards and updating them.

From a cultural perspective, designers can be seen as outsiders relative to a community of users. As mentioned above, co-design aims to reduce the gap that exists in any act of design between the sets of intentions of these two collective actors. When users are the community of a specific place, co-design can help to reduce the distance between the cultural mindsets of insiders and outsiders of that community, whether those outsiders are the designers themselves or another group of users (e.g. tourists, such as the main end-users of the information boards in Marsaxlokk).

The inside/outside dynamic must be carefully considered when choosing and designing a community practice. This is not only in connection to the cultural vitality of a community but also to the economic viability that is linked to cultural sustainability. This is particularly relevant in those cases in which the resources needed to revitalise a community and to reveal its cultural capital can only be brought in from outside, through strategic choices aiming to attract tourists or new active cultural producers such as artists (Duxbury, 2013). Balancing endogenous and exogenous cultural stimulation is crucial in order to aim to achieve cultural sustainability, minimising unexpected outcomes. This often requires a large strategy that involves several complementary practices.

Conclusions

We have attempted here to bring the debate on territorialisation more down to earth by presenting a theoretical and empirical framework for cultural mapping and co-design. Researcher-practitioners who aim to understand and promote a community's appropriation of space must make several strategic choices that have a critical impact on the final outcome of the process. We hope to have contributed to raising their awareness of the implications of such choices. Our model provides a framework for identifying the foremost challenges inherent in any intervention, which means that this model can be generalised to some extent. But one must never forget that all cultural mapping or co-design projects are highly contextual and must be treated on a strictly case-by-case basis. Only an approach highly sensitive to local circumstances can aspire to avoid failure or irrelevancy.

Credits

This chapter is the result of a collaboration between the two authors. Leonardo Chiesi wrote the following parts: Introduction; Design in a social perspective; Relation with action-research; Territorialisation; Strategic choices: three key dimensions; Conclusions. Paolo Costa wrote the following parts: Cultural mapping and co-design; Raising children's awareness about cultural heritage in Bethlehem; Reconnecting people to their place in San Pedro de Macorís; Involving citizens to co-design their own place; Discussion of the three cases in relation to the three dimensions; How cultural mapping, co-design and the three dimensions play out in relation to cultural sustainability and territorialisation.

Acknowledgements

The Bethlehem Area Conservation and Management Plan (BACMP) was coordinated by architect Goffredo Serrini and was funded by the Italian Cooperation programme, under the supervision of UNESCO and the collaboration of the three municipalities of Bethlehem, Beit Jala and Beit Sahour, and of the Centre for Cultural Heritage Preservation of Bethlehem. The workshop in San Pedro de Macorís was organised by architect Francesco Gravina, Dean of the School of Architecture of the Universidad Central del Este. The workshop in Marsaxlokk was part of the activities of the EU co-financed project 'Mare Nostrum: A Heritage Trail along the Phoenician Maritime Routes and Historic Port-cities of the Mediterranean Sea' (2009–13), coordinated by professor Carlo Alberto Garzonio, University of Florence. The participating students were involved with the help of professors Anton Grech, Antoine Zammit and Lino Bianco of the University of Malta. Architect Fabio Ciaravella facilitated the design process of both the workshops in San Pedro de Macorís and in Marsaxlokk. We are sincerely grateful to all participants who were directly and indirectly involved in the three community processes analysed in this chapter. This work could not have been possible without them.

References

Adorno, T.W. (1967). *Funktionalismus heute. Ohne Leitbild. Parva Aesthetica*. Suhrkamp, Frankfurt am Main.

Bourdieu, P. (1998). *La domination masculine*. Seuil, Paris.

Bradbury, H. and P. Reason (2001). *Handbook of action research: Participative inquiry and practice*. SAGE Publications, London.

Chiesi, L. (2010). *Il doppio spazio dell'architettura: Ricerca sociologica e progettazione*. Liguori, Naples.

Chiesi, L. (2015). Territoriality as appropriation of space: How 'engaging with space' frames sociality. In: this book, Chapter 6.

Chiesi, L. and P. Costa (2015). One strategy, many purposes: A classification for cultural mapping projects, pp. 69–85 in: Duxbury, N., Garrett-Petts, W.F. and D. MacLennan (eds), *Cultural mapping as cultural inquiry*. Routledge, London.

Clifford, S. and A. King (eds) (1996). *From place to PLACE: Maps and parish maps*. Common Ground, London.

Corbett, J. (ed.) (2009). *Good practices in participatory mapping. A review prepared for the International Fund for Agricultural Development (IFAD)*. IFAD, Rome.

Duxbury, N. (ed.) (2013). *Animation of public space through the arts: Toward more sustainable communities*. Almedina, Coimbra.

Duxbury, N. and E. Gillette (2007). *Culture as a key dimension of sustainability: Exploring concepts, themes, and models*. Working Paper 1. Creative City network of Canada. Centre of Expertise on Culture and Communities, Vancouver.

Duxbury, N., Garrett-Petts, W.F. and D. MacLennan (eds) (2015). *Cultural mapping as cultural inquiry*. Routledge, London.

Friedman, V.J. and T. Rogers (2009). There is nothing so theoretical as good action research. *Action Research*, 7 (1): 31–47.

Gustavsen, B. (2008). Action research, practical challenges and the formation of theory. *Action Research*, 6 (4): 421–437.

Hague, C. and P. Jenkins (eds) (2004). *Place identity, participation and planning*. Routledge, New York.

Hardina, D., Middleton, J., Montana, S. and R.A. Simpson (2007). *An empowering approach to managing social service organizations*. Springer, New York.

Hawks, J. (2001). *The fourth pillar of sustainability: Culture's essential role in public planning*. Common Ground, Melbourne.

Kosko, B. (1993). *Fuzzy thinking: The new science of fuzzy logic*. Hyperion, New York.

Lynch, K. (1960). *The image of the city*. MIT Press, Cambridge, MA.

Poonamallee, L. (2009). Building grounded theory in action research through the interplay of subjective ontology and objective epistemology. *Action Research*, 7 (1): 69–83.

Rapoport, A. (2005). *Culture, architecture and design*. Locke Science Publishing Company, Chicago.

Sanders, E.B.-N. and P.J. Stappers (2008). Co-creation and the new landscapes of design. *CoDesign*, 4 (1): 5–18.

Serrini, G. (ed.) (2012). *Bethlehem area conservation and management plan: The plan as an alphabet*. UNESCO, Paris.

Simonsen, J. and T. Robertson (eds) (2013). *Routledge international handbook of participatory design*. Routledge, London.

Soini, K. and I. Birkeland (2014). Exploring the scientific discourse on cultural sustainability. *Geoforum*, 51: 213–223.

Stewart, S. (2007). *Cultural mapping toolkit*. Creative City Network of Canada and 2010 Legacies Now, Vancouver.

Stringer, E.T. (2007). *Action research*. SAGE Publications, New York.

Whyte, W.F. (1989). Advancing scientific knowledge through participatory action research. *Sociological Forum*, 4 (3): 367–385.

11 How to scale a territory

Experiences from the United States

Frans Padt

Introduction

This chapter describes how territories can purposefully be designed to attain greater sustainability at the territorial level and beyond. Consider these possibilities: Indian reservations as innovation hubs for an energy transition in the Southwestern United States. The historic city of Pittsburgh, PA, moving away from historic preservation of selected monuments to the revitalisation of all its vernacular neighbourhoods. A multi-modal transportation system in the Denver Region. Highway corridors in Massachusetts that integrate highways into natural territories. Restoring the water cycle in California at multiple levels of scale. All these examples are explained in this chapter to illustrate active human interaction with the environment, spurred by the desire for greater sustainability. Are these initiatives real? To a certain extent they are: stakeholders have come together, real initiatives are under way, money is invested and rules are adapted. We have studied these initiatives during a research seminar for fifth-year and graduate landscape architecture students at Penn State University. We discovered new design opportunities at the territorial level and beyond, and imagined how these initiatives could develop in the long run. This chapter presents our findings. The challenges and design opportunities for each initiative are explained, as well as the rescaling strategies and the role of 'culture' and 'sustainability' therein. We will also present the working method we developed for designing such strategies. The following section introduces theoretical background on the relationship between territories and scale, the concept of scale as a social construction and the process of territorialisation as a struggle between multiple actors.

Theoretical background

Different types of scales can be used to characterise territories (Cash *et al.*, 2006). The spatial scale is the most straightforward. This scale relates to the spatial extent of a territory and can include one or multiple landscapes, ecosystems, cities and infrastructures. The temporal scale is relevant as well to understand how the territory came into being. Typically a territory has a cultural and ecological history that helps to explain the specific qualities of the territory. The governance scale comprises the jurisdictions and institutions that govern the territory. Governance levels are typically tied to a specific actor such as a neighbourhood association, a municipality, a 'province', a national government or a supra-national entity (such as NAFTA or the European Commission). A territory can also be described by a management scale, that is the scale at which the resources of a territory are physically managed. Such management can range from large-scale sweeping radical interventions (e.g. demolition of old buildings), to projects (e.g. historic preservation), to specific tasks (e.g. tree maintenance). Finally, the knowledge scale of a territory is helpful to understand a territory. For example, is knowledge received from outside (typically abstract scientific knowledge) or created as indigenous knowledge (Fischer, 2000; Stoecker, 2013)?

One research challenge is how to assess the scales of a territory. Two basic approaches can be discerned: the positivistic and the social-constructivist approach. In the positivistic approach researchers measure scales with a measuring rod. They measure landscape characteristics like the drainage area of a stream, the size of bird habitats, the distribution of air pollution, commuter distance, landscape perceptions, soil characteristics, income distribution and the location of historic and cultural sites. Such landscape characteristics are holistically analysed and neatly classified into territories (Steiner, 2008). The essence of a positivistic attitude is that territories are already there and that the 'only' task of the researcher is to discover, measure and map them. The positivistic tradition is dominant in many spatially oriented disciplines in natural and social sciences. The social-constructivist approach differs in that it does not consider the researcher as an outside observer. According to this approach researchers observe space through a specific lens, or 'scale frame' (Hospes and Kentin, 2014). The researcher's preference for a particular scale is informed by, among other factors, the researcher's education and worldview, cultural background, academic and professional experiences, research traditions in the field and the institution the researcher is affiliated with. Demographers tend to look at large-scale demographic patterns, landscape architects typically prefer to work at the site scale and community workers often feel most comfortable at the local level. Scale here acts as a 'comfort zone'. These are of course generalisations because professions are not necessarily tied to one level of scale. Anthropologists can study large-scale cultural trends, village traditions and anything in between. More generally, the scale of observation influences what is observed, which makes it difficult to assess what the 'true' scale of a territory is. The 'observational scale' (scale frame) guides the decisions the researcher makes in every step of the research process, from problem definition to conclusions and recommendations. The social-constructivist attitude is that reality can neither be directly assessed nor objectively and universally known (Padt and Arts, 2014). For a social-constructivist studying territories this is extremely interesting because it opens the way to explore how and why people, organisations and society at large frame territories at a particular scale (Gupta, 2014). We have examined the case studies using this approach.

Until now, we have treated territories as a research object and we have seen that this research object is not pre-given but actively shaped by researchers. In disciplinary teams this process might not be noticeable if its members share the same scale frame, but in multi-disciplinary teams there will most likely be a debate on how to scale a territory. Some will emphasise large-scale geological or demographic patterns, others a particular set of landscapes or governance structures and others specific ecological or cultural sites. At some point the team will utilise a 'cookie cutter' and cut out a territory out of the overlapping and related layers of that territory. Unfortunately, rather than informing the reader of the scientific publication about the choices made, the chosen territory is typically presented as a plain scientific fact.

Actors outside academia that have a stake in the territory (politicians, community organisations, businesses) will also have a scale frame, but one that might not necessarily coincidence with the scientifically framed territory. When scientific territories become real territories to be governed they will bring in their own scale frames, such as administrative boundaries, watersheds, neighbourhoods and business zones. The question then arises whether scientific or 'public' considerations should be leading in the final definition of a territory. In practice, both considerations play a role, and often already do so during the research. From a social-constructivist point of view this is not necessarily a problem because scientists frame reality just like others and should thus not have precedence in the process of territorialisation.

We can now say that territories are not there waiting to be discovered, measured and mapped, but rather come into being through discourse. Territories-as-discourse are shaped by a multitude of actors, each bringing their own scale frame, discursively wrapped as a scalar narrative (Gonzáles, 2006; Hajer, 1995). These narratives are supported by scientific evidence, anecdotes and metaphors (such as 'compact city'). It is in a process of 'discursive struggle' that a compromise is reached on the definition of the territory, at least for the time being. The definition of a territory is a strategic decision. After all, in the 'agreed-upon' territory roads and houses are built, forests are cut down and preservation areas and resorts are fenced; these aspects in their totality make the territory-as-discourse into something real.

The word 'struggle' is used intentionally here because territorialisation (defining and shaping territories) is exactly that: a struggle between powerful and less powerful scientists, policy makers, politicians, citizens, business people and their organisations. Powerful actors have more resources (money, scientific reports, reputation, land, access to decision making, etc.) and more influence in the process of territorialisation than the less powerful. How is power and influence actually exercised? Territories are discursively formed, thus one smart strategy is to tell a persuading narrative and to pursue this narrative in the process of territorialisation (a 'sticky story', see Van der Stoep, 2014). The task for the researcher is to identify, unravel and understand how such narratives serve the values and interests of actors who tell them. Such research smoothly translates into the normative question whether the narrative is good or bad in itself or in its consequences. Every decision on the boundaries of a territory includes and excludes people, plants, animals, landscapes and the like and can therefore create 'spatial injustice' (Soja,

2010) and unsustainabilities when the territory only serves the interests of a few (think of gentrification pushing out tenants, nature conservation pushing out local tribes or large-scale economic development pushing out local retailers). The act of defining territories and territorialisation is thus not only a research issue but also a highly normative and political one.

In the context of this book we focus on territories as the focal level of analysis. Yet, as explained above, any territory is embedded in scalar relationships, both upwards (for example the global level) and downwards (for example the household level). It is extremely important to keep an eye on these wider scalar relationships when designing territories. This relational view on scale (Sayre, 2009) underlies our research, as explained in the next section.

Methods

This chapter describes research performed during a research seminar for fifth-year and graduate landscape architecture students at Penn State University. Besides the educational goal of the seminar (acquainting the students with scale-sensitive design), the primary research goal of the seminar was to define a rescaling strategy for an area currently facing sustainability challenges. The secondary goal was to develop a working method to develop such a strategy. The empirical material included five case studies selected to cover a wide range of scales, topics and geographical environments. From small to large, these case studies were: Kampoosa Fen (Massachusetts), Historic Districts in Pittsburgh (Pennsylvania), *Power Paths* (Arizona), High Speed Rail in the Denver Region (Colorado) and Ecosystem Services in California. The method used was a collaborative learning approach, using group work, interaction, role play, experimenting and reflection. This method was chosen not only because the research was done with students, but also because collaborative learning resembles the real world learning (and negotiation) process that is typically involved in the process of territorialisation (see above). Our method included a review of scale frames, a critical evaluation thereof and defining a rescaling strategy for the area. The details of this method were developed along the way and will for this reason be explained after the case studies.

Case studies and scalar strategies

We have supplemented our description of these case studies with a *post factum* reflection on the role of culture in the process of territorialisation for each case study. For our reflection we use the symbolic, reification and institutional cultural dimensions of territorialisation as outlined in Chapter 1 of this book.

Kampoosa Fen

Kampoosa Fen is located near Stockbridge in Berkshire County of the state of Massachusetts. The story of Kampoosa Fen starts thousands of years ago, at the bottom of this ecologically diverse fen. This small area of peaty wetland

(160 acres), currently overlooked by many in the surrounding communities, receives its water from streams and calcareous cold groundwater in the surrounding watershed. The fen is protected under the Massachusetts Wetlands Protection Act. The fen is in danger of being disturbed by salt runoff from the Massachusetts Turnpike I-90 that runs just north of the fen, right through its drainage basin. Runoff from snowmelt in the winter months carries the large applications of road salt into the fen, resulting in subtle changes in the chemistry of the fen and a decline in rare, native species.

While this seems a relatively small problem to solve, the actual operations causing this issue are working at a much larger scale. The transit system in Western Massachusetts is heavily dependent on cars and interstate highway travel. Because of this connection to all destinations and landscapes, the fen is the perfect opportunity to rebalance the transportation and ecological scales. By framing the ecological problem as a small-scale problem it is unlikely that the problem will be solved, considering the scalar and power imbalances between the transportation and state agencies and the local preservation groups. By scaling up in the ecological scale from the fen to the larger (Housatonic) watershed, the ecological interests become tantamount to the transportation ones. Rather than seeing infrastructure and ecology as opposite interests at different levels of scale, a new tri-state highway corridor could be created that integrates the two, celebrates the cultural landscape (the reification dimension) and helps the public to appreciate the local fen ecology (the symbolic dimension). Such a highway corridor would require close collaboration between the relevant departments of Massachusetts, Connecticut and New York and relevant organisations in the watershed (the institutional dimension). Such collaboration is not new: the Housatonic Greenway and the Berkshire Taconic Landscape are examples of multi-stakeholder projects across state boundaries that can serve as an example for developing highway corridors.

Historic Districts in Pittsburgh

Pittsburgh, Pennsylvania, is a city enriched with over 250 years of heritage, dating back to 1758 when British General John Forbes named the city after British Secretary William Pitt. Today the city is growing and looking to move towards the future while still trying to stay true to its historic past. Pittsburgh offers residents, communities and visitors thirteen city-designated Historic Districts and many nationally designated sites, park, and places. These places bring forth the history of Pittsburgh as well as celebrating the many nationalities that have come to make Pittsburgh home. A disconnect occurs, however, between three main actors within this preservation process: the city services, the national services and the communities and neighbourhoods. The city declares one series of designations, then the national level declares others. Communities and neighbourhoods do not have much say in the designation of historic places, and communities without historic designations are excluded from the preservation project.

Pittsburgh has great potential to become a cultural territory, especially if each neighbourhood were to be considered for its historic and vernacular value instead of considering only needlepoint places or unconnected chunks of the city. Scaling preservation to the neighbourhood level would enhance a sense of community and celebration of the unique qualities of each neighbourhood (the symbolic and reification dimensions). Yet a problem persists in the institutional dimension. Besides the disconnect between the city, national government and communities in designating historic places, the preservation of these places seems to be driven by a local 'growth machine' (Logan and Molotch, 1987) of politicians, local entrepreneurs, professionals, local media and conservation groups with vested interests in cultural preservation. This growth machine excludes community groups or entire communities from the preservation project. No common agreement about the rules of the game for historic preservation can be found. This lack of the institutional dimension may seriously hinder a more spatially just Pittsburgh as a cultural territory.

Power Paths

Power Paths (Boudart *et al.*, 2008) is a documentary that tells the story of coal mining in the Navajo and Hopi reservation in Arizona. The coal was piped as 'slurry' to the Mohave Generating Station that supplied energy to Phoenix, Las Vegas and Los Angeles. Coal mining brought revenues to the Navajo Nation in the form of royalties and employment, but also caused air pollution, groundwater depletion and dried-up springs. Moreover, many Navajo and Hopi families were not connected to the electric grid and had no running water. This situation illustrates the disconnection between the territory of the Navajo and Hopi reservation and the rest of the American Southwest, as well as the scalar imbalance between the gas and oil industry, the cities, and the reservation and its tribes. In the early 2000s, resistance grew against this situation. Some tribe members joined forces, organised protests and formed a coalition with environmental organisations (who were concerned about the air pollution in the nearby Grand Canyon) to end the coal mining. In 2005, the permit of the Mohave Generating Station was not renewed and the power plant was shut down and dismantled. The newly formed coalition ('Just Transition') perceived this as an opportunity to make a transition to sustainable energy as well as to compensate for the loss of jobs and royalties caused by the closing of the power plant and the mines. Nevertheless, coal is still mined in the reservation to operate the nearby Navajo Generating Station that is anticipated to run until 2044.

This case study is relevant in this book because 'culture' is an important mediator in this effort. The tribes motivate their activism by referring to their ancestors who had lived there for centuries and to the spiritual aspects of water. As one of the activists says in the documentary: 'We need to create a way of life where a community is not forced to cannibalise their mother in order to live' (Boudart *et al.*, 2008). This quote illustrates the importance of place for the tribes. The documentary also shows how wind and solar energy is a natural choice, considering the importance of natural elements in the Native American culture. These symbolic and reification dimensions characterise the Navajo and Hopi reservation as a 'territory'. In the institutional dimension the community has developed the capacity for self-organisation. They initiated and organised action and were able to mobilise widescale support and resources. Luloff (1990) refers to this capacity as the 'capacity to act', which develops as a result of both an internal drive and an external threat. The capacity to act is not bound to the territory of the tribes: the documentary suggests scaling out the Navajo and Hopi initiative to other Indian reservations and other already existing comparable initiatives across the southwestern part of the United States. Taken together, by further working on these cultural dimensions, the Navajo and Hopi 'territory' has the potential to become an important innovation hub for a future-oriented energy transition in the Southwestern United States.

High Speed Rail in the Denver Region

The Denver Region and the Southwestern United States face booming population growth within the next twenty-five years. As these cities develop, it will be very important to give consideration to the management of infrastructure, including transportation networks. Currently Denver, Colorado, is investing in a High Speed Rail (HSR) network to address issues of urban growth and to encourage sustainable, automotive-independent travel between nearby cities. In the long run, HSR can accommodate travel between cities at distances between 50 and 175 miles with total networks up to 500 miles, where HSR is much more efficient and economic than automobiles and planes. Tunnelling the HSR would make travelling through the mountains safer and faster and would provide reliable access to the ski resorts from Denver International Airport.

In scalar terms, the HSR requires long-term management and collaboration between governmental agencies in Colorado and the neighbouring states. However, local taxpayers and city dwellers might be sceptical about the benefits of HSR. A 'scale jump' exists between the interstate transportation network and the Denver neighbourhoods. The jump can be made smaller by 'scaling in' from this interstate network to create a multi-modal transportation system in the Denver Region. Such a system would make the Denver Region more sustainable, but a challenge remains because 'thinking big' characterises the institutional dimension of the Denver Region. In order for the Denver Region to become a real territory, in future planning the human scale should be brought back to maintain a sense of community and vital neighbourhoods (the symbolic and reification dimensions).

Ecosystem services in California

California currently faces severe drought – one of the many recurrent droughts documented in written records and climate data from the 1800s onward. Despite continued practice of conservation standards that developed out of necessity during these periods of drought, a sustained and increasing human population puts irreversible stress on a limited water table. The existing fresh water supply cannot support increased development, agricultural production, energy industries and a public/private sector without taking away from animal and plant habitats that depend on a certain quality and quantity of water. Losing the biodiversity provided by these natural ecosystems means a loss of ecosystem services that further compounds drought and climate extremes, and compromises landscape performance.

This situation cannot be fixed at one particular level of scale. Rather, we imagine a new regime of ecosystem services at different levels of scale: provisioning, regulating, supporting and cultural. Provisioning water services are based on the extraction of water for farmers, residents, tourists and industry. Water can be extracted from terrestrial fresh water systems or from the Pacific Ocean through desalinisation. Because the fresh water systems are under stress, desalinisation could be a relatively sustainable alternative if it is wind and solar powered and placed at the right locations. Regulating ecosystem services aim to fix and maintain the water system. This is typically done at the watershed level. Technical measures such as erosion and flood control, water quality protection, water purification and recycling of grey and black water for primary reuse can be part of such an effort. Typically, provisioning and regulating ecosystem services optimise the water system within existing land uses. Supporting ecosystem services, the third category, question this premise and seek to restore the regional hydrologic and nutrient cycles, including evapotranspiration, precipitation, infiltration, water storage, surface runoff and groundwater discharge. Rather than optimising water use, parts of the American Southwest would be reclaimed to restore basic ecological processes. In the light of future climate change, this would require a fundamental rethinking of the ecology, settlement patterns and demography in the region. Cultural ecosystem services, finally, focus not only on the water or ecological functions of the area but also on larger issues of human health, a well-functioning society, quality of life and altruism (knowing that in the future humans and non-humans alike will have access to nature's benefits). From this analysis it follows that there is no specific level at which territories can be defined. The current challenges in the Southwest require a multi-scale and multi-level approach. The watershed would be an obvious candidate as a territory, but we have seen that a watershed approach would be too limited for restoring the hydrological and nutrient cycles in the region.

Table 11.1 summarises the main findings of the case studies. The overall conclusion is that through 'scaling up, scaling in and scaling out', new culturally mediated territories can be created that help the case of sustainable development. These new territories all appeal to the human scale of ecological awareness, sense of community and spirituality (the symbolic dimension). They can become places where communities thrive and culture and the wider landscape is celebrated (the reification dimension). Finally, they require collaboration between institutions and may enhance the community's capacity to act (the institutional dimension). We hypothesise that territories that meet these criteria of the human scale, 'placefullness' and the community's capacity to act are more likely to establish spatial

Table 11.1 Overview of the cultural territorial dimensions, scalar strategies and sustainability benefits for the rescaled territories in each case study

Case study	*Cultural territorial dimensions*			*Scalar strategy*	*Sustainability benefit*
	Symbolic	*Reification*	*Institutional*		
Kampoosa Fen	ecological awareness	celebrates the cultural landscape	institutional collaboration	scaling up from the fen to create a highway corridor	balance of ecology and transportation
Pittsburgh Historic Districts	sense of community	celebration of neighbourhood qualities	problematic disconnect between organisations	scaling up from historic monuments to vernacular neighbourhoods at the city level	spatial justice between neighbourhoods
Power Paths	spiritual aspects of water and land	Native American culture	capacity to act	scaling out sustainable energy initiatives to other Indian reservations and the wider Southwest	energy transition
HSR Denver Region	sense of community	vital neighbourhoods	problematic mega planning	scaling in from the multi-state HSR network to create a multi-modal transportation system at the neighbourhood level	sustainable transportation
Ecosystem Services California	N/A			building multi-scalar and multi-level relationships	restoration of the hydrological cycle

justice and sustainability than culture-less territories. But territorialisation is not the silver bullet for sustainable development. As the California case study demonstrates, the complex multi-scale and multi-level problems cannot be solved at the territorial level only. Lagendijk *et al.* (2009) have referred to the tendency to reduce complex problems and solutions to the territorial level as the 'territorial trap'. For the other cases where appropriate territories could be identified, we should also keep in mind the relationships with higher and lower levels of scale or, in short, the relational nature of scale (Sayre, 2009; Massey, 2005). Territories, paradoxically, are both a means and a goal for sustainable development.

A working method

Our case study research method included a review of scale frames, a critical evaluation thereof and defining a rescaling strategy for the area. Along the way we developed a more specific working method that we think can be applied more generally in cases where scalar unbalances exist. This method is outlined below.

Review of scale frames

The very first step is to identify the research topic, the case study, the problem and the focal level of analysis. However, there is a potential problem in defining a focal level of analysis: it may be an artefact of one's own observation (see Introduction above). Moreover, because of the relational nature of scale, it is artificial to pinpoint an analysis at a particular level of scale without knowing exactly how that level relates to other levels of scale. One way out of these dilemmas is what Hackman (2003) has called 'bracketing'– a process by which the researcher examines 'influences on a focal phenomenon that are located one level of analysis above and one level below the focal phenomenon' (Ford and Sullivan, 2008: 427). As applied to spatial analysis, this means that a focal spatial level, its larger context and its smaller units are mapped at the same time. In the Pittsburgh case, for example, we made a reflective choice (see Introduction above) for 'Pittsburgh' as the focal spatial level, the greater Pittsburgh area as the context and the neighbourhoods as the smaller units. We could have also chosen the greater Pittsburgh area as focus, Northern Appalachia as context and Pittsburgh and other cities as the smaller units. Or, moving down, we could have chosen the neighbourhoods as focus, Pittsburgh as context and the housing blocks as the smaller units. Because there is no way to be absolutely sure that the correct brackets are chosen, we believe that reflecting on the choices should be an essential part of step 1. Such a reflection could include the problem at hand, the social and biophysical aspects of the region, one's own scale frame ('comfort zone'), expectations of others and available resources. It is important to note that during this step no territories are delineated because no critical evaluation of scale frames has taken place yet (see below). More fundamentally, there is a risk that one might select an obvious territory that represents the interests of the powerful (Callon and Latour, 1981), but one that is not necessarily just and sustainable.

We have adopted the scale matrix of Cash *et al.* (2006) to explore the scale frames of the actors that appeared to be relevant in each case study for the defined brackets. The word 'frames' means that at this stage we were primarily interested in the scales that the relevant actors put forward, rather than in our own scale interpretations. For the *Power Paths* case we relied on the documentary and background information found on the internet. For the other case studies, literature reviews were performed. Each case study revealed many scale frames and we found the Cash scale matrix a useful tool to show this and to unravel the complex cross-scale and cross-level relationships. We used the matrix as a heuristic tool, rather than as rigid analytical scheme, in order to not lose sight of these relationships. Because we were examining scale frames of actors we introduced the actor scale as a separate scale. We also decided that the actor scale could replace the jurisdictional and institutional scales because of the close relationship between these three scales. The spatial and temporal scales were used in each case study, but the levels were different in each of them. The network and management scales were used in most case studies, but again with case-specific levels. For some case studies a cultural scale, an ecological scale and a transportation scale were added. The result of this step is an overview of actors and the levels of scale they use. We deployed different creative methods to visualise this relationship: a separate matrix for each actor, colour coding, labelling each level of scale with an actor and a narrative account. Overall, a scale matrix, which should include the actors, is useful for the review of scale frames when used in a heuristic, flexible and creative manner.

Critical evaluation

Having mapped the scale frames of actors, the next step was to clarify how they related and whose scale frame was more or less dominant. During our case study research the scale matrix turned out to be unsuitable for this. Instead we crafted a 'creative map' for each case study. The goal of these maps was to identify how actors and their scale frames related spatially. First, places and actors were mapped and represented with symbols, shapes, labels, colours, brief narratives and sketches. Some maps were to scale and others represented spatial relationships in a more abstract way. Relationships were visualised with arrows. Second, the scale frames were added and their dominance was visualised with bigger or smaller bubbles, the labels XS to XXL or other means. Scale dominance was assessed qualitatively, according to the power and influence of the related actor (based on the information sources). Third, we assessed the scalar configuration and identified winners and losers, which could include people, organisations, ecosystems, cultural sites and other elements that were visualised on the map. On some maps the winners and losers were represented with emoticons.

During the next step, the actual territories were carved out of the complex web of relations. The basic criterium for the scale of the new territory was: can the new territory help sustainable development at multiple levels of scale, including the territorial? In the previous section territorial and non-territorial rescaling strategies had been presented. A review of the cultural dimensions of these new territories revealed that the human scale, placefullness and the community's capacity to act are the bonding factors for such territories.

Conclusions

Territorialisation is one of the scalar strategies actors can deploy to achieve greater sustainability at multiple levels of scale. Because there is no absolute measure by which to delineate the appropriate territory, territorialisation should be seen as a negotiation process between actors who each bring different scale frames to the table. Having an overview of the actors' scale frames is an important first step for successfully negotiating the appropriate territory. Herein lies an important task for the researcher. The next step is to review these scale frames against criteria for spatial justice and sustainability to prevent the negotiated territory serving only the interests of the powerful. We hypothesise that territories that represent the human scale, placefullness and the community's capacity to act are more likely to establish spatial justice and sustainability than culture-less territories. There is a close relationship between these three territorial dimensions. The human scale connects people materially and spiritually to their local ecology and community. In this way a territory is no longer an abstract notion but a real, placefull place where communities thrive and culture and the landscape are not a decor but a place where people live their real lives. Leo Tolstoy, in Anna Karenina, illustrates this point well when he writes:

> To Konstantin Levin the country was the background of life, that is of pleasures, endeavors, labor. To Sergey Ivanovitch the country meant on one hand rest from work, on the other a valuable antidote to the corrupt influences of town, which he took with satisfaction and a sense of its utility. To Konstantin Levin the country was good first because it afforded a field for labor, of the usefulness of which there could be no doubt. To Sergey Ivanovitch the country was particularly good, because there it was possible and fitting to do nothing.
> (Tolstoy, 2003: 223).

It is likely that territories to which people are really connected enhance their capacity to initiate and organise action and to mobilise widescale support and resources for the development of their territory. The rich literature on community development in the United States (e.g. Wilkinson, 1991) supports these observations and could give deeper insight into the processes of territorialisation and sustainability.

Acknowledgements

The case studies for this study were performed as a part of a research seminar for fifth-year and graduate landscape architecture students at the Department of Landscape Architecture at The Pennsylvania State University. I am grateful to Abhinandan Bera, Eric Gabriel, Lara Nagle, Patrick Nelligan and Emma Pritchett for their original ideas, creative work and inspiring discussions during the seminar.

References

Boudart, B., Abbe, J., Coyote, P. and P. Michelson (2008). *Power Paths*. Native American Public Telecommunications, Inc., Menlo Park.

Callon, M. and B. Latour (1981). Unscrewing the Big Leviathan: How actors macro-structure reality and how sociologists help them to do so, pp. 277–303 in: Cetina, K.K. and A.V. Cicourel (eds), *Advances in social theory and methodology: Toward an integration of micro- and macro-sociologies*. Routledge and Kegan Paul, Boston.

Cash, D.W., Adger, W.N., Berkes, F., Garden, P., Lebel, L., Olsson, P., Pritchard, L. and O. Young (2006). Scale and cross-scale dynamics: Governance and information in a multilevel world. *Ecology and Society*, 11 (2): 8–19.

Fischer, F. (2000). *Citizens, experts, and the environment: The politics of local knowledge*. Duke University Press, Durham and London.

Ford, C.M. and D.M. Sullivan (2008). A multi-level process view of new venture emergence, pp. 423–470 in: Mumford, M.D., Hunter, S.D. and K.E. Bedel-Avers (eds), *Multi-level issues in creativity and innovation*. Elsevier, Oxford and Amsterdam.

Gonzáles, S. (2006). Scalar narratives in Bilbao: A cultural politics of scales approach to the study of urban policy. *International Journal of Urban and Regional Research*, 30 (4): 836–857.

Gupta, J. (2014). 'Glocal' politics of scale on environmental issues: Climate change, water and forests, pp. 140–156 in: Padt, F.J.G., Opdam, P., Polman, N. and C. Termeer (eds), *Scale-sensitive governance of the environment*. John Wiley & Sons, Oxford.

Hackman, J.R. (2003). Learning more by crossing levels: Evidence from airplanes, hospitals, and orchestras. *Journal of Organizational Behavior*, 24 (8): 905–922.

Hajer, M.A. (1995). *The politics of environmental discourse: Ecological modernization and the policy process*. Oxford University Press, Oxford.

Hospes, O. and A. Kentin (2014). Tensions between global-scale and national-scale governance: The strategic use of scale frames to promote sustainable palm oil production in Indonesia, pp. 203–218 in: Padt, F.J.G., Opdam, P., Polman, N. and C. Termeer (eds), *Scale-sensitive governance of the environment*. John Wiley & Sons, Oxford.

Lagendijk, A., Arts, B. and H. Van Houtum (2009). Shifts in governmentality, territoriality and governance: An introduction, pp. 3–10 in: Arts, B., Lagendijk, A. and H. van Houtum (eds), *The disoriented state: Shifts in governmentality, territoriality and governance*. Springer, Heidelberg.

Logan, J.R. and H.L. Molotch (1987). *Urban fortunes: The political economy of place*, University of California Press, Berkeley and Los Angeles.

Luloff, A.E. (1990). Community and social change: How do small communities act?, pp. 214–227 in: Luloff, A.E. and L.E. Swanson (eds), *American rural communities*. Westview Press, Boulder.

Massey, D.B. (2005). *For space*. SAGE Publications, London.

Padt, F.J.G. and B. Arts (2014). The concept of scale, pp. 1–16 in: Padt, F.J.G., Opdam, P., Polman, N. and C. Termeer (eds), *Scale-sensitive governance of the environment*. John Wiley & Sons, Oxford.

Sayre, N.F. (2009). Scale, pp. 95–108 in: Castree, N., Demeritt, D., Liverman, D. and B. Rhoads (eds), *A companion to environmental geography*. Wiley-Blackwell, Oxford.

Soja, E.W. (2010). *Seeking spatial justice*. University of Minnesota Press, Minneapolis.

Steiner, F.R. (2008). *The living landscape: An ecological approach to landscape planning*. Island Press, Washington DC.

Stoecker, R. (2013). *Research methods for community change: A project-based approach.* SAGE Publications, London.

Tolstoy, L.N. (2003). *Anna Karenina.* Barnes & Noble Books, New York. Original work serialized in Russian between 1875 and 1877.

Van der Stoep, H. (2014). *Stories becoming sticky: How civic initiatives strive for connection to governmental spatial planning agendas.* PhD thesis, Wageningen University, Wageningen.

Wilkinson, K.P. (1991). *The community in rural America.* Greenwood Press, New York.

12 Culture matters. Planning processes and approaches towards urban resilience in European cities and urban regions

Two examples from Brussels and Ljubljana

Jenny Atmanagara

Introduction

Today 75 per cent of the European population lives in cities and urban regions (EEA, 2012). City-dwellers represent a melting pot of different social groups with diverse interests, attitudes and values. Because citizens spend their daily life on the local level, identity and sense of place can lead them to increase their commitment to the design of their living environment. Both the cultural diversity and the commitment of local players are important factors to consider when discussing the adaptability of urban systems.

Global challenges such as climate change, loss of natural resources and increasing urbanisation are becoming more apparent. More frequent and extreme heat waves in southern and central Europe are forecast, while precipitation is expected to increase in northern Europe (Greiving *et al.*, 2011; IPCC, 2007). How can the stakeholders of European cities and urban regions cope with the impacts of global challenges? Which approaches, strategies and measures do they already apply?

Local communities must be sensitised to the need to adapt to changing circumstances. New roles for the municipalities are emerging to foster the capabilities of these local groups. Urban planning provides strategic governance towards an adaptive management of cities and urban regions by developing and implementing adequate responses and workable solutions. In doing so, urban planners constantly work in an ambivalent stress field: on the one hand, as planning experts they are expected to produce knowledge and insight on a planning case; yet – unlike most fundamental researchers – planners are involved in the related political process; they have to set certain goals in a normative way and they must balance these with the reasonable interests of various groups of civil society.

Urban planners find the concept of resilience attractive for two reasons: 1) it addresses the need for adaptive management of urban systems, including social learning on the local level, and 2) it offers a combination of analytic and normative settings.

From diverse concepts of resilience to place-based approaches and territorialisation

Since its beginnings in the 1970s, the concept of resilience has evolved from discipline-specific definitions, such as found in environmental psychology (Werner, 1971) or ecology (Holling, 1973), to a broader approach covering diverse phenomena that is now used in various disciplines. Urban planners have chosen the concept of socio-ecological resilience as most applicable because they usually work at the human-nature interface and have to solve social and environmental problems at the local or regional scale.

Socio-ecological resilience is understood as the ability of a system to learn from catastrophic events and to adapt to changing environmental conditions, both reactively and proactively (Pickett *et al.*, 2004; Folke, 2006; Walker and Salt, 2006; Birkmann *et al.*, 2011; Christmann *et al.*, 2012). Other definitions, such as the concept of 'engineering resilience' (Hollnagel, 2006), stressed the ability of a system to absorb shocks and restore itself (i.e. to 'bounce back') to its initial state (Holling, 1973). In contrast, the concept of socio-ecological resilience turns to an approach of 'bouncing forward' or transforming the system to suit the changed circumstances (Table 12.1).

The increasing popularity of the term 'resilience' may lead to it becoming another buzzword, similar to 'sustainable development', with its vague definition and numerous fields of application (Scoones, 2007). Although the concept of resilience and the concept of sustainable development show certain similarities, such as their elastic character (Porter and Davoudi, 2012), they must be clearly distinguished (see Table 12.2). To enhance resilience in social-ecological systems, change rather than constancy must be embraced (Walker and Salt, 2006; Rees, 2010). This implies a dynamic form of sustainability. Resilience can be either desirable or undesirable, unlike sustainability, which implies maintenance of preferable system states (Carpenter *et al.*, 2001). Resilience, a system's ability to act, has uncertain results; in contrast, sustainability often follows a more normative approach (Redman, 2012). Ahern (2011) equates sustainability with a

Table 12.1 Types of resilience (source: Atmanagara *et al.*, 2013)

Types of resilience	
Ecological	which disturbances can be tolerated while the system remains functional (Walker *et al.*, 2005)
Engineering	the ability to return to a stable equilibrium point after disturbance (Pickett *et al.*, 2004)
Spatial	how different areas have varied responses to a disturbance (Walker *et al.*, 2005)
Socio-ecological	the ability of a system to adapt and adjust to disturbance (Pickett *et al.*, 2004)

Table 12.2 Comparison of the terms 'sustainability' and 'resilience' (source: Atmanagara *et al.*, 2013)

Sustainability	*Resilience*	
Elastic concept	Elastic concept	Porter and Davoudi (2012)
Embraces constancy	Embraces change	Rees (2010)
Preferable	Desirable or undesirable	Carpenter *et al.* (2001)
Outcome specified in advance	Uncertain results	Redman (2012)
Fail-safe	Safe-to-fail	Ahern (2011)
Control change and growth	Adaptive capacity for reorganising and recovering without changing state	Ahern (2011)

'fail-safe' approach that aims to achieve stability, manage systems effectively and control change and growth. In contrast, the 'safe-to-fail' approach of resilience accepts change and uncertainty and builds an adaptive capacity for reorganising the system and enabling recovery. Increased resilience is considered a prerequisite to achieving sustainability (Ahern, 2011). Resilience can therefore be understood to reconfigure and facilitate the basic principles of sustainability in response to a particular temporal or spatial context, accepting that the only constant is change. With its focus on sudden, unexpected events and the societal responses to them, the concept of resilience is primarily connected to short-term periods. Yet in the long run, the combination of many adaptive cycles and the evolution of (new) systems can also contribute to enhanced sustainability.

The concept of resilience has come into planning science only recently. The recent emergence of urban resilience in planning policy discourse has been highlighted by Wilkinson (2012), who stressed the necessity to understand what the integration of social-ecological resilience ideas into urban planning means in practice. Urban resilience prioritises the identification of the unpredictable, non-deterministic processes and disturbances to which a city might be vulnerable, learning about the past and possible future scenarios in terms of direct and indirect consequences, frequency and scale (Ahern, 2011). Folke *et al.* (2005) refer to this continuous process of learning, adapting and adjusting as 'active adaptive management', where policies are regarded as hypotheses and management actions become experiments to test those hypotheses, recognising the inevitability of change and uncertainty. The aim is to achieve an understanding of the dynamics of a system so that it can be managed 'towards a desirable trajectory', in spite of the significant social and institutional barriers to realising adaptive co-management (Wilkinson, 2011). Adger *et al.* (2009) has even argued that issues of value, ethics, risk, knowledge and culture construct societal limits to adaptation, but that these limits are mutable. Adger *et al.* (2013) has demonstrated how culture mediates changes in the environment and society and has elucidated the shortcomings in contemporary adaptation policy.

Huitema *et al.* (2009) set out aspects of adaptive co-management including an emphasis on the role of local governance, public participation, an experimental approach to resource management and management at a bioregional scale. Urban resilience therefore recognises a key role for municipalities. It supports public participatory action research, which builds social capital by setting up a 'mutually respectful dialogue' (Pickett *et al.*, 2004) that recognises the knowledge people have of local systems and their own actions.

The link between the concept of resilience and the concept of culture becomes evident here. Soini and Birkeland (2014) identified seven storylines on 'cultural sustainability' in the scientific discourse over the last decade. The storyline of eco-cultural resilience emphasises the need to consider both cultural and ecological aspects in the development process and to require inter- and trans-disciplinary collaboration at a territorial regional level. The storyline of eco-cultural civilisation illustrates a certain distrust of environmental management systems and programmes to solve environmental problems, and stresses the importance of education and the role of bottom-up initiatives for enhancing cultural evolution (Soini and Birkeland, 2014). These notions present the link that connects urban resilience, placed-based approaches and territorialisation.

As seen in the section below presenting the empirical results, place-based approaches are always developed and implemented in a certain local and/or regional context. The activities and interventions implemented by key agents in European cities and urban regions can be interpreted as cultural practices of the local stakeholders. The processes of development and implementation of these practices are influenced by certain cultural characteristics of the local and regional institutions. Since the concept of resilience refers to the adaptability to changing environmental conditions and the capability of urban systems and societies, this contribution also addresses the co-production of society and environment with regard to the impacts of global challenges.

Objective, approach and methodology

Our goal was to generate a better understanding of the role of culture in planning processes working toward urban resilience. We explore relevant planning approaches, strategies and measures in diverse European cities and urban regions. Since to date only a few cities or urban regions have embraced the concept of resilience in their public policies and formal planning, the focus of this survey was on informal planning and bottom-up initiatives from various members of civil society. In such planning processes, collaboration between various stakeholders and transfer of knowledge play important roles.

This contribution is based on empirical results from surveys conducted during the years 2012 and 2013 as part of the FP7 project 'TURAS – Transition towards Urban Resilience and Sustainability' (TURAS, 2011). The main objective was to explore the approaches, strategies and measures of European cities and urban regions in regard to urban resilience and sustainability. We carried out a survey that captured related programmes, projects and initiatives during the last decade in the cities of Aalborg, Brussels, Dublin, Ljubljana, London, Nottingham, Rome, Rotterdam, Seville, Sofia and Stuttgart. The questionnaire comprised 19 questions on the cities' objectives of sustainable development and urban resilience, the key agents' actions on settlement development and urban resilience, the main strategies and measures related to land use and urban regeneration, and an idea of the cities' future activities. At the time of writing, the response rate had reached 73 per cent (8 questionnaires).

The objective behind the survey was not to be statistically representative, but rather to map the different planning contexts in a number of European cities and urban regions. The aim of the survey was to understand better the impact of different contexts on planning. It should be treated as a baseline investigation of the cities' political strategies and measures in regard to urban resilience and sustainability. The limited number of respondents as well as the high heterogeneity of the answers to the questionnaire make it nearly impossible to make a systematic comparison of the approaches, strategies and measures in the European cities and regions.

Finally, the potential transferability of the approaches, strategies and measures between European cities and urban regions can be questioned or should at least be tracked more closely. Tangible assets, such as design ideas, are quite easy to transfer to other places, but planning processes and approaches do not transfer so easily. Transferability to other local contexts can be limited by these factors:

- the diverse foci and different areas of application of public policies and planning (European, national, regional, local);
- the coherence of the related laws or lack thereof (despite great efforts to harmonise European legislation, coherence is not always found);
- the various traditions, routines and cultures of the different planning systems and local administrations;
- the diversity of the local contexts in regard to economy, society, culture, ecological systems; and
- the different meanings and understanding of concepts and terms in the various European languages.

Heterogeneity of planning approaches in European cities and urban regions

The survey revealed a high level of heterogeneity of approaches, strategies and measures in the participating European cities and urban regions. Using a bottom-up methodology, we identified four main planning approaches:

i) formal transformation approach;
ii) integrative planning approach;
iii) experimental land use approach;
iv) participative approach.

i) The formal transformation approach represents the classical way of 'top-down planning' by the state and its public authorities. The overall objectives related to this planning approach are sustainable and balanced urban development, economic growth and competitiveness, social balance and participation of civil society, and the protection of the natural environment. The instruments to implement these objectives are mainly legislation, plans on different scales, architecture competitions, etc. The focus of this approach is to limit urban sprawl; in the foreground are measures related to house building, improving the technical infrastructure and promoting the social and cultural infrastructure. Resilience, a relatively new concept in urban planning, is hardly recognised in many public policies and related planning documents. If it is considered at all, the concept is mainly used in regard to risk management and natural hazards, by developing emergency plans for certain urban districts and departments. Quite often it is used in a similar way to sustainability.

ii) The integrative planning approach tries to combine different uses and functions for the same area. The overall objectives are to build resilient infrastructures and to upgrade recreation areas. For example, when constructing public green infrastructure (e.g. parks or public green spaces), planners try to integrate retention areas for flood prevention or preserve cold air lanes. In order to reduce the flow of traffic and to improve the quality of life, the promotion of sustainable mobility is promoted and supported, e.g. by expanding the network of bike paths. This approach is often initiated and co-financed by the public authorities; however, true success depends on the involvement of civil society and a variety of social groups.

iii) Over the last decade, a certain distrust of official planning interventions has given rise to the experimental land use approach. The European financial crisis has revealed the low economic resilience of many European cities and urban regions. As a result, investments in construction projects are declining in many European countries, particularly in northwestern Europe, where construction projects have often been financed by private investors or by public-private partnerships. Currently, various projects and measures are being developed and implemented in an experimental way on the neighborhood level. Measures such as the temporary use of empty buildings or urban gardening aim to improve urban quality of life, create attractive and livable cities and strengthen the participation of civil society. These projects, which are often initiated and implemented by artists and designers who explore the urban space for their art activities and temporary interventions, typically involve citizens or social groups from the start.

iv) Besides formal participation in planning processes, the public authorities of a number of European cities and urban regions have developed certain strategies and measures to increase participation. Whereas formal meetings and workshops are often limited to a selection of representatives, the participative approach involves members of civil society from the very beginning of planning processes, to reach as many citizens as possible (including marginal groups) and develops strategies and measures in a bottom-up manner. The instruments applied are round table meetings, open space workshops, online platforms, etc.

The planning approaches outlined above are part of the different planning systems in European cities and urban regions. They serve as guiding principles for transforming society towards urban resilience. Because social transformation requires cultural evolution, these planning approaches are always developed and implemented within a certain regional and/or local context. Cultural determinants such as the intensity of collaboration between key agents, education, knowledge transfer and access to information shape the evolution of urban planning. In practice, however, European cities and urban regions mostly apply more than one of these approaches in order to solve their problems.

Examples of strategies and measures towards urban resilience in European cities and urban regions

How can European cities and urban regions build more resilient structures to address the impacts of climate change, loss of natural resources and urban sprawl? How does culture mediate these processes? For urban planning, three main issues are determinant:

- urban management with regard to urban resilience is characterised by a high complexity due to the diversity of sometimes competing sub-systems within cities, e.g. energy production systems and water supply;
- urban planning can no longer be applied in a top-down manner, but must consider the interests, attitudes and values of diverse groups of civil society;
- available space is often limited in European cities and urban areas, especially in locations with a strong economic infrastructure.

The planning approaches that seem most promising for fostering urban resilience are those that try to integrate different functions for the same area, involve local citizens and manifold social groups, and constantly evaluate and redevelop the existing strategies and measures. Urban space should be seen as a laboratory for testing and continually improving certain projects and measures to enhance urban resilience. This evolutionary way of planning is illustrated by the two examples below of European cities and certain areas within those cities.

Parckdesign Project in Brussels, Belgium

Parckdesign is a biennial project dedicated to public space planning and initiated by Brussels Environment and the Brussels Ministry for Environment, Energy and Urban Renovation. Editions of Parckdesign prior to 2012 emphasised the creation of eco-designed urban furniture for existing Brussels parks. In contrast, the 2012 edition, called Parckdesign2012–GARDEN, aimed to reinterpret industrial wastelands, leftover spaces and interstices in Brussels (Parckdesign, 2012). This edition was coordinated by Architecture Workroom Brussels and a multidisciplinary team of curators. The scope of action focused on Anderlecht and Molenbeek, districts where the residents have the least access to green spaces. Contemporary landscape architects, designers and artists designed and implemented ten urban interventions on former 'wastelands'. The aim was to create a circuit of areas where people could meet and spend time together by either activating vacant areas or reactivating abandoned urban sites and public spaces. By linking up these vacant spaces, a network of public spaces and green spaces emerged at regional level that emphasised the potential of these sites.

This biennial project illustrates both the experimental approach and the participatory approach mentioned above. By selecting multidisciplinary team members who are familiar with the place and by proposing cooperation with inhabitants and local stakeholders, Parckdesign 2012 has become an integral part of the mechanism of local dynamics. This cultural event brings projects to life, some of which achieve long-term viability thanks to the involvement of different local partners and associations. The aim of these interventions is to question the value of these new public spaces, open them up and subtly transform them.

More than a cultural event alone, the Parckdesign2012–GARDEN event is an opportunity to test another method of city-making. It creates a setting where the role of deserted spaces can be considered and the capacity for transforming the city is increased by working on the smallest urban units – the neighbourhoods. By reusing vast tracts of wasteland, involving the inhabitants, bringing the issue of biodiversity into focus, and by providing *in situ* teaching, it contributes to the diverse dimensions of sustainability. With its experimental and participative approach on the local level, including inter- and transdisciplinary collaboration as well as education and bottom-up initiatives, it covers both the storyline of eco-cultural resilience and the storyline of eco-cultural civilisation in regard to cultural sustainability (Soini and Birkeland, 2014). Hence, this project provides flexible and adaptable solutions and therefore strengthens urban resilience in the short term. If the building of resilience is indeed a prerequisite of achieving sustainability (Ahern, 2011), this project then contributes to the diverse dimensions of sustainability in the long term.

The concept of territorialisation and the role of culture are reflected in this project in several dimensions. By involving the inhabitants and local stakeholders actively and from the very beginning, this project adds to the sense of place, place-making and place attachment, identification and identity of people, valorisation and the commitment of people to certain places, as described in the symbolic dimension of territorialisation. This project refers to the reification dimension of territorialisation in two ways: first, the project areas are structured through occupation, use and transformation of the land; and second, certain cultural practices are applied on the spot in an artistic and creative manner for community vitality and community planning. Finally, its participatory approach, which includes collaboration and self-governance, changes the rules of the game and routines of institutions and organisations as described in the institutional dimension of territorialisation.

Community District Tabor in Ljubljana, Slovenia

The project 'Bottom-up Urban Regeneration through Cultural Industries' is located in the neighbourhood of Tabor in Ljubljana city. Its aim is to revitalise the community district (Marn, 2011). A number of local organisations gathered together to enhance the quality of life in this area. The main objectives are to improve identity and a sense of community, to foster social cohesion and to create an attractive living and meeting place for the inhabitants. The project is financed indirectly through the Municipality of Ljubljana, the district community budget and European funds.

In the centre of this neighbourhood, Tabor Park has been revitalised as the core of a comprehensive renewal of the Tabor district (Prostoroz, 2013). The local inhabitants could express their needs and wishes for the design of the public space to the mayor of the municipality of Ljubljana. The implemented measures included installing park equipment such as tree lights and bird houses, tables and Wi-Fi to work in the park, a hammock and canvas chairs for relaxation, playground equipment and renovated sport areas. During the late spring and summer months, daily sports, cultural and social activities were organised, such as literature reading, slackline and table tennis tournaments, bowling and other cultural and social events.

The programme was designed in close cooperation with local people and organisations as well as institutions involved in culture, education and sustainable and spatial development. Among others the Cultural Quarter of Tabor Society (KČT – Društvo Kulturna Četrt Tabor) has been set up with the aim of strengthening the cooperation between individuals and organisations in the field of culture and encouraging activities in the neighbourhood. This society addresses the problems of sustainable development with expert support from the Institute for Spatial Policies and publishes the *Tabor* magazine, which contains information and stories about the neighbourhood and the KČT.

This project revitalises public space in the city centre and encourages the local community to participate in the design and use of the park. Various activities throughout the year for inhabitants and tourists (e.g. cultural, sports and educational events, market days, educational workshops, etc.) contribute to urban regeneration through cultural industries in a bottom-up manner. Similar to Brussels, this project uses an experimental and participative approach on the local level. By fostering inter- and transdisciplinary collaboration, providing education activities and fostering participation, it refers primarily to the storyline of eco-cultural civilisation in regard to cultural sustainability, but also includes elements of the storyline of eco-cultural resilience (Soini and Birkeland, 2014). It builds a sense of responsibility and community on the neighbourhood level, thereby generating social capital, which is regarded as an important prerequisite for urban resilience (Pickett *et al.*, 2004; Huitema *et al.*, 2009).

The concept of territorialisation and the role of culture are addressed here in different ways. The active involvement of local inhabitants and stakeholders in developing Tabor Park and the surrounding district installed a new form of community planning and certain cultural practices that refer to the reification dimension of territoriality. By occupying, using and transforming the area, the local people created a new place to live. When considering the role of art, creativity and cultural activities, agency is seen to mediate the planning process and interventions. The place-making approach and valorisation process of this project also refer to the symbolic dimension, where people commit themselves and bind themselves to a certain place. In doing so, they also change the norms, rules and routines of organisations and institutions, thereby addressing the institutional dimension of territorialisation.

Discussion and conclusions

In this chapter we have used the concepts of urban resilience and cultural sustainability to examine the role of culture in planning processes and planning activities of European cities and urban regions. The empirical research within the TURAS project led us to discern four main planning approaches (formal, integrative, experimental and participative), which are often observed in combination. These planning approaches can help to foster urban resilience and transform local and regional societies. In the two examples from Brussels and Ljubljana, planning focused on urban regeneration, land redevelopment and place-making by local stakeholders.

The municipality and/or the neighbourhood appear to be the appropriate level for action to combat global challenges such as climate change, loss of natural resources and urban sprawl. However, in planning practice, the required processes often take too long to cope with sudden and unexpected events such as natural disasters. Existing planning instruments, e.g. local development plans, can help to identify suitable areas for particular uses. But the political process to implement such plans and weigh the interests of diverse stakeholders is time-consuming, which makes these instruments quite inflexible and incapable of dealing with new, sudden problems. The next step is to find a more flexible and adjustable framework which can be implemented in stages.

The municipality and its neighbourhoods can serve as a laboratory to test new ideas and solutions. In this perceivable and valued environment, the diverse stakeholders from public administration, civil society and the economy can generate workable solutions for future urban development. The experimental land use approach seems to be the most advanced approach to thinking 'out of the box' and to enhancing urban resilience. In this approach, social learning, creativeness and innovation are initiated and social capital is assembled, which are considered important prerequisites for urban resilience. Many of the local projects can be interpreted as building urban resilience in the short term, which contributes to sustainability in the long term.

European cities and urban regions share a common triad of objectives including economic vitality, quality of life and social balance, but they follow different planning approaches and processes. Depending on the specific impact of global challenge(s) and the local context of the cities and regions, specific strategies and measures are developed and implemented. The experimental and participative planning approaches used in the cases of Brussels and Ljubljana show a number of elements related to cultural sustainability, e.g. inter- and trans-disciplinarity, high creativity, bottom-up approach, etc. These planning approaches, strategies, and measures refer first to the symbolic and reification dimension of territorialisation, but can influence the institutional dimension in the long term as well.

In this context, culture serves as a mediator (Adger *et al.*, 2013) to develop adequate problem-solving to combat the impacts of global challenges and to foster urban resilience. When urban planners use experimental and participative approaches to design their concepts and plans, they support co-production of workable solutions together with the stakeholders who live and work in the specific area. As shown by the cases from Brussels and Ljubljana, such an understanding of urban planning comes close to the storylines of eco-cultural resilience and eco-cultural civilisation within the concept of cultural sustainability (Soini and Birkeland, 2014). Planners mostly work at the human-nature interface and therefore have to consider both natural and cultural issues. Their work is determined by both the natural environment as well as the requirements of society. A better understanding of the specific cultural factors and the cultural context in planning areas would improve the planners' concepts, plans and designs. But to date this knowledge has been mostly absent in the education and training of urban planners.

Urban resilience of European cities and regions requires both short-term strategies and measures to adapt immediately to sudden events and changing conditions, as well as a long-term transformation of society. The latter is deeply determined by cultural factors. Social transformation requires a paradigm shift, leaving the stability-oriented concept of sustainability behind, and reaching instead for an adaptive and more flexible approach (Wilkinson, 2012). The concept of urban resilience is now well-known in the Anglo-Saxon countries, but most of the other European countries have either just started to consider this concept in their public policies or do not use the term at all. Professional bias among many urban planners and designers hinders the implementation of a concept that questions their own profession, which is highly stability-oriented and normative. Integrating this cross-sector concept into the daily routines of urban planning and adjusting it to the existing administration will be a major task, as the majority of the administration is still organised in sector-related departments. However, more and more European municipalities are embedding the idea of continuous change, which goes along with emerging new roles for municipalities and urban planners.

The approaches, strategies and measures of European cities and urban regions reveal the culturally-determined social capital that currently exists in many European cities and regions. The cases from planning practice imply a high level of creativity and innovation, which are regarded as preconditions for an evolutionary way of planning, and a social transformation towards urban resilience. Still, more attention should be paid to the back-loops of these interventions, the evaluation and continuous improvement of planning processes and results, as well as to the limited transferability of planning solutions due to diverse planning systems and cultural diversity in European cities and urban regions.

Acknowledgements

I express my sincere thanks to my colleagues from the TURAS project, in particular Philip Crowe from the University College Dublin and Eva-Maria Stumpp from the University of Stuttgart for their input on the concept of urban resilience, and the many fruitful discussions that helped to focus my thoughts. In addition, I thank the project leaders Johann Jessen (University of Stuttgart) and Karen Foley (University College Dublin) for sharing their knowledge and professional experience.

References

Adger, N., Barnett, J., Brown, K., Marshall, N. and K. O'Brien (2013). Cultural dimensions of climate change impacts and adaptation. *Nature Climate Change*, 3: 112–117.

Adger, N., Dessai, S., Goulden, M., Hulme, M., Lorenzoni, I., Nelson, D.R., Naess, L.O., Wolff, J. and A. Wreford (2009). Are there social limits to adaptation to climate change? *Climatic Change*, 93: 335–354.

Ahern, J. (2011). From fail-safe to safe-to-fail: Sustainability and resilience in the new urban world. *Landscape and Urban Planning*, 100 (4): 341–343.

Birkmann, J., Böhm, H.R., Buchholz, F., Büscher, D., Daschkeit, A., Ebert, S., Fleischhauer, M., Frommer, B., Köhler, S., Kufeld, W., Lenz, S., Overbeck, G., Schanze, J., Schlipf, S., Sommerfeldt, P., Stock, M., Vollmer, M. and O. Walkenhorst (2011). *Klimawandel und Raumentwicklung. E-Paper der ARL nr 10.* Akademie für Raumforschung und Landesplanung, Hannover. Available at: http://shop.arl-net.de/glossar-klimawandel-raumentwicklung.html (accessed 19 March 2012).

Carpenter, S., Walker, B., Anderies, J.M. and N. Abel (2001). From metaphor to measurement: Resilience of what to what? *Ecosystems*, 4: 765–781.

Christmann, G., Ibert, O., Kilper, H. and T. Moss (2012). *Vulnerability and resilience from a socio-spatial perspective: Towards a theoretical framework.* Leibniz Institute for Regional Development and Structural Planning, Erkner. Available at: www.irs-net.de/download/wp_vulnerability.pdf (accessed 21 September 2012).

EEA – European Environment Agency (2012). *Urban adaptation to climate change in Europe: Challenges and opportunities for cities together with supportive national and European policies*. EEA Report No. 2/2012. Office for Official Publications of the European Union, Luxembourg.

Folke, C. (2006). Resilience: The emergence of a perspective for social-ecological systems analyses. *Global Environmental Change*, 16: 253–267.

Folke, C., Hahn, T. and P. Olsson (2005). Adaptive governance of social-ecological systems. *Annual Review of Environment and Resources*, 30: 441–473.

Greiving, S., Csete, M., Davoudi, S., Fleischhauer, M., Holsten, A., Kropp, J., Kruse, S., Langeland, O., Ligtvoet, W., Lindner, C., Lückenkötter, J., Peltonen, L., Jacqueline, R., Sauri, D., Schmidt-Thomé, P. and K. Schneller (2011). *ESPON climate: climate change and territorial effects on regions and local economies.* The ESPON 2013 Programme. Available at: www.espon.eu/export/sites/default/Documents/Projects/AppliedResearch/CLIMATE/inceptionreport_final.pdf (accessed 30 November 2012).

Holling, C.S. (1973). Resilience and stability of ecological systems. *Annual Review of Ecology and Systematics*, 4: 1–23.

Hollnagel, E., Woods, D.D. and N. Leveson (eds) (2006). *Resilience engineering: Concepts and precepts*. Ashgate, Aldershot.

Huitema, D., Mostert, E., Egas, W., Moellenkamp, S., Pahl-Wostl, C. and R. Yalcin (2009). Adaptive water governance: Assessing the institutional prescriptions of adaptive (co-) management from a governance perspective and defining a research agenda. *Ecology and Society*, 14 (1): 26

Marn, T. (2011). *Bottom-up urban regeneration through cultural industries*. Institute for Spatial Policies, Ljubljana. Available at: http://ipop.si/en/2011/11/30/bottom-up-urban-regeneration-through-cultural-industries (accessed 6 November 2014).

IPCC – International Panel on Climate Change (ed.) (2007). *Fourth assessment report: Climate change 2007 (AR4)*. Intergovernmental Panel on Climate Change, Cambridge.

Parckdesgin (2012). Available at: www.parckdesign.be/en/content/parckdesign-2012 (accessed 7 May 2015).

Pickett, S.T.A., Cadenassso, M.L. and J.M. Grove (2004). Resilient cities: Meaning, models, and metaphor for integrating the ecological, socio-economic, and planning realms. *Landscape and Urban Planning*, 69: 369–384.

Porter, L. and S. Davoudi (2012). The politics of resilience for planning: A cautionary note. *Planning Theory & Practice*, 13 (2): 329–333.

Prostoroz (2013). *Park Tabor*. Available at: http://prostoroz.org/eng/index.php?/the-tabor-park/about (accessed 6 November 2014).

Redman, C. (2012). Resilience and sustainability. Keynote lecture at the *1st International Conference on Urban Sustainability and Resilience*. London: University College London. Available at: www.ucl.ac.uk/stream/media/swatch?v=158a9dcac4ef (accessed 6 November 2014).

Rees, W.E. (2010). Thinking 'resilience', pp. 25–40 in: Heinberg, R. and D. Lerch (eds), *The post carbon reader: Managing the 21st century's sustainability crises*. Watershed Media in collaboration with Post Carbon Institute, California.

Scoones, I. (2007). Sustainability. *Development in Practice*, 17 (4–5): 589–596.

Soini, K. and I. Birkeland (2014). Exploring the scientific discourse on cultural sustainability. *Geoforum*, 51: 213–223.

TURAS (2011) *Transitioning towards urban resilience and sustainability*, Seventh Framework Programme. Large-scale integrating project. Theme Env. 2011.2.1.5-1: Sustainable and Green Cities, Brussels.

Walker, B. and D. Salt (2006). *Resilience thinking: Sustaining ecosystems and people in a changing world.* Island Press, Washington DC.

Werner, E. (1971). *The children of Kauai: A longitudinal study from the prenatal period to age ten*. University of Hawaii Press, Honolulu.

Wilkinson, C. (2011). Social-ecological resilience: Insights and issues for planning theory. *Planning Theory*, 11 (2): 148–169.

Wilkinson, C. (2012). Urban resilience: What does it mean in planning practice? *Planning Theory & Practice*, 13 (2): 319–324.

13 Re-creating and celebrating place(s) in designated space(s)

The case of Wales

Eifiona Thomas Lane, Siân Pierce, Arwel Jones and Ian Harris

Introduction

The cultural history of Wales is broadly understood as that of changing patterns of Welsh language usage and often media commodified (and stereotypic) images of historical activities associated with the heavy, carbon-based industries of coal and slate extraction and processing of raw materials, e.g. steel and aluminium, on which the UK's industrial revolution was greatly dependent. Use of the Welsh language within communities across Wales records a contraction in the numbers of Welsh speakers, yet global networks of Welsh communities persist. During the historical period of industrialisation, the drive for greater and cheaper productivity led to tensions and voicing of protest which decimated communities across Wales geographically and socio-culturally, and led to stagnation of the economy, outmigration of young people and a loss of social and cultural capital.

The declining extractive industries and heavy, metal-based manufacturing heralded an increasing shift post 1945 towards protection and designation of significant swathes of the Welsh countryside, guarding against development whilst extending the areas available to recreation and for conservation of landscape and nature (for instance, turning farm lands into the three National Parks). Reactions to and resistance of the pressures for designation, protection and conservation are evinced by long-standing (and ongoing) local and national campaigns to withstand external development, imposition of policy and regulation. Across Wales, a coalition of campaigners have emphasised the themes of housing and work with particular focus placed upon community and linguistic priorities.

In this chapter we look at the relationship between cultural processes and defined places and their dynamic interaction within multi-layered policy contexts committed to sustainable development. In the empirical part of the chapter, a range of recent case studies illustrate sustainable community-scale development which celebrates the local and strongly resonates with multidisciplinary definitions of cultural sustainability: 'The relationship between place and space as well as the relationship between humans and their environment seem to be among the crucial concerns when conceptualising cultural sustainability' (Stylianou-Lambert *et al.*, 2013). Finally, in the discussion, we highlight the need for local resourcing and actions to engage all stakeholders in celebrating the locally defined significance of place, space and cultural sustainability while maintaining resilience through developing local economic gain.

Place, space and the significance of a sense of place has been the focus of academic discourse, when 'space feels thoroughly familiar to us, it has become place' (Tuan, 1977: 73) whilst Dale *et al.* (2008: 268), writing about sustainable community development initiatives in three Canadian communities, note the lack of discussion of the 'interplay of space, place and sustainability'. At the same time, the United Nations acknowledge that 'culture is a source of enrichment and an important contributor to the sustainable development of local communities, peoples and nations, empowering them to play an active and unique role in development initiatives' (United Nations, 2011: 1).

The cultural place called Wales

In 2002, the Welsh Assembly Government published the document 'Creative Future – A Culture Strategy for Wales' which made a number of significant assertions:

> Culture is not a luxury in our lives, or a mere embellishment to the material tasks of daily existence. It is the texture of our living. Our culture is the aggregate of our actions and aspirations, interests and passions, values and beliefs [...] This cultural strategy has two starting points: first, that culture is a central rather than a peripheral issue in public policy, second, that a cultural strategy must release the energies not only of individuals but also of our local and national communities ...
>
> (Welsh Assembly Government, 2002: 3 and 41)

The 2014 Welsh Government report 'Culture and Poverty' investigated harnessing the power of the arts, culture and heritage to promote social justice in Wales and acknowledged the Power of Place, *Cynefin* and Community:

> *Cynefin* has no equivalent in English. It means to have both a sense of place, and time; to be conscious of identity, and of belonging. It is a term which is already coming into use as an indicator of the intent and character of public programmes linked to their physical surroundings ... In many parts of Wales, as the years of industrialisation recede and the landscape changes, and as rural life is invaded by modernism in all its forms, many children do not know, or are losing touch with, the history of the place they live'.
>
> (Welsh Government, 2014c: 49)

Rodwell (2007) and Sinclair (1998) offer explanations of *Cynefin* which are on a par with the German phrase *heimat* as being a deep connectedness between place and individual – where one is born and brought up and also the 'environment to which one is naturally acclimatised' (Dale *et al.*, 2008: 269). Much of the visual arts, written culture and landscapes of Wales remain iconic, often arising from a notion of *Cynefin* which we contend is wider than simply attachment to place.

They are also increasingly being utilised as bases from which many festivals, local, national and international, are being developed. Literature and performance festivals (*eisteddfodau*) are exclusively and purposively Welsh medium competitive events and differ in their orientation to traditional festivals. They are locationally specific, have national significance and are reinvigorating social and cultural capital on a national and local scale – especially within the creative and performing arts. Festivals and agricultural shows, particularly thematic food heritage festivals, have burgeoned in the past decade or longer, with celebration of indigenous skills and landscapes of food production that are distinctive and local. Despite the opportunities for showcasing new policy initiatives and funding streams – as well as opportunities for sharing policy initiatives and networking across sectors – a great debate continues about the value of funding such activities in respect of their future sustainability from a European Union grant support or aided perspective. However, celebrating such local cultural outpourings has become a mainstay of the understanding of distinctiveness and its role in promoting the conservation of cultural diversity, including networks of similarity across Europe and beyond. Pierce *et al.* (1997) describe the traditional celebrations of The Welsh Heartland – *Y Fro Gymraeg* – and the need for a sensitive policy framework to support cultural local dynamism, while 'safeguarding amenity and wildlife conservation and which would derive its priorities from the socio-cultural characteristics of the communities it serves' (Pierce *et al.*,1997: 317).

Describing the 'space' called Wales

Since 1997, the 20,779 km^2 area of Wales (of which roughly 80 per cent is devoted to agriculture) is now a devolved region of Britain. There have been three phases of devolution – the first two of which operated under the Government of Wales Act 1998. The subsequent 2006 Act introduced two models of devolution and the National Assembly elected from May 2011 to May 2015 operates under the second model. Wales has fewer powers than Scotland and Northern Ireland and is the only country in the Union in which powers are 'conferred', or given, by the United Kingdom Parliament.

Measuring 274 km from north to south, and 96 km from east to west at its shortest points, with a 1200 km coastline, it has three National Parks, five Areas of Outstanding Natural Beauty (AONB), 33 Blue Flag beaches and six UNESCO World Heritage sites (Welsh Government, 2013). The population of Wales has been estimated at 3.1 million, up from 2.7 million in 1971 and predicted to rise to 3.5 million by 2081. The rise has been attributed to natural growth, and a net inflow of migrants from other parts of the United Kingdom to the country in 2012 was 5,300 (Welsh Government, 2014a).

Local governance across the political region is currently administered through 22 Unitary Local Authority Areas with the three National Parks under statute having devolved powers for planning and the effective management of the area through a strategic policy framework which allows 'relevant organisations to comply fully with their statutory responsibility to have regard for National Park purposes'.

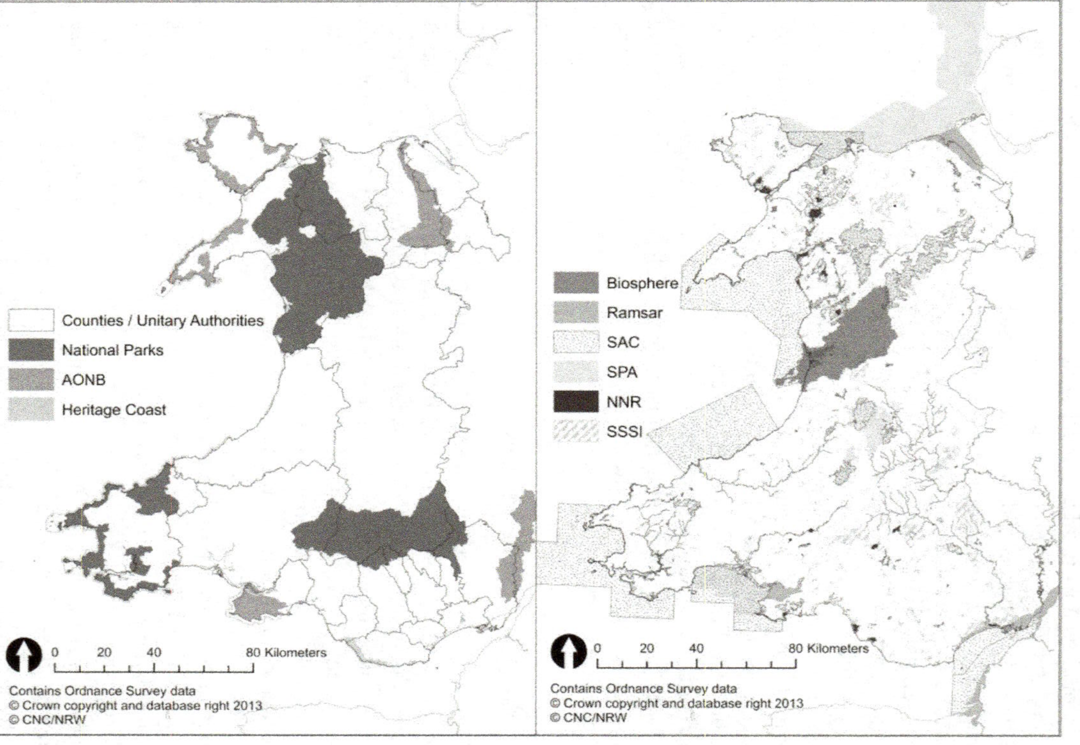

Figure 13.1 Wales: administrative areas with landscape (international, EU and UK) biodiversity designations.

Key: AONB = Area of Outstanding Natural Beauty, SAC = Special Area of Conservation, SPA= Special Protected Area, NNR = National Nature Reserve, SSSI = Site of Special Scientific Interest.

Source: contains Ordnance Survey data © Crown copyright and database right 2013

Being predominantly mountainous in character and having a highly dispersed population across the north-west and central area, the whole of Wales can be termed rural with the exception of the major population centres of Cardiff, Newport and Swansea. The definition of 'rural' is based on the OECD guidelines, which classify local areas as rural where their population density is below 150 inhabitants/ km^2 (Welsh Assembly Government, 2008).

Wales continues to be typified by the patterns of rural and urban inequality, an ageing population, outflow migration of people of working age and a greater inflow of people beyond working age, coupled with a decline in rural services and characterised by uneven development. There have been substantial changes in many parts of Wales, with many communities now 'transient' with increased migration and a growth in 'dormitory towns' adjacent to the East/West transport axes. Since the 1970s there has been an aggressive pursuit of policies relating to inward investment; however in its recent review of regeneration (2013), the Welsh Government recognised that the current economic situation militates against the property led initiatives of forty years ago:

> During recent years there has been greater realisation of the contribution that the natural environment can play in terms of regeneration … managed as a multifunctional resource holistically with other regeneration activities through a strategically planned and delivered approach, this resource is capable of delivering a wide range of economic, social and environmental solutions …
>
> (Welsh Government, 2013a: 29)

The most recent economic profile for Wales shows that there is a tentative recovery. GVA (Gross Value Added) in 2012 was £47.3 billion but much of the growth was based on retail consumption not production. An estimated 70,000 people are employed in the agricultural supply chain and up to 230,000 jobs are linked to the Welsh food and drinks economy (Welsh Government, 2014a, 2012).

With the reforms of the European Structural funds in 1988, the sparsely populated rural counties of Wales covering 75 per cent of the landmass – yet with only 25 per cent of the population – were designated as Objective 5B areas. The recent iterations of European funding (1994–1999, 2000–2006, 2007–2013) allowed the drawing down of funding from varied sources. The budget for the 2014–2020 Wales Rural Development Programme, recently announced at £953 million, is the largest ever budget allowing the government to 'recognise that challenges facing people living in rural communities are different from challenges that exist in the more populated areas of Wales (enabling) … response and solutions to local needs' (Welsh Government, 2014c, d).

Within the Government of Wales Acts, a 'legal binding duty' was made to Sustainable Development as a cross-cutting theme for the activities of government. One of the first acts to be established following devolution established frameworks which located relevant strategies for sustainability at the heart of all practices. This culminated in the publication of the 'One Wales: One Planet

Sustainable Development Scheme' (Welsh Assembly Government, 2009), its subsequent implementation reviews and a Sustainable Development White Paper.

In July 2013, the First Minister of Wales announced an update to the Welsh Legislative Programme for 2011–16, which included the government's commitment to legislate to make sustainable development the central organising principle of all devolved public service. The Sustainable Development Bill (2012) was recast as the Future Generations (Wales) Bill:

> Sustainability lies at the heart of the Welsh Government's Agenda for Wales; it also lies at the heart of this legislative programme … it will promote the economic, social and environmental well-being and enhance people's quality of life in Wales. It is about defining the long term development path for our nation. It means healthy, productive people; vibrant, inclusive communities; a diverse and resilient environment and an advanced and innovative economy.
>
> (Welsh Government, 2013a, b)

Local Authorities and the state-sponsored public bodies across Wales have a statutory duty to draw up and to implement environmental and natural resource management, conservation and sustainable development policy and to monitor how the scheme is delivered. In October 2013, a draft Environment Bill was introduced in Wales for a consultation period of three months. The purpose of the Bill was to:

> look again at the legislation that affects the environment and natural resources in Wales. We want to introduce new legislation through the Environment Bill to make sure we have the right legislative framework in place to manage our natural resources in a way that will deliver lasting benefits for now and for future generations.
>
> (Welsh Government and Cuthbert, 2013)

A unique policy and governance context exists in Wales that should be celebrated in terms of its potential to facilitate financial and other types of support for maintaining the hidden stores of resilience in these communities where globalisation influences have to date not overthrown local understanding of sustainability and traditional values. However many of these areas were designated before the emergence of a regional governance led by a commitment to the sustainability imperative/paradigm, for their beauty and instrumental priorities of conservation of aesthetic beauty or biodiversity, rather than for sustaining resilience, livelihood or community.

Wales: designations and sustaining a sense of place

Most of the hidden places of Wales are remote, distinctive repositories of the traditional centres of resilience protected by International-, European- and UK-based legal designations, e.g. Biosphere, Special Protection Areas and Special Areas of Conservation or National Park Status. These high-quality landscapes or special spaces correspond to the level of IUCN Category V, which is:

> A protected area where the interaction of people and nature over time has produced an area of distinct character with significant, ecological, biological, cultural and scenic value: and where safeguarding the integrity of this interaction is vital in protecting and sustaining the area and its associated nature conservation and other values.
>
> (IUCN, 2015)

Many of the spaces and places within Wales have a uniqueness attributable to a perceptual relationship between landform, ecosystem, community and cultural heritage. These areas are managed based on the concept of multi-functionality that co-prioritises a combination of landscape-, biodiversity- and amenity-conservation measures, all of which recognise the value of ecosystems services in the process of their management planning and development of places. Wales' three National Parks share two statutory functions: 'to conserve and enhance the natural beauty, wildlife and cultural heritage of the area and promote opportunities for the understanding and enjoyment of the special qualities of the area by the public' (Snowdonia National Park, 2010).

These are territories bounded by the physical limit of their landscapes and biodiversity interest, and are identified by a specific conservation-focused community for their material dimension in direct contrast to the local relations formed within their communities (Amin, 2009).

Until the emergence of the discourse on sustainable development with an expanded legislative responsibility for the economic well-being of National Parks and their communities, these areas had been considered primarily by the policy community which manages and regulates them as physical entities or protected spaces. These spaces are, however, sustained by the language, economic and social policies of local governance and constrained by the requirements of the Wales Spatial Plan and other strategic management plans which are formulated through a consultation process leading to a regional/national spatial strategy.

Biodiversity conservation is also a prominent element of Welsh governance; the natural, built and cultural resources of Wales are conserved as being of significant benefit for tourism- and leisure-based activities – in short, Wales' green economic potential based on the careful management of its natural capital. Thus designation of space has a massive potential in terms of its influence on conservation activities for both natural areas and places such as villages and settlements across Wales, many of which have undergone a period of decline and uneven development since the mid 1970s.

The link is now being made at policy level in Wales that place protection and designation is insufficient in itself and often too narrow in its application and that overlapping agendas for conservation, rural development, regeneration, cultural expression, health and well-being and anti-poverty measures offer scope for more integrated and complete people- and place-based approaches, ensuring rural resiliences.

This ties in to some extent with the ecosystems approach adopted by the agency Natural Resources Wales, including the integrated management of land, water and living resources that promotes conservation and sustainable use in an equitable way (Convention on Biological Diversity, 1992). The 2011 UK National Environment Assessment describes different ecosystem services and looks at how they relate to each another – these include provisioning, regulating, supporting and cultural services.

The ecosystem approach (Potschin and Haines Young, 2013) is, however, much more than accepting ecosystems as the core of environmental management. It recognises that people and society are integral components of ecosystems and their management and conservation. Within a Scottish context, however, this approach has been described as 'One that is gaining in popularity and relevance as it combines the place-based approach with a systematic and integrative approach to environmental management and links communities with decision making' (UK NEA, 2011: 65).

This necessitates a way of working and decision-making that cuts across traditional policy and institutional boundaries. It brings consideration of natural, economic and social sciences into a single methodological framework, although Plieninger *et al.* (2013: 118) contend that 'cultural ecosystems services are rarely fully considered in ecosystems services assessments'. All of this serves to confirm the often complex dynamic cultural process linking people and place and the challenge posed by taking a whole landscape (be it a catchment, community or other natural or human system-based) approach to managing and celebrating rural areas and ensuring their continued and balanced vibrancy and viability.

Case studies

In order to illustrate the dynamics and tensions extant in designated and otherwise defined rural areas in relation to their protection, development and regeneration, three carefully selected case studies are presented. They are all practical field projects based on personal experience and applied involvement in regional development consultancies.

Reporting for each case study is based on recent consultancy activities and has been an integral part of each project's actual inbuilt monitoring and review process during project development in a field-based context rather than based purely on theoretical/academic analysis. The purpose of each project was to facilitate best practice development *in situ* and utilises the authors' own analyses based on past experience of participative development methods and project evaluation.

The case studies below demonstrate real world lessons learned from several different perspectives, including their modes of cooperation and engagement, community-based economic and social value added/multipliers and broader contributions to local scale sustainable development in terms of building resilience. The sources from which these examples emerged are discussed in relation to the longer-term capacity and infrastructure improvements offered by these projects.

Clwydian Range and Dee Valley Area of Outstanding Natural Beauty (CR&DeeAONB)

In November 2011, Welsh Government confirmed the extension of the Clwydian Range AONB to include the Dee Valley in recognition of the area's distinctive landscape, biodiversity, cultural heritage and historic environment. Such areas, along with National Parks, have recently been identified by the Minister for Culture and Sport as 'Areas which should be in the vanguard of demonstrating how Wales can secure healthy, biologically diverse and productive environments that are managed sustainably, with communities that are safe and sustainable, and where people choose to live and work' (Welsh Government, 2013d: 1).

In addition to traditional land uses such as agriculture and forestry, tourism that fits with this approach is being developed in the area. The Dee Valley Sustainable Tourism Project Action Plan (Jones, 2012) identified a series of key elements for development:

- Branding: increasingly, place branding is used to distinguish and differentiate a destination from its competitors. There should therefore be one overarching brand identity.
- Transport: a need to develop and promote an integrated network of transport links has been identified.
- Niche tourism: opportunities exist for targeting and offering specific tourism products, including:
  - cultural heritage tourism – this could include existing historical attractions/cultural activities and events. Special packages could be developed by accommodation providers, supported by orientation and training on the area's cultural heritage resource.

Figure 13.2 View overlooking Clwydian Range AONB and Castell Dinas Bran, Llangollen, Wales

Source: © Denbighshire County Council, 2014.

  - food tourism – the AONB is already exploring food aspects with farmers and other producers. Further developments could celebrate local produce/cuisine, and create special itineraries and trails based on local food products.
  - outdoor tourism – this focuses on the rural sports and recreation facilities.
- Events: these can be incorporated into the themes developed above, using existing and redeveloped venues.
- Information technology: the area is currently served by two different visitor websites. Some basic work is required to ensure greater clarity and develop a common portal.

UNESCO Man and the Biosphere Programme – Bro Ddyfi/Dyfi Valley Marketing Strategy (BroDMS)

Half a million visitors come to the Dyfi Valley each year to experience the area's unique 'natural' character and beauty. The ethos of sustainable living is reflected throughout the community – which is home to a number of 'green' businesses and an internationally renowned ecotourism centre, the Centre for Alternative Technology.

Figure 13.3 Two young beach scientists in the Biosphere Reserve

Source: Robin Farrar

The awarding of UNESCO modern Biosphere status has elevated the area onto a world stage on a par with Uluru and the Camargue, demonstrating the high environmental standards and equally demanding management and development challenges. The ambition is to become a model integrated living landscape where tourist activities complement those of the local population and land managers.

Taking the green tourism route is not a narrow niche decision, but a sensible way of managing resources, running businesses, providing a quality service and gaining market edge. The eco-imperative is becoming an increasingly significant factor in people's everyday lives, with major impacts such as climate change, resource depletion and global equity featuring strongly in the serious media. Those who might want to make a difference in their own lives, e.g. energy-saving and resource recycling, might also desire to slow down for a while to focus on quality of life.

Opportunities arise for sending these powerful messages to potentially receptive audiences:

- Look at the everyday: quality local produce, slow food, green activities, green retail, wildlife activities, benign transport – for locals and visitors.
- Stress-busting and recreation: eco-retreats, holistic medicine, complementary therapies, yoga and meditation.
- Connect with wild nature: innovative guided wildlife watching and walks, mountain biking and coasteering.

Cambrian Mountains Initiative (CMI)

The Cambrian Mountains form the upland backbone of Wales. Running from the borders of the Snowdonia National Park in the north to the Brecon Beacons National Park in the south, they are an area of unspoilt upland landscape (originally identified for designation as a National Park). The area supports valued upland habitats and species with some farming traditions maintained since the Middle Ages.

Launched in June 2008, this was a broad partnership to deliver Integrated (Sustainable) Rural Development for the landscape area and surrounding communities. It aims to bring a sustainable development approach, focusing on growing the local economy through the promotion of – and adding value to – quality local produce and tourism, and enhancing the provision of ecosystem services. It also seeks to build a sense of place through a common brand and a community development network that engages local communities. Some of the main issues are:

- Farming and land management: low profitability and uncertainty, an economy disproportionately affected by declining agricultural incomes and changing policies. An ageing farm population, many leaving the industry; young people leaving the area leads to a loss of traditional skills and capacity.
- Community: lack of affordable housing, with population age balance skewed towards the elderly; in-migration, out-migration and lowering birth rates results in limited employment opportunities; closure and poor access to services.

- Business: lack of support, business skills, research and development, lack of ICT infrastructure, critical mass of businesses and limited business collaboration.
- Tourism: limited high-profile environmental attractions, lack of coherent branding, marketing and promotion of traditional Welsh cultural activities, low profile of national trails and poor accommodation links, limited supply of high quality serviced accommodation, resultant low spending.
- Renewable energy: little retention of profits and development of community renewables in the local community.
- Water management and carbon sequestration: lack of payment for the management of ecosystem service delivery.
- Landscape and biodiversity: deterioration in habitats, uncertainty over the future of agricultural support, intrusive energy developments and lack of understanding of landscape change and its likely effects.
- Cultural heritage and the built environment: loss of Welsh language and culture with demographic change, lack of understanding of the area's past history, neglect of the historic resource, many derelict properties.

Against this background the vision for the area is of

> self-sustaining, resilient and environmentally sustainable businesses and communities enjoying a high quality of life and proud of their place … with a high quality environment adapted to the effects of climate change, delivering vital ecosystem services of value to the nation, and a region that is nationally and internationally recognised as a distinct tourism destination and producer of high quality foods and other products that reflect their mountain provenance.
>
> (Land Use Consultants Ltd *et al.*, 2012: 11)

Discussion: lessons learned from the case studies

All three case studies have demonstrated degrees of innovation and of working together differently on a landscape scale in an integrated manner (see Table 13.1). They show to some extent how overlapping agendas affecting rural resilience, such as public services, employment, social inclusion, cultural identity, land use, environmental and heritage management, can be looked at together and tackled collectively. They also reveal administrative and structural challenges in inter-departmental and cross-sector collaboration. Examples such as these illustrate both the merits and some of the difficulties of treating defined spaces as meaningful places. Each area has been defined as an integrated land unit either by designation or landform consideration and each can lay claim to having a unifying cultural identity based on the relationship between people and place. In order to ensure that these cultural communities retain their resilience, more integrated rural development (including social, cultural, economic and environmental reinforcement) is required to make and nurture this living and

Table 13.1 Lessons learned from the case studies

	Case 1 (CR&DeeAONB)	*Case 2 (BroDMS)*	*Case 3 (CMI)*
Resourcing	The project might have been better resourced, in terms of direct funding and staff availability	Marketing does not stand alone from other area management and tourism development considerations	Clearer, more realistic business planning was required
Integration	Need for greater integration with other initiatives in the area	There is a strong overlap with other agendas affecting residents, i.e. quality of life and social inclusion (economic, cultural and linguistic)	Initial lack of focus or strategic approach
Cooperation	Stronger working link with public bodies and existing work programmes is needed	Other relevant areas of activity include sustainable transport, local food production and management of the protected living landscape	Wider land use issues – needs to develop its engagement with upland management, nature conservation, historic buildings, recreation and tourism activity
Longer term viability	Must have more local embedding, with a greater project presence on the ground	Green lifestyle, healthy living and environmental awareness are strong underlying principles (for residents and visitors)	Original emphasis was on upland Welsh organic lamb, but now expanded to include other food and non-food products and activities
Landscape and designation	Collaboration developed several viable landscape related sub-projects	Strong catchment/watershed management boundary, rather than administrative area	CMI not a designated area – it crosses several administrative boundaries; this makes working together a challenge

working relationship and enable people to continue leading viable and rewarding lives enriched by their sense of place.

As some of these case studies were pilot initiatives or took new and innovative approaches towards land management, both positive and negative lessons were learned, communicated to stakeholders and applied to future projects and onward policy recommendations.

Making and re-making 'places' for regeneration

Wales is more than a bi-cultural place as defined by its Welsh-English language pair. It is a multi-faceted cultural mix of the urban and the rural, the traditional and contemporary, the global and the local – and is more complex and inter-related even than those seeming dichotomies.

This chapter has explored an alternative celebration of the local that recognises the value of the places and the special, environmental, cultural and linguistic spaces of Wales – but there are now challenges to be addressed. Proposed changes to planning legislation mean that improving the economy is now cited as a priority action. Rhetoric is moving from the protection of the landscape at 'all costs' to a form of partnership working where there are:

> Positive benefits for the natural and historic environment of the AONBs and parks, and for the local communities in terms of sustainable socio-economic development. They are wonderful assets for the whole of Wales and must increasingly ensure their work reaches and benefits our most deprived communities, playing an effective role in supporting Welsh Government's tackling poverty agenda.
>
> (Welsh Government, 2013d: 1)

Partnership working and co-design have been explored as contributors to Wales' acknowledged potential for growth of its green economy and the associated benefits to reduce rural community vulnerability. As has been discussed, much of this activity was driven by European funding. However, a lack of coordination meant that often local regeneration initiatives did not focus on long-term community resilience but instead on entrepreneurial ability to draw down available funds for project-driven rather than strategic sustainable development, as happened in so many of the inward investment initiatives of the 1970s and 1980s.

From the case studies presented, there is an obvious need to attend to the disconnection between strategic interventions and community interest. This often stems from an urbanised often city-region perspective on decision making and funding for rural Wales which is very much focused on ecosystem assessments, e.g. carbon sinks and recreational experiences. Adopting a more localised cultural landscape scale approach to governance would be more appropriate. Selman (2006: 19) states that 'Landscape scale governance will draw upon a blend of strategies and tactics whereby partnerships of actors work together to protect and re-create distinctive places and spaces'.

From the overview of the case studies discussed, past priorities have been based on maximising the natural capital of designated spaces with little appreciation of the fundamental need to build on the broader social and cultural capital, whereby places would be better sustained. Funding for the broader rural good needs to understand the common life experiences and cultural heritage or future aspirations of those who are able to choose to stay within their own *Cynefin*, to live and maintain an increasingly challenging lifestyle. The diversity of such locally constructed territories across Wales continues to challenge generic metropolitan approaches to formulating strategies for maintaining such spaces and places described above. Many of the celebration-worthy communities and hidden places are in decline, or in some cases derelict, existing only within heritage memory and cannot thus be re-created.

The explanation of patchy success and areas to be addressed to develop best practice in the case studies described might be due to the individual and uniquely challenging community and cultural context within which each study exists. Such a broad diversity of contexts presents very specific challenges to agencies responsible for allocating project funding or organising relevant, successful and sustainable developments or for measuring their success, especially through more traditional targeted outcome. What can work for one community project might not at all be as easy or as effective in a different community dynamic. It might be possible to achieve improvements to the limited outcomes through more creative proactive initiatives that enable locally driven and monitored regeneration targets and actions. A comment also is directed towards a more strategic needs-based geographical spread of funding for regeneration to sustain viable communities, especially those attempting to maintain their distinctiveness. Globalisation forces influencing these communities are not best faced by applying outdated and defunct spatial planning zones or through development by opportunistic bids for short-term European funding.

Bringing regeneration under the local control of the communities, where the socio-cultural influence and the natural and physical constraints of the places closely inform the development process, would address the problematic notion of territoriality in these special places that are claimed by all as 'breathing spaces' but are owned by few, such as National Parks and Special Protected Areas in Europe.

References

Amin, A. (2009). Doreen Massey: Space, place and politics. Available at: http://media-podcast.open.ac.uk/feeds/doreen-massey/transcript/doreen_massey_track_003.pdf (accessed 27 July 2013).

Dale, A., Ling, C. and L. Newman (2008). Does place matter? Sustainable community development in three Canadian communities. *Ethics, Place & Environment: A Journal of Philosophy & Geography*, 11 (3): 267–281.

IUCN (2015) Available at: www.iucn.org/about/work/programmes/gpap_home/gpap_quality/gpap_pacategories/gpap_category5 (accessed 7 May 2015).

Land Use Consultants Ltd in association with Jones, A. and S. Hughes (2012). *A business plan for the Cambrian Mountains Initiative (CMI).*

Office for National Statistics (2014). *Regional labour market bulletin.*

Ordnance Survey Open Data Meridian 2 1:50,000 vector. Available at: www.ordnancesurvey.co.uk/opendatadownload/products.html (accessed 21 January 2015).

Organisation for Economic Cooperation and Development (1994). *Creating rural indicators for shaping territorial policy.* OECD, Paris.

Pierce, S., Rennie, G. and E. Lane (1997). Will Wales stay green in the absence of rural policy?, pp. 302–321 in: Byron, R., Walsh, J. and P. Breathnach (eds), *Sustainable development on the North Atlantic margin.* International Society for the Study of Marginal Regions. Ashgate, Brookfield.

Plieninger, T., Djiks, S., Oteros-Rozas, E. and C. Bieling (2013). Assessing, mapping and quantifying cultural ecosystems services at community level. *Land Use Policy*, 33: 118–129.

Potschin, M. and R. Haines-Young (2013). Landscapes, sustainability and the place-based analysis of ecosystem services. *Landscape Ecology*, 28: 1053–1065.

Rodwell, J. (2008). Forgetting the land. *Studies in Christian Ethics*, 21 (2): 269–286.

Selman, P. (2006). *Planning at the landscape scale.* Routledge, London.

Sinclair, N. (1998). Preface. In: K. Williams (ed.), *The land and the sea.* Gwasg Gomer, Dyfed.

Snowdonia National Park (2010) *Cynllun rheolaeth ACPE 2010-2015 management plan*, p. 10. Available at: www.nationalparks.gov.uk/eryri2010/snpa_mp_2010 (accessed 28 April 2015)

Stylianou-Lambert, T. Churchman, A. and K. Sioni (2013). *Investigating cultural sustainability: Experts and multidisciplinary approaches.* COST, Brussels.

Tuan, Y.F. (1977). *Space and place.* Edward Arnold, London.

UK NEA (2011). *The UK national ecosystem assessment: Synthesis of the key findings.* UNEP-WCMC, Cambridge.

United Nations (2011). *Resolution adopted by the General Assembly on 20 December 2010* [on the report of the Second Committee (A/65/438)] A/Res/65/166. Available at: www.un.org/en/ga/search/view_doc.asp?symbol=A/RES/65/166 (accessed 21 November 2014).

United Nations (1992) *Convention on biological diversity.* Available at: www.cbd.int/convention/text (accessed 28 April 2015)

Welsh Assembly Government (2002). *Creative future: A culture strategy for Wales.*

Welsh Assembly Government (2008). *Rural development plan for Wales: The situational analysis.*

Welsh Assembly Government (2009). *One Wales: One planet. The sustainable development scheme of the Welsh Assembly Government.*

Welsh Government (2013a). *Vibrant and viable places: A new regeneration framework.*

Welsh Government (2013b). *Future Generations Bill: Better choices for a better future.* Press Release, July 2013.

Welsh Government (2013c). *Towards the sustainable management of Wales' natural resources.* Consultation on proposals for an Environment Bill, October 2013.

Welsh Government (2013d). *Taking the long view, Welsh Government Consultation on the draft Policy Statement for Protected Landscapes in Wales.*

Welsh Government (2014a). *Towards the sustainable management of Wales' natural resources. Consultation on proposals for an Environment Bill. White paper – summary of responses*, March 2014.

Welsh Government (2014b). *The Wales we want factsheets: Economy & employment; Our population; Culture, heritage and language.*

Welsh Government (2014c). *Culture and poverty: Harnessing the power of the arts, culture and heritage to promote social justice in Wales.*

Welsh Government (2014d). Ministerial statements. *Ministers taking action to build vibrant communities*, April 2014.

Welsh Government and J. Cuthbert (2013). *Written statement – Future Generations Bill – Better choices for a better future*. Report.

14 Local maize practices and the cultures of seed in Luoland, West Kenya

Paul Hebinck, Nelson Mango and Hellen Kimanthi

Introduction

To explore the relation between culturally embedded development situations and sustainable development, we have focused on a range of interventions that aimed to replace or substitute local maize varieties with 'modern', science driven varieties. Despite the prevalence of such efforts worldwide, many of them do not stand the test of time. But why not? Our answer hinges on the dissonance between the social-material realities of the new maize varieties that arrived in West Kenya through a series of 'external' interventions and what we understand here as the 'culture of seed'. Seed practices in Luoland in West Kenya are well embedded and structured by cultural beliefs and associated kinship based practices. This culture of seed is not one homogenous practice but is, rather, heterogeneous and fragmented. 'Luoland' is operationalised here as a heterogeneous, fragmented landscape constituted by an assemblage of different seed and land-related practices and rural livelihoods derived from such assemblages. This assemblage of practices does not stand on its own and cannot be understood with reference to tradition and custom only. The current assemblage of practices are to an extent, and in many different ways, also shaped and structured by what we conceptualise as socio-technical networks. These networks are constituted by multiple social actors, their ideas, ideologies and practices, and material objects such as maize seeds with their specific bio-physical properties. The networks are multiple and coexisting, but also fluid and dynamic: they transform each other. They serve to connect – in our case – Luoland to different sources of genetic material originating in different geographical areas, e.g. Central America (McCann, 2005). Tsing (2000: 353) eloquently relates these networks to a configuration of an 'interconnected, but not homogenous, set of projects'.

Many of the maize varieties that are planted and consumed today came to Luoland through a variety of networks. These are either intentional breeding programmes or famine and relief programmes or labour migration connected to maize breeding and selection programmes in the United States of America, South Africa and, later, in Kenya. Whereas some of these networks continue to use traditional methods of seed exchange via traders and farmers, others have been purposefully initiated by 'external' intervention programmes that are backed by the (colonial and postcolonial) state and foreign donors. The 'external' networks are clearly moulded by a combination of ideas and ideologies which state that the best strategy to secure one's current and future food provisioning and get out of poverty is to adapt 'modern' hybrid varieties of maize. The ideas and ideologies we refer to here are known in literature, among development practitioners and in the villages as the Green Revolution and the Millennium Village Project (MVP) approach.

Recurrent food shortages are one of the major challenges for Luoland. As early as 1911 the colonial authorities responded to the frequent famines through emergency food aid packages, which included various maize varieties. State interventions such as the Green Revolution and MVP have focused on increasing productivity through introducing improved seed such as hybrid maize varieties, but Luo farmers have historically responded to food shortages by diversifying their crops to include 'local' maize, cassava and to, an extent, sorghum. They do not necessarily adopt 'modern', hybrid varieties of maize that have been introduced over the years. By 'local' maize (also called 'land races'), we mean maize varieties that are open-pollinated and have been enriched in the field through selection and production by Luo family farmers. By 'modern' varieties we mean varieties that have been bred under special circumstances and selected by seed companies according to scientific standards. 'Modern' in contrast to 'local' varieties originate from exogenous and imported germplasm (mostly from Mexico), bred for their higher yielding capacity or better suitability to some of Kenya's agroecological conditions. Both types of seed, like any technology, have specific requirements for use; we will return to this aspect later.

Methodologically, our approach derives from Paasi's (2010) argumentation that regions such as Luoland are social constructs constituted by a fragmented or heterogeneous assemblage of (in our case) seed related practices. Paasi (2010) and also Li (2007) associate this with agency. The agency that constitutes these assemblages is located in the social actors that are involved (farmers, intervening agents) and their various knowledge repertoires and experiences. This agency manifests in a specific narrative whereby a specific grammar (Rip and Kemp, 1998; Hebinck, 2001) is used to socially defend and legitimise one's choice of which maize to plant. The 'grammar of maize' contains specific clues and explanations as to why certain 'local' varieties are predominant in the landscape and are continuously enriched while new, 'modern' varieties are present to a much lesser extent. The agency cannot be solely attributed to social actors, but lies also in the material objects, i.e. the various kinds of maize varieties and their specific biophysical properties. Seed practices are thus conceptualised as outcomes of a coproduction between the human and nonhuman elements (Anderson and McFarlane, 2011; Woods, 2007) which 'do not emerge casually nor can they be easily engineered' (Long, 2001: 39), which in turn generate heterogeneous and highly fragmented development situations (Umans and Arce, 2014). Moreover, manifestation of the interactions between the social and material tend to be locally specific. This interpretation finds much support in the recent literature on place and space (Escobar, 2001, 2006; Massey, 2004, 2005; McGee, 2004) as well as in the broader literature on re-assemblages (Latour, 2005; De Landa, 2006; Woods, this book, Chapter 3). It also builds on interpretations of development and change that are well established in the sociology and anthropology of development literature (Arce and Long, 2000; Long, 2001; Oliver de Sardan, 2006). This article builds on these interpretations and extends this by arguing that culture, to paraphrase Rip and Kemp (1998: 30), stands for making the configuration of the social and material work.

We set out to show empirically that re-assembling does not follow a single logic or one master plan. We unpack the assemblage of seed practices by exploring maize production, focusing on what kind of varieties are produced and consumed and why.

The structure of the chapter follows the timeline of maize seeds that have gradually arrived via a variety of networks in the region over the last 120 years. We highlight three distinct phases of maize related interventions, to explain the different dynamics emanating from these interventions. In the conclusion, we point out the patterns of assembling and relate this to the debate on the role of culture in territorialisation and sustainability.

This chapter draws on longitudinal research in Luoland (van Kessel, 1998; Mango, 2002; Hebinck, 2001; Mango and Hebinck, 2004; Kimanthi, 2014), which started in 1996 and focused on three villages in Siaya district in West Kenya: Nyamninia, Muhanda and Muhoho. Historical data on the spread and use of maize varieties were combined with more recent data (1996–2002, 2003–2004, 2013–2014) on the intensity of the use of local and modern (hybrid) maize varieties. Data were collected in the form of recurrent interviews with key informants (including farmers and extension agents) and intense field observations over the years. Some still remembered the introduction of the different maize varieties to the area. Detailed, follow-up case studies of farmers and fields were conducted to unpack maize seed related practices. Historical records and traveller stories were consulted specifically to trace the histories of maize during the early colonial period.

Maize networks

Luo agriculture has seen major transformations over the last 100–150 years. Sorghum and millet have been gradually replaced by maize and land use moved from shifting cultivation to a stage of permanent cultivation. Based on colonial records and oral history, the gradual shift from sorghum and millet to maize can be ascribed to a series of famines that occurred in the late nineteenth and early twentieth century. Roughly since the 1940s, agriculture has been transformed through the processes of commoditisation and intensification. More recently (from the 1970s onwards) commoditised agriculture is in decline, and production for home consumption and localised trade predominate. The pursuit of off-farm income opportunities and careers outside agriculture have led to labour migration, which has been accompanied by population growth, a reduction in field sizes and a decline in soil fertility (Mango, 1999).

Although maize had been grown in small quantities well before the beginning of the twentieth century, it only came into prominence with the distribution of improved varieties of white maize during World War I (Heyer, 1975: 146) followed by a range of new maize varieties, both 'local' and 'modern' (Mango and Hebinck, 2004; Hebinck, 2001). By 1930, maize was well established in West Kenya. In areas with satisfactory rainfall and free-draining soil, maize became popular because of its higher yielding potential compared to indigenous cereals.

The start of maize cultivation in Luoland can be traced back to the late nineteenth century, although the exact date is unknown. Through *trade networks* various maize varieties arrived in Luoland and have been propagated since then. Neighbouring Uganda was a major source of maize varieties that found and still do find their way to Siaya through trade relationships. Through contacts with *Waswahili* (people from the coast) and Arab traders in the late nineteenth century, maize almost certainly found its way to Siaya. Through such trade routes, varieties like *radier* and *rachich* (the multicoloured varieties of maize) entered Luoland. At the turn of the century other varieties surfaced in the region. The most recent local maize variety that is popular and still widely grown can be traced back to 1982/1983 (the famine of *Goro-goro).* It is called *nyauganda* (Uganda white); it came to Kenya through traders that went to Uganda to purchase maize during that great famine.

Food and famine relief programmes by the colonial and postcolonial state also brought specific maize varieties. Most of the yellow maize that we still find today has been imported from the United States to deal with acute food shortages. Some was reserved as seed for the next planting season and then planted. Two white varieties first arrived in the context of famine relief and are still being planted today, namely the *oking* and *ababari*. *Oking* was introduced during the great famine of 1906–1907. *Ababari*, and possibly other white varieties, were introduced following the great famines of 1917–1919. Farmers still plant these two varieties of maize today, identifying them by their physical (phenotypic) characteristics. At a later stage, the government introduced Hickory King maize and other varieties originating from South Africa to replace the yellow maize varieties. These introductions fit the general pattern of the colonial state being actively engaged in trying to introduce industrial crops (such as sesame and cotton in Nyanza) and improved varieties of food crops (Kitching, 1980).

An important maize network is associated with a range of maize *research, selection and breeding programmes.* The Department of Agriculture of the colonial and postcolonial state and the white settlers were always looking for new varieties that were better suited to the inland climate, which were invariably found in South Africa. The yellow maize varieties imported from the United States as part of famine relief programmes are also derived from breeding programmes. Recently, some NGO-like institutions have started maize breeding programmes with quite a different emphasis to those linked to formal research and breeding networks. From the mid-1960s onwards various varieties of hybrid maize (such as H512, H511, H622 and H614) were introduced in (West) Kenya. These (white-only) varieties are closely associated with planned state intervention and involve maize breeders and their breeding programmes in Kenya or elsewhere, as well as extension, credit and marketing agencies. These maize breeding programmes are discussed in the next section of this chapter. At the time, these varieties were all bred by the Kenya Seed Company (KSC) in Kitale. KSC held a monopoly position on the Kenyan seed market until market liberalisation in the early 1990s following Structural Adjustment, when other seed companies were allowed to sell seeds to farmers. This resulted in more recent entries of hybrid varieties such as PAN5195 and PH1, bred by maize seed companies in South Africa (Pannar) and the United States (Pioneer). Both varieties were issued to farmers in Siaya at almost no cost. As confirmed by our interviews with local farmers, neither of these performed very well: the seeds germinated poorly and the fields where they were planted had a desolate appearance.

Patterns of maize production

In the 1960s, with the beginning of the Green Revolution, the spread of maize in Luoland entered a significantly different phase. The Green Revolution was designed to improve the productivity of maize by introducing high-yielding varieties as well as to modernise maize production. The goal was not only to exchange more maize through intensifying and expanding market relationships, but also to transform the production process in such a way that new and science based inputs would become predominant. The Green Revolution preached and fuelled the use of hybrid varieties of maize, the spread of inorganic fertiliser and replacing some manual labour with machines (e.g. tractors). Provision of agricultural credit was a main vehicle in the planned transformation. The programmes to modernise agriculture were implemented by the state with support from international organisations like CIMMYT (Centre for the Improvement of Maize and Wheat) and more broadly with foreign aid. As mentioned above, the Green Revolution brought a range of new, mostly white, hybrid varieties.

Despite all the efforts coordinated by the state and the international aid community, the adoption rate of hybrid maize in Siaya district was never very high in comparison to other parts of West Kenya. In 1973 the uptake of hybrid maize for the whole of Siaya was still below 20 per cent, while in districts like Trans Nzoia and Kakamega it had reached almost 100 per cent (Gerhart, 1976: 27). In other words, most farmers in Siaya district decided not to adopt the presented hybrid maize package. Furthermore, the farmers who did adopt the technology package did not, in most cases, adopt the total package. They adjusted or redesigned the package in many different ways (see below).

The Green Revolution was supposed to make a major contribution to increased productivity and food production, and thus to be a major landmark in social transformation and development. Ideally, Green Revolution types of maize should have replaced 'local' maize varieties because of their superiority in terms of productivity. This has not happened, however. Various types of 'local' maize are still widely grown and continuously reappear. This has occurred despite major efforts (past and present) in Luoland by the so-called Millennium Village Project (MVP) approach to strengthen the hybridisation of maize production. The MVP was designed by Jeffrey Sachs and Pedro Sanchez (Sanchez *et al.*, 2007, 2009) with the support of a range of donors in the context of the Millennium Development Goals. The MVP approach was implemented in Luoland in Sauri village from 2004 onwards. Key to this approach is making seed and fertilisers available at almost no cost and brokering new market institutions in collaboration with farmers' unions and village leaders. MVP also stepped up extension to farmers in an effort to rejuvenate agriculture extension which, due to lack of government funding, has virtually collapsed. The objective of the MVP approach was to reduce poverty by re-energising the Green Revolution and to achieve a renewed uptake of hybrid maize varieties in Luoland. Like the Green Revolution, it has only partly succeeded. A short spike in the use of hybrids was indeed observed, but the degree and intensity of planting modern maize has since returned to pre-MVP levels. In the next sections we will briefly explain why.

Between 1998 and 2000 we conducted a survey in our three research villages – Nyamninia, Muhanda and Muhoho – to determine the patterns of maize cultivation and document which varieties were planted. The survey took place approximately three years before MVP was initiated in Sauri village. Due to time and other constraints, we were not able to survey the same group or even an equal number of farmers again. Instead we performed a follow-up series of the same cases studies done between 1998 and 2000 (Kimanthi, 2014).

In 2000, 40 farmers were selected at random and asked what type of maize they were growing at the time of research (Table 14.1). This pattern unfolded over time and revealed varying and rather contrasting strategies. We encountered people over the years who, after initially enthusiastically embracing the new maize varieties, began to gradually distance themselves from such new practices and returned to local seed. Almost one-third of the farmers pointed out that they had never planted hybrid maize, which was not surprising given

Table 14.1 Type of maize grown by farmers in three villages in 2000

Type of maize grown	*Villages*			*Total*	*%*
	Nyamninia (N = 40)	*Muhanda (N = 40)*	*Muhoho (N = 40)*		
Farmers combining hybrid and local maize	10	7	2	19	15.8
Farmers stopped planting hybrids	20	22	21	63	52.5
Farmers that never planted hybrids	10	11	17	38	31.7
Total	40	40	40	120	100

Source: adapted from Mango and Hebinck, 2004: 306.

the low level of adoption in Luoland. These contrasting strategies are treated as empirical manifestation of various processes of assembling and re-assembling, continuously producing new practices. These do not coexist but rather interact and mutually shape each other via the dynamic exchange of maize seed amongst and between people. The pattern that emerges is not static despite the resurgent efforts of the MVP.

The majority of farmers had stopped planting hybrid maize that was introduced in the 1970s. One difficulty with interpreting the responses to the survey is farmers who have planted hybrid maize once in their lifetime often say that they had always planted hybrid maize. To avoid problems of interpretation we used purposive sampling to select 23 of these farmers to interview in more detail, trying to understand the processes at work. We combined this information with field observations, which provided basic information to help us understand why the initial adopters had distanced themselves in one way or another from planting hybrid maize. Of the sample, 22 farmers had at some time cultivated hybrid maize, but only six of them were still growing it, all in combination with local maize varieties. Sixteen had stopped planting hybrids and reverted to growing only local maize, and one farmer had never grown hybrid maize. Most young farmers, and particularly women farmers, had never grown hybrid maize. Detailed discussions with these 23 farmers gave a series of reasons why the great majority of farmers do not prefer hybrid varieties.

In the most recent study that also explored the intensity of the use of hybrid seeds among the farmers in the Sauri MVP, 99 per cent of the farmers within the village planted hybrid seeds at the beginning of the project as they accepted free hybrid seeds and fertilisers given by the project to all farmers. Now an equal number of farmers use hybrids and local varieties. During the study, 16 farmers were interviewed (four of whom were follow-up cases from the previous study). The results showed that six of the farmers have adopted the use of hybrid seeds and modern farming practices, five farmers have redesigned the package and are now 'inbetween' as it were; they plant both local and hybrid maize seeds and do not always follow the modern ways of farming as required by the interventionists. The remaining category of farmers is comprised of farmers who, for the various reasons as discussed below ('distancing'), have gone back to planting only local seeds. It is important to note that in all the households visited, local maize varieties are grown at least each year by someone within the household, and more so during the short rainy seasons. During a follow-up case study, one farmer grew only hybrid seeds during both long and short rainy seasons for commercial purposes while his wife grew local varieties mainly for subsistence use and to fulfill the cultural purpose of *golo kodhi* and *duoko cham* ('first sowing' and 'first harvest'; see below). Some of the older generation maintain growth of local varieties especially if their children practise 'modern' farming, thus according to the farmers hybrid varieties cannot replace local varieties. The pattern that emerged is that 'local' maize is and remains predominant despite all the heavyweight interventions to replace 'local' by 'modern' maize. In the following section we provide a succinct analysis to explain this process.

The 'grammar of maize': why local maize predominates

The data collected via repeated interviews and field observations over the last 15 years point to three main arguments for the preference of 'local' maize. There are *institutional issues,* but also *agronomic properties* that play a key role and, more importantly perhaps, we find *cultural values and repertoires* that resonate with the planting, harvesting and consumption of 'local' maize. We first summarise the first two arguments and then expand on the last argument.

Institutional issues

Market related issues do not necessarily disqualify hybrids agronomically and/or culturally, but, rather, hinge on the quality of relationships between maize cultivation and the set of institutions surrounding and supporting it. For some people failures of this type do not constitute a reason to reject hybrid maize but rather to package and redesign the set of prescriptions that form the technology package surrounding hybrid maize (see Mango (2002) for a more detailed discussion of this issue). For others, these failures provide sufficient reason to distance themselves from the hybrids and the markets. One of the arguments for distancing (moving away from hybrid maize) is the relatively high monetary costs of inputs such as seed and fertiliser. Hybrid maize does not grow well without applying fertiliser and purchasing new seeds each year. This counters the arguments (presented by the six farmers still growing hybrids alongside local maize in 2000 and the six farmers growing them in 2014) that hybrid maize is a profitable crop to grow in Luoland. Lack of money or credit to purchase the necessary inputs are pertinent issues. Difficulty in obtaining inputs and the perception that they (seeds especially, but also fertilisers) deteriorate in quality were also mentioned as reasons to stop growing hybrid maize. Abednego, one of our key informants and a knowledgeable and experienced farmer, stated that 'growing maize as a commercial crop is not very economical. You use a lot of inputs and the output is not very encouraging. The farming practised here has got a lot of risks'.

Selina, a female farmer, expresses a general distrust of the market since Structural Adjustment:

> Since there is market liberalisation, most of our good quality maize seeds are marketed in countries like Uganda, Tanzania and Rwanda ... Anybody can sell anything to you as hybrid maize seeds as long as it is dusted with the green chemical they use for real hybrid maize.

Moreover, since the Structural Adjustment Programme was implemented in the 1990s, government support for agriculture has dwindled. The ratio of farmers to extension workers has since steadily increased. MVP has practically monopolised extension since it started operations in the region. Their focus is to propagate hybrid maize; they ignore the farmers' reluctance to grow hybrids. The few extension workers present in the region grow local maize from self-selected seeds they generate themselves. Despite having a stable salary to purchase inputs, they cite the same reasons for growing local instead of hybrid maize. The inputs-for-free approach that MVP followed till recently increased the planting of hybrid maize varieties only temporarily. 'Never refuse a gift' was commonly given as an answer. Now that MVP is virtually defunct, the number of farmers planting hybrids has dropped to nearly pre-MVP levels.

Agronomic properties

One of the most powerful and commonly heard arguments to discontinue planting hybrids and to 'return' to local varieties is that local maize outyields hybrids when only farmyard manure is applied. Moreover, experience with local maize, the so-called *zero-type*, provides a counter-argument to the claims of plant breeders that hybrids are superior in terms of productivity. When we visited James Otieno during one of our maize variety collection tours, he pointed at the samples of maize that we held in our hand, he gave us one of his zero-type cobs and said: 'Look here. See for yourself. This cob is much bigger than the hybrid you have in your hand. So what is your judgement?'

Farmers also claim that hybrid maize lodges more than local varieties; that the cobs from hybrids open, resulting in cob rot and bird damage; and that hybrids are less resistant to weeds, pests, diseases and sudden changes in weather conditions. Hybrid maize also takes too long to mature. In contrast, 'local' maize is an early maturing variety. Hybrid maize also does not store very well and is easily attacked by weevils. Our informant Monye pointed out that the advantage of local maize is that they are early maturing:

> The fact is that local maize is as good as hybrid maize. It does not demand a lot of input and is not as labour intensive as hybrid. Sorghum is even better as one weeding is sufficient for it. Local varieties are hardy and can resist pest attack during storage. They can even be stored up to three years. Normally when I see local maize somewhere, I bring it to this place.

Soil fertility and the application of fertilisers is a major issue. Soil fertility and maintaining it is critical in Luoland. Official recommendations for maintaining soil fertility through the application of fertiliser are strongly contested. People claim that 'fertilisers spoil the soil', and that 'the soil becomes addicted to fertiliser' and that fertilisers stimulate the growth of striga, a parasitic weed. Farmers thus prefer the use of compost and farmyard manure to inorganic fertilisers. Organic manure resonates better with the production of local maize than hybrid maize and suppresses striga growth.

Cultural repertoire and taste preferences

Culturally embedded notions of how and why to grow 'local' maize are supported by strong and oft-voiced claims. Women in particular claim that the porridge (*ugali*) they make from hybrid maize is light and less satisfactory than the *ugali* made from local maize. They argue and are convinced that *ugali* made from hybrids requires twice as much maize as *ugali* from local maize. This claim is important because the assumed yield superiority of hybrids is beaten by the much higher nutritious quality of the 'local' maize varieties. Hybrid maize is also said to be less sweet than local maize. Certain local varieties are excellent and taste good when boiled; others are perfect when roasted. Furthermore, most female farmers mention that local varieties have harder seed coats as compared to the hybrid variety. They store well when dusted with ash from burnt bean stovers. Hybrid maize grains are attacked heavily by weevils, even after dusting with the same ash, because their seeds are very soft. The hybrid maize that is grown within homesteads is grown for sale. Some farmers mentioned that they quickly sell their hybrids to buy local maize in the markets. This is not a common practice, however.

Women who brew local beer (*busaa*) mention that local maize produces higher quality beer than hybrid maize and that the drink is sweeter when local maize is used. Extension agents we talked to confirm this and they attribute it to the heavier starch content in local maize as compared to hybrid maize. They say hybrid maize is light and that is why its brewing quality is low. The unique qualities of local maize are lacking in hybrid maize, which is why farmers prefer local maize. High yield alone has failed to attract farmers towards hybrids. Colour is another argument in favour of local maize.

A second crucial element in the analysis is that hybrids are perceived as not resonating with Luo culture. The practice of first sowing (*golo kohdi*) and first harvesting (*duoko cham*) is incompatible with hybrid seed. Hybrid maize is perceived as a strange seed and unlike local maize does not become part of the family seed, and is therefore incompatible with Luo cultural repertoires. It remains an 'outside seed' (*nyareta*). The *golo kodhi* principle is an essential and shared cultural repertoire among the Luo. Abednego, a fervent hybrid maize grower, explains why:

> I have to follow the Luo customs. I am the eldest son in my father's family and failure to do so might impede the progress of my other brothers in farming as they cannot put any seed in the soil before I do so. Once my mother has planted, then I can also plant, followed by my two younger brothers. (…) In the ceremony of *golo kodhi*, it is required that you use family seeds. Most people do not understand what family seeds are but today I want to tell you the secret behind it. Family seeds are the ones that were passed on to us by our ancestors. They are the ones that we try to regenerate and in case of any calamity, we can use them to offer sacrifices to the ancestors. They are able to recognise them. Furthermore the first harvest comes from these seeds we use to brew beer from and that we offer back again to our ancestors during the ceremony known as *fuachra*.

But, as always with local cultural repertoires, they are sometimes contested and reworked. It seems that if the relationship between relatives is good, a solution can more easily be found for solving (some of the) problems generated by *golo kodhi*. For instance, when the mother of Oketch Bundmawi and Oduor Lomo was delayed in her land preparation activities and therefore could not sow in time, she just sowed a few square metres of maize, after which her sons started sowing their plots. When there are disputes between relatives – which occur frequently – elders can use *golo kodhi* to display and continue their authority or to punish youngsters who, in their opinion, do not show respect to them. One other informant specifically mentioned that one way to circumvent the *golo kodhi* ceremony is to purchase seed on the market and plant it immediately, without bringing those seeds into the homestead.

Conclusion: cultural sustainability

The heterogeneous practices of maize growing are well explained when referring to the cultural repertoires. Re-assembling is not just a practice that responds to the material specificities of the objects of labour (e.g. seed, fertilisers). It is also shaped by socio-cultural beliefs and views, by history, taste and by experience. The notion of family seed appears as a key element in the explanation why local maize prevails – and probably always will – and why it resurfaces even after and during times of high-powered interventions such as MVP. Family seed brings together the cultural practices like *golo kodhi* and *duoko cham,* the continuous presence of ancestors and the authority of elders, but also the strongly expressed belief and practice that selecting own seeds from previous harvests provides a good basis for renewed production and continuous reproduction. This provides a strong belief in own seeds and lays a claim that the saving and selection of own seeds enriches their own maize without relying on commoditised relations with markets and their agents. 'Local' implies autonomy from markets and provides a good basis for food security. When we appreciate the arguments that 'local' seed is more nutritious, more colourful, sweeter, stores better and is more palatable, which is the core of the Luo maize grammar, we are witnessing the further unfolding and legitimisation of a pathway to sustainable development which is clearly rooted in a dynamic cultural repertoire of practices. This cultural repertoire gives hands and feet to a configuration that works in the daily practice of farming. Despite these cultural notions not being universally shared by the Luo, they do not upset the social fabric of rural life in Luoland. They rather provide continuity and a non-commoditised basis for achieving social and food security that would otherwise be maintained through commodity relations. 'Local' maize proves to be a pathway that is well embedded in the local agroecology and one which reduces financial expenditures.

This chapter underlines that culture is an essential element of sustainability. Interventions and expert knowledge, even if paved with good intentions, must be cognisant of cultural notions of development. The Luo grammar for maize provides substantial proof for the argument that culture does not stifle development. Culture is one of the connecting elements between society and the environment. Moreover, this chapter underlines that development does not unfold according to one single logic, as the Green Revolution and MVP protagonists have assumed and practised; development stands for a multitude of practices that are continuously reassembled in time and space. These data provide overwhelming proof that belies the widely shared belief vested in sociotechnical networks of international research, renowned universities and donors that the Green Revolution has made a significant inroad in regions like Luoland. Despite the massive investment in terms of time, status, manpower and money over the last 80 years – roughly since the colonial state attempted to change the Luo agricultural landscape – the Green Revolution has failed to make lasting inroads in Luoland. This is not unimportant, given the recent upsurge in calls to invest more and more resources in a reworked Green Revolution. The story of maize in Luoland and the grammars of maize displayed there, like other regions in the world, provide ample evidence for a culturally embedded agroecological perspective of agricultural and rural development. Such a perspective holds more promising prospects for sustainable mitigation of Luoland's recurrent food shortages than introducing a next generation of hybrids and/or genetically modified maize.

References

Anderson, B. and C. McFarlane (2011). Assemblage and geography. *Area*, 43: 124–127.

Arce, A. and N. Long (2000). *Anthropology, development and modernities: Exploring discourses, counter-tendencies and violence*. Routledge, London.

De Landa, M. (2006). *A new philosophy of society: Assemblage theory and social complexity*. Continuum, London.

Escobar, A. (2001). Culture sits in places: Reflections on globalism and subaltern strategies of localization. *Political Geography*, 20: 139–174.

Escobar, A. (2006). Difference and conflict in the struggle over natural resources: A political ecology framework. *Development*, 49: 6–13.

Gerhart, J.D. (1976). *The diffusion of hybrid maize in Western Kenya*. Princeton University Press, Princeton.

Hebinck, P. (2001). Maize and socio-technical regimes. In: P. Hebinck and G. Verschoor (eds), *Resonances and dissonances in development: Actor, networks and cultural repertoires*. Royal Van Gorcum, Assen.

Heyer, J. (1975). The origins of regional inequalities in smallholder agriculture in Kenya, 1920–73. *East African Journal of Rural Development*, 8 (1/2): 142–181.

Kimanthi, H. (2014). *Interlocking and distancing processes: An analysis of farmers' interactions with introduced crop production technologies in Sauri Millennium Village, Kenya*. Unpublished Master's thesis, Wageningen University, Wageningen.

Kitching, G. (1980). *Class and economic change in Kenya: The making of an African petite-bourgeoisie, 1905–1970*. Yale University Press, New Haven.

Latour, B. (2005). *Reassembling the social: An introduction to actor-network-theory*. Oxford University Press, Oxford.

Li, T. (2007). Practices of assemblage and community forest management. *Economy and Society*, 36: 263–293.

Long, N. (2001). *Development sociology: Actor perspectives*. Routledge, London.

Mango, N. (1999). *Integrated soil fertility management in Siaya District, Kenya*. Managing Africa's soils No.7. NUTNET Publication, Russell Press, Nottingham, United Kingdom.

Mango, N. (2002) *Husbanding the land: Agrarian development and socio-technical change in Luoland, Kenya*. Unpublished PhD thesis, Wageningen University, Wageningen.

Mango, N. and P. Hebinck. (2004). Cultural repertoires and socio-technological regimes: A case study of local and modern varieties of maize in Luoland, West Kenya. In: Wiskerke, H. and J.D. van der Ploeg (eds), *Seeds of transition: Essays on novelty production, niches and regimes in agriculture*. Royal Van Gorcum, Assen.

Massey, D. (2004). Geographies of responsibility. *Human Geography*, 86: 5–18.

Massey, D. (2005) *For space*. SAGE Publications, London.

McGee, R. 2004. Unpacking policy: Actors, knowledge and spaces. In: Brock B., McGee R. and J. Gaventa (eds), *Knowledge, actors and spaces in poverty reduction in Uganda and Nigeria*. Fountain Publishers, Kampala.

McCann, J. (2005) *Maize and grace: Africa's encounter with a New World crop, 1500–2000*. Harvard University Press, Cambridge, MA.

Olivier de Sardan, J.P. (2006). *Anthropology and development: Understanding contemporary social change*. Zed Press, London.

Paasi, A. (2010). Regions are social constructs, but who or what 'constructs' them? Agency in question. *Environment and Planning A*, 42: 2296–2301.

Rip, A. and R. Kemp (1998). Technological change. In: Rayner, S. and E.L. Malone (eds), *Human choice and climate change: Resources and technology*. Batelle Press, Columbus, Ohio.

Sanchez, P., Denning, G. and G. Nziguheba (2009). The African green revolution moves forward. *Food Security*, 1: 37–44.

Sanchez, P., Palm, C., Sachs, J., Denning, G., Flor, R., Harawa, R., Jama, B., Kiflemariam, T., Konecky, B. and R. Kozar (2007). The African millennium villages. *Proceedings of the National Academy of Sciences*, 104: 16775–16780.

Tsing, A. (2000). The global situation. *Cultural Anthropology*, 15: 327–360.

Umans, L. and A. Arce (2014). Fixing rural development cooperation? Not in situations involving blurring and fluidity. *Journal of Rural Studies*, 34: 337–344.

van Kessel, C. (1998). *Adoption, adaptation, distancing and alternative networks. An analysis of farmers' responses to a hybrid maize technology package in Yala Division, Western Kenya*. Unpublished Master's thesis. Dept. of Development studies, Nijmegen Catholic University, Nijmegen.

Woods, M. (2007) Engaging the global countryside: Globalization, hybridity and the reconstitution of rural place. *Progress in Human Geography*, 31: 485–507.

Woods, M. (2015). Territorialisation and the assemblage of rural place: Examples from Canada and New Zealand. In: this book, Chapter 3.

15 *Les jardins partagés* in Paris

Cultivating space, community and sustainable way of life

Monica Caggiano

Introduction

The popularity of urban gardens in Europe has increased since the nineteenth century, in parallel with the industrialisation processes and the associated migration from rural to urban areas. Urban workers with rural origins 'naturally' cultivated non-built areas and saved lands from urbanisation. This not only strengthened their bond with their origins and culture, but also provided some insurance against income loss and social exclusion. These modern urban gardens were first understood as gardens for underprivileged people, based on the names *migrant gardens* (UK) or *jardins ouvriers* (France). During the Second World War, so-called 'war gardens' proliferated.

In the postwar period, along with the economic boom, gardening in cities gradually lost its importance. Urban gardens became an element of landscape degradation and a symbol of poverty and sociocultural resistance owing to the modernisation processes. In the 1980s, agriculture in the cities began to flourish again. Some local institutions started showing an interest in these urban gardens, and the first municipal regulations were adopted to control squatting on unused land.

Recently, the demand for cultivable land in the city has exploded. All age groups and walks of life are getting involved in urban gardening. Along with the most classic form of gardening, new types are also emerging: terrace vegetable gardens, rooftop gardens, vertical vegetable gardens, mobile gardens and recyclable gardens, to name a few. The recent attention on urban agriculture covers different and multifaceted needs and tendencies, and involves a great diversity of political, environmental, economic, social and educational issues.

The growing number of individual garden plots is paralleled by the rise of community gardens. They are considered as an expression of collective action with the aim of recovering the urban public space to develop environmental practices and economic and social innovations.

Urban agriculture has shifted from being a sign of social backwardness to becoming an instrument of political claims. One example is the global 'Guerrilla Gardening' movement, which grows plants on vacant public or private lands without permission. The movement aims to promote reconsideration of environmental policies or land ownership to assign the land a new purpose or to reclaim land perceived as neglected or misused. *Poor people's gardens* have been transformed into so-called *agricivism:* integrating agriculture in the urban landscape as one of the main ways to improve urban environmental quality and human well-being (Ingersoll, 2004).

Urban agriculture has also become a key element in the recent debate on urban-rural integration. The classic dichotomy of rural versus urban is crumbling and in certain cases has become irrelevant due to the growing and diversified dynamics of *urbanisation of rural areas* and *ruralisation of urban areas*. Traditional concepts are not able to describe and rediscover the *sense of place* (Pascale, 2009); thus researchers are seeking new categories, symbolic and operational, to analyse the territory in a systemic way without the approach being either conflictual or functional (Bauer and Roux, 1976; Donadieu and Fluery, 2003; OECD, 2013).

The urban agriculture flourishing in densely-populated Paris is an excellent example of these dynamics. Reflecting the great popular demand, more than 70 *jardins partagés* (JPs) have been created in Paris. A JP designates a collective garden that is set up on small public plots granted by the local authorities; local associations manage the gardens. '*C'est la culture à la culture!*' ('It is cultural (horti)culture!'), said the president of the 'Auguste Renoir Square' garden. He added, 'The JPs are spaces where material and intellectual culture mix.'

Framing the case as a cultural and physical reappropriation of territory (Escobar, 1998), we aim to analyse the experience of JPs in Paris as a place-based development pathway, enhancing community self-organisation by connecting symbolic, material and structural dimensions (Turco, 1998). We aim to highlight the meanings, values, strengths and limitations of these experiences as emerging *place-based processes*. Our research was based on qualitative data collection via field surveys implemented in three phases: autumn 2008, autumn 2011 and spring 2014.

More than 40 JPs were visited and 18 JP referents were interviewed using an open-ended questionnaire. In many cases, we interviewed several garden members per JP. Other qualified witnesses were also consulted: politicians, members of the associations that help the JPs and other persons with special expertise on the subject. This chapter represents the results of that study. The short quotes from anonymous interviews reference the name of the garden to which the interviewee belongs; they were translated into English by the author.

Cultivating Paris

The JPs stem from a strong French tradition of *jardins ouvriers* ('workers' gardens'). Since 1952 these have been re-named *jardins familiaux* ('family gardens'); however, this new urban space-sharing form draws its inspiration from the New York and Montreal community gardens. In 1997, the *Fondation de France* referred to the community gardens in an invitation for bids that ultimately led to the creation of the first community garden in Lille.

Historically in Paris, family gardens were installed by the workers along the old city walls, far from the centre of town. The spirit of the modern JPs is to locate the garden inside the densely-built urban areas. This location facilitates their exploitation and most importantly promotes the concept of collective management of the local environment.

In 2001, after the election of the Paris Mayor, Bertrand Delanoë, the City Hall launched the *Charte Main Verte* ('Pact of the Green Thumb') project with the objective of regulating, sustaining and promoting the community gardens located within the city limits. This project was embedded into a larger 'City Greening' programme that was sustained by a left-wing coalition with a strong influence from *Les Verts* (the Green Party). However, as an environmental consultant at the Paris City Hall explains:

> The JPs were a response to a structured and precise citizens' request. The project started under the first Delanoë administration, but some gardens had been created previously. In some cases, the gardens spontaneously rose up on public plots and were squatted by the inhabitants. Through the Green Thumb programme we tried to create discipline and provide a legal and institutional framework to this phenomenon.

The new administration adopted public participation in decision-making processes as a key point of its electoral programme and the number of applications for public space use and green areas were numerous.

The City Hall created a convention that the associations then signed. The members were granted a plot to garden for one to five years, under certain conditions such as opening hours, organisation of public events, creating a management plan, communication and showing respect for the environment by adhering to the rules of organic gardening. The municipality provides the garden with adapted soil, guarantees the water supply and provides an enclosure around the garden. The city created a department for 'Green Space and Environment' that helps to create gardens and provides follow-up activities such as training sessions, gardeners' seminars (*Les cafés-jardins*), organises days for seed trade and exchange of know-how, and the like.

Cultivating urban wasteland

JPs are small plots varying from 70 m^2 (*1001 Feuilles* garden) to around 1000 m^2 (*Jardin de l'Aqueduc,* one of the largest inner-city gardens), with creative names such as *Le Poireau Agile* (The Agile Leek), *Papilles et Papillons* (Papillae and Butterflies), *Potager des Oiseaux* (The Birds' Vegetable Garden), *Aligresse* (the garden is located next to Aligre square, thus the name is a play on words based on *Allégresse,* meaning 'joy'). Sometimes the JPs are situated in public parks, a location meant to stimulate citizens to care for the gardens.

The JPs are usually managed by neighbourhood associations, either pre-existing or created on an ad hoc basis. These associations either follow the citizens' or the *quartier* council initiative, or are formed ad hoc directly by the local municipality. If pre-existing, they have other activities in the *quartier* (leisure, social integration, training, etc.); in other cases their activities are limited to the garden management alone.

The number of members of the associations ranges from 20 to 200 persons, or even more for some associations, but in cases of larger associations the task of managing the garden is just one part of the association's activities; the JP Alligresse is an example of this. The number of actual gardeners is usually lower, with an average of 35 per JP.

The JPs are mainly located on the northern and eastern parts of Paris; about 60 per cent are in the XVIII, XIX and XX *arrondissements* (administrative districts), because these have a greater availability of urban wasteland and lower real estate prices than other areas. These traditionally working-class neighbourhoods are now populated by a new middle class that includes many immigrants. Most of the local governments have left-wing administrations. A spatial map of the JPs shows a striking co-location with the outline of the last barricades of the *Commune de Paris* in 1871, which still symbolises the great utopia of a government of the people.

In the current process of economisation and privatisation of social life, which is resulting in a decline of the public and community realm, the JPs assume a role of what Ray Oldenburg calls 'third places': public places on neutral ground where people can gather and interact (Oldenburg, 1999). Third places are positioned between the home (first place) and the workplace (second place); they allow the informal social relations that are important for community development and social cohesion. 'Nowadays, living in a city means being considered either as a user or a consumer, whereas in a JP everyone can be themselves' (Interview, 'Charming Little Urban Campaign').

The gardens are located on public areas that are usually owned by the Paris municipality, but in other cases they are found on plots belonging to public real estate entities such as *Paris Habitat* or the *Réseau Ferré de France* (the state-owned entity that manages France's railway infrastructure). The sites have often been abandoned: sometimes permanently or sometimes temporarily, for example before a planned construction project or new assignation. In these cases, they form an ephemeral reality, which is sometimes reflected in the name: 'Nomad Garden' or 'Ephemeral Garden'. Despite their planned short lifespan, they successfully gather attention and human energy. The transient and ephemeral nature of JPs represents a weakness in the context of place-based development, however, because these processes require a non-ephemeral amount of time to flourish.

Cultivating territory

'The JPs are highly symbolic places where people can (re)connect with nature in a magical and surreal context, between buildings and asphalt' (Interview, *Jardin de Falbala*). In the JPs, the *process* of territorialisation starts with physically enclosing the garden, thus delimiting a specific place in the urban landscape. This enclosure opens a common area inside the city. This creates a marked contrast with the classical enclosure of the commons in order to privatise or nationalise common land in an attempt to avoid the so-called 'Tragedy of the Commons'

(Hardin, 1968). The definition of boundaries allows a 'symbolic control of space', adding value to a zone which was perceived as urban wasteland but which now, through a collective appropriation of urban space, has become a garden.

The gardeners perceive being part of the community as an important advantage of participating in a JP. They see it as a form of 'symbolic public good', which might be considered as an important driver of collective action. The new individual and community imaginaries blooming on the garden activate a social construction of the place, where the sense of place is the product of interactions involving the individual, the setting and their social worlds (Hay, 1998).

The enclosure also legitimises a 'material control of space', empowering people to have the control and ownership of a garden and to consider it *their* space. The possibility for citizens to actively transform a space outside of their own home – a space that is often perceived as alien and outside of their control – further strengthens the dynamics of identification between the community and its lived space.

Finally, the enclosure structures a place under a specific regulatory framework. It results from a negotiation process in which land users interact among themselves and with the institutional rules defined by the Pact of the Green Thumb. In this way, every garden can adapt the regulatory framework to its own needs, exploring innovative practices and institutional arrangements within the overall regulations.

Cultivating identities

These processes of sensemaking create similar but unique places. Each JP is distinctive and the local government admits this high level of diversity: 'Each JP is very different from the other. The City Hall does not have a dogmatic attitude towards this, but rather recognises the existence of deep differences in their management and organisation' (Interview, Environmental Consultant at Paris City Hall). Nevertheless, the municipality is still a dominant actor in the process, limiting the citizens' power in decision making.

There are great differences even within the same garden. The JPs involve a rich and varied archipelago of individuals: senior citizens, children, managers, unemployed people, professionals, illegal immigrants and so on, all of them linked by their common passion for gardening. The richness of this situation confirms the transversal nature of agriculture and horticulture, thus enabling intercultural and intergenerational unions. In addition, 'when running the garden activities, there's no need for appointed leaders. Everyone can take this role in turn' (Interview, *Jardingue*, Archipelia Association).

Gardeners participate in the project with their own agricultural vision, depending on their culture, social origins, personal background and experiences. For instance, the high incidence of female gardeners from Southeast Asian countries (such as Vietnam or Cambodia) is remarkable; in those cultures, women are traditionally in charge of the family garden.

For some people the JP is 'a home extension, the garden that we don't have, a little paradise in a *quartier* with little green space' (Interview, *Association*

Cultures et Potager 17/18, *Jardin des deux Néthes*). These gardeners enjoy its relaxing and therapeutic nature, as well as the opportunity to do physical labour outdoors. Others have highlighted how much this activity has a deep value: 'gardening is a vital need' (Interview, *Jardin de Falbala*) or it

> concerns the relationships between mankind and nature, people, culture and beauty. Cultivating tomatoes is learning again about the original human values, growing what you need yourself, rediscovering the value of caring for the earth in the beauty of a flower.
>
> (Interview, *Jardingue*, Archipelia Association)

For other participants (French natives or foreigners) coming from a rural area, cultivating a garden means keeping their own roots alive. They bring their past know-how and experience to the JP: the gardener from Maghreb cultivates mint, whilst the Breton cultivates artichokes. The JPs are therefore also a tool to preserve and transmit knowledge and traditions among different generations and cultures.

The majority of gardeners, however, do not have previous experience in gardening. Every JP has one or two persons with real knowhow; these become points of reference for the group. Nevertheless, they all remain eager to obtain information and suggestions. Fellow association members, family members, bystanders and the ever-present internet are mostly used as an alternative source of information.

Cultivating diversity

The gardeners' social context reflects the area where the garden is located. Some JPs are social and cultural melting pots, while others are characterised by a unique people typology, mainly middle-class urbanites: 'to say it simply, we ... are mainly White Europeans' (Interview, *Jardin d'Alligresse*) that does not explicitly represent the sociocultural local context. However, two important dynamics that frame the Paris urban landscape (the increasing gentrification of the city and the growing numbers of individuals with multicultural/cross-cultural identity) influence how JPs deal with multiculturality. Generally speaking, in JPs located further from the city centre, the garden is more open to the context, both physically and figuratively. When the JPs are located inside public gardens and have no physical fence, they organise activities with the local community, and multiculturalism flourishes. Foreign-born gardeners often use crops and cultivation techniques originating in their native countries (Daniel, 2012).

Divergences are evident in the way people from different cultures participate in the life of the garden and in the association that manages it. In general, the project sponsors – who manage and take official responsibilities in the associations – are well-integrated middle class persons who are able to deal with the institutions, while foreign citizens are less involved in association life.

Figure 15.1 A small *jardin partagé* in a working-class neighbourhood

Sources: © Antonio Calone (upper and bottom right); © Zohra Bouabdallah (bottom left)

> It's not outright that many of the Africans or Asians living in this *quartier* would take part in the garden activities, as well as in other association activities, maybe due to the fact that the bureaucratic and associative mechanisms require language and certain modalities that are typically occidental.
>
> (Interview, *Jardingue,* Archipelia Association)

Or:

> Those Kabylian women always meet on that bench, and can stay for hours to observe the JP; it is the part of the park they prefer the most. We invited them to cultivate their own plot, but they declined.
>
> (Interview, *Le Poireau Agile*)

Communication channels play a crucial role in the integration process of foreign citizens. Part of this population has hardly any access to the information, and this lack of access is sometimes accentuated by their lack of knowledge of French, although this does not always prevent people from participating: 'Some JP members I have seen are completely illiterate extra-communitarian women' (Interview, *Graine de Jardins*).

The different meanings, attitudes and values of gardeners generate a diversity of practices and internal rules, which are reflected in different perceptions of the places. We have distinguished the following differences in perceptions.

First, the idea of agriculture is considered as a means to create and strengthen social links between citizens. This objective, explicitly included in the Pact of the Green Thumb, as well as in some association by-laws, can be more or less strong and evident, and is often prioritised:

> As far as we are concerned, gardening is an alibi, a pretext to recreate what the city has taken from us: a meeting place. We are less interested in counting the carrots we have produced than the number of persons we have included. We want this garden to become a space for meeting and dialogue among different generations and cultures.
>
> (Interview, *Les Haies Partagés*)

In the past, the *jardins ouvriers* also had a two-pronged objective: the more materialistic objectives linked with food cultivation/production were joined with the moral/political ones, as synthesised by the famous sentence of Priest Jules Lemire, the father of the French *jardins ouvriers*: 'The garden is the means, the family is the purpose' (*La terre est le moyen, la famille est le but*, Cabedoce and Pierson, 1996: 11). This quote expresses the opinion that gardening is not only an alimentary and economic resource, but also a healthy and honest way to spend time with the family.

Another perception concerns the tension between a private and collective vision on space, expressed both at the garden and plot level. 'Our slogan is: "Here there is nothing to take and everything to share". Any visitor can plant something;

they do not need to be a registered member' (Interview, *Les Haies Partagés*). This 'sharing vision' is not homogeneously present among JPs; clear differences arise starting from plot management strategies. The JP plots can be individual, collective or mixed, where individual areas are next to collective ones, often reserved for the schools and neighbourhood children. Some are also semi-collective areas, cultivated by two to four people with different criteria for how the plots are assigned. In the JP *Cité Prost*, for instance, 'we have a waiting list from which we gradually assign the plots. The interesting thing is that people sharing the same space don't know each other, so this is a way to meet new people' (Interview, *Jardin Partagé Citè Prost*).

For collective plots, the key management rules are set during a general assembly or other informal meeting, and then each member is free to implement his or her own solution variations: 'We have the vegetable plot, the one for medicinal plants, and so on … Every parcel has one person who manages and coordinates the others' work' (Interview, *Jardin Fessart*). The collective management works well when the associates share joint goals and efficient communication tools, such as board diaries, are used.

The shift from individual to collective plots has been observed in several gardens:

> We now want to transform some individual areas into collective ones, devoted to a common and shared project, which everyone could stick to. We aim to increase the conviviality in the relationships between the associates, and to enable the participation of the many others who are on the waiting list.
>
> (Interview, *Jardin des deux Néthes*)

This trajectory reflects a maturation process and increasing consciousness of the idea of sharing. However, this can happen in a rather painful way, such as seen when some members resist giving up their own plot. 'I garden this parcel with my daughter and for her it would be strange to share it. We have invested in it sentimentally and emotionally and this is too important to give up' (Interview, *Jardin des deux Néthes*).

In some cases, the evolution to a collective gardening is due to practical reasons:

> There are almost ten individual plots and the rest is collective. In the beginning, we decided to let the members choose their option. Now, on the contrary, we are urging them to make the second choice. It has been a natural evolution since some families didn't take care of their individual plot. Above all, the collective management is more likely to fulfil our objective, which is to meet each other and not only the harvest.
>
> (Interview, *Jardin de Falbala*)

In some cases, the JPs' nature could be misunderstood, with a real risk of privatisation of public space:

> Some gardeners' visionis influenced from the tradition of the *jardin ouvrier*, which runs very deep in France. In that case, they contact us to be granted a plot that they can exploit in an exclusively private way. They start to create many defence barriers, rarely interact with others and never participate in the life of the association.
>
> (Interview, Environmental Consultant at Paris City Hall)

Different visions generate different practices and rules. This can also generate various conflicts within the JPs, especially concerning the general management, running the association, and what to do with unsupervised children.

> The JPs are frequented by many African kids; the parents very often work and cannot attend to them during the day – some gardeners don't want to welcome them in the garden.
>
> (Interview, Environmental Consultant at Paris City Hall)

Other conflicts relate to the vision of proper cultivation: 'Some people would like a perfect garden without a blade of grass, while others would prefer to foster biodiversity and devote more space to spontaneously-growing plants' (Interview, *Graine de Jardins*). Conflicts are often resolved through negotiation; they often end with the departure of individuals from the garden or with the closure of their own plots.

This diversity, both at the level of individuals and gardens, activates several processes of social and community change, which affects cultural sustainability in different ways.

Cultivating cultural sustainability

The JPs may contribute to various forms of cultural sustainability, improving different visions and practices of place, community, urban life and landscape, and resulting in a blooming of 'place-consciousness' (Magnaghi, 2010) and reterritorialisation processes (Deleuze and Guattari, 1980).

A JP is an instructive example of how resources are combined with individual self-interest to create favourable conditions for collective action, simultaneously providing interlinked individual or club goods and purely public goods. The JPs do not contribute significantly only to the quality of life of the gardeners; they also provide various ecological, social and cultural advantages for the whole population. Such advantages affect the social well-being and public happiness, restoring the urban space for social relation, proximity and better environmental quality.

First of all, the JPs add territorial value to the urban area through its social management. The JPs ensure the enjoyment of green spaces and often save them from negligence and social degradation: 'Before the garden, there was a playground for kids. Little by little, fewer and fewer kids came to play there, and it became a place to sell drugs' (Interview, *Jardin de Falbala*). In addition, the municipality saved money on cleaning and maintenance of the area:

> For the municipality, maintaining a free space has a cost – people dump everything in it, and it becomes a garbage container. In a JP, on the contrary, people get involved in the space management and cleaning it; moreover, they organise activities for the *quartier*.
>
> (Interview, *Jardin Fessart*)

The basic costs for a JP vary from case to case. For example, 'In our municipality the investment was between 20,000 and 60,000 euros' (Interview, City Representative of the XIV *arrondissement*). There are some factors that particularly influence the costs, for example if the plot is public or has to be acquired. However, the main impact results from drainage costs, depending on the plot's level of pollution. 'Recently, we made an evaluation of a JP which resulted in an estimated cost of 5,000 euros for 100 m^2. Regardless, when considering the long term, the initial investment is less than the recurring maintenance costs for a green space' (Interview, Environmental Consultant at Paris City Hall). Another element to be considered is that the incidence of acts of vandalism is much lower in JPs compared to other public assets, green spaces included. 'In Paris, acts of vandalism episodes on public properties are very frequent. The JPs, however, are much more respected, probably because they are created by the inhabitants, therefore considered as peers, marking a clear difference with what is created by institutions' (Interview, *Graine de Jardins*). In addition, the JPs are often the fruit of children's work, so an awareness campaign is being implemented, including through the schools. The direct participation therefore produces a civic consciousness and a social control.

> The garden is open and accessible to everybody even when the association members are absent. We've never had damage or any other problems. I'd go as far to say that the more open a garden is, the less it is a target for vandalism, as people feel more responsible.
>
> (Interview, *Les Haies Partagés*)

The JPs not only create a garden community, but they strengthen social links between the other citizens with the result of improving social integration and social capital, which are considered as strategic key resources for place-based development (Magnaghi, 2010). A JP, despite the fence, remains a public space. When the gate is open, everyone can pop in. This open space encourages conviviality and dialogue: 'There's always someone who, passing by the garden, comes in, asks something, then we start chatting about any subject, not only gardening, but also about life in the *quartier*, politics and so on' (Interview, *Jardin Fessart*).

Moreover, the JPs are frequently the stages for shows, parties, children's activities and opportunities to involve other citizens, especially the neighbourhood residents, who often contribute to the garden's life by donating plants, gardening tools and other furniture: 'The JP is a component of life in the *quartier* and is regularly frequented by some people that are not members but are very active in the management of the garden' (Interview, *Les Haies Partagés*). From an environmental perspective, even though these projects are on a small scale, the JPs contribute to the landscape's beauty and to the enhancement of ecosystem services in various ways. For instance, they improve the air quality in a polluted urban context, and they close the nutrient cycle by recycling organic waste and, through the use of compost, improve nutrients and soil structure. They increase the biodiversity within the city limits, since the JPs encourage pollination and are a refuge for wildlife such as soil organisms, wild plants, insects, birds, etc.

Furthermore, the JPs contribute to the diffusion of a *culture* of *environmental sustainability,* reconnecting urban residents to nature, promoting organic farming and environmentally respectful practices. In addition, they preserve and improve tacit knowledge and skills as part of the so-called 'social ecological memory for ecosystem management' (Barthel *et al.*, 2010), transferring it among different generations and cultures.

In this way, the JPs might be effective laboratories to experiment with and disseminate citizen practices to encourage sustainable exploitation of the environment and conservation of biodiversity.

Cultivating commons

The JPs can play an important role in community development as well as raise the quality of life of inhabitants and their civic sense.The JP often evolves into a catalyst for participation in public life, hosting debates around local issues. In some cases, this political mould is more conscious and claimed:

> The JP, as far as we are concerned, is a social network factory for local resistance. It is a shared and direct democratic space; we are convinced that only a small geographic stage could be a landscape for possible social changes. The JP makes it possible for people to reappropriate public awareness.
>
> (Interview, *JP Alligresse*)

Sometimes, the political connotation is obvious from the outset; often the JP is a result of a long lasting social mobilisation to conquer public green spaces, such as the JP *Cité Prost*, which is situated in the middle of a public park.

> On this field, there was a plan to build a seven-storey social housing project. From 1996, we began organising demonstrations and petitions to request the creation of a garden in this densely inhabited neighbourhood with few green spaces. When the city administration changed, we thought that the time had come to give a legal form to our movement and to negotiate with the public authorities. This process succeeded and in a short time, we obtained a public park, with a space for the JP in the middle of it.
>
> (Interview, *Cité Prost*)

The JP of *Rue des Coulmiers* is another example of social mobilisation: a neighbourhood resident managed to create a pressure group, posting notices on the fence of an abandoned piece of land owned by the French railway company, inviting the residents to come every Saturday morning to squat and reappropriate it. At these times, the plot was being invaded by the inhabitants who started planting different plants. In the beginning, the activities were performed under the railway officers' and police watch, and indeed, the railway company intended to sue the group for private property violation. But after long negotiations with the mediation of the XIV *arrondissement,* which supported the project, the JP was officially created in May 2008, after almost one year of illegal Saturday gardening sessions.

The JPs can even affect citizenship itself, improving the inhabitants' quality of life as well as their civic sense. 'Very often, those who first approach the garden don't have the slightest idea of how to deal with institutions, how the city is organised and what the institutions are that manage it' (Interview, *Graine de Jardins*).

Sometimes the JPs can arouse interest in community life and trigger learning mechanisms on how to take part in it: 'Thanks to the JPs, the citizens realise that by working together they gain voice and power. Many persons, who frequented the garden got interested in municipal life, started attending the quartier councils; in short, they gained self-confidence as citizens' (Interview, City Representative of XIV *arrondissement*). The JPs also offer important suggestions for the institutional dimension of cultural sustainability. The JPs' community management belongs to the experiences that show a middle road between the state and market in public asset management (the commons) and in the local governance.

Several studies, like those of the Economy Nobel prize laureate Elinor Ostrom (Ostrom, 1990), have enlightened the validity of collective management and the community's ability to generate endogenous institutional arrangements (community rules, systems and tools), compliant with an environmentally and economically sustainable management of common-pool resource.

Finally, the JPs can improve the imaginaries of cultural sustainability. Taking part in a JP, or merely visiting it, in an urban high-density European city, creates a sort of *V-effekt* (*Verfremdungseffekt*, the alienation effect) used in Brecht's theatre to provide a 'bond' of alienation between performer and audience in the play through jolting reminders of the artificiality of the theatrical performance (Brecht, 1964). The *V-effekt* turns the spectator into an observer, arousing his capacity for action, forcing him to make decisions. Similarly, a JP creates a perceptual sense of dislocation in the viewer: 'The JPs enable people to get disconnected from any surrounding event' (Interview, *Jardin de Falbala*). Their special ability to break with the surrounding environment pushes citizens to think about the natural, cultural and social degradation commonly taking place.

> A JP is a privileged space of exchange, a way to open and make enlived places. This is a place where we can enjoy staying with other people. If we would meet these same persons in a bus, they would not talk to each other; however in the JP they do, because it's a special place, also for its beauty.
>
> (Interview, *Potager des Oiseaux*)

As the *V-effekt* should encourage the audience to see the possibilities for actions in the world outside the theatre, the JPs' effect of increasing awareness should stimulate a critical view and a will to manifest change that goes beyond its limits. Instead of providing only temporary relief from the uneasiness of city life, JPs suggest scenarios for sustainable futures, promoting community management where urban agriculture becomes an urban planning tool for sustainable urban planning (Donadieu, 1998).

Conclusions

JPs present interesting insights for the debate on place-based development in the urban context and on cultural sustainability. The gardens integrate rurality into cities, creating an aesthetic function that inevitably includes ethical, productive, social and cultural functions. Contrary to the functionalist urbanism, assuming urban qualities through zoning and functional separation, urban gardens express the vision of multifunctional space (Donadieu, 1998). Viewed from a broader perspective, JPs could be a real project of local development (Hirschman, 1958). These projects mobilise resources and capabilities that are hidden, scattered or under-utilised, promoting a collective well-being based on (and improving) an awareness of place, according to the territoriality approach (Magnaghi, 2010).

Albeit to varying degrees in different actors and different JPs, the gardeners produce a community and individual empowerment in urban planning and reappropriation of public space. The people in many urban areas often experience their territory as foreign and/or constrictive, outside of their effective control. In the case of JPs, the sharing of experiences, knowledge, memories and imagination allows new narratives of place to emerge, facilitating the processes of territorial transformation.

Gardens are an example of processes of co-production between society and the environment, including concrete and symbolic dimensions, according to the vision of place as a set of relationships, a relational space, instead of a mere physical space or geographical area (Dematteis, 1985; Horlings *et al.*, 2015).

These processes of territorialisation develop at a different pace depending on the garden. We cannot consider the JPs as a homogeneous notion with regard to their meanings and their practices. This uniform vision tends to hide the great varieties of symbols, motivations, spatial configurations, meanings and organisations as well as the particular and contextualised practices which make any garden unique. This remarkable heterogeneity is manifested both between different JPs and within gardens, involving meanings, practices and organisational frameworks.

A general weakness of all these experiences is their space and time limits, the ephemeral nature of many gardens and their structured boundaries that limit the social construction of territory and the community-building that takes place within and outside the gardens.

The institutional framework in which the gardens are embedded can represent another limitation to the territorialisation processes, as illustrated in the *Jardin*

Solidaire experience. Although it became a reference in the *quartier* for its critical role in the local activities and social integration, it has been closed after a long struggle between the population and the authorities. Similarly different gardens of the XVIII *arrondissement* are currently under threat of closure despite their important activities in the social life of their neighbourhood. In these cases, the relationship with the city authority has become very conflictual. The institutional framework allows the development of JPs and fixes their practices within defined borders.

The gardeners add value to the urban landscape, transforming 'non-places' (Augé, 2008) of the urban area into 'hyperspaces' that provide a multiplicity of possibilities (Ascher, 2008), or rather into 'hyper territories' as qualified by the reconstruction of community relations of solidarity and social bonding (Magnaghi, 2007). However, no generalisations are possible. The trajectories through which these potentials are realised (or not) are unique for each *jardin partagé*.

References

Ascher, F. (2008). *Les nouveaux compromis urbains: Lexique de la ville plurielle*. Éditions de l'Aube, La Tour d'Aigues, Vaucluse.

Augé, M. (2008). *Nonluoghi, introduzione a una antropologia della surmodernità*. Eutherpa, Milan.

Barthel, S., Folke, C. and J. Colding (2010). Social-ecological memory in urban gardens: Retaining the capacity for management of ecosystem services. *Global Environmental Change*, 20 (2): 255–265.

Bauer, G. and G.M. Roux (1976). *La rurbanisation ou la ville éparpillée*. Éditions du Seuil, Paris.

Brecht, B. (1964). *Brecht on theatre: The development of an aesthetic*. Hill and Wang, New York.

Cabedoce, B. and P. Pierson (1996). *Cent ans d'histoire des jardins ouvriers*. Éditions Créaphis, Paris.

Daniel, A.C. (2012). *Comment les jardiniers des jardins associatifs contribuent-ils à la construction de paysages alimentaires? Mémoire M2*. Ingénierie des Territoires, Agrocampus Ouest, Angers.

Deleuze, G. and F. Guattari (1980). *Mille plateaux*. Les Éditions de Minuit, Paris.

Dematteis, G. (1985). *Le metafore della terra: La geografia umana tra mito e scienza*. Feltrinelli, Milan.

Donadieu, P. (1998). *Campagnes urbaines*. Actes Sud, Arles.

Donadieu, P. and A. Fleury (2003). La construction contemporaine de la ville-campagne. *Revue de Géographie Alpine*, 91 (4): 19–28.

Escobar, A. (1998). Whose knowledge, whose nature? Biodiversity conservation and the political ecology of social movements. *Journal of Political Ecology*, 5: 53–82.

Hardin, G. (1968). The tragedy of the commons. *Science* (AAAS), 162: 1243–1248.

Hay, R. (1998). Sense of place in a developmental context. *Journal of Environmental Psychology*, 18: 5–29.

Hirschman, A.O. (1958). *The strategy of economic development*. Yale University Press, New Haven.

Horlings, L., Battaglini, E. and J. Dessein (2015). Introduction: The role of culture in territorialisation. In: this book, Chapter 1.

Ingersoll, R. (2004). *Sprawltown*. Meltemi, Rome.

Magnaghi, A. (2007). Il territorio come soggetto di sviluppo delle società locali. *Etica ed economia*, Vol. IX, 1/2007.

Magnaghi, A. (2010). *Progetto locale: Verso la coscienza di luogo*. Bollati Boringhieri, Turin.

OECD (2013). *Rural-urban partnerships: An intergrated approach to economic development*. OECD Publishing, Paris.

Oldenburg, R. (1999). *The great good place: Cafes, coffee shops, bookstores, bars, hair salons, and other hangouts at the heart of a community*. Marlowe, New York.

Ostrom, E. (1990). *Governing the commons: The evolution of institutions for collective action*. Cambridge University Press, Cambridge.

Pascale, A. (2009). Coi concetti di urbano e rurale non si riscopre il senso dei luoghi. *Agriregionieuropa*, n. 18 September.

Turco, A. (1998). *Verso una teoria geografica della complessità*. Unicopli, Milan.

16 A 'European Valley' in South America

Regionalisation, colonisation and environmental inequalities in Santa Catarina, Brazil

Luciano Félix Florit, Lilian Blanck de Oliveira, Reinaldo Matias Fleuri and Rodrigo Wartha

Introduction

The Brazilian state of Santa Catarina is widely viewed as being the most European of the Brazilian states, due to the nineteenth-century colonisation by European immigrants. Nevertheless, the construction of the regional identity as 'European' implies the invisibility of other sociocultural and ethnic identities that have been historically subalternised or excluded, resulting in inequities that usually remain unrecognised.

In this chapter we analyse how the tourist regionalisation process known as the 'European Valley' updates and reinforces these inequities, thus contributing to the maintenance of a colonial relationship. We base our reflections here on the territorialisation process of the state of Santa Catarina by analysing the colonisation process and the state government's construction of regional divisions. Regionalisation is considered here as a form of territorialisation. The analysis focuses on the symbolic and institutional dimension of territorialisation; the latter is expressed in the drawing of administrative policy boundaries on behalf of the state.

We use the term 'territorialisation' to refer to the process by which the territory has been defined and reified over the course of history, thereby rooting the communities' cultural identities. In our case study, the territorialisation process is described as highly conflict-laden owing to the colonial occupation of indigenous peoples' territories. The conjunction between colonisation and the territorial configuration process resulted in the stereotypical opposition between social groups identified as 'Brazilian' and the people of European descent. Although this process appears to have been completed during the nineteenth century, we illustrate how it is still ongoing as revealed through contemporary tourist regionalisation.

We argue that the tourist regionalisation labelled as the 'European Valley' is a specific form of territoralisation that reifies a naturalised territorial construction which began with a colonisation process characterised by violence against the indigenous peoples of the region. We use reification here in a sociological way meaning 'to give reality', which refers to an understanding of regions not as pre-given but as socially and historically constructed. In Santa Catalina (SC) this regional construction occurred in a context of conflict. This reification maintains and updates the relations typical of coloniality, while at the same time reinforcing the invisibility of regional indigenous concerns. From the indigenous peoples' point of view, the fundamental problem is the disastrous effects of the state's flood-control policy as exemplified in the dam built on indigenous territory. The dam's construction and its effect on the indigenous people is just one of the unrecognised inequalities (in this case, an environmental one) represented in the state of Santa Catarina.

Coloniality and territorialisation in Santa Catarina

Brazil is one of the largest countries in the world, occupying almost half of the continent of South America with an area of 8.5 million km². Diversity is a hallmark of Brazilian society. It has more than two hundred indigenous ethnic groups which together comprise about 2 per cent of the population. More than half of all Brazilians are descendants of people from various African countries; while another significant portion of the population is made up of the descendants of immigrants from different continents, cultures and religions.

The state of Santa Catarina (SC) is located in southern Brazil, bordered to the north by Paraná (PR), to the south by Rio Grande do Sul (RS), on the east by the Atlantic Ocean and on the west by the Republic of Argentina. It occupies nearly 96,000 km² (1.12 per cent of the country) and is divided into 295 municipalities. With a population of slightly more than 6 million inhabitants (2010), it represents 3.28 per cent of the Brazilian population. In 2010, the gross domestic product (GDP) of SC was R$152 billion, the seventh greatest in the country and 4 per cent of Brazil's total GDP.

From the beginning of the occupation of Brazil in 1500 until the eighteenth century, Santa Catarina remained little explored. Because it possessed neither gemstones nor other major attractions for the Portuguese Crown, the area remained largely undisturbed, covered by native forest and inhabited by indigenous peoples. At the beginning of the eighteenth century, Santa Catarina was divided in two main regions. The coastal cities of Laguna, San Francisco do Sul and Desterro (currently Florianópolis) became important cities for supplying Portuguese ships heading further south to Colonia del Sacramento, Uruguay. The second region, called the *Caminho das Tropas* (The Way of the Troops), was one of the major Brazilian economic routes during the eighteenth and nineteenth centuries. This important economic route connected the southeast to the south, mainly for trading mules, which were indispensable for the work of the gold mines of Minas Gerais.

By the 1820s, slavery had started to fall out of favour, and some measures against the practice had already been taken in Brazil, although it would not be fully outlawed until 1888. At the same time, the government initiated attempts to attract European immigrants to work on new projects. The influx of European immigrants gave the area a strong background of European colonisation, culture and religion. The legacy of this history is revealed in the cultural diversity of

Santa Catarina, as exemplified by the different languages, identities, traditions of knowledge and territorialities. European colonisation manifests itself through strategies of control over certain areas or space to reach and influence people and resources (Sack, 1986). This control has resulted in the imposition of behavioural rules, modes of speaking, and so on, along with the uses and valuations of nature that construct the landscape, both symbolically and materially.

The territorialisation was decisively determined by the history of colonisation. Territorialisation is implied in the dense ethnic content, which was constructed through a process of conflict, especially in relation to indigenous peoples who lived in the region. According to Bonnemaison and Cambrézy (1996: 13–14, author's translation), the symbolic and cultural load which is present in a territory integrates and constructs the identity of human beings:

> We belong to a territory. We do not have it, we do not keep it; we dwell in it, we impregnate ourselves with it. [...] In short, the territory is not just about its functions or possession, but about its being. To forget this spiritual and nonmaterial principle is to be doomed to not understand the tragic violence of many struggles and conflicts that affect the world today: to lose territory is to disappear.

In this conflict-laden process, some histories and cultures were privileged over others via processes of cultural homogenisation that were initiated during colonisation. In the Itajaí Valley in Santa Catarina, oral and written celebrations of the heroism of European immigrants are among the discourses that fill the memory of the people, who maintain relationships, knowledge and regional experiences. This enhances European culture while rendering invisible other groups that are in fact part of Santa Catarina and the Itajaí Valley, such as indigenous peoples, people of African descent, African-Brazilians, *caboclos*, *sertanejos* and *quilombolas* (Oliveira *et al.*, 2014).

The original inhabitants of Santa Catarina are the indigenous Xokleng Laklanõ, Kaingang and Guarani peoples. These were semi-nomadic and, in the case of the Xokleng Laklanõ, moved freely through an area stretching from Porto Alegre (RS) to Curitiba (PR). The movement of pioneers and, later, troops into these areas led to the indigenous populations being fixed in place, mainly on account of the trade carried out by the *tropeirismo*. By the beginning of the nineteenth century, SC had several established cities around this route. However, the current borders of the territory as a state in the Republic were not defined until the twentieth century, after the Contestado War (1912–1916).

In this context, the Portuguese Crown began a violent policy of occupation of the traditional indigenous spaces. King João VI, by Royal Charter (1808), declared war on Xokleng Laklanõ residing in the domains of Lages and Guarapuava (Pereira *et al.*, 1998). In parallel, the government established several groups to advance colonisation and throughout the nineteenth century promoted systematic policies of occupying indigenous territory. The government thereafter enforced multiple polices that aimed directly at defining the population groups and, in many cases, (re)creating stereotypes and stigmatising cultures. What had previously been officially defensive wars against indigenous populations became wars of spatial occupation (da Cunha, 2009) aimed at imposing a colonial cultural vision.

To replace slave labour, the government acted to attract European immigrants. In 1824, the first groups of German immigrants arrived in São Leopoldo (RS) and, in 1829, a large contingent settled in San Pedro de Alcantara (SC). Both cities were close to their state capitals to provide them with agricultural support. From 1870 on, Italian immigrants began to arrive. Dos Santos (1998) indicates that the indigenous people who occupied the southern region of Brazil at the beginning of colonisation were gradually driven into the interior by the threat of diseases and *bugreiros* (hunters of indigenous people).

In Brazil, the creation of laws relating to land ownership and the replacement of slaves with European immigrants occurred throughout the nineteenth century. These moves aligned with the interests of large landowners, mainly coffee producers in the southeast, who held their production base on large properties using slave labour. The land and labour force have always been considered from the economist's bias of development of the territory and its integration into the market economy, a view that was emerging in that century. This strategy conceived the stages of economic development in land policy and the management of the labour force to be inseparable (da Costa, 1979).

In 1850, a few days after the promulgation of the Eusébio de Queiroz Law that prohibited the slave trade, the Land Law was passed, establishing purchase as the only form of access to land. This law was conceived for colonisation and for the deployment of immigrants and settlers (an official category, synonymous with *peasant*, and in the south assumed to refer to individuals of European origin), as well as for the consolidation of properties, thereby establishing all the legal structures and the land development pattern (Seyferth, 1974). Both laws were formulated in the context of the structure of the National States, whose borders defined population distributions that gave immigrants a large majority. This resulted in the demand for new laws to ensure domination and control over population and territories.

By creating a land market and encouraging the expansion of settlements by Europeans, the Brazilian government increased the differences between the existing populations and the settlers, triggering conflict and disputes. The consolidation of Santa Catarina as a state took place in the context of this political and administrative structure, where the presence of European settlers, through government action on land sales, came gradually. It led to the expropriation of indigenous traditional territories and the initiation of new regional development processes, with new concepts of nature and natural resources, new agents and new territorial configurations.

From the sociocultural point of view, this conjunction between colonisation and the territorial configuration process resulted in the stereotypical opposition between social groups identified as 'Brazilian' and '*de origem*', which in this context means 'of European origin'. Those who were '*de origem*' identified themselves as descendants of European immigrants, specifically of Italians and Germans. This was opposed to other ethnic groups, generically called 'Brazilian', which included indigenous peoples, people of African descent and mestizos (people of mixed racial descent), also known as *caboclos*.

The groups that identified themselves as '*de origem*' introduced a revised view of the history of the area, in which immigrants, 'full of spirit, vigor, health, intelligence and faith, implanted [...] religion and progress everywhere where it is established' (Dall'Alba, 1987: 152, author's translation). This historical narrative endorses the notion of a pioneering conquest of the region, which strengthens the self-esteem and the spirit of unity among the '*de origem*'.

The attributes given to this group were essential in establishing an intervention plan for the environment they found because the 'natural barriers' demanded tenacity and commitment. The problem was that these characteristics were celebrated, as opposed to the traits assigned to the 'Brazilians', who were represented as 'lazy', 'lacking fibre', 'discouraged', 'slow in thought and speech' and 'shy', or as typifying 'rustics' and 'hicks' (Thomé, 1992). This belittling of the original and native ethnic groups went as far as identifying them with barbarians, legitimising their extermination or assimilation to civilisation. The migration policy also had a racial component, insofar as it promoted the whitening of the population. This was aligned with Brazilian imperial policy intended to stimulate miscegenation so as to increase the proportion of white people.

The cultural festivals and landscapes defined in this process are exalted even today for the purposes of tourism and to affirm the identity, serving as a factor that demarks the Italian–German cultural territory in Santa Catarina. Those moments of celebration strengthen the sense of belonging. The appreciation of the traditions, insofar as it reflects a sense of the group, also updates the coding of the differences held to exist between 'Brazilians' and the '*de origem*'. One of the territories with the most pronounced ethnic demarcation is the Itajaí Valley (Vale do Itajaí).

Regionalisation, regional vocations and the 'European Valley'

The above-described regional development process that has been taking place since the time of the colonial construction reflects a system of social relations and conflicts, consolidating economic and political orders consecrated by and reproduced by the state. This system is constituted in economic, political and cultural patterns, which link economic arrangements to sociocultural values, supported by normative and symbolic parameters.

From an environmental point of view, this has resulted in the transformation of the landscape and the appropriation of resources, both supported by socially defined conceptions of nature. The term 'patterns' refers to a set of practices that tend to be routinely reproduced (Giddens, 1989) and are associated with a territory that, in turn, is also a product of these practices. These economic and political-cultural patterns are connected with a 'region' that indicates the specific geographic area in which they operate and from which the means of their reproduction is obtained (Theis, 2008).

Essential to the regional development process were some regionalisation practices in which symbolic power (Bourdieu, 1993) is exercised by planning officers, whether state or non-state. For these planning officers, some references are usually taken as given elements, reifying them, although they are the product of historical, economic, cultural and landscape transformation processes in which different social actors had relationships, often conflictive. In this process, borders are designed starting from an abstract and conceptual scheme of the region, giving concrete contours that cause the mental construction of the planners to become understood as a real entity with intrinsic existence.

These practices of regionalisation inadvertently favour essentialist understandings, ignoring the fact that the ontological status of these regions derives from the very act of regionalisation. These operations have been crucial to the process of reification of the regions in Santa Catarina, which was complemented by the imputation of specific functions and features, and which are in turn appropriated or incorporated by agents with power to shape the territory by their practices.

Regionalisations are a particular way of symbolically exercising power to draw boundaries between geographical areas from points of view that are functional for the agents with specific placements in the social space. Such operations constitute territorialisation practices that are more effective the more convincing they are in selecting the material and cultural geographic references that give them empirical support, and the greater the recruitment of interests and identities that find themselves included under this definition.

In Santa Catarina, these regionalisation operations are diverse, and have been based on different logics and intentionalities, some of which refer to the national scale and others to the state scale. In both, the relationships and interest systems do not necessarily coincide. The most widespread official regionalisation in Brazil, incorporated into the national system of statistics – and as a consequence providing fundamental support to decision making and implementation of federal public policies – is the regionalisation of the Brazilian Institute of Geography and Statistics (IBGE). This institution divides states into meso-regions and micro-regions based on generic economic and social similarities. With respect to Santa Catarina, this division gathers the 295 municipalities in six meso-regions, which are divided in their turn into micro-regions.

Another important regionalisation that articulates the national point of view of agents with state-wide perspective is the River Basins regionalisation of the National Water Agency (ANA) and the National and State Councils of Water Resources. Within the administrative boundaries of the state of Santa Catarina lie ten hydrographic regions, covering 17 basins and their respective Basin Committees (National Water Agency, 2014). Some other common forms of regionalisation that strictly relate to the area are the geo-economic regions and the tourist regions. The geo-economic regions divide the state into seven parts, and the tourist regions into nine parts. The geoeconomic regionalisation does not have any official definition, but is usually used both for policy implementation and by economic agents associated with the activities that are identified on the objective basis of that regionalisation.

The region considered here is the Itajaí Valley, dubbed the 'European Valley' by the tourist industry. The Itajaí Valley is the sole regional division that appears in all of the abovementioned regionalisation operations. This region is considered therefore as an administrative meso-region, a river basin district, a geo-economic region and tourist region. In other words, it appears justified on various bases, including the physical, economic and cultural aspects. It thus produces a strong conjunction of agents that have their interests included and, in turn, leaves little opportunity for agents whose positions in the social space do not support this regionalisation.

The name of the Valley comes from the river Itajaí, which was the access route of European immigrants. This river drains the region and is formed from the fusion of the South Itajaí and Western Itajaí rivers. In its course, it also receives waters from its tributary the North Itajaí. At the point of the Itajaí–Mirim confluence, it begins to be called the Itajaí. For the municipalities that compose the Itajaí Valley, the river has played a key role since the time of colonisation, and continues to play such a role in the present for the development of economic activities in the region. The colonisation of the Valley began with the city of Itajaí, which was the first municipal cluster. It was followed by the establishment of the Blumenau colony and later by the formation of the settlement in Rio do Sul, municipalities in the Itajaí Valley, larger rivers of the Itajaí basin, and the state and federal roads crossing the region (Figure 16.1).

The tourist regionalisation that labels much of the contemporary Itajaí Valley as the 'European Valley' was defined by the State Board of Tourism, following the guidelines of the National Plan for the sector. This plan has employed the tourist region as the structuring axis of the national policy through the Tourism Regionalisation Program: Routes of Brazil. It is a management model that combines the notion of territory with local clusters as a way of ordering, promoting, qualifying and diversifying the touristic opportunities offered (Bortolossi, 2008; Ministry of Tourism, 2004). According to Beni, this operation consists of the 'organisation of a geographic space into regions for the purposes of planning, managing, promoting, and integrating in order to share the tourist activity' (Beni, 2006: 30, author's translation).

The promotion of tourism in the European Valley exalts the characteristics and customs of European settlers, emphasising the German and Italian, as well as the natural beauty favourable to ecotourism, adventure tourism, and so on. This is expressed as follows on the website of the state government:

> The cultural heritage of the German, Italian, Austrian, Polish and Portuguese colonizers is the great mark of this region of Santa Catarina, located in the Vale do Itajaí (Itajaí Valley). Famous for hosting the largest German festival in the Americas, the Oktoberfest of Blumenau, the Vale Europeu has many other attractions: from the typical architecture to the cuisine, celebrated in great style during the October Festivals; from the purchasing routes in the towns and cities of the Santa Catarina textile industry region to the religious celebrations which take place in several of its municipalities; from ecotourism to rural tourism. Choose your route and have a good journey.
>
> (Santa Catarina, 2014)

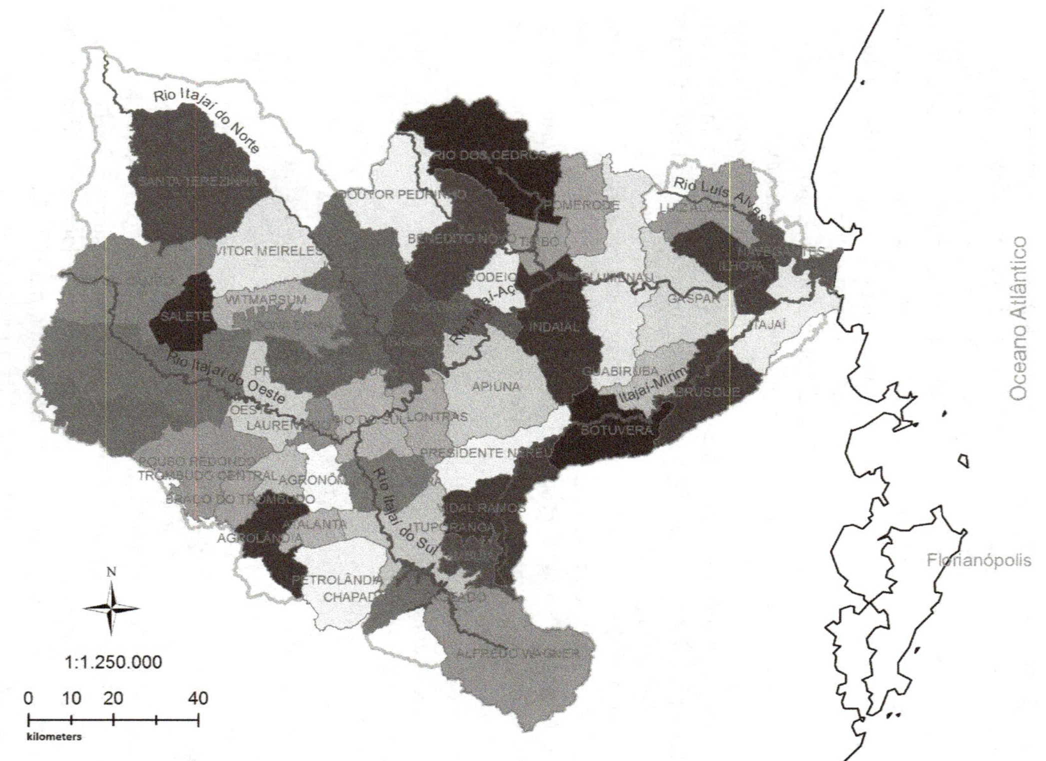

Figure 16.1 Municipalities in the basin of the Itajaí River

Source: SISGA (2014)

More specifically, another website expresses the official historical discourse on the origins of these attractions:

> The Itajaí Valley was colonised by European immigrants, particularly Germans, who founded Blumenau in 1850. In the last quarter of the nineteenth century, Italians settled near the existing German settlements. The descendants of these people preserve the customs of their ancestors in their culinary traditions, architecture, folklore, dances, and festivals. The privileged nature of the region provides numerous options for ecotourism and adventure tourism.
>
> (Santur, 2014)

The omission of any reference to the indigenous peoples who inhabit(ed) this valley, with their own conceptions of nature, values and ways of living, is not accidental. It simply reaffirms the conception that the tourist regionalisation of the European Valley consecrates.

For this reason, the European Valley is a regional designation whose implications go far beyond the planning of tourist activities. It consumes and consecrates the reification of the region as possessing characteristics which, although they are imputed and the product of historical and conflict-laden relationships, appear as self-evident and naturally given, and are therefore received as 'vocations'. The so-called regional vocation refers to the idea that, in a region, one supposed intrinsic tendency prevails as an unavoidable potential for a certain activity, supposedly determined by the territorial characteristics, natural or cultural, which results in their supposed 'vocation'.

Such reification takes place because an abstract representation of the region is accepted and incorporated by economic and political agents, which holds symbolic power to spread their representation as a natural and an historical reality. In other words, such representation of the region denies that it is derived from power relations and landscape transformations due to conflictive historical processes. In fact, the occupation of the European Valley entailed the modelling of the landscape based on the concepts, values and needs of the settlers. This took place through the delimitation of plots of land according to European systems, deforestation, and the 'cleansing' and gardening of areas near villas. Marcos Mattedi (2001), referring to the views of nature that were dominant throughout the Itajaí Valley's development process, emphasises that, for the settler, the local nature appeared as a clear threat, as an enemy to be subdued through deforestation, the removal of certain species and the elimination of the *bugres* (indigenous people). Despite this, the landscapes constructed in this way are now considered as evidence of the 'touristic potential' of the region, whose territorial configuration enables a balanced way of conciliating agricultural and non-agricultural activities with industry and services, attracting urban populations by their 'natural amenities' (da Veiga, 2000).

According to Kate Soper (1996), the most serious consequence of the abstraction of the role of human agency in the production of a space that is exalted as 'natural' or 'traditional' is the neglect of the social relations, often conflict-laden and exploitative, from which the environment was established and that are marked in the physical territory. Indeed, much of what the tourist impulse exalts as the scenic value of the landscape, or tries to promote as experiences associated with a more harmonious order of a traditional lifestyle, is in fact a product of class, gender and race relations, which are usually disregarded in the formal constitution of such regions, or when the virtues of the landscape are exalted.

The exaltation of the European Valley for tourism therefore has a political effect, involving a rhetoric that obscures much of the landscape that is known for its attractiveness for tourism. It takes this form because of centuries of human activity in the material sense. It is the product of a history filled with violence and arbitrariness. This includes not only the historical buildings, but also much of the landscapes of scenic value and 'natural nooks and crannies'. This leads to an uncritical and anachronistic legitimation of the historical process that defined this situation. This happens through the dimming of unworthy aspects of the historical process and the invisibility of the submitted and subjugated subjects in that process.

This naturalisation and the concealment of conflict in the production of the landscape mingle very well, paradoxically, with a certain rhetoric of environmental common sense that reduces the problem of sustainability to energy efficiency issues, technological innovations and (especially in the Itajaí Valley) environmental control through infrastructure projects. This common sense focuses on the metaphorical and abstract conflict between the rights of the present and the future generations, ignoring the existing conflicts between co-present subjects. These subjects are the ones who suffer the environmental inequality that results from the disproportionate exposure to the risks due to their different ability to escape from the sources of these risks (Acselrad, 2010). This unequal distribution of environmental impacts tends to reproduce the social inequalities of Brazilian society (class, ethnicity, gender, and so on). From the territorial point of view, this dynamic is associated with the operation of the land market, which leads to harmful practices being located in devalued areas. In turn these are treated by state planning and regionalisation operations as 'sacrifice zones' (Bullard, 1994, cited in Porto, 2013, author's translation), in which people are forced to live in dangerous or degrading conditions and exposed to major risks.

Environmental inequities in coping with floods

Since the beginning of colonisation, immigrants have had to deal with the threat of flooding in the Itajaí Valley. This was a recurrent phenomenon but did not prevent European settlement of the area, which has had to cope with the effects of flooding on increasingly large scales.

The main way found to 'solve' the problem was through structural engineering projects, especially the building of dams. These began to be constructed in the 1960s and were planned in the Alto Vale do Itajaí region, since the dynamics of the flooding were then understood to be related to the rainfall in that region.

It was decided that three dams would be built in the cities of Ituporanga, Taio and José Boiteux, which at the time belonged to the municipality of Ibirama. The construction of two of these (the South Dam in Ituporanga and the West Dam in Taio) began in the 1960s and was completed in the 1970s. On the other hand, the North Dam in José Boiteux (Ibirama) was begun in 1972 (during the military dictatorship in Brazil) and was not completed until the 1990s. The municipality that benefited the most from these structural interventions was Blumenau.

In the past, Blumenau hosted the colony, and covered almost the entire territory of the Valley. Today, however, the city has a much smaller territorial extension due to the creation of several municipalities, but still preserves the greatest economic and political importance of any in the region (Kohls Schubert, 2014). This project has effectively undone the work of setting up the indigenous territory that had been reconstituted and reorganised in an atmosphere of difficulty and hostility, but which had nonetheless been successful in re-establishing the existence of indigenous communities with their own culture and ways of living.

The construction and subsequent use of the North Dam – Brazil's largest dam for flood control – drastically and irreversibly changed the lives of the Xokleng Laklanõ people. Although the project 'affected over 900 hectares of indigenous land, […] their best lands, representing 95 per cent of their fertile land for agriculture' (Pereira *et al.*, 1998: 66, author's translation), the indigenous population was excluded from any decision process regarding the dam. No studies of environmental or social impact were done and to date, compensation for the land occupied by the dam waters has not been paid in full. The dam creates problems for the Xokleng Laklanõ people in a number of different areas. This second historic loss of territory is now added to the problems of non-demarcation of the land, the difficulty of getting along with the settlers, timber extraction and problems with health and education.

In 1978, the first flood on indigenous land 'occurred due to the construction of the North Dam' and 'for the first time, the community [of the Xokleng Laklanõ people] realised the full extent of the drama caused by this engineering project. The reaction that followed was mostly one of panic and disorientation' (Müller, 1987: 53, author's translation). The North Dam occupied not only the best agricultural area, but also the flat land of the people, the location of huts, houses, etc.; thus, it brought not only material losses, but also social and cultural losses. The union of the Xokleng Laklanõ people was historically grounded in that territory, where their experience was guided in a close relationship promoting relationships and interactions for generations. The North Dam caused the loss of the Xokleng Laklanõ people's best land and the social disintegration of the group.

Today, among their multiple claims, there are two urgent demands: the demarcation of the indigenous land and compensation in relation to the North Dam. Indigenous land currently covers an area of 14,000 ha, which should be extended to 37,000 ha (Pereira *et al.*, 1998). By not demarcating this (which would require indemnifying the settlers who have been using these lands for generations), the government creates a problem, because it supports the expectations of both sides and prevents the effective creation of public policies for the development of the indigenous settlement.

In this context, Walsh (2012) defends the intercultural perspective that is configured as a political, social, epistemic and ethical project of transformation and decoloniality. For the author, interculturality will only have meaning, impact and value when taken critically as actions, projects and processes that seek to intervene in the restructuring and reorganisation of the social foundations that racialise, undermine and dehumanise – that is, in the very matrix of the coloniality of power so present in today's world.

As distinct from colonialism – the political and economic domination of one people by another anywhere in the world – *coloniality* describes the pattern of relationships that emerges in the context of European settlement in the Americas and which has become a modern and permanent power model. Coloniality penetrates into almost every aspect of life and locates itself, among other places, in power relations and by imposing conceptions of nature based on a binary division of nature from society that denies the ancient relationship between biophysical, human and spiritual worlds, treating the landscape with merely instrumental conceptions.

Conclusion

The European colonisation process that configured the territory in the state of Santa Catarina, especially in the Itajaí Valley, is today a consequence of coloniality, given the pattern of relationships that tends to perpetuate in the context of the modern management of nature and landscape.

On one hand, the flood control strategy emphasises infrastructure projects, focusing on minimising the occurrence of flooding in the city of Blumenau by sacrificing other areas, especially those occupied by indigenous peoples. On the other, the exaltation of European identity and of the cultural landscapes associated with it are politically and economically consecrated through the regionalisation of the European Valley, which, beyond being a merely tourist regionalisation, reaffirms the historical subordination of the colonised populations. The reifying of the territorial construction takes place through a violent colonisation process. This reification updates the relations of coloniality while reinforcing the invisibility of regional indigenous issues and reproducing historical environmental inequities.

The North Dam has irreversibly altered the daily life of the Xokleng Laklanõ people yet they were not permitted to participate in the decision process. This project not only took their best agricultural areas and their houses, but also disregarded their conception of nature and landscape that involves a long-standing relationship between biophysical, human and spiritual worlds. Their worldview encompasses ways of life and knowledge systems that deeply rely on a spiritual and social–cultural relationship with nature, which underlies the construction of the landscape from their own cultural perspective. The conception of coloniality, reaffirmed by the control of nature through infrastructure projects and the exaltation of the European Valley, is praised from the state, with only a few voices advocating greater reflexivity, these essentially being located in academia and social movements.

This analysis focuses on territorialisation via processes of symbolisation – the labelling of the area as European Valley – and institutionalisation. The touristic regionalisation has been described as a practice of territorialisation where power is exercised. This exercise of power took place in the form of drawing administrative policy boundaries with far reaching consequences: these policies and planning exercises do not represent the interests and cultural values of the population as a whole, as they exclude those of the indigenous population.

Acknowledgements

The authors thank Dr Elena Battaglini for her helpful readings and suggestions and Professor Marina Beatriz Borgmann da Cunha and the FURB Idiomas for their valuable assistance in the translation of this chapter. We are also grateful to Debora Fittipaldi Gonçalves for her timely technical assistance.

References

Acselrad, H. (2010). Ambientalisação das lutas sociais – o caso do movimento por justiça ambiental. *Estudos avançados*, 24 (68): 103–119.

Beni, M. (2006). *Política e planejamento de turismo no Brasil.* Aleph, São Paulo.

Bortolossi, S. (2008). *Regionalisação do turismo no Vale Europeu, Santa Catarina: uma abordagem institucional.* Unpublished Master's thesis, Universidade Regional de Blumenau, Santa Catarina, Brazil.

Bonnemaison, J. and L. Cambrézy (1996). *Le lien territorial: Entre frontières et identités. Géografies et cultures.* L'Harmattan, Paris.

Bourdieu, P. (1993). *Cosas dichas.* Gedisa, Barcelona.

Bullard, R. (1994). *Dumping in Dixie: Race, class and environmental quality.* Westview Press, Boulder.

da Costa, E. (1979). *Da monarquia à republica, momentos decisivos.* Editora Ciências Humanas, São Paulo.

da Cunha, M.C. (2009). Política indigenista no século XIX, pp. 133–154 in: M.C. da Cunha (ed.), *História dos índios no Brasil.* Companhia das Letras, Secretaria Municipal de Cultura, FAPESP, São Paulo.

da Veiga, J.E. (2000). *A face rural do desenvolvimento.* Editora da UFRGS, Porto Alegre.

Dall'Alba (1987). Imigrantes italianos em Santa Catarina. In: L. De Boni (ed.), *A presença italiana no Brasil.* EST, Porto Alegre.

dos Santos, S.C. (1998). Os índios Xokleng e os imigrantes, pp. 57–70 in: Fleuri, R.M. (ed.), *Intercultura e movimentos sociais.* Mover/NUP, Florianópolis.

Giddens, A. (1989). *A constituição da sociedade.* Martins Fontes, São Paulo.

Kohls Schubert, V. (2014). *Medo desigual: um estudo sobre as iniquidades intra-regionais no enfrentamento das enchentes no Vale do Itajaí (SC).* Unpublished Master's dissertation, Universidade Regional de Blumenau, Santa Catarina, Brazil.

Mattedi, M.A. (2001). Notas sobre as visões de natureza em Blumenau: mais um capítulo da trágica história do sucesso humano. *Revista de Estudos Ambientais*, 3 (1): 29–39.

Ministry of Tourism (2004). *Programa de regionalisação do turismo: roteiros do Brasil.* Brasília.

Müller, A.S. (1987). *Opressão e depredação: A construção da barragem de Ibirama e a desagregação da comunidade indígena local.* FURB, Blumenau.

National Water Agency (2014). *Comitês de Bacias Hidrográficas, Santa Catarina. 2014.* Available at: www.cbh.gov.br/DataGrid/GridSantaCatarina.aspx (accessed 30 October 2014).

Oliveira, L.B., Kreuz, M. and R. Wartha (2014). *Educação, história e cultura indígena: desafios e perspectivas no Vale do Itajaí.* Edifurb, Blumenau.

Pereira, W. da Silva, *et al.* (1998). *Laudo antropológico de identificação e delimitação de terra de ocupação tradicional Xokleng: história de contato, dinâmica social e mobilidade indígena no sul do Brasil.* Funai, Porto Alegre.

Porto, M.F.S. (2013). Ecologia, Economia e Política: contradições, conflitos e alternativas do desenvolvimento, pp. 1–75 in: Randolph, R. and H.M. Tavares (eds), *Política e planejamento regional, uma coletânea*, Vol. 1. UP Gráfica, Brasília.

Sack, R. (1986). *Human territoriality: Its theory and history.* Cambridge University Press, Cambridge.

Santa Catarina (2014). Available at: http://turismo.sc.gov.br/destinos/vale-europeu (accessed 30 October 2014).

SANTUR (2014). Available at: www.santacatarinaturismo.com.br/destinos.php?id=26 (accessed 30 October 2014).

Seyferth, G. (1974). *A colonisação alemã no Vale do Itajaí-Mirim: um estudo de desenvolvimento econômico.* Editora Movimento, Porto Alegre.

SISGA (Information System Applied to Environmental Management System) (2014). FURB. Available at: www.inf.furb.br/sisga (accessed 30 June 2014).

Soper, K. (1996). Nature/'nature', pp. 21–34 in: Robertson, G., Mash, M., Tickner, L., Bird, J., Curtis, B. and T. Putnam (eds), *Future natural: Nature, science, culture.* Routledge, London and New York.

Theis, I.M. (ed.) (2008). *Desenvolvimento e território: questões teóricas, evidências empíricas.* Edunisc, Santa Cruz.

Thomé, N. (1992). *Sangue, suor e lágrimas no chão do contestado.* Edições/UnC, Caçador.

Walsh, C. (2012). Interculturalidad y (de)colonialidad: Perspectivas críticas y políticas. *Revista Visão Global*, 15 (1–2): 61–74.

17 Conclusion

Territorialisation, a challenging concept for framing regional development

Elena Battaglini, Lummina Horlings and Joost Dessein

Several strands of literature highlight the regional dimension of development processes: neo-institutional economics, the study of regional versus national competitiveness, the theory of comparative advantages and the focus on industrial districts. Despite a body of studies that, until the first half of the twentieth century, had not taken the variables of time and space in their analysis of development into account, places are taken in their specificity as the founding element for describing (and for some authors, interpreting) the constraints and opportunities of regions for their historical, cultural and socioeconomic conditions. The neoclassical theory of growth, based on the model of the Nobel laureate Robert Solow, expunges the spatial variable and is then gradually questioned in favour of the so-called endogenous regional development approach (Stimson *et al.*, 2011).

Over time, places take on the role of a favourable (or unfavourable) environment for business, making the creation of external economies (or diseconomies) possible, and giving rise to specific forms of cooperation between companies and developmental actors. At least some authors assert that development and innovation in certain successful regions are not produced by the assertion of a single company but rather by the competitiveness of the entire territory as expressed through the synergies between institutions and socioeconomic actors. These synergies are the basis of the processes of accumulation of knowledge and the dissemination of information and opportunities useful for supporting development in the context of effective planning (Battaglini, 2014).

Debates on regional development have described the relevance of social networks, proximity and organisational models to point to the importance of cooperation and trust between actors on the regional scale. Since the 1950s scholars seeking the roots of local competitiveness have progressively shifted their emphasis to the less material aspects of development. The central role initially attributed to the presence of infrastructure (1950–1960) was subsequently assigned to exports (1960–1970), to endogenous development, to small and medium enterprises (SMEs) and to districts (1970–1980). Later, it shifted to innovation, to technology transfer, to innovative milieux (1980–1990), to the learning economy of intangible factors and collective learning (1990–2000) and finally, to relational capital and local culture (from 2000 to the present day).

In the latter stages in particular, the milieu has become a key concept – the focus of interesting ongoing debate. 'That something in the air', meaning the ideas and secrets inherent in all work that children can learn in an unconscious way (Marshall, 1890) can be understood as the local atmosphere that explains and interprets the networks of cooperation – the *untraded interdependencies* (Storper 1993, 1995). These are expressed in the specific diffusion of knowledge, the organisation of production and the division of labour, the reproduction of professional skills and in forms of social regulation (Camagni, 2008; 2009).

Although culture has been recognised as an element of milieu, its role has not been described explicitly in literature on regional development. Our book therefore attempts to analyse how culture in its interplay with environment strongly contributes to a local specific milieu.

Why territorialisation?

The cases described in this book highlight the time-space dimension of development and the ways in which people use resources. Culture, in its interplay with nature, influences the ways in which people shape their territories. It mediates practices and institutions but also the senses; it is expressed in subjective perceptions, sense-making and the construction of narratives and regional identities, pointing to how people assign value to their resources and thus influence sustainable local and regional development. Culture further influences ways of life and human intentionality, thus providing insights about why people would contribute to change.

The role played by culture in regional development and sustainability is discussed using case studies from North and South America, Europe, Africa, Asia and Australasia. The role of culture implicitly and explicitly relates to what we intend by territorialisation – it provides us with a lens to understand how culture influences multi-scale spatial development. All the case studies focus on concepts such as region and place. Despite their varied etymologies and meanings, all share the focus on and the significance of how space is represented, performed and thus bound to the natural, cultural and social characterisation of a specific context.

The main aim of this book is to bring the semantic efficacy of the concept of *territory* to the fore as compared to the notions of *region* and *place*. The word *territory* has an etymological link to 'terrain', through the Latin *terrēnum* (ground) and *terra* (earth). It therefore offers a clear reference to the natural features of places (see also Horlings *et al.*, 2015).

In our view, when engaging with development processes in the light of sustainability, the word *territory* – much more than *region* or *place* – stands for the complex relationship between local communities and their environment, and between nature and culture. If we take our investigation further, territory possesses this semantic power in the way in which it alludes to the dynamic of appropriation of space as a key to understanding social life, its processes and its social and economic development. We thus agree with Chiesi (2015) in conceiving of territorialisation 'as the core of many social dynamics'. It relates to the primary set of experiences of perception, symbolisation and valuation that actors develop with their immediate surroundings or larger spaces, as 'low-level processes are the constituents of high-level ones, and not vice-versa … (because) any territorial experience, regardless of scale, happens with the engagement of the body–mind system with the surrounding environment' (Chiesi, 2015: 76). Territorialisation thus allows us to ground the analysis of higher-scale concepts – such as region, development and globalisation – to the microscale of these primary experiences.

Measuring these different scales is also crucial for what we have called the 'institutional dimension' of territorialisation (Horlings *et al.*, 2015), its organisation and planning towards sustainability (Padt, 2015). Here territorialisation is intended from the point of view of researchers or planners and their modalities for framing and constructing territories through 'scientific evidence, anecdotes and metaphors'. From this perspective, territorialisation as a discourse of defining and shaping territories is 'a struggle between powerful and less powerful scientists, policy makers, politicians, citizens, business people and their organisations' (Padt, 2015: 164).

The process of territorialisation has relevant bottom-up dynamics, which are almost always pluralistic and often conflicting. They hardly fit into GDP or other indexes that measure development or well-being. Grasping the symbolic dimension of place or intangible culture from the top down is either a conceptual or a methodological challenge, as Cicerchia discusses in Chapter 9:

> 'Feeling at ease' in different places (home, neighbourhood, school, workplace, city, etc.), the awareness of the *genius loci* or of the cultural meanings of places, landmarks, etc., the ability to access and to take full advantage of the resources locally available are basic requirements for sustainable endogenous development. Measuring them and transforming them into policies is the challenge that lies ahead.
>
> (Cicerchia, 2015: 142–143)

Chiesi and Costa, in Chapter 10, discuss how community practices, as co-design and cultural mapping, can foster many forms of territorialisation. Here this concept is intended 'as bottom-up appropriation of space' (Chiesi and Costa, 2015: 148) by collective and deliberate intentions ascribed to it. These methodologies are excellent instances of participatory action research: they could improve territorial planning at any level of scale by the increase of the 'degree of congruence' between the conceptual word of planners and designers and that of users and citizens, promoting place-attachment.

Assemblage theory, as discussed by Woods in Chapter 3, has the strength and the consistency to parallel the main arguments of our book by focusing on the material components 'both natural and manufactured, but also technologies and people' (Woods, 2015: 30) and the expressive components that drive the affective modalities of how assemblages are perceived and managed. By adopting assemblage theory, rurality or urbanity as social constructs (previously detached) are reconnected to territories as place identity, either urban or rural, could refer to the same space. Claiming that the properties of an assemblage cannot be reduced to the properties of its components – and that a place cannot be reduced to, or be constrained by, its territory or environment – Woods stresses the role of the theory in countering the environmental determinism of early geographical traditions.

In theorising spatiality, sociologists – like geographers – have traditionally confronted the epistemological black box of the nature–culture divide. On one hand, sociology has favoured the concept of space over that of place, with the latter being considered lacking generality, as it relates to the context in which it is used rather than having a meaning per se (Manuel-Navarrete and Redclift, 2010). On the other hand, with the need to locate sociological analysis in values, interests and practices, the concept of space had been depreciated (or even neglected) with the concern either of falling into some form of environmental determinism or compromising the explanatory power of mainstream sociological variables and the capacity for generalisation possessed by the social sciences (Chiesi, 2010).

In defining territorialisation 'as coproduction of society and environment where both have agency' (Horlings *et al.*, 2015) we refer to the mutual constitution of the social and the natural, of communities and their living environment, thus challenging the debate over the nature–culture divide.

Territorialisation and human agency: the mediation of culture

Culture is a crucial 'vector' (Redclift and Manuel-Navarrete, Chapter 2) of these dialectics, mediating how society negotiates the definition of space and marking the direction of how space defines the possibility for social behaviour. Redclift and Manuel-Navarrete define culture as 'the opportunities and limits inherent in the local environment within which human agency works' (Redclift and Manuel-Navarrete, 2015: 19). In this perspective, places are not simply the product of human agency but are 'cultural products' that could be 'reinvented' and 'reshaped' within the changing context of policy discourses and the 'rhetoric of sustainability'.

Horlings (Chapter 4) conceives of culture as rooted in human values. She understands territorialisation in different spans of time and space as the expression of individual and collective cultural values (Horlings, 2015: 104). She thus adds an important fourth dimension of territorialisation: 'worldview', referring to people's intentionality and way of life. She describes how the worldview and symbolic dimension of territorialisation offer insights into how values drive people's place-specific motivations, cultural sense-making and sense of place.

In this line of reasoning, Kivitalo *et al.* (Chapter 7) discuss how culture manifests itself in the everyday life of rural people and communities in Finland, and how these people construct trajectories of development and give meaning to rural places in the light of sustainability. Sustainable development processes are thus to be considered as related to 'recognition, dialogue and negotiation between diverse cultural meanings, values and identities' and rooted in 'traditions and emotional bonds toward the place, which are handed down through the generations' (Kivitalo *et al.*, 2015: 104).

The recognition of the specific natural and cultural characteristics of places is also stressed by Thomas Lane *et al.* in Chapter 13, where the resilience of Welsh communities is challenged by 'generic metropolitan (planning) approaches' that fail to take into account the local need to maintain their distinctiveness in terms of social and cultural capital.

In Chapter 14, the case of seed practices in Luoland (West Kenya) is described as 'embedded and structured by cultural beliefs and associated kinship based practices' (Hebink *et al.*, 2015: 206). These practices are shaped (and challenged) by external interventions that are backed by the state and foreign donors driving local farmers to adopt new, hybrid varieties of maize. Conflicting ideologies about food security socially defend and legitimise farmers' choice of which maize to plant. The authors build on these different conceptions of territorial development, arguing that culture 'stands for making the configuration of the social and material work' (Hebinck *et al.*, 2015: 208).

Culture also matters in the planning processes and in the approaches to urban resilience as Atmanagara discusses in Chapter 12. Building on the empirical results of a European FP7 project survey, she contributes to the understanding of territorialisation by exploring the planning and regulatory strategies of different European cities in regard to urban resilience and sustainability. Here, culture is understood as the intensity of collaboration between key agents, education, knowledge transfer and access to information. These cultural factors play a crucial role in shaping the evolution of urban planning in the selected cases. Urban resilience is a result fostered by planning approaches that 'try to integrate different functions for the same area, involve local citizens and manifold social groups, and constantly evaluate and redevelop the existing strategies and measures' (Atmanagara, 2015: 182) on the basis of territorial specificities.

Another interesting case of urban territorialisation is described in Chapter 15 by Caggiano, who refers to collective gardens set up and run in Paris by local associations on small public plots granted by the local authorities. These *jardins partagés* convey rurality into the city, creating an aesthetic function that inevitably includes ethical, productive, social and cultural functions, and mobilising 'resources and capabilities that are hidden, scattered or underutilised, while promoting a collective well-being based on (and improving) an awareness of place' (Caggiano, 2015: 232). The way this accords with our book's approach to territorialisation is seen in the empirical evidence of processes of coproduction between society and the environment as realised in the gardens through the sharing of experiences, knowledge, memories and imagination. This facilitates the processes of urban transformation, adds value to the urban landscape and reconstructs community relations of solidarity and social bonding.

In Chapter 16, Florit *et al.* analyse how patterns of symbolisation and reification that were imposed during the colonial age in the Brazilian state of Santa Catarina still inform the institutionalising dimension of territorialisation. The examples of tourism and regional branding here are understood in terms of how they update and reinforce environmental and cultural inequities, contributing to the maintenance of a colonial relationship.

The complex issue of development is addressed in this book in terms of space and time and the cultural specificities of the local communities who are confronted with the affordances and potentialities of their endogenous resources, the pressures of the external market and extensive networks over a global scale.

In essence, we locate ourselves in the theoretical perspective inaugurated by Weber in his work *Protestant Ethic and the Spirit of Capitalism*, which highlights the role of cultural factors in the rise of capitalism. Facing the bi-directional relationship linking culture to society, Weber identifies the horizon of meaning of human action in the cultural system. In his methodological writings, he defines culture as:

> a finite segment of the meaningless infinity of the world process, a segment on which human beings confer meaning and significance. This is true even for the human being who views a particular culture as a mortal enemy and who seeks to 'return to nature'.
>
> (Weber, 1994 (1922): 540)

As for Weber, for us the selection of what is valuable (even in trajectories of territorialisation) is an act of identity in a double sense. It refers primarily to the personal and social dimensions of the identity of a subject, to its multiple memberships that transcend the socialisation process that results. Selection is also an act that connects to the cultural identity of an individual who, in the distinction between the self and the other, is based on the meaning and feeling of a common origin that is also territorial.

Agency of nature or nature of agency?

The meaning of nature is continuously negotiated in relation to its supposed counterpart, and is usually defined as 'the other' vis-à-vis human society and culture. Culture is often equated with all human artefacts, and nature with the external environment; that is, culture and nature are distinguished from each other as if they were two separate realms of reality (Haila, 2000: 155). In early sociological efforts to explain human consciousness and the mind, animals were frequently used to describe the uniqueness of humankind; it is in relation to such counterparts that the uniqueness of human agency stands out. In this sense, nature serves to define what being human implies (Uggla, 2010: 81).

To corroborate the hypothesis of coproduction introduced by our book (Horlings *et al.*, 2015), Battaglini and Babović attempt in Chapter 5 to challenge this nature–culture divide by discussing the empirical findings stemming from their Serbian case study. The main aim of their contribution was to understand the process of territorialisation as a co-production of nature and culture in which both have agency. They rely on the concept of affordances (Gibson, 1986) to underpin nature's agency, and on the concepts of cognitive, affective and selective values (Kluckhon, 1951) to operationalise the role of culture in the symbolisation and reification stages of territorialisation. Their analysis shows that access to land, its type, quality and morphology act to afford and strongly define everyday practices as well as the long-term processes of territorialisation. At the same time, the distribution of land, as well as its valuation by actors during these processes, is influenced by cultural factors, specifically by social norms and values.

The other authors of this book also refer to cases and practices that support our hypothesis of coproduction where both nature and culture have agency. Redclift and Manuel-Navarrete, in Chapter 2, refer to how *ejido* communities convey the natural attraction of the *cenotes* into sustainable forms of tourism, conferring value on their territory and culture. Chiesi then devotes an entire section of Chapter 6 to discussing the heuristic power of the concept of affordances (which Redclift and Manuel-Navarrete might have referred to in the case of the *cenote*) as 'an opportunity for action mediated by the environment' (Chiesi, 2015: 78). He claims that the interminable catalogue posed by the environment and objects

> allows us to get rid of the problematic notion of 'function': the object itself is no longer seen as having one or more functions, but rather the subject is the one who *discovers affordances in the object*. This completely inverts the perspective: our capacity to individuate opportunities in space becomes key, rather than some objective qualities that predetermine its function(s).
>
> (Chiesi, 2015: 78, emphasis added; see Gibson, 1986: 127–129)

In this sense, this challenges the very nature of agency and the constructivist bounding of culture defined as 'the opportunities and limits inherent in the local environment within which human agency works' (Redclift and Manuel-Navarrete, 2015: 19).

Hebinck *et al.* in Chapter 14 argue that certain local maize varieties and their specific biophysical properties afford specific local agricultural practices. Modes of seed cultivation are thus to be conceptualised as the dynamic interaction connecting the human and non-human elements; processes that 'do not emerge casually nor can they be easily engineered, and generating in turn heterogeneous and highly fragmented development situations' (Hebinck *et al.*, 2015: 207).

In Chapter 8, Dessein elaborates further on the encounter, interaction and mutual transformation between communities (each with their system of values, norms, beliefs and symbols) and living nature, framing two different practices of saffron cultivation in Morocco. He connects these culturally embedded modes of production to the local natural conditions through a model where territorialisation can be understood as the combined processes of endogenous regional development and coproduction, defined as the interplay of the social and natural environment. Therefore,

> strong territorialisation can be found with a balance between the endogenous and exogenous forces influencing development in a context of a strong human-nature interrelation (i.e. strong co-production). Weak territorialisation, by extension, occurs under conditions of an unbalanced relation between exogenous and endogenous forces combined with a disconnected human-nature nexus.
>
> (Dessein, 2015: 110)

Arguing for the nexus between nature and culture in processes of territorialisation, we thus stand for a different nature of agency, one related not only to human intentions but meant to connect the limitations and possibilities inherent in nature to the aims and expectations of human practices. We therefore join Nash (2005) in the need to think about agency in different terms, such as Latour's (1993) notion of 'relational' agency dispersed among humans and natural hybrids in what he terms an actor network. We also go along with Ingold's (1987) efforts to challenge constructionism in the social sciences by analysing organisms in their environment, rather than as 'self-contained individuals with their culture confronting nature as the external world' (Battaglini and Babović, 2015: 70).

Territorialisation: main theoretical challenges

In this book, we deal with territoriality and territorialisation through reference to frames of time and space and to the cultural specificities of local communities in how they tackle either the endogenous potential of their local heritage or the external pressures of the market and globalisation. We have confronted local communities, seen as human subjects who relate to their biologically and culturally inbuilt 'species-being'. Perceptions, meanings and values are therefore understood as part of their embodied experience of relations with their own species and more widely with nature (Dickens, 1992, 2000). Drawing on Dickens, nature is claimed here to resemble that construct of the Chicago School, the 'biotic level' whose characteristics 'open themselves to the senses of observers who initially perceive the materiality and physicality of such resources insofar as they might affect the actors' representations and actions' (Battaglini and Babović, 2015: 61).

The economic activities of the third sector, such as local exchanges and trading schemes, consortia, organic agriculture and other cases examined in our book, seem to attempt to establish new locally controlled ways of working together, 'attempting to realise the biologically-based need of people for a sense of association, security, social identity' (Dickens, 2000: 161) in both urban and rural contexts.

Attention to practices in the way we have framed it on the territorial level goes along with Bourdieu's analytical effort to deny the opposition between subjectivism and objectivism. Emphasising only the role of culture in constructing actors' experiences does not allow us to understand the affordances of natural resources, and therefore the 'material' conditions of their symbolisation and reification – in other words, the 'real' conditions of the possibility of action. On the other hand, stressing only the structural and physical limits and opportunities afforded by the environment might have driven us to the determinism which we avoided through the notion of co-production.

The international cases discussed here make clear that different natures and cultures exist in relation to diverse territorialisation processes. We could therefore assert that the conceptual strength of 'territorialisation' lies precisely in the possibility that it can frame different coproductions of nature–culture within specific strands of time and space. Unlike the broader and normative concept of sustainable development (which could be located in any place and at any time), the reference to the coproduction of natures–cultures in territorialisation offers an improved understanding of the process underlying regional development, allowing scholars to better analyse the interests at stake, the stakeholders in play, the valued resources to be taken into account for development initiatives and paths and the local efforts to challenge external pressures of the market and globalisation. Its conceptual density permits us to better frame the social climate, the type of coordination or mutual control between development agents and firms, the direction of contacts led by trust and the common sense of belonging to a community – even a business community – that shares similar values and attitudes. The findings in this book can therefore inform the debates on cultural sustainability, providing more insights on how culture mediates practices, symbolisation, reification and institutionalisation in multi-scale spatial development.

With this perspective, the notion of 'territorialisation' further challenges regional studies, especially in economics and sociology. By defining the crucial role that culture and knowledge play, territorialisation reconnects the study to state, market and social dynamics within specific time and space frames, while increasing the adherence of economic structures to historical–empirical reality. In the sociological strand, it challenges the disciplinary divisions among urban and rural social scientists. Physical, biological, social, economic and political relations, processes and practices involving the built and the natural environment – still considered outside the social construction of reality – need to be recognised by both urban and rural sociology in order to avoid ineffective forms of strong constructionism that could lead to disciplinary reductionism.

More knowledge is needed to analyse the type and quality of territorial co-productions, mediated by milieu, but this is a story for another time and perhaps another book.

References

Atmanagara, J. (2015). Culture matters. Planning processes and approaches towards urban resilience in European cities and urban regions: Two examples from Brussels and Ljubljana. In: this book, Chapter 12.

Battaglini E. (2014). *Sviluppo territoriale: Dal disegno di ricerca alla valutazione dei risultati.* Franco Angeli, Milan.

Battaglini, E. and M. Babović (2015). Nature and culture in territorialisation processes: Challenges and insights from a case study in Serbia. In: this book, Chapter 5.

Caggiano, M. (2015). *Les jardins partagés* in Paris: Cultivating space, community and sustainable way of life. In: this book, Chapter 15.

Camagni, R. (2008). Towards a concept of territorial capital, pp. 33–47 in: Capello, R., Camagni, R., Chizzolini, B. and U. Fratesi (eds), *Modelling regional scenarios for the enlarged Europe.* Springer, Berlin.

Camagni, R. (2009). Territorial capital and regional development, pp. 118–132 in: Capello, R. and P. Nijkamp (eds), *Handbook of regional growth and development theories*. Edward Elgar, Cheltenham (UK) and Northampton (USA).

Chiesi, L. (2010). *Il doppio spazio dell'architettura. Ricerca sociologica e progettazione.* Liguori, Naples.

Chiesi, L. (2015). Territoriality as appropriation of space: How 'engaging with space' frames sociality. In: this book, Chapter 6.

Chiesi, L. and P. Costa (2015). Making territory through cultural mapping and co-design: How community practices promote territorialisation. In: this book, Chapter 10.

Cicerchia, A. (2015). Is there a place for place? How spaces and places are included in the measures of sustainable development and well-being. In: this book, Chapter 9.

Dessein, J. (2015). Territorialisation in practice: The case of saffron cultivation in Morocco. In: this book, Chapter 8.

Dickens, P. (1992). *Society and nature: Towards a Green Social Theory.* Harvester, Hemel Hempstead.

Dickens, P. (2000). Society, space and the biotic level: An urban and rural sociology for the new millennium. *Sociology*, 34: 147–164.

Florit, L.F., Blanck de Oliveira, L., Fleuri, R.M. and R. Wartha (2015). A 'European Valley' in South America: Regionalisation, colonisation and environmental inequalities in Santa Catarina, Brazil. In: this book, Chapter 16.

Gibson, J. (1986). *The ecological approach to visual perception*. Psychology Press, Taylor & Francis Group, New York and Hove, UK.

Haila, Y. (2000). Beyond the nature: Culture dualism. *Biology and Philosophy*, 15: 155–175.

Hebinck, P., Mango, N. and H. Kimanthi (2015). Local maize practices and the culture of seed in Luoland, West Kenya. In: this book, Chapter 14.

Horlings, L.G. (2015). The worldview and symbolic dimensions in territorialisation: How human values play a role in a Dutch neighbourhood. In: this book, Chapter 4.

Horlings, L.G., Battaglini, E. and J. Dessein (2015). Introduction: The role of culture in territorialisation. In: this book, Chapter 1.

Ingold, T. (1987). *The appropriation of nature: Essays on human ecology and social relations.* University of Iowa Press, Iowa City.

Kivitalo, M., Kumpulainen, K. and K. Soini (2015). Exploring culture and sustainability in rural Finland. In: this book, Chapter 7.

Kluckhohn, C. (1951). Values and value-orientations in the theory of action: An exploration in definition and classification, pp. 388–433 in: Parsons, T. and E. Shils (eds), *Toward a general theory of action.* Harvard University Press, Cambridge, MA.

Latour, B. (1993). *We have never been modern.* Harvard University Press, Cambridge, MA.

Manuel-Navarrete, D. and M. Redclift (2010). The role of place in the margins of space, pp. 334–348 in: Redclift, M.R. and G. Woodgate (eds), *The international handbook of environmental sociology*. 2nd edn. Edward Elgar, Cheltenham (UK) and Northampton (USA).

Marshall, B. (1890). *Principles of economics.* 1st edn. Macmillan, London.

Nash, L. (2005). The agency of nature or the nature of agency? *Environmental History*, 10 (1): 67–69.

Padt, F. (2015). How to scale a territory? Experiences from the United States. In: this book, Chapter 11.

Redclift, M. and D. Manuel-Navarrete (2015). 'Sustainable places': Place as a vector of culture. Two cases from Mexico. In: this book, Chapter 2.

Stimson, R.J., Stough, R.R. and P.J. Njikamp (eds) (2011). *Endogenous regional development: Perspectives, measurement and empirical investigation.* Edward Elgar, Cheltenham.

Storper, M. (1993). Regional 'worlds' of production: Learning and innovation in the technology districts of France, Italy and the USA. *Regional Studies*, 27 (5): 433–455.

Storper, M. (1995). The resurgence of regional economics, ten years later: The region as a nexus of untraded interdependencies. *European Urban and Regional Studies*, 2 (3): 191–221.

Thomas Lane, E., Pierce, S., Jones, A. and I. Harris (2015). Re-creating and celebrating place(s) in designated space(s): The case of Wales. In: this book, Chapter 13.

Uggla, Y. (2010). What is this thing called 'natural'? The nature–culture divide in climate change and biodiversity policy. *Journal of Political Ecology*, 17: 79–91.

Weber, M. (1994). *Sociological writings*, ed. W. Heydebrand, Continuum, New York (Weber, M., 1922, *Gesammelte Aufsätze zur Religionssoziologie*. Mohr, Tübingen).

Woods, M. (2015). Territorialisation and the assemblage of rural place: Examples from Canada and New Zealand. In: this book, Chapter 3.

Index

Page numbers in **bold** indicate tables and in *italics* indicate figures.

CPSIA information can be obtained
at www.ICGtesting.com
Printed in the USA
LVHW011925150319
610815LV00005B/89/P